THE SHAPE OF THE PAST

JOHN WARWICK MONTGOMERY, Consultant to the Christian Legal Society, Oak Park, Ill., is one of the leading theologians of our time.

He holds earned doctorates from the Universities of Chicago and Strasbourg (France) and is the author of more than thirty books, including *Jurisprudence: A Book of Readings* (Strasbourg: International Scholarly Publishers; distributed in the U.S. by Lerner Law Books, Washington, D.C.).

He is a founding member of the World Association of Law Professors; a member of the American Society of International Law, and the Evangelical Theological Society; a fellow of the American Scientific Affiliation; and is listed in *Who's Who in America, Who's Who in France, Who's Who in Europe*, and *Who's Who in the World*.

A complete listing of Dr. Montgomery's books appears on page 391 of this edition.

THE SHAPE OF THE PAST

A CHRISTIAN RESPONSE TO SECULAR PHILOSOPHIES OF HISTORY

John Warwick Montgomery

BETHANY FELLOWSHIP, INC.
Minneapolis, Minnesota

To
Herman John Eckelmann, B.E.E., B.D.,
Ithaca, New York,
a watchman upon the wall (Isa. 62:6, 7)

Copyright © 1975
Bethany Fellowship, Inc.
All rights reserved

Original edition copyright © 1962
John Warwick Montgomery

Published by Bethany Fellowship, Inc.
6820 Auto Club Road, Minneapolis, Minnesota 55438

Printed in the United States of America

Library of Congress Cataloging in Publication Data:

Montgomery, John Warwick.
  The shape of the past.

  Includes bibliographical references and index.
  1. Historiography. 2. History—Philosophy.
3. History (Theology) I. Title.
D13.M65 1975   907'.2   75-26651
ISBN 0-87123-535-8

Courses in the History Department are, as a rule, the university's most perfect type of the fact-loaded, idea-absent, academic exercise. Here the wood is everywhere lost among the trees; and it is the rare professor who can show the student any thing but a close-clustered thicket of details. While the professor lectures on the Battle of Cowpens, the strategy of the Battle of Cowpens, the tactics of the Battle of Cowpens, the logistics of the Battle of Cowpens, the personalities of the opposing generals in the Battle of Cowpens, the classroom swims around, and the great ideas and forces of history are lost in the flood of facts. Certainly, facts are interesting in themselves, facts about the Battle of Cowpens should be preserved, and specialists in military history should know all about this battle. But need a student spend his time learning all the known facts about it? Cannot history be taught so as to have a meaningful relationship to law, literature, philosophy, religion, art, architecture; and a meaningful relationship to the fundamental motives, habits, aspirations, psychological peculiarities, self-deceptions, hypocrisies, and grandeurs of human nature; and a meaningful relationship to the present?

- George Williams, <u>Some of My Best Friends Are Professors:
  A Critical Commentary on Higher Education</u>
  (New York and London: Abelard-Schuman, 1958), p. 226.

ACKNOWLEDGMENTS

The following persons kindly read portions of this book and offered valuable criticisms: Mario Einaudi, Professor of Government, Cornell University; Edwin A. Burtt, Susan Linn Sage Professor of Philosophy, Cornell University; W. D. Allbeck, Wittenberg Synod Professor of Historical Theology, Hamma Divinity School of Wittenberg University; J. Igor Bella, Professor of Exegetical Theology, Hamma Divinity School of Wittenberg University; and T. A. Kantonen, Frederick Gebhart Professor of Systematic Theology, Hamma Divinity School of Wittenberg University. I myself, however, am wholly responsible for interpretations appearing in the published work.

Readers will observe my debt to the many previous authors who have concerned themselves with philosophy of history and related subjects; the notes at the end of each chapter will identify by author and publisher all copyrighted (as well as non-copyrighted) books employed. Biblical quotations generally follow The New English Bible for the New Testament, and the Authorized Version for the Old Testament, but in several instances I have modified or independently translated verses in the interest of greater fidelity to the Hebrew and Greek originals.

I am especially indebted to my friend and former colleague, E. J. Barnes, B.A., M.A., for allowing me to publish in this volume his valuable essay, "The Dependability and Value of the Extant Gospel Manuscripts."

* * *

Five printings of The Shape of the Past over a twelve-year period have fully justified a second edition under the auspices of my genial theological publisher, Bethany Fellowship, Inc. Dr. Paul D. Feinberg of the Division of Philosophy of Religion at the Trinity Evangelical Divinity School has kindly permitted the reprinting of his defense of my historical apologetic which appeared first in the pages of Christian Scholar's Review.

John Warwick Montgomery

Easter Day:
The Festival of the Resurrection of our Lord:
1975

CONTENTS

PART ONE

PHILOSOPHICAL HISTORIOGRAPHY

"And now," I said, "let me show in a figure how far our human nature is enlightened or unenlightened:- Behold! human beings living in an underground den. . . ."

"You have shown me a strange image, and they are strange prisoners."

"Like ourselves," I replied; "and they see only their own shadows, or the shadows of one another, which the fire throws on the opposite wall of the cave."

- Plato, The Republic, VII, 514 A ff.

"It is raining harder than ever," said John from the mouth of the cave.

"It will not stop to-night," said Father History. "You must stay with me till the morning."

- C. S. Lewis, The Pilgrim's Regress; an Allegorical Apology for Christianity, Reason and Romanticism (London: Bles, 1950), p. 156.

FOREWORD

It is safe to say that practically all of the history you have read in the past and much of the history you will read in the future attempts to answer <u>What</u> questions. What happened at the battle of Thermopylae? What kind of a man was Napoleon? What were the causes of the Russian revolution? Such questions as these - we call them <u>What</u> questions - comprise much of present-day historical study and thinking, and, perhaps unwittingly, give the impression that the historical field is one where memorization and antiquarian curiosity count for much, but where the pursuit of "right reason" and the concern for larger issues of meaning have little place. No doubt the common stereotype of the historian as a harmless, superannuated gentleman, devoted to tombstone rubbings or the plumbing system of ancient Rome, derives at least in part from single-minded concentration upon the <u>What</u> of history.

However, <u>What</u> questions are by no means the only questions that the student of history can ask. Moreover, they are not even the most basic questions that can be asked, for the answers to them depend upon prior answers to <u>Why</u> questions. By <u>Why</u> questions we mean questions touching on all the larger issues of meaning and purpose that underlie specific historical investigations: Why should history be written and studied? Is there ultimate purpose in history? Does history "repeat itself"? Can history be "objective"? Is history an art or a science? Answers to these and other basic <u>Why</u> questions are being given <u>implicitly</u> every day by those who write history, for history cannot be written without considering them. But the very fact that the answers are usually implicit rather than explicit creates a grave danger - that students will assume either that the questions can be ignored in practice, or that "common sense" will provide a satisfactory approach to them. Here, as in all other realms, the Socratic axiom is applicable: "The unexamined life is not worth living."[1] In this book an attempt will be made to stand back from the historical task and examine it from the <u>Why</u> standpoint - from the standpoint of philosophical meaning and significance.

The novel (and probably disturbing) character of this approach ought to be emphasized at the outset. The following statements by the eminent Cambridge historian Herbert Butterfield point to a level of tension in the Why realm which seldom exists on the What level:

> Our final interpretation of history is the most sovereign decision we can take, and it is clear that every one of us, as standing alone in the universe, has to take it for himself. It is our decision about religion, about our total attitude to things, and about the way we will appropriate life. And it is inseparable from our decision about the rôle we are going to play ourselves in that very drama of history.[2]

History viewed solely as What seldom if ever requires decision - at least conscious decision. Indeed, there are undoubtedly many who have entered the historical field and have made a career of history in order to live in a placid, insular land where decision would not be required, and where "the facts and nothing but the facts" exist.[3] The very word "decision" suggests revival campaigns rather than rare book rooms - Billy Graham rather than Professor Toynbee. But history is in fact a sphere of decision, as this book will be at pains to point out. The reader may not (and needless to say, need not) agree with the author in the position he takes, but he will find that a "sovereign decision" must be made by all readers and writers of history, and that the most dangerous historians are those who think no decision is necessary when in reality they have already made one.

NOTES

1. Plato, Apology of Socrates, 38a:
   "Ho de anexetastos bios ou biõtos anthrõpõ(i)."
   Cf. Eduard Zeller, Outlines of the History of Greek Philosophy, ed. Wilhelm Nestle, trans. L. R. Palmer (13th ed.; London: Routledge & Kegan Paul, 1931), pp. 97-104; and E. L. Allen, Guide Book to Western Thought (London: English Universities Press, 1957), pp. 13-16.

2. Herbert Butterfield, Christianity and History (London: Collins' Fontana Books, 1957), p. 39.

3. That this is becoming less and less possible is evident from the recent resurgence of interest in philosophy of history, as manifested in the new scholarly journal, History and Theory. For a listing of current contributions in this field, see John C. Rule (ed.), Bibliography of Works in the

Philosophy of History, 1945-1957 ("History and Theory Beihefte," No. 1; 's-Gravenhage, The Netherlands: Mouton, 1961).

CHAPTER ONE

HISTORY AND HISTORIOGRAPHY

"When I use a word," Humpty Dumpty said, in a rather
scornful tone, "it means just what I choose it to mean -
neither more nor less."

"The question is," said Alice, "whether you can make
words mean so many different things."

"The question is," said Humpty Dumpty, "which is to be
master - that's all."

"Impenetrability! That's what I say!"

"Would you tell me, please," said Alice, "what that
means ?"

"Now you talk like a reasonable child," said Humpty
Dumpty, looking very much pleased, "I meant by 'impenetrability' that we've had enough of that subject, and it would be
just as well if you'd mention what you mean to do next, as I
suppose you don't mean to stop here all the rest of your life."

"That's a great deal to make one word mean," Alice said
in a thoughtful tone.

"When I make a word do a lot of work like that," said
Humpty Dumpty, "I always pay it extra."[1]

In this passage Humpty Dumpty demonstrates not only his
essentially belligerent character, but also a commendable degree of philosophical sophistication, for he recognizes (1) that
words require specific definition by the user, and (2) that one
word, precisely defined, can do the work of many others. Although Humpty Dumpty is no more than a nursery-rhyme egg-
head, we shall follow his approach over against those who argue
that initial definition of a subject creates dangerous limitations,
and over against others who would define merely by example.
The former make the same error as the man who argued that
train tracks should be abolished because they unnecessarily
limit the freedom of trains; and the latter beg the question, for
to choose examples at all one must have some criteria (i.e., an
implicit definition) in mind. We therefore begin with an analysis of the fundamental terms "historiography" and "history"; by
means of such preliminary discussion we will achieve some

6

degree of orientation to the subject field of this book, and at the same time come to an appreciation of the complexity of the problems in the field and the need for "sovereign decision" with regard to them.

Historiography

Etymologically, the word "historiography" means "the writing of history" (Gk., historia, "history," and graphein, "to write"), and so Webster defines it. Thus an "historiographer" becomes a "writer of history," i.e., an historian. This identification of historiographer and historian, of historiography and history, existed for centuries, as is well illustrated by the old office of "royal historiographer," that is, royal historian.[2] Today, however, the term "historiography" is used in a more specialized sense. In his review of Harry Elmer Barnes' History of Historical Writing, Carl Becker wittily commented:

> Forty years ago I was fascinated by the study of history - the mechanics of research, of that sort of research at all events (there are other kinds) which has been defined as "taking little bits out of a great many books that no one has ever read, and putting them together in one book that no one will ever read." Later I became less interested in the study of history than in history itself - that is to say, in the suggestive meaning that could be attributed to certain periods or great events, such as that "the spirit of Rome is an acid which, applied to the sentiment of nationality, dissolved it," or that "the Renaissance was the double discovery of man and the world." Now that I am old the most intriguing aspect of history turns out to be neither the study of history nor history itself, in the above noted senses, but rather the study of the history of historical study. The name given to this aspect of history is the unlovely one, as Mr. Barnes says, of Historiography.[3]

Here Becker distinguishes historiography ("the study of the history of historical study") both from history itself and from pedestrian research techniques. Later on in his review, he expresses a desire that "historiography would become a history of history rather than a history of historians."[4] In the present book, and in the other volumes of this series, we shall employ the expression historiography in the broad sense of "history of history" - as embracing both the Why (philosophical historiography) and the How (methodological historiography) of the historical task. Though we will discuss many individual

7

historians and philosophers of history who have contributed to this area - and indeed have created it - we shall focus attention on the problems and issues at the heart of all historical work. In a word, for us historiography might be considered a depth analysis of the historian's task. But, needless to say, such analysis will have little meaning apart from a clear understanding of what we mean by history itself.

History

The word "history" is used every day without definition in our newspapers, magazines, books, and conversations; are we therefore to conclude that it is a transparent term, the meaning of which is obvious? If this is the reader's view now, it most certainly will not be his opinion when he has reached the end of this section! Here we will see how complex a term "history" is, and how the very process of defining it brings us into a sphere of vital problems concerning man and life which require personal and individual decision.

We begin with a simple but important distinction:

The word "history" has two meanings. It may mean either the record of events or events themselves. We call Cromwell a "maker of history" although he never wrote a line of it. We even say that the historian merely records the history which kings and statesmen produce. History in such instances is obviously not the narrative but the thing that awaits narration. The same name is given to both the object of the study and to the study itself. The confusion is unfortunate. Sociology, we know, deals with society; biology with life; but history deals with history! It is like juggling with words.[5]

"History," then, can refer either to events or to the study of these events. Here we shall concentrate on the latter, but the former must never be lost sight of. We must not make the mistake of identifying events with the human records or interpretations of them; at a minimum this constitutes historical arrogance (history is no more than my understanding of it), and at a maximum, solipsism (I acknowledge no objective reality outside myself). The Marxist "rewritings" of history in our own time are gross examples of this fallacy; they assume that outside of party politics and official interpretations there is no objective reality - no history which deserves to be recorded and understood whether it agrees or disagrees with personal

8

and corporate beliefs. Examples of this kind of "memory hole" are legion.

New distortions and omissions of fact continue to occur. The subscribers of the Great Soviet Encyclopedia - a very important tool - were advised in 1954 "carefully to cut out" the page referring to Lavrenti Beria, the purged chief of the police, and to substitute for it an item equal in length on the Bering Strait . . . . The same practice obtained when Viacheslav Molotov was dropped from the Party Presidium last June [1957]. Already the August issue of Problems of History, the historical journal, in enumerating the members of the Central Committee elected in August, 1917, omitted Molotov's name without explanation.[6]

Such denials of the objective reality of history remind one of George Orwell's nightmare depictation of life in the ultimate totalitarian collective.

"There is a Party slogan dealing with the control of the past," he said. "Repeat it, if you please."
"'Who controls the past controls the future; who controls the present controls the past,'" repeated Winston obediently.
"'Who controls the present controls the past,'" said O'Brien, nodding his head with slow approval. . . .
"I tell you, Winston, that reality is not external. Reality exists in the human mind, and nowhere else. Not in the individual mind, which can make mistakes, and in any case soon perishes; only in the mind of the Party, which is collective and immortal. Whatever the Party holds to be truth is truth."[7]

The student of history needs to realize from the very outset of his work in the field that events must never be confused with interpretations of them, and that historical truth is not to be identified with the judgment of individual or Party.

Since we are concerned here primarily with history as a study rather than as events subject to study, we need to distinguish this particular field of intellectual activity from others. Our procedure will be to build up a comprehensive definition by considering several common (but inadequate) definitions.

"History is the study of the past." Here the obvious question arises, "the past of what?" Does the historian concern himself with the changes in position of Halley's comet through the centuries? Obviously not, unless he is studying human reactions to the appearance of the comet - or unless, with the astrologers, he is convinced that the heavenly bodies influence human affairs!

"The good historian is like the giant of the fairy tale. He knows that wherever he catches the scent of human flesh, there his quarry lies."[8] History, as we are using the term, must be distinguished from natural history.

"History is the study of man in the past." Is history then an attempt to define human nature by examining past human activities? Is it an attempt to discover the nature of man? As we shall see, historical study ideally provides insight into human nature, but this is not the object of the historian's task. Moreover, as we shall also see, a prior knowledge of human nature is required in order to arrive at any meaningful historical interpretations.

> Our great forebears, such as Michelet or Fustel de Coulanges, taught us to recognize that the object of history is, by nature, man. Let us say rather, men. Far more than the singular, favoring abstraction, the plural which is the grammatical form of relativity is fitting for the science of change.[9]

The historian is properly concerned with human beings rather than human nature; he is not an antiquarian philosopher in disguise.

"History is the study of past human societies." In this definition we see another abstraction (society) substituted for the previous abstraction (man) - and this abstraction has no more in its favor than the other. Here we have an implied reduction of the role of the individual; as Bloch well notes, "Man in society, and societies, are not precisely equivalent ideas."[10] Especially in our day of mass society, mass culture, mass media, and mass man[11] - a day in which half the world is tending toward absolute collectivism and the other half toward sociological other-directedness[12] - the significance of the individual must not be soft-pedaled. We have just indicated that history is not antiquarian philosophy; neither is it antiquarian sociology.

"History is the attempt to answer questions about human actions done in the past" (Collingwood's definition).[13] Here the difficulty lies in the stress placed upon human action, for it suggests too man-centered, anthropocentric a view of history. Man not only acts in history; he also reacts. It is true that the historian is interested in the non-human only insofar as it is relevant to the human, but this does not mean that the acting human being must or should occupy the historian's complete attention. The New Testament critic and philosophical theologian

10

Rudolf Bultmann presents a valid criticism of Collingwood's approach when he writes:

> His definition of history as the history of human actions seems to me to be one-sided. For human life goes its way not only through actions, but also through events which encounter us through that which happens to one. And the reactions to these events are also actions in a certain sense. Man is responsible in his reaction too, and his behaviour or conduct in the face of such events is also decision.[14]

Bultmann's criticism of Collingwood warns us against all hyperhumanizations of the historical task. Shotwell correctly points out that historical study cannot be absolutely restricted to human affairs, for "the body and mind of man belong to the animal world and have antecedents that reach far beyond the confines of humanity, while the natural environment of life, - food, climate, shelter, etc., - are also part of the human story."[15] The great military historian Oman echoes this sentiment when he writes: "One cannot eradicate physical phenomena in the world from the sphere of historical inquiry, though man is not responsible for earthquakes, or volcanic explosions, or tidal waves."[16] It is possible - and indeed necessary in our era of enlarged horizons due to Einsteinian relativity and space travel - to go beyond even the qualifications stated by Shotwell and Oman. History may soon also embrace the study of non-human but rational creatures with whom earthly space travellers come into contact. Moreover, Christian theology has always asserted that man is not the only spiritual being in the universe - angels, demons, and God himself are included as well in the historical drama. If it is true (or even possible, and in a relativistic universe nothing but logical self-contradiction is impossible) that "the devil, as a roaring lion, walketh about, seeking whom he may devour" (II Pet. 5:8), that "some have entertained angels unawares" (Heb. 13:2), and that "when the fulness of the time was come, God sent forth his Son" (Gal. 4:4), then we must broaden the definition of historical study at least to allow for these possibilities. Human beings will still constitute the focus of the historian's effort, but they will not be his sole concern.

"History is a plain narrative of past events in human experience." This definition errs (to use Croce's terminology in his Theory and History of Historiography) by confusing chronicle with history. Chronicle may be regarded as a "simple narrative," but history, properly so called, needs to be a significant narrative. W. H. Walsh, who uses the latter term, says in its defense:

> The historian is not content to tell us merely what happened; he wishes to make us see why it happened, too. In other words, he aims . . . at a reconstruction of the past which is both intelligent and intelligible. It is true that historians often fail to reach this high level: they lack either the evidence or the insight required for an adequate reconstruction, and find themselves in consequence driven to recite isolated facts without being able to fit them into a coherent picture. But their doing so testifies only to the general difficulties under which historians work, not to any inherent weakness in the historical ideal. The truth is that history is a much more difficult subject than it is often taken to be, and that its successful pursuit demands the fulfilment of many conditions, not all of which are in the power of historians themselves.[17]

Shotwell nicely makes the chronicle-history distinction when he writes: "The antiquarian preserves the fragments of the great machinery of events, but the historian sets it to work again, however faintly the sound of its motion comes to him across the distant centuries."[18] This is not to say, however, that the task of history is to fit events into some prearranged logical sequence of development; to create a significant narrative is not necessarily to create a logical or progressive one.

> The fact is that History is not a tale of logical processes or necessary evolutions, but a series of happenings - some of them so startling as to deserve to be called cataclysms. One has to study these happenings with a cautious conviction that they might have happened otherwise, and that no word is so dangerous as the word "inevitable," and no conception so dangerous as the idea "progress" - unless (of course) one takes progress in the literal sense, and makes it mean no more than movement in one direction, e.g. Hogarth's "The Rake's Progress." For movement may mean motion towards a precipice no less than towards a paradise. When I read certain authors I am reminded of the schoolboys whom I used to examine forty years ago, and who always answered the familiar question, "Are we better than our ancestors?" with the cheerful reply, "Yes, certainly, for they were ignorant of steamers, railway trains, and electric lighting."[19]

Such näiveté, though perhaps excusable in the schoolboy, is inexcusable in the historian. The student and the writer of history must not confuse doubtful evolutionary presuppositions with the unquestionable fact of change in human affairs and with the necessity of interpreting that change adequately. The twin pitfalls to be avoided here are a cowardly refusal to do more than record disparate facts, and a presumptive attempt to force the facts into logical-progressive schemes. In neither case is the result history; in the former instance it is chronicle, in the latter dogma.

Having considered five partial but inadequate definitions of the historical task, can we now incorporate the foregoing insights into an inclusive formulation? History, regarded as a study rather than events subject to study, will here be defined as: <u>An inquiry focusing on past human experience, both individual and societal, with a view towards the production of significant and comprehensive narratives embracing men's actions and reactions in respect to the whole range of natural, rational, and spiritual powers.</u> Note that this definition fulfils the conditions set down in the discussion which has preceded it: attention is centered on man in the past - but not on mankind in the abstract or society in the abstract, and not on man the actor to the exclusion of the personal and impersonal forces to which he must or may react; and the interpretative function of the historian receives considerable emphasis. Note also that history is conceived of not as a closed body of knowledge but as an "inquiry" (the basal meaning of the ancient Greek word <u>historia</u> is "a learning by inquiry or investigation"); and that the historian's task is viewed comprehensively, embracing all phases of past human experience, not merely certain traditional areas such as political and economic life.

Three Problems Necessitating "Sovereign Decision"

Owing to its specificity, the above definition underscores several problems which have thus far been only implicit. Three difficulties arise, and it will be seen that the final resolution of all three must await the presentation of an adequate philosophy of history in succeeding chapters.

First, there is the matter of human nature. The historian, we have said, "focuses his inquiry on past human experience" and studies "men's actions and reactions" in the past. But how does the historian arrive at his interpretations of human motivation? How, for example, does he determine what caused a Luther or a St. Paul finally to break with the predominant religious position of his culture? Or what caused William to carry out the Norman invasion of England? Obviously, the student of history obtains all the information he can from the written statements of the principals themselves and from the assertions of their contemporaries. But, just as obviously, the historian does not accept any of these data uncritically. One's contemporaries may not have understood him, and one may not clearly recall the bases of his own decisions! The historian clearly operates with a prior conception of human nature, and even though ideally this conception will be enlarged and refined in the very course of historical research and reading, it is always present at the outset of an investigation, or no judgments of consequence would be made at all.

> In addition to the specific generalizations which historians assume, each for his particular purposes, there is also for each a fundamental set of judgments on which all his thinking rests. These judgments concern human nature: they are judgments about the characteristic responses human beings make to the various challenges set them in the course of their lives, whether by the natural conditions in which they live or by their fellow human beings. No doubt some of them are so trivial as to be scarcely worth formulating: no one, for instance, needs to set out formally the truth that men who undergo great physical privations are for the most part lacking in mental energy. But that the body of propositions as a whole is extremely important is shown by the reflection that it is in the light of his conception of human nature that the historian must finally decide both what to accept as fact and how to understand what he does accept. What he takes to be credible depends on what he conceives to be humanly possible.[20]

The question thus arises: What is the final source of the historian's conception of the "humanly possible"? Where does he derive his idea of human nature? The answer to this cannot be "from his historical studies," for we have just said that the historian has to have such a conception prior to engaging in any specific investigation. The true answer is that the historian's conception of human nature stems from his general philosophy of life - which is implemented, but not created, by his historical studies, and which lies behind all of his inquiries into the past. It goes without saying, therefore, that a sound personal philosophy is of crucial importance for sound historical work. If - to take a negative example - the historian holds the view expressed by the modern religious leader Mrs. Mary Baker Glover Patterson Eddy, that "man is incapable of sin, sickness, and death" and "evil is but an illusion, and error has no real basis," He will almost certainly be incapable of adequately

14

interpreting Hitler's career. One's conception of human nature ultimately derives from one's religio-philosophical beliefs, and these need to be solid or one's historical study will suffer in the gravest possible degree.

The same may be said about a second problem suggested by our definition of historical inquiry: the problem of significance. It has already been emphasized that history differs from chronicle in that it constitutes a significant narrative, and that "significant" does not necessarily mean logical or progressive. But what does it mean? Evidently the historian must have some idea of what constitutes a significant interpretation, or he would not attempt to produce one. A comparison of history and chronicle readily indicates in what respect they differ. The chronicle lists events without regard to relative importance, e.g.,

29 B.C. The closing of the temple of Janus for the first time since 235

15 B.C. The defeat of Lollius by the Germans

14 A.D. Death of Augustus Caesar

33 A.D. Jesus crucified

36 A.D. Artabanus, king of Parthia, makes peace with Rome

In order to turn chronicle into history, it is necessary to stress some events and deemphasize others to produce a meaningful narrative. But notice that such emphasizing is inevitably based upon value judgments as to what is important and what is not (or better, what is more important and what less important). In terms of the above illustration, it is clear that one's personal value-system, which is related to one's religio-philosophical beliefs, will make all the difference in the world as to what kind of history he will write on the basis of the chronicled events. A Christian and a non-Christian will not put stress at the same points; to the secularist, Augustus' death will almost certainly have preeminence (or, if the history of Parthia is his main concern, Artabanus' peace with Rome?); to the Christian, the death of Christ causes all the other events to pale by comparison. Thus the problem of significance, no less than the problem of human nature, requires - and in fact presupposes - decision with regard to ultimate issues.

The third problem which is pointed up by an attempt to define the nature of historical study is a particularly difficult one - so difficult, in fact, that it will require our attention in the next chapter as well as here. This problem has to do with the word "past", which inevitably appears in definitions of

15

history. Everyone agrees that the historian is essentially a
student of the past, but what does this really mean ? In a sense,
it can be argued that all students, whether of history or of other
disciplines, are students of the past, for neither the future nor
the present is subject to study. The future is unpredicable, and
so cannot be studied, and the present moves into the past so
rapidly that it can only be experienced, not studied.[21] The
French poet-satirist Boileau put it well when he wrote:

> Le temps fuit, et nous traîne avec soi:
> Le moment où je parle est déjà loin de moi.[22]

"Time flies and draws us with it; the moment in which I am
speaking is already far from me": this is true in formal study
as well as in ordinary life. Even the analyst of current opinion
finds that by the time he has taken his poll he is working with
past opinion. It follows that no sharp line can be drawn between
students of the present and students of the past, or between
history as the study of the past and other subjects which study
the present.

But is it possible to think of historical study as beginning at
a constantly moving point at a fixed distance from the present,
and extending back in time from that point ? That this is the
popular solution to the problem is well illustrated by Marc
Bloch's story of one of his high-school teachers who was very
old when Bloch was his pupil, and who said on one occasion:
"Since 1830, there has been no more history. It is all politics."[23] Obviously this subjectivistic approach solves nothing,
for it provides no criterion for determining where the supposed
line between past and present should be drawn. Moreover, it
may even imply that the closer to the present the historian's
field of interest, the less a historian he is; thus the scholar of
World War II might be considered to have less right to the
designation of historian than a scholar of World War I ! The
approach just described also lends support to the common
stereotype of the historian as a drab antiquarian whose involvement in the remote past has caused him to lose all touch with
the world of his own day.

If it is true that "the fabric of history is woven upon one
loom,"[24] then one cannot make qualitative distinctions between
present and past, or define the historian's task in such a way
that he is excluded from the present. In the definition of historical study set forth above, we have said that history is "an
inquiry focusing on past human experience" - not an inquiry
limited to past human experience. The historian differs from
other scholarly inquirers not in that he limits himself to the

past while they study the present, but in that he focuses his attention on the past, and brings the resources of both present and past to bear upon the past in an effort to understand it. While other students are interested in the past only insofar as it can be specifically applied to the present, the historian is concerned to understand the past as a meaningful phenomenon. The historian, in other words, is willing to sacrifice his own personal needs and goals in the present to understand the needs and goals of those who cannot articulate them any longer. He is willing to shift out of the center of focus the landscape of his own personality, and shift into focus what Tennyson has called "the eternal landscape of the past."[25] This certainly does not mean that historical study has no applicability to the present, but it does mean that the historian receives benefits from the past as a by-product and not as a goal of his studies. It is clear that the historian, to do his work properly, must be willing in a sense to "lose himself" in the lives and time-environments of others. But to do this is not easy, and requires a radical change in the egocentric self, which is always more concerned with its own psychology and needs than with anything else. Egocentrism and the countering of it constitute at root a religious problem, and thus once again the process of defining history leads to the realm of ultimate religious concern. The student who is a slave to his own personality will face an insuperable barrier to understanding the men of the past and the issues which moved them; in the realm of historical inquiry particularly, only the one who loses his life will ever find it.

The historian "focuses his inquiry on past human experience," and the past cannot finally be separated from present or future. We thus cannot escape one of the most perplexing of all issues: the relation between the past which the historian studies, the present in which he lives, and the future which he continually enters. Here we find ourselves involved in the fundamental concept of Time, and it is to this concept, and its connection with the historian's task, that we must next direct our attention.

NOTES

1. Lewis Carroll, Through the Looking-Glass, chap. vi.

2. E.g., Johannes Locken (Loccenius), 1597-1677, was appointed royal historiographer (i.e., historian) by Queen Christina of Sweden (see John Warwick Montgomery [ed.], A Seventeenth-Century View of European Libraries

[Berkeley: University of California Press, 1962], p. 136).

3. American Historical Review, XLIV (October, 1938), 20.
Reprinted in Carl L. Becker, Detachment and the Writing of
History: Essays and Letters, ed. Phil L. Snyder (Ithaca,
N.Y.: Cornell University Press, 1958), p. 65.

4. Ibid., p. 75.

5. James T. Shotwell, An Introduction to the History of History
(New York: Columbia University Press, 1922), pp. 2-3.

6. Alexander Dallin, "The Soviet Social Sciences after Stalin,"
Library Quarterly, XXVIII (October, 1958), 310.

7. George Orwell, 1984: A Novel, Pt. 3, chap. ii.

8. Marc Bloch, The Historian's Craft, trans. Peter Putnam
(Manchester, Eng.: Manchester University Press, 1954),
p. 26.

9. Ibid., pp. 25-26.

10. Ibid., p. 25, n. 2.

11. Cf. George P. Grant, Philosophy in the Mass Age (Van-
couver, B.C.: Copp Clark, 1959).

12. Cf. David Riesman, The Lonely Crowd (New Haven: Yale
University Press, 1950).

13. R. G. Collingwood, The Idea of History (New York: Oxford
University Press' Galaxy Books, 1956), pp. 9-10.

14. Rudolf Bultmann, The Presence of Eternity: History and
Eschatology; the Gifford Lectures 1955 (New York: Harper, 1957), pp. 136-37. It should not be necessary to add
that this quotation does not imply a general imprimatur for
Professor's Bultmann's theological-philosophical orientation; the present writer greatly appreciates Bultmann's
emphasis on existential decision, but totally disagrees with
his unhistorical attempts at "demythologizing" the New
Testament documents.

15. Shotwell, op. cit., p. 5.

16. Charles Oman, On the Writing of History (London: Methuen, 1939), p. 2.

17. W. H. Walsh, Philosophy of History: An Introduction (New York: Harper Torchbooks, 1960), p. 32.

18. Shotwell, op. cit., p. 6.

19. Oman, op. cit., p. 9.

20. Walsh, op. cit., p. 65.

21. This is true even if we agree with William James when he says, in his Principles of Psychology, that the present is experienced as a "saddle-back" rather than a "knife-edge," i.e., that the present contains something of the "no longer" and something of the "not yet," and is thus a unitary piece of duration.

22. Nicholas Boileau-Despréaux (1636-1711), Épîtres, III, 47.

23. Bloch, op. cit., p. 37.

24. Reinhold Niebuhr, "The Unity of History," Christianity and Crisis, II (May 4, 1942), 1.

25. In Memoriam, Pt. XLVI.

CHAPTER TWO

HISTORY AS TIME TRAVEL

On the Nature of Time

Our discussion of the meaning of the past has inexorably led us to a discussion of the meaning of Time, of which the past comprises one aspect. The difficulty in understanding the nature of Time has been well stated by Augustine: "Si nemo a me quaerat, scio, si quaerenti explicari velim, nescio" (I know what it is if no one asks me, but if I want to explain it to an inquirer, I do not know how). As the great astronomer Sir Arthur Eddington pointed out, Time appears all the more mysterious by reason of our intimate contact with it:

> Our knowledge of space-relations is indirect, like nearly all our knowledge of the external world - a matter of inference and interpretation of the impressions which reach us through our sense-organs. We have similar indirect knowledge of the time-relations existing between the events in the world outside us; but in addition we have direct experience of the time-relations that we ourselves are traversing - a knowledge of time not coming through external sense-organs, but taking a short cut into our consciousness. When I close my eyes and retreat into my inner mind, I feel myself <u>enduring,</u> I do not feel myself <u>extensive.</u> It is this feeling of time as affecting ourselves and not merely as existing in the relations of external events which is so peculiarly characteristic of it; space on the other hand is always appreciated as something external. That is why time seems to us so much more mysterious than space. We know nothing about the intrinsic nature of space, and so it is quite easy to conceive it satisfactorily. We have intimate acquaintance with the nature of time and so it baffles our comprehension. It is the same paradox which makes us believe we understand the nature of an ordinary table whereas the nature of human personality is altogether mysterious. We never have that intimate contact with space and tables which would make us realize how mysterious they are; we have direct knowledge of time and of the human spirit which makes us reject as

inadequate that merely symbolic conception of the world which is so often mistaken for an insight into its nature.[1]

Because of the element of mystery and paradox involved, most historians and historiographers prefer to leave the problem of Time to the philosophers. For example, Professor John McIntyre, in his recent work, The Christian Doctrine of History, restricts his discussion of Time to three generally-accepted characteristics of Time (the irreversibility of Time, and the consequent uniqueness and importance of the "now"; the influence of past upon present and present upon future, and the unavoidable conditions and limitations which the past always imposes upon current activity; and the growth-and-decay character of all of life); concerning the nature of Time he says merely: "We are not obliged to make a decision from among the various views of the nature of time which have been offered in the history of the study of this subject, by physicists and philosophers - as to whether time is an absolute concept (Newton), a relativist concept (modern physics), an intuition of sense (Kant), an unreality characteristic of the realm of appearance (Hegel and Bradley), or an element in a serial universe (J. W. Dunne)."[2] It is certainly true that the historian need not concern himself with the nature of Time in order to interpret the past in a satisfactory manner, but the better acquainted he is with the Time problem, the more he will be able to view his academic task in philosophical perspective. Moreover, the very fascination which Time holds for every thinking person - and particularly for those whose studies focus on the past - provides sufficient reason to discuss the subject here.

The basic question with regard to Time is whether it is essentially "objective" or "subjective." By "objective" we mean existing independent of the observer; by "subjective," a product of the observer's mind.[3] Andrew K. Rule poses the problem thus:

> Psychological time refuses to fit into the tidy patterns of objective time; and yet the two must somehow be related. Psychological time must be real because we can be aware of it as a purely inner experience to consciousness; but is it the only real time, the objective time being merely an "artificial" schematization for some limited purpose? Or is objective time the only real time, psychological time being the result of some subjective warping? Are both real time; and, if so, how are they related? Or is time as such unreal?[4]

21

On the "subjective" or "psychological" side of the argument, we have the ordinary experience of men in every age, as expressed by the younger Pliny: "Tanto brevius omne, quanto felicius tempus" (The happier the time, the quicker it passes).[5] This point requires no belaboring if we think of how rapidly academic vacations and holidays speed by! It is obvious that regardless of the regular, measured movement of Time suggested by our clocks and calendars, Time is experienced much differently by different people, and even by the same person at different times. The question is whether "clock-time" is no more than a civilized attempt to reduce individualistic madness by imposing order on temporal chaos, or whether Time has an objective flow outside of subjective experience. The most influential statement of the non-objective view of Time is given by Immanuel Kant, who regards Time as an essential presupposition (a priori) of human thought:

> Time is not something which exists of itself, or which inheres in things as an objective determination, and it does not, therefore, remain when abstraction is made of all subjective conditions of its intuition. . . . Time is nothing but the form of inner sense, that is, of the intuition of ourselves and of our inner state. It cannot be a determination of outer appearances; it has to do neither with shape nor position, but with the relation of representations in our inner state. And just because this inner intuition yields no shape, we endeavour to make up for this want by analogies. We represent the time-sequence by a line progressing to infinity, in which the manifold constitutes a series of one dimension only; and we reason from the properties of this line to all the properties of time. . . . Time is the formal a priori condition of all appearances whatsoever.[6]

Kant effectively shows that the time-idea is fundamental to human thought, but does he also prove that Time has no reality outside of the human consciousness? The answer here must be No, for even if we grant (as we do) the a priori, presuppositional character of Time in human thought, it does not follow that consciousness or mind creates the time-idea; it may be that Time is fundamental to human thought because Time is objectively a fundamental reality in the very composition of the universe.

A more recent philosophical claim that Time is subjective was made by the French philosopher Bergson. He argued that our inner experience of Time is far different from objective clock-time, for in our experience of Time the moments

22

interpenetrate each other, whereas in the outside world they are divided into self-contained units. Clock-time should be viewed as our utilitarian attempt to divide Time up so that we can master it, not as a true representation of the nature of Time. But Bergson is not saying that Time is unreal because it is subjective; quite to the contrary, it is "the very stuff of reality":

> No stuff [is] more resistant nor more substantial. . . . Duration is the continuous progress of the past which gnaws into the future and which swells as it advances. And as the past grows without ceasing, so also there is no limit to its preservation. Memory, as we have tried to prove, is not a faculty of putting away recollections in a drawer, or of inscribing them in a register. . . . In reality, the past is preserved by itself, automatically. In its entirety, probably, it follows us at every instant; all that we have felt, thought and willed from our earliest infancy is there, leaning over the present which is about to join it, pressing against the portals of consciousness that would fain leave it outside.[7]

On the "objective" side of the Time argument we find a formidable protagonist: modern science. To the scientist, as to Bergson, Time is real; but he would not agree with Bergson that it is in essence a mental process or that clock-time misrepresents its true nature. Newtonian physics categorically asserted time's objectivity; Eddington humorously contrasts philosophical notions of time with this objective "Astronomer Royal's time," and suggests that even if Bergson won an argument with the Astronomer Royal by showing that his idea of time was "quite nonsensical," the philosopher "would probably end the discussion by looking at his watch and rushing off to catch a train which was starting by the Astronomer Royal's time." Eddington goes on to say that the Astronomer Royal's time (i.e., ordinary, objective clock-time) "permeates every corner of physics. It stands in no need of logical defence; it is in the much stronger position of a vested interest. It has been woven into the structure of the classical physical scheme."[8] Classical physics refused to be troubled by Zeno's paradoxical criticisms of objective Time,[9] and Einsteinian relativity in this respect follows and builds upon the Newtonian approach.

It is sometimes claimed that the theory of relativity has revolutionized our concepts of space and time. The theory of relativity relates the observations made by an observer O to the observations made by an observer O' moving with

23

respect to O. It does not say anything about space and time itself.[10]

If anything, modern relativistic physics stresses the objective nature of Time to a greater extent than Newton did, for it associates Time with the three dimensions of Space to form a Space-Time continuum of four dimensions. Present-day Einsteinian physics is proceeding on the assumption that Time is objective in nature, and some very exciting possibilities are beginning to appear:

> If it turns out that motion will really slow down clocks and leave a permanent mark in the form of lost time, that could have an interesting effect on the possible adventures of future generations of men in space. If a speed near that of light could be maintained, time would slow for the space voyagers. They might reach a distant destination and return in what seemed to them weeks, though on the earth many centuries would have passed. If time really slows in motion, a person might journey even to a distant star in his own lifetime. But of course he would have to say good-bye to his own generation and the world he knew. He would return to a world of the future.[11]

The implications of the objective view of Time for philosophy of history are no less fascinating. If Time exists as an objective entity apart from the observer, and travel into the future is a conceivable possibility, what about travel into the past?

Time Travel

The idea of travelling in Time has so appealed to human beings that it appears as a theme in numerous literary works. In Charles Williams' novel, Many Dimensions, the existence of a strange stone permitting "movement in time and place and thought" leads one of the characters in the story to reflect:

> A Stone that could . . . deal as it had dealt with space ought to be able to deal in some way or other with time. For time was the same thing as space, or rather duration was a method of extension - that was elementary. "Extension," he thought, "I extend myself into - into what? Nothingness; the past is not; it doesn't exist." He shook his head; so simple a solution had never appealed to him. Every infinitesimal fraction of a second the whole universe pealed off, so to speak, and passed out of consciousness, except for the

24

extremely blurred pictures of memory, whatever memory might be. Out of existence ? that was his difficulty; was it out of existence ? . . . The past might, even materially, exist; only man was not aware of it, time being, whatever else it was, a necessity of his consciousness. "But because I can only be sequentially conscious," he argued, "must I hold that what is not communicated to consciousness does not exist ? I think in a line - but there is the potentiality of the plane." This perhaps was what great art was - a momentary apprehension of the plane at a point in the line. The Demeter of Cnidos, the Praying Hands of Dürer, the Ode to a Nightingale, the Ninth Symphony - the sense of vastness in those small things was the vastness of all that had been felt in the present.[12]

Such thoughts as these have caused other writers - particularly those in the popular field of science fiction - to depict Time Travel in bold strokes. Undoubtedly the best such example, and a prototype for more recent works of similar content but less artistry, is H. G. Wells' Time Machine. Here the "Time Traveller" argues:

"Any real body must have extension in four directions: it must have Length, Breadth, Thickness, and - Duration. . . . There is no difference between Time and any of the three dimensions of Space except that our consciousness moves along it. . . . Here is a portrait of a man at eight years old, another at fifteen, another at seventeen, another at twenty-three, and so on. All these are evidently sections, as it were, Three-Dimensional representations of his Four-Dimensioned being, which is a fixed and unalterable thing." . . .

"But the great difficulty is this," interrupted the Psychologist. "You can move about in all directions of Space, but you cannot move about in Time."

"That is the germ of my great discovery. But you are wrong to say that we cannot move about in Time. For instance, if I am recalling an incident very vividly I go back to the instant of its occurrence: I become absent-minded, as you say. I jump back for a moment. Of course we have no means of staying back for any length of Time, any more than a savage or an animal has of staying six feet above the ground. But a civilized man is better off than the savage in this respect. He can go up against gravitation in a balloon, and why should he not hope that ultimately he may be able to stop or accelerate his drift along the Time-Dimension, or even turn about and travel the other way?"[13]

Is such a hope chimerical? Even on the physical level, we must not be too quick to discount it. Relativity theory has opened up amazing possibilities; we now live in a thought-world where the atheist-type mentality - the mentality that makes a philosophy out of denial - has become a bit anachronistic. The universe is now seen to be too vast and teeming with too many potentialities to be limited by negative assertions. Specifically, one cannot deny the physical possibility of Time Travel on the ground of entropy (that since all processes run off in such a manner that there is a continual diminution of available energy, the flow of events is unidirectional and irreversible),[14] for even if one holds (and one need not) that the universe is a closed system to which no energy is being supplied from the outside,[15] Time Travel would not reverse the general flow of history. Further, the common argument that Time Travel is impossible because one could thereby alter the past - and therefore the present as well - is compelling only if one denies the freedom of the will and holds to a thoroughgoing determinist philosophy. Likewise, the claim that Time Travel is absurd because one could meet himself in the past - a true Doppelgänger situation - loses force if we see that on a more limited scale we encounter our past selves constantly - through old photographs, old diaries, and old friends and relatives who see and treat us as we were once but (probably) are no longer. On the positive side of the Time Travel argument, we have the striking investigations of J. W. Dunne, who, on the basis of experiments with prevision, affirms the "serial" character of Time - that Time consists of a series of fields related in the manner of "Chinese boxes" with each field contained within a field one dimension larger, "the larger field covering events which are 'past' and 'future,' as well as 'present,' to the smaller field."[16] Dunne experimented only with anticipations of the near-by future, but his work does lend support to the view that the universe is really "stretched out in Time," and that the past might theoretically be reached by movement into its dimension.

Whether or not physical Time Travel will ever become a reality, Time Travel in a non-physical sense is both a theoretical possibility and a practical actuality. Consider the too-common phenomenon of "old movies" on television. When one watches these films, one actually travels into the past. Gone with the Wind is shown: Clark Gable lives again - his

26

mannerisms precisely as they were when the film was made; Vivien Leigh is young again - her features exactly as they were decades ago. The viewer is in the same position he would be if, by physical Time Travel, he were transported to the scene of the original filming. If it is objected that the viewer cannot see all that went on at the original filming, and that he cannot ask the film stars questions or influence the course of the filming, the answer is that even if he were transported to the original scene, such limitations would still exist for him. He could not see everything or converse with anyone he liked; his position as observer would set limits for him then as it does now.[17] Granted the limitations are different now, and in a sense more severe, but they do not differ in nature from the limitations placed upon all observation. Moreover, the present-day observer of the film can experience much the same emotion as the physical Time Traveller would experience; note in this connection S. Alexander's remarks on the enjoyment of the past:

> We may now ask ourselves what is really present in the strict sense when there is a past enjoyment; what it is which lends colour to the belief that the remembered state of mind is actually present. The answer is that the underlying neural process is present, and that process is partially at least the same whether the act of mind be a perception of a present or a memory of a past object.[18]

But let us consider the film illustration further. How effective a Time Machine is a film? On the one hand, it provides remarkably effective knowledge of externals (e.g., documentary films give us first-hand knowledge of how Nazi soldiers marched and how Civil War cannons were loaded and fired); on the other hand, the restricted scope of a film leaves us with only a partial view. The well-known film footage of the capture of Paris during the Second World War is a case in point: everyone is touched by the scenes of weeping Frenchmen; but how meaningful is this momentary trip into the past if one does not understand the background of the fall of France - the Maginot line, the French victory in World War I, the long history of German-French conflict extending back to the decentralized Holy Roman Empire of the German nation and the powerful, absolutist France of Louis XIV? Obviously, Time Travel gains in effectiveness as the scope and detail of the journey increase.

Here we see that the best Time Machine of the present-day is the field of historical study - history as defined in the previous chapter. Admittedly not all historical writing achieves the ideal - or, to carry our analogy further, not all historical works are Time Machines of equal effectiveness; but so many powerful examples of historical Time Machines do exist (for example, Karl Brandi's biography of Emperor Charles V) that their reality cannot be discounted. Wedgwood illustrates the matter well both for the reader and for the writer of history:

> We only have to go a few centuries back in the history of Europe, to the Middle Ages, to find men framing their thought and action on entirely different assumptions. For them the individual life was set not in time, but in eternity; ideas and actions were to be thought of not in terms of time past and time future, but in terms of eternity in Heaven or Hell . . . . The historian who fails to make allowance for these deep changes in ways of human thought is unlikely to develop an illuminating sense of the past. Without the capacity for entering into the fervour of our ancestors' beliefs we shall never gain any real understanding of the Reformation.[19]

Great historical works will capture this "sense of the past" - will act as Time Machines by doing what Charles Williams' above-quoted character said of great art: "apprehending the plane at a point in the line." Like "the Ninth Symphony," the ideal historical production provides "a sense of the vastness of all that had been felt in the present."[20]

The achieving of this sense of the past depends upon a consideration already noted in the previous chapter: the ability to subordinate one's own interests to those of others. This is exceedingly difficult in present time; how much more so where men of the past are involved - who can so much more easily be bent to the personal interests of the student! The fact is that human beings are naturally self-centered, as the great depth psychologists have discovered;[21] and a remedy for this problem of self-centeredness is not to be found in human nature itself. Here we find ourselves faced with one of the most serious of all issues in historical study: a Time Machine of tremendous capacity exists for our use, but we cannot use it unless we have effectively overcome the problem of self. Only one remedy for the disease of self-centeredness is experientially satisfactory, and it should not be strange that that remedy is a religious one, since human personality is a basic religious concern. The essential problem, religiously defined, is that man has alienated himself from his Creator, and because of that alienation he has made a god of himself and prefers self-worship to real understanding of others. The religious answer is God's self-giving Act in Jesus Christ, whereby man is reconciled to God, and thus freed from himself.[22] In this world-view, objective Time becomes the totum simul - the eternal present - of God's love,[23] and the Christ-event becomes meaningful for men of past ages who looked forward to this salvation as well as for men of our present era who look back to it. And written over the entrance of the historian's Time Machine are the words of Christ: "I am the door: by Me if any man enter in, he shall be saved, and shall go in and out, and find pasture."

NOTES

1. Sir Arthur Eddington, The Nature of the Physical World [the Gifford Lectures of 1927] ("Everyman's Library," No. 922; London: J. M. Dent, 1935), p. 60.

2. John McIntyre, The Christian Doctrine of History (Edinburgh: Oliver and Boyd, 1957), p. 22.

3. No attempt will be made here to justify the use of the objective-subjective distinction. The distinction is introduced in spite of its philosophical difficulties because (as modern empirical science so well indicates) it must be employed in order to carry out any meaningful scholarly investigation.

4. Andrew K. Rule, "Time," in Twentieth Century Encyclopedia of Religious Knowledge, An Extension of the New Schaff-Herzog Encyclopedia, ed. L. A. Loetscher (Grand Rapids, Mich.: Baker Book House, 1955), II, 1116.

5. Epistles, VII, 14.

6. Immanuel Kant, Critique of Pure Reason, tr. Norman Kemp Smith (London: Macmillan, 1933), pp. 76-77.

7. Henri Bergson, Creative Evolution, tr. Arthur Mitchell (London: Macmillan, 1911), pp. 4-5. Cf. Bergson's Time and Free Will, and Wildon Carr's Henri Bergson.

8. Eddington, op. cit., p. 46. Cf. the following assertions by L. Susan Stebbing: "It is important to insist that neither

time nor causation is subjective. There may be said to be 'subjective times' dependent upon conditions relative to the percipient; there is a subjective causality also dependent upon conditions relative to the percipient. But these conditions are in the world, i.e. are really conditions. In communicating with each other, and in scientific speculation, we seek to ignore these conditions in order to attain statements of universal significance" ("Some Ambiguities in Discussions concerning Time," in Klibansky and Paton [eds.], Philosophy & History; Essays Presented to Ernst Cassirer [Oxford: Clarendon Press, 1936], p. 123).

9. The most famous of Zeno's paradoxes concerning objective motion (and thus concerning the ideas of objective Space and objective Time) is the so-called "Achilles-and-the-tortoise" problem: If in a race the tortoise has the start on Achilles, Achilles can never come up to the tortoise, for while Achilles traverses the distance from his starting-point to the starting-point of the tortoise, the tortoise moves forward, and while Achilles traverses this distance, the tortoise moves forward again, and so on. Thus Achilles can run forever and never win the race. But our everyday experience is at variance with this argument, and so we must conclude that our normal, objective concepts of Space and Time are fallacious. As Zeller states, the "fundamental error" in this and other paradoxes of Zeno dealing with Space and Time is "the confusion of the infinite divisibility of space and time with infinite dividedness" (Eduard Zeller, Outlines of the History of Greek Philosophy, ed. Wilhelm Nestle and trans. L. R. Palmer [13th ed.; London: Routledge & Kegan Paul, 1931], p. 53). Zeller means that although Zeno's premise really states only that Achilles must traverse an infinity of subdivisions of a spatial and temporal interval which is finite, Zeno's conclusion introduces an infinity of Space and Time. Thus he confounds a finite time interval infinitely divided with an infinite time (i.e., he confuses what is infinitely divisible with what is infinitely extensive), and his paradox must be discounted.

10. Aldert van der Ziel, The Natural Sciences and the Christian Message (Minneapolis: T. S. Denison, 1960), p. 111.

11. Isaac Asimov [Associate Professor of Biochemistry, Boston University], The Intelligent Man's Guide to Science

(2 vols.; New York: Basic Books, 1960), I, 286-87. It is
important to note that the concept of a "time-retarding
journey" involves no logical contradiction or semantic
"trick"; it is assuredly not a modern Zeno's paradox.
Stebbing writes: "From neglect of the peculiar conventions
of physics, there arise such paradoxes as the paradox of
'the time-retarding journey.' But, like all paradoxes, this
paradox is due to a confusion of standpoints. The paradox
is deduced from the general theory [of Relativity], and may
be regarded as an example of an equation of the form

$$\int_{t_1}^{t_2} dt \left(1-u^2/c^2\right)^{\frac{1}{2}} = \left(1-u^2/c^2\right)^{\frac{1}{2}} \left(t_2-t_1\right).$$

It is true that $\int_{1}^{2} dt$ is the same both for the observer who
leaves the earth with a very high velocity and for the stationary observer, whereas the time each has lived, which
would be represented by $\int_{1}^{2} ds$, will be different. But the
time is the same for the observers not as observers but
only as objects observed. The whole point of introducing
'physical time,' as contrasted with 'lived time,' is to secure
this consistency. In physics 'time' is a fourth dimension;
in experience it is not: in physics time is no less relative
than space; in experience there is an absolute now and an
absolute here" (Stebbing, in Klibansky and Paton [eds.],
op. cit., pp. 122-23).

12. Charles Williams, Many Dimensions (London: Faber &
Faber, 1947), pp. 53-54. All the works of this modern
Christian writer deserve high commendation - not only his
metaphysical-supernatural novels, but also and especially
his poetry (e.g., Taliessin through Logres, and The Region
of the Summer Stars), his drama (e.g., Seed of Adam), and
his non-fiction (e.g., Witchcraft, and The Descent of the
Dove: A History of the Holy Spirit in the Church).

13. H. G. Wells, The Time Machine (London: William
Heinemann, 1911) chap. i, pp. 2-3, 5-7.

14. This has been called "die Geschichtlichkeit der Natur" (the

historic character of nature) by C. F. von Weizsäcker
(History of Nature [Chicago: University of Chicago Press,
1949]), and "time's arrow" by H. F. Blum (Time's Arrow
and Evolution [Princeton: Princeton University Press,
1951]).

15. The Christian must hold that at least in a spiritual sense
energy is continually being supplied to the human situation
by God's regenerating activity through the Holy Spirit. (I
owe this valuable point to my colleague, Professor H. A.
Gram.)

16. J. W. Dunne, An Experiment with Time (3d ed.; London:
Faber Paper Covered Editions, 1958), p. 158.

17. In a recent television play by Rod Serling on his program
The Twilight Zone, this point was well illustrated by a Time
Travel situation in which the Traveller attempted to foil
Lincoln's assassination; he was unsuccessful (a succession
of unforeseen circumstances prevented him), though his
entrance into the past did result in a small change (as to
the social status of a minor character) in the present.

18. S. Alexander, Space, Time, and Deity; the Gifford Lectures
at Glasgow 1916-1918 (2 vols.; London: Macmillan, 1927),
I, 130.

19. C. V. Wedgwood, Truth and Opinion; Historical Essays
(London: Collins, 1960), p. 36.

20. The close connection between historical study and Time
Travel is well brought out in Henry James' unfinished novel,
The Sense of the Past (London: W. Collins, 1917), where
the hero's love of the past is the vehicle by which he is
transferred a century back in time. Cf. Wedgwood, op. cit.,
pp. 19 ff.

21. This is obvious with regard to Adler, but it is no less true
of Freud, whose libido concept is thoroughly egocentric,
and restates in psychological terms the Classical Greek
Eros-idea of love (which we shall discuss later and contrast with the Christian concept of love).

22. Historical evidence in support of this contention is given in
chap. v, and in essays included in Pt. II of this book.

23. On the totum simul, and our partial human experience of it,
    see A. Seth Pringle-Pattison, The Idea of God in the Light
    of Recent Philosophy; the Gifford Lectures Delivered in the
    University of Aberdeen in the Years 1912 and 1913 (Oxford:
    Clarendon Press, 1917), pp. 354-55. The most concrete
    and striking interpretation of Time from a Christian view-
    point appears in Nathan R. Wood's Secret of the Universe
    (9th ed.; Boston: Warwick Press, 1936), pp. 42-47, where
    an "identity, not of substance, but of principle" is posited
    between the Triune God and triune Time: the Father paral-
    lel with the future, the Son parallel with the present, and
    the Spirit parallel with the past, for "the Past issues, it
    proceeds, from the Future, through the Present," just as
    "the Spirit issues, He proceeds, from the Father, through
    the Son." In this connection it should be noted that in the
    familiar Biblical passage concerning the end of the age,
    "there should be time no longer" (Rev. 10:6), the Greek
    word employed is chronos ("durative time"), not kairos
    ("dynamic, existential, decision-time"), and both the
    American Standard Version of 1900-1901 and the Revised
    Standard Version of 1946 here quite properly translate
    chronos by the word "delay"; but more on the kairos con-
    cept later.

CHAPTER THREE

THE CLASSICAL-CHRISTIAN HERITAGE IN
HISTORICAL WRITING

History itself has a history. Men through the ages have written history in different ways as a consequence of the different philosophies of life that they have held. Now that we have gained some insight into the meaning of such basic terms as "history" and "time," and have begun to see the degree to which "sovereign decision" enters into the historian's work, we are in a position to survey the major types of historical writing through the ages. By such a survey - even though necessarily a rapid one - we shall encounter the central problems of philosophical historiography which have troubled and fascinated men from the beginning of time; and having seen how the great thinkers of the past have dealt with these problems, we will be better fitted to deal with them ourselves.

Our discussion of the "history of history" will, for convenience, extend over two chapters. The present chapter treats the history of Western historical writing to the end of the seventeenth century, and the next chapter will continue the narrative to the present day. The reader may well ask why a division is being made at the year 1700 rather than at a more traditional and seemingly more convenient point, such as the end of the Middle Ages, or the discovery of America, or the beginning of the Reformation. The answer is that the most fundamental "break" in the history of Western civilization came at the time when the great heritage of Classical and Christian ideas lost its place as the central focus of Western life, and was replaced by a fundamentally different approach to life characterized by depersonalization and materialism. No single completely satisfying date can be set for this change, since elements of materialistic depersonalization appeared early and the Classical-Christian heritage is by no means dead even today, but the year 1700 seems to provide the best division point, for it recognizes Scientism and the eighteenth-century "Enlightenment" as the true progenitors of the new age.[1] Probably the best argument for the use of the 1700 date is that a definite change in over-all scholarly interests can be seen at that point;[2] but the date is not as important as the fact that in early modern times the Classical-Christian cement which had held society together for thousands of years lost its hold on large segments of Western culture, and was replaced by a philosophy of life of a vastly different character. In this chapter we shall see how history was conceived and written by "Old Western Man"[3] - a species not yet completely extinct, and one which may well deserve to be cultivated in preference to more recent varieties.

Metaphysics and Myth

Concern for history is not a universal human characteristic. We of the West find historical thinking so natural to us that we often assume that all men in all times and places likewise have thought in historical terms. In actual fact, it is the twin heritage of Greco-Roman and Judeo-Christian culture that has given the West its historical orientation.[4] Non-Western cultures have centered their attention not on man's action in time, but on eternal truths outside of time (i.e., on metaphysical speculation), and on representations of these truths in mythical dress. An important recent article on the Indian conception of history points out that Indian thinkers have been preoccupied not with history as such, but with the non-permanence both of individuals and of the material evidences of their civilization, and with the unchanging spirit of man rather than with his historical activities.[5] Even the Chinese, with their strong sense of familial loyalty and tradition, have not gone beyond a belief in the "absolute relevance of the past" - the past as absolute and permanent - a reflection of the ideals of the "six classics" which are felt to sum up all history.[6]

In the ancient Near East, "Egypt and Mesopotamia possessed records which amounted to a kind of chronicle, but the decisive step to a real historical literature seems never to have been taken there."[7] The Egyptian and Mesopotamian cultures approached life mythologically and liturgically rather than historically.

These two ancient cultures are textbook examples of the fact that considerable technological and administrative, moral, spiritual, and intellectual complexity, vitality, political power, practical and theoretical sophistication can develop without the kind of a systematically rational and critical spirit that characterized Greece, which never did

35

rate for long as a first-class political power. Positively speaking, the self-understanding of these cultures was predominantly mythological (expressing itself in imaginative ideas) and cultic (expressing itself in conduct and liturgical practices) . . . . The most important aspect of a predominantly mythological self-understanding is the experience of spontaneous oneness of man with his total environment, social, natural, and temporal. Therefore it becomes a very real question, as the relevant articles in this volume have shown, whether we can at all speak of an Egyptian or Mesopotamian idea of history, in spite of the fact that we are rightly confident that we can understand their history of which they who made it had no such understanding.[8]

Certainly there was a sense of history among these early peoples, but for a definite conception of history, and indeed for the first examples of historical writing worthy of the name, we must turn to Athens and to Jerusalem.

Classical Historiography

Herodotus is termed the "father of history," and it has been well said that "all our historical writing rests on foundations laid by the Greeks."[9] But "even among the Greeks this development came late."[10] The mythical and metaphysical approaches to life which we have just discussed are evident in the Homeric poems and in Hesiod. Indeed, one of the most remarkable characteristics of Greek historical thought is the use of a mythical-metaphysical concept to give meaning to the historical process.

This concept is the cyclical pattern, the idea of "history repeating itself." The idea of cyclical recurrence is by no means peculiar to the Greco-Roman world; it is, in fact, one of the most fundamental of all mythical concepts, as my former colleague Professor Eliade has so trenchantly shown.[11] But Greek and Roman thinkers, in an effort to see meaning in the apparent diversity of historical events, applied the cycle myth to history, thereby lifting history-writing above the level of mere chronicle.

On the surface, and taken in isolation, the Greek myth of eternal return is difficult to appreciate; by some it has even been regarded as unworthy of Greco-Roman culture. Yet the myth looms large in the writings of the great Classical philosophers and historians. We find Plato telling us of a twofold motion of the universe which at intervals produces tremendous cataclysms resulting in the destruction of almost all human beings - cataclysms followed by regenerations in which "the white hair of the aged darkens."[12] Aristotle said that in another age there might be another Plato, and that Troy would fall again.[13] Polybius tells us that when Scipio Africanus burned Carthage he wept - not out of regard for the fate of the survivors about to be enslaved - but because the wheel of time would ultimately bring Rome to the same end.[14]

There is a sense in which such cyclical interpretation has a negative and antihistorical character. Eliade asserts that the Greek reinterpretation of the myth of eternal repetition was an attempt to "defend the self from history" and constituted "a supreme attempt toward the 'staticization' of becoming, toward annulling the irreversibility of time."[15] But this does not really do justice to the Greek use of the idea. Let us hear Edith Hamilton's defense of the use of cyclical pattern by the greatest of all Greek historians, Thucydides.

> Historians to-day generally reject the idea that history repeats itself and may therefore be studied as a warning and a guide. The modern scientific historian looks at his subject very much as the geologist does. History is a chronicle of fact considered for itself alone. There is no pattern in the web unrolled from the loom of time and no profit in studying it except to gain information. That was not the point of view of the Greek historian of the war between Athens and Sparta, whose book is still a masterpiece among histories. Thucydides would never have written his history if he had thought like that. Knowledge for the sake of knowledge had little attraction for the Athenians. They were realists. Knowledge was to be desired because it had value for living; it led men away from error to right action. Thucydides wrote his book because he believed that men would profit from a knowledge of what brought about that ruinous struggle precisely as they profit from a statement of what causes a deadly disease. He reasoned that since the nature of the human mind does not change any more than the nature of the human body, circumstances swayed by human nature are bound to repeat themselves, and in the same situation men are bound to act in the same way unless it is shown to them that such a course in other days ended disastrously.[16]

When Eliade says that as a result of the Greek emphasis on cycles, "among all the forms of becoming, historical becoming too is saturated with being,"[17] he is quite right - but this is properly an evidence of the Greek genius, not a criticism of the

37

Greek mind. The Greeks insisted upon discovering being -
unity, meaning - in the flux and "becomingness" of history.
They realized that without pattern there is no history, only
chronicle, for history must be a significant narrative. Admittedly, the cyclical concept taken by itself can produce antihistorical attitudes, but this does not militate against its proper
use; indeed, as we shall see, it can take on unexpected value
when combined with a particular motif of even greater significance stemming from the Judeo-Christian tradition.

Mention has been made of several great historians among
the Greeks and Romans. We would not be doing justice to
Classical historiography if we did not give some identifying information about them, and if we did not acquaint ourselves with
two other writers of comparable importance. Herodotus (5th
C. B.C.), the "father of history," recorded the conflict between
the Greeks and the Persians, and in the course of it (because
the Persians conquered Egypt) he presented a detailed description of Egypt.[18] His greatest weakness is his credulity;
but on the positive side his work is characterized by intelligent
curiosity, structural unity, and a consummate mastery of literary style and of the art of story-telling. Moreover, as his
opening sentence demonstrates, he recognized the dignity inherent in the historian's task: "These are the researches of
Herodotus of Halicarnassus which he publishes in the hope of
thereby preserving from decay the remembrance of what men
have done, and of preventing the great and wonderful achieve-
ments of the Greek and Oriental worlds from losing their due
meed of glory. . . ." Herodotus teaches the present-day writer
of history that the historian's work is a noble one, and that
great historical writing must also fulfil the standards of great
literature.

Thucydides (also 5th C.) did not suffer from the credulous-
ness that marred Herodotus' writing. His History of the
Peloponnesian War is a pragmatic work untouched by myth,
legend, or questionable tradition. "Thucydides in a word applied the principles of Greek critical philosophy to history, and
this is his greatest eminence."[19] We have already seen that he
utilized the cyclical view of history in order to give meaning to
his narrative. He himself tells us that he relied chiefly upon
the accounts of eyewitnesses to insure reliability; in doing so,
he was applying the Socratic-dialogue technique to historical
scholarship. As is the case with many other historians who
came after him, his major failing was related to his major virtue: in applying a philosophical approach to history, he became
convinced that he knew human nature well enough to reconstruct

the past where records were lacking. Thus when he knew that
a speech had been delivered on an occasion, he sometimes re-
created the speech himself and put it into the mouth of the orator; Pericles' magnificent "Oration on the Athenian Dead" is
probably of this nature - but it remains one of the world's profoundest utterances nonetheless.[20] Thucydides made the mistake of not recognizing the uniqueness and unpredictability of
much of human action; but here he erred less than Freud and
other "psychoanalytic historians" who more than once have actually perverted the data of history to fit their predetermined
conceptions of human nature.[21]

The Greeks were philosophers first and historians second;
and the Romans were political rulers and administrators first,
and historians second. Moreover, as has been repeated so often that it has become almost banal, "when Rome conquered
Greece, Greece conquered Rome." In the Roman historians we
should thus expect to find the Greek approach to history coupled with an added practicality; and this is what we do find. The
transition figure between Greek and Roman historiography is
Polybius (2d C. B.C.), who wrote in Greek concerning the expansion of Rome to the status of a world power. He came to
Rome as a Greek hostage, and there saw that the universal
dominion of Rome would forever displace the old Greek city-
state. His History, which depicts the momentous events of his
own times from 221 to 146 B.C., reflects his conviction that
"fortune has caused the whole world and its history to tend toward one purpose - the empire of Rome." Thus, like
Thucydides, Polybius believed that historical writing must provide a significant narrative, not mere chronicle; and as one
who recognized the true genius of Rome, he was convinced that
history should have a practical, utilitarian aim. In his own
words:

> The special province of history . . . is to learn why it was
> that a particular policy or argument failed or succeeded.
> For a bare statement of an occurrence is interesting indeed,
> but not instructive; but when this is supplemented by a
> statement of cause, the study of history becomes fruitful.
> For it is by applying analogies to our own circumstances
> that we get the means and basis for calculating the future;
> and for learning from the past when to act with caution, and
> when with greater boldness, in the present.[22]

Livy (59 B.C. - A.D. 17) was a member of the distinguished
circle of men of letters associated with the emperor Augustus;
his literary friendships thus included the lyric poet Horace and

the epic poet Vergil. Livy stated his aim as that of writing
"the history of the Roman people from the foundation of the city
down to my own time." The result was a colossal production
which has come down to us only in part (we have 35 of the original 142 books). Its significance lies in the fact that it was the
first great general history of Rome - the first to deserve a
place in Latin literature. Livy's Roman predecessors had emphasized the "annalistic method," which consisted of recording
events in strict chronological sequence, without much regard
for style and even less regard for interpretation. Livy, however, produced a literary masterpiece.

> His language is rich, clear, harmonious, - in its higher
> flights comparable to the eloquence of the greatest ora-
> tors. . . . He excels in painting the great scenes in the na-
> tion's life, the bitterness of party struggles, the passions of
> the masses, the joy and dread of multitudes. Stroke by
> stroke his periods seem to grow under his hand till he final-
> ly makes us almost see with our bodily eyes the scenes he
> portrays. To read his "pictured page" is like wandering
> down a long, stately gallery, the walls all glowing with the
> rich colors of historical paintings. He lives with his char-
> acters, and makes their feelings his own.[23]

Like Polybius, Livy wrote history with a utilitarian purpose;
the didactic, ethical, and patriotic tone of his entire work can
be seen in his prefatory remarks. "What chiefly makes the
study of history wholesome and profitable is this," he writes,
"that you behold the lessons of every kind of experience set
forth as on a conspicuous monument; from these you may
choose for yourself and for your own state what to imitate,
from these mark for avoidance what is shameful in the conception and shameful in the result."[24]

The Classical historian who will conclude our brief catalog
is Tacitus (ca. 54 - ca. 116), "the greatest name in Roman
historiography, comparable to Thucydides in Greek historiography."[25] We possess about one-third of Tacitus' writings,
the most important of which are the Annals (the history of the
Roman emperors from Tiberius to Nero), the Histories (an
account of the author's own time, from the accession of Galba
to the death of Domitian),[26] and the Germania (an invaluable
source of information concerning the ancient Germans). The
great strength of Tacitus' historical writing has been well
stated by Macaulay in his Essay on History: "In the delineation
of character Tacitus is unrivalled among historians, and has
very few superiors among dramatists and novelists." Also,

Tacitus is master of the pithy (and frequently cynical) observation - for example, "The more corrupt the state, the more
numerous the laws," and "The greatest crimes are perilous in
their inception, but well rewarded after their consummation."
Modern historians have often criticized Tacitus for his anti-
imperial bias, and the fact of this bias cannot be gainsaid.
Tacitus was an advocate by profession, and he wrote history as
an advocate - not as a bloodless observer. His portraits of the
emperors are undoubtedly too black, and his depictation of the
primitive Germans is almost certainly too utopian; but he is
honest enough to record many facts that do not fit his interpretations, and, indeed, the facts he gives have on more than one
occasion provided the basis for interpretations at variance with
his own. It is fair to say that "he writes as an advocate, but as
one who appeals, not as one who aims to convince."[27] Tacitus
can teach us that history written from a definite point of view
can be infinitely superior to so-called "unbiased" history. The
latter, as we shall see, is often no more than a mask covering
presuppositions of a most gratuitous sort. It cannot be emphasized too strongly that the most dangerous historians have not
been those with definite convictions, but those who have been
unaware of their convictions.

The Classical contribution to historiography lies in its determined attempt to find meaning and stability in history
through eternal cyclical patterns, and in its effort to produce
great historical works which were at the same time works of
enduring stylistic and literary merit. As the Classical age
drew to a close, these virtues were pushed to such an extreme
that they became vices; clever literary technique came to substitute for solid content, and an overwhelming desire for permanence and "substantiality" brought about an impatience with
and lack of interest in the multifarious details of the past.[28]
Philosophy, the first love of the Classical world, became its
last love as well; and history lost out in the process. But while
the curtain was coming down on the Classical age, the veil of a
certain temple was rent from top to bottom,[29] affording a new
perspective on history - and indeed on the universe as a whole.
Tacitus himself unconsciously heralds the new age when he
writes in passing of a "Christus, who in the principate of
Tiberius had been put to death by the procurator Pontius
Pilate."[30]

Biblical Historiography

For the philosophers and historians of Greece and Rome,

history had had no beginning and would have no end; and in the eternal cyclical pattern of the universe, Socrates would drink the hemlock again and again. The Biblical writers, however, viewed history as beginning at a definite point, and as moving toward a definite conclusion. The Old Testament opens with the assertion that "in the beginning God created the heaven and the earth" - and this was a creation out of nothing,[31] not merely (as in the case of Plato's Demiurge in the Timaeus) a shaping of pre-existent material. Moreover, the Old Testament looks forward to a Messiah and to a Messianic kingdom. In the New Testament, this same linear conception of history is presented, but with an important addition: a focal point has been added on the time line, for Messiah has come, in the person of Jesus. The New Testament writers recognize two streams of prophesy in the Old Testament, not just one; the predictions of a "suffering servant" are fulfilled in Jesus' earthly life and His death on a Roman cross,[32] but the predictions concerning the final Messianic fulfillment await His Second Coming "in glory, to judge both the quick and the dead." Thus if we regard the Classical concept of history as cyclical, and the Old Testament idea of history as linear, we can designate the New Testament view as "linear, but centered."[33] Expressing these concepts diagrammatically, we have

The Classical View:

The Old Testament View:

The New Testament View:[34]

The importance of the Biblical conception cannot be overstressed. Here for the first time Western man was presented with a purposive, goal-directed interpretation of history. The Classical doctrine of recurrence had been able to give a "substantiality" to history, but it had not given it any aim or direction. It is not strange that Classical man lost interest in history when it represented for him no more than eternally repetitious events. But for the "people of God" in Israel and in the Church, history was definitely "going somewhere." All our modern conceptions of historical progress - whether religious or materialistic, Christian or Marxist - take their origin ultimately from the Biblical idea of history.[35]

The specific New Testament contribution to historical thinking lay in its provision of a dynamic center for the historical process. Because the Old Testament "reached no final conclusion as to how salvation was to be achieved,"[36] it offered no supreme event by which other events could be evaluated. Israel had her historical foci, to be sure, and the most significant of them was the deliverance from Egypt. When Israel celebrated the Passover, she commemorated God's liberating act in Egypt when He destroyed her enemies but "passed over" those Hebrew families who placed blood on their doorposts at His command.[37] But this act did not remove the collective sin of Israel or the sins of individual Israelites; rather, it pointed forward to a final blood Sacrifice that would liberate all men from all the powers of evil. When "Christ our Passover was sacrificed for us,"[38] a focal center was provided for human history. The B.C. - A.D. time division is a constant reminder of the New Testament influence on historiography and world history.

In recent years much effort has been expended, especially by scholars of the so-called "Biblical theology movement," to draw as powerful a contrast as possible between Hebrew and Greek thought.[39] This movement has been influenced, as has the theological activity of Karl Barth and the "Neo-Orthodox," by a laudable desire to crush the fallacious belief of Protestant liberalism that Biblical religion is in no sense uniquely revelatory. Our preceding discussion has certainly shown a marked contrast in basic historical motif between Classical and Biblical thought; but we must be warned not to allow ourselves to sharpen this distinction to an absolute degree. The revolutionary work of James Barr[40] demonstrates clearly that the Biblical theology movement has badly misused philological evidence in supporting its position, and the implication is unavoidable that absolute contrasts between Hebrew and Greek thought cannot be sustained any longer.

Are we now saying that no essential distinction exists between Classical and Biblical conceptions of history? Certainly not; but we are saying that they need not be regarded as mutually exclusive. It may come as a surprise to some that a cyclical pattern of history appears as a definite, though secondary, motif both in the Bible and in early Church teaching and practice. In the Old Testament, we find cyclical interpretation especially obvious in the historical books.

> The Biblical narrative is built around the great cases of emergence, and gains its dramatic movement in detail as the story of recessions from, and returns to, levels of meaning already achieved. Genesis establishes the dramatic pattern of emergence and recession of meaningful order.

It opens with the creation of the world, culminating in the creation of man; and it follows the account of the original emergence of order with the story of the great recession from the Fall to the Tower of Babel. A second level of meaning emerges with Abraham's migration . . . to Canaan. That is the first Exodus . . . . Genesis is clearly the prelude to the main event whose story is told in Exodus, Numbers, and Joshua - that is, to the second Exodus, the wandering in the Desert, and the conquest of Canaan. . . . The pattern established by Genesis simply runs on with its alterate recessions from, and recapturings of, the level of meaning achieved by the Conquest. The book of Judges is a model of this type of historiography, with its . . . repetition of the formula: "So the Israelites did what was evil in the sight of Yahweh in that they forgot Yahweh their God, and served the Baals and Ashtarts," followed by accounts of prompt punishment through military defeat at the hands of Midianites, Amorites, or some other neighbor, by the repentance of Israel, and by the rise of a major judge who restores independence.[41]

In the early Church, we find regular liturgical services that represent and re-present the life and death of Christ, and the gradual development of a "church calendar" in which the events of Jesus' life are celebrated in rotation year after year.[42] One of the greatest theologians of the early Church, Irenaeus (2d C.) set forth a theory of "recapitulation" (anakeō(i)alaiōsis) based on Pauline doctrine,[43] in which he states that Christ, as the "second Adam," remedied the disobedience of the first Adam through His death on the Cross, and in doing so reconciled the human race to God and sanctified all stages of human life by His life; thus to Irenaeus the lives of all Christians are influenced by the divine pattern of Christ's life, and Christ's history "repeats itself" in the personal history of believers.[44]

If we examine carefully the corporate cycles of the Old Testament and the individualized cycles in Paul and Irenaeus, we shall see that they have in common the stages of sin, judgment, and grace; and that these stages are conceived of as existing within (not without) the "linear, but centered" pattern which is foundational for the Biblical view of history. We may schematize the combination of motifs thus:

INCARNATION
(FIRST COMING)
OF CHRIST

CREATION ⟨-⟩-⟨-⟩-⟨-⟩-⟨-†-⟩-⟨-⟩-⟨-⟩-⟨-⟩ SECOND COMING
OF CHRIST;
LAST JUDGMENT

CYCLES REFLECTING SIN, JUDGMENT, AND GRACE

Here a spiral combines the basic linear pattern with a secondary cyclical pattern; a repetition of sin, judgment, and grace
occurs throughout history, but such cycles are part of a movement directed toward a definite goal, and the whole pattern is
focused on a single event, the Cross, where judgment against
sin takes place and "all sufficient grace" to cancel out sin is
made available.

It will be noted that a closer examination of the Biblical idea
of history has provided a legitimate ground for reconciling the
Greek cyclical pattern with the unique linear conception which
is the great contribution of Biblical religion to historiography.
Instead of setting Classical and Biblical thought in diametric
opposition, we have been able to view them as complementary.
And is this really so strange, from a Christian perspective?
Simone Weil is not the only eminent thinker to find "intimations
of Christianity among the ancient Greeks";[45] and Paul himself
once presented Christianity to Greeks with the argument, "As
certain of your own poets have said. . . ."[46] The same Apostle
preached on another occasion that God "left not Himself without
witness" among the pagan peoples of the world.[47] In our day
just as in the first century, "Greeks" come constantly with the
request, "Sir, we would see Jesus";[48] they will be more likely
to find Him when His followers realize that He has not contra-
dicted unbelievers' gropings toward truth and meaning as much
as He has fulfilled them.

The Middle Ages

At the watershed between Classical times and the Middle
Ages stands St. Augustine (354-430), bishop of Hippo. In his
City of God Augustine set forth an explicit Christian philosophy
of history on the basis of Biblical teaching, and his work has
become one of the all-time Christian classics. The fact that
the book was Charlemagne's favorite[49] is an indication of its
profound influence on medieval Christendom. Augustine was
prompted to write the work because of the sack of Rome in 410

by Alaric (this date is still taken by some to mark the end of the Roman world) and by the pagan argument that Rome had fallen from its former glory as a result of embracing the Christian superstition. In reply, Augustine exposed the evils of the old Roman religion, and stressed the noble character of Christianity; but he went beyond this particular issue to the great conflict of God's kingdom (or City) and man's kingdom in history. The two "cities" are not identified with earthly institutions (it has been mistakenly argued that Augustine was simply contrasting the Roman Church with the Roman Empire); rather, the cities represent two different realms of allegiance.[50] The city of man resulted from the Fall; because of sin, human government, with its coercive powers, has become necessary. The city of God is the creation of God's free grace, and its membership consists of those who have received the salvation made available through Christ's death for the sins of the world. "Two cities have been formed by two loves," Augustine writes, "the earthly by the love of self, even to the contempt of God; the heavenly by the love of God, even to the contempt of self. The former, in a word, glories in itself, the latter in the Lord."[51] The Christian is necessarily involved in the life of both of these cities, but he must never confuse the one with the other, and must seek to win men to citizenship in the Heavenly City. Seen in this light, the fall of Rome is not the supreme tragedy, for the creations of man's world are ever rising and falling; the tragedy of all tragedies is to set one's heart on an earthly city when an eternal citizenship, purchased at infinite cost, is available for the asking.[52]

Augustine had been a Neo-Platonist before he became a Christian, and in his writings one sees his effort to utilize the best insights of the Classical age to illuminate the Christian Gospel. He has been frequently criticized for corrupting the Biblical faith through blending foreign elements with it,[53] but in actuality he should be praised for a realistic attempt to make Christianity relevant to the intellectual life of his day. Thus Augustine did not stop with the Christ-centered historical philosophy just described; within the "linear, but centered" Biblical conception, he set forth a periodization of history related to the natural and spiritual experience of individuals.

On the basis of this theological framework Augustine distinguishes six epochs, according to the six days of creation. The first extends from Adam to the great Flood; the second from Noah to Abraham, and the third from Abraham to David, with Nimrod and Nimus as their wicked counterparts.

46

The fourth epoch extends from David to the Babylonian
Exile, the fifth from there to the birth of Jesus Christ. The
sixth and last epoch, finally, extends from the first to the
second coming of Christ at the end of the world. . . .
Augustine refrains from any apocalyptic calculation of the
duration of the last epoch. What matters from an eschatological viewpoint is not the negligible difference of a few
hundred or a few thousand years but the fact that the world
is created and transient. Besides the division into six
epochs, and their analogy with six individual ages (infancy,
childhood, youth, early manhood, later manhood, old age),
there is also a division into three epochs according to the
spiritual progress of history: first, before the law (childhood); second, under the law (manhood); and third, grace
(old age).[54]

Augustine's effort to coordinate human history with personal
history - corporate life with individual life - is of great significance, for it suggests that the answers to perennial problems in the philosophy of history may depend squarely upon
answers to basic questions concerning human nature. In biology, an analogous principle is widely accepted - that "on-
togeny repeats phylogeny," i.e., that a general correspondence
frequently exists between the embryologic development of an
individual and the history of the development of the race as a
whole.[55] Perhaps in the historical realm a viewpoint reiterated by Billy Graham has more validity than is usually as-
cribed to it: the view that only when individuals experience
regeneration is there any hope for the regeneration of society.

Mediaeval historiography after Augustine usually identified
his city of God with the Roman Church and his city of man with
secular life; this resulted in a lack of interest in the world,
and a concentration upon church life and ecclesiastical institutions. Most historical works were annalistic in character, and
naïvely uncritical. This was not, however, the result of the acceptance of the Christian faith (as one frequently hears from
critics unsympathetic to Christianity); it was due rather to the
breakdown of society and the severing of lines of communication after the fall of the Western Roman Empire. Long centuries of feudal and manorial decentralization had an inevitable
effect on scholarly activity; it was only natural that historical
studies should have suffered as did all other aspects of life.
Notable exceptions existed, however; the Venerable Bede (673-
735), in his Ecclesiastical History of the English Nation, produced a historical masterpiece utilizing excellent sources and

47

critical acumen.[56] Joachim of Floris (ca. 1145-1202), an
Italian mystic theologian who was unsatisfied with mere chronicle, set forth a striking periodization of history in three
epochs: the reign of the Father (the pre-Christian era), the
reign of the Incarnate Son (the Christian era), and the reign of
the Holy Spirit (the future millenial age).[57]

The chief merit of mediaeval historiography lay in its universal perspective - a perspective which grew out of the universal character of the Christian Gospel. "Even in the Middle
Ages nationalism was a real thing; but an historian who flat-
tered national rivalries and national pride knew that he was
doing wrong. His business was not to praise England or
France but to narrate the gesta Dei."[58] Sometimes this universal perspective is expressed in ways difficult for us to appreciate - as in the case of the numerous monastic chronicles
that begin, not with the founding of the monastery under discussion, but with the Creation of the world and the Fall of our
first parents; but even this should be understood as a laudable
effort to see local and particular events in the light of the
whole history of the race - and indeed, sub specie aeternitatis.
In our day, when national rivalries so often determine (and
pervert) historical writing, and when doctoral dissertations so
often merely transplant bones from one academic graveyard to
another, we ought not to be too quick to discount the panoramic
perspective of our Christian forefathers. And even if we have
difficulty in giving the men of mediaeval times their proper
due in this regard, we must not forget that had it not been for
their careful preservation and transcription of the records of
antiquity, present-day historical analysis of the ancient world
would be a virtual impossibility.[59]

Renaissance and Reformation

In spite of their many differences, the Renaissance and the
Reformation had at least two important common characteristics: an attempt to "go back to sources" (fontes) of Western
life, and a concentration on the individual person. In the case
of the Renaissance (and we speak here primarily of the
Renaissance in Italy), the point-of-view was anthropocentric
(man-centered), whereas in the case of the Reformation, it
was theocentric (God-centered); thus the Renaissance took an
interest in the sources of pagan Classical antiquity and in individual personality per se, while the Reformation concentrated
on the Biblical sources and on individual personality before
God (coram Deo). Mediaeval civilization had been

48

society-orientated, not individual-directed (the feudal, manorial, gild, and ecclesiastical systems fitted men into predetermined community patterns), and the established character of
society had given to all activities a timeless quality and a lack
of concern for sources. In opposing this mediaeval frame of
reference, the Renaissance and Reformation made some distinctive contributions to historiography.[60]

The men of the Renaissance were so vitally interested in re-
covering the civilizations of ancient Greece and Rome that they
engaged in numerous and protracted searches for Greek and
Latin manuscripts and antiquities, and by their discoveries they
put all future generations of historians in their debt.

> Manuscripts were worshipped by these men, just as the
> reliques of Holy Land had been adored by their great-
> grandfathers. The eagerness of the Crusades was revived
> in this quest of the Holy Grail of ancient knowledge. Waifs
> and strays of Pagan authors were valued like precious gems,
> revelled in like odoriferous and gorgeous flowers, consulted
> like oracles of God, gazed on like the eyes of a beloved mis-
> tress.[61]

The urge to return to the sources also produced a critical
spirit that questioned accepted documents and sources and laid
the basis of modern textual criticism. Thus Lorenzo Valla
(15th C.) demonstrated that the so-called "Donation of Con-
stantine" was a forgery, and that the papacy had no right to
base its authority in temporal affairs upon it.[62] Renaissance
individualism resulted in a conception of the past as "the history of human passions,"[63] and a stress on biography and
autobiography. The success of such works as Boccaccio's
Life of Dante (14th C.) and Benvenuto Cellini's egotistical
history of himself (16th C.) are accurate indicators of the
spirit of the age.[64] Along with biographical works came personal accounts of contemporary life, for example the political
Memoirs of the great French chronicler-historian Commines
(ca. 1447-ca. 1511).

Moreover, in its attempt to understand Classical antiquity,
the Renaissance provided Western man with "a sense of perspective on the past, the ability to place oneself in time with
respect to an age as a whole, the awareness of historic distance."[65] In the Middle Ages, as the eminent art historian
Panofsky points out, a divorce had occurred between artistic
form and thematic content; Classical and Biblical figures were
represented in mediaeval dress, for mediaeval man was not
aware of the distance in time between the ancient period and

his own era.[66] With the coming of the Renaissance, a new awareness of the reality of time brought about a reintegration of ancient form and content, and a definite attempt was made to understand the original historical meaning of Classical and Biblical forms. "The development of a sense of historical distance was one of the most distinguishing marks of the cultural movement in Renaissance Italy, and this sense of distance paralleled the growth of a sense of perspective in painting and the general interest in archeology."[67]

Reformation historiography has been woefully neglected - as is evidenced by the complete absence of reference to it in Collingwood's Idea of History, and by Shera's irresponsible assertion that "the struggles that characterized the Reformation and Counter-Reformation arrested and finally destroyed this humanistic interest [in historical antiquity], and once again history became the hand-maiden of theologic dogma."[68] In actuality, the Reformation did for Biblical and theological studies what the Renaissance did for Classical studies: it reorientated them in terms of the sources. No longer could commentaries and late tradition be successfully appealed to; proper method demanded that one study the authoritative documents at the basis of the Christian faith. Such an emphasis had an inevitable and salutary effect on Reformation historical studies, so that alongside the polemical, anti-Romanist Magdeburg Centuries, edited by Matthias Flacius Illyricus (16th C.; Lutheran), there appeared such monuments of scholarship as the History of the Augsburg Confession by David Chytraeus (16th C.; Lutheran), and the impartial, factual Commentaries of Johann Sleidan (16th C.; Lutheran) which covers the history of the Reformation period from 1517 to 1555 by presenting a "voluminous collection of original documents," and which constitutes "the most important single source of the Reformation era."[69] Moreover, because of their regard for learning, the Reformers actively promoted the establishment of libraries, and thus contributed to later historical scholarship.[70]

Ideologically, the Reformation concerned itself with the individual in the presence of God. For Luther and for Calvin it was inconceivable that a man could stand before God except as a result of God's own gracious acceptance of the man; no longer would participation in the communal religious life of the mediaeval church be accepted as a substitute for a personal relationship with God based on His own gift in Jesus Christ. Salvation thus came to be described in Biblical terms rather than ecclesiastical terms, in personal terms rather than in collective terms, and in a theocentric terms rather than

50

anthropocentric terms. This perspective can well be summed up in a single New Testament assertion, frequently quoted by all the Reformers: "By grace you have been saved through faith; and this is not your own doing, it is the gift of God - not because of works, lest any man should boast."[71] This understanding of the proper relation between man and God led to a radically God-centered view of history.

Luther's theology of history[72] involved the convictions that (1) God is the omnipotent creator of the historical process, and historical events are the masks or cocoons behind which He is concealed; He works in every man but does not thereby violate man's personality and will; (2) The evils of history are the result of the activity of Satan and of human sin; the latter are realities permitted by God during the course of the present age but are destined to suffer final defeat at Christ's Second Coming;[73] (3) God's creative and preserving activity places men into institutional orders of community (Gemeinschafts- ordnungen) - marriage and family, the state, vocation, art, science, etc. - which protect human beings from destroying themselves in their sin and from reducing human life to chaos;[74] (4) "The meaning of history, according to Luther, consists in this that it is the field in which God's Word performs the work of salvation. . . . Every event in world history, whether it be great or small, is only willed and worked by God in order that His Word might accomplish its saving work among mankind."[75] It should be noted that Luther, on the basis of Scriptural teaching, set himself against all philosophies that try to find an immanent goal for the historical process - that see ultimate historical meaning in the attempts of sinful man to create utopias through human self-improvement; to Luther, history's center lies not in man's continual efforts to outrun his sin, but in Christ's judgment upon sin. Heinrich Bornkamm well describes the Christocentric emphasis in Luther's position when he writes:

> God's message amid the tumult of history is the same as that preached in His revealed Word: mercy and judgment. Even today we find these two incomprehensively interwoven, as they will also be on the Day of Judgment. . . . Behind the thin wall of time, the wall separating us from God, Luther, with a longing that had conquered all fear, heard Him approaching. But without the Divine Word, without Jesus Christ, we could not understand the voice of God in history. . . . At the very spot where men committed their greatest sin He opened the gates to the Father's house from

51

which they had fled. And wherever individuals and nations crucify Christ anew, not only God's punitive justice awaits them but behind His angry countenance the Father's beckoning voice as well. For Luther Christ's cross was a pledge of God's wonderful, hidden rule in history; and in it he found, as every Christian finds, the help not indeed to understand history but to bear it and to be victorious over it.[76]

Calvin shared Luther's central insights into the meaning of history; indeed, though Calvin's "theological presuppositions often dictated his historical interpretations," he held "a startlingly dynamic conception of history."[77] The sovereign God of Calvin was "not such as is imagined by sophists, vain, idle, and almost asleep, but vigilant, efficacious, operative, and engaged in continual action."[78] In the last chapter of the Institutes he thus describes God's action in history:

> Here is displayed His wonderful goodness, and power, and providence; for sometimes He raises up some of His servants as public avengers, and arms them with His commission to punish unrighteous domination, and to deliver from their distressing calamities a people who have been unjustly oppressed: sometimes He accomplishes this end by the fury of men who meditate and attempt something altogether different. Thus He liberated the people of Israel from the tyranny of Pharaoh by Moses. . . . Thus He subdued the pride of Tyre by the Egyptians; the insolence of the Egyptians by the Assyrians; the haughtiness of the Assyrians by the Chaldeans; the confidence of Babylon by the Medes and Persians, after Cyrus had subjugated the Medes. The ingratitude of the kings of Israel and Judah, and their impious rebellion, notwithstanding His numerous favours, He repressed and punished, sometimes by the Assyrians, sometimes by the Babylonians. . . . Whatever opinion be formed of the acts of men, yet the Lord equally executed His work by them, when He broke the sanguinary sceptres of insolent kings.[79]

To the Reformers, God's sovereignty over history and His great act of mercy in entering history for man's salvation provided the only bases for hope and the only remedies for meaninglessness in historical interpretation.[80]

The Age of Systematization

I have shown elsewhere[81] that the seventeenth century was

primarily a systematizing era which grew out of the Renaissance and the Reformation. During the age of classical and theological revival, men were intoxicated with the heady wine of new discovery; in the succeeding century they made sober efforts to collect, arrange, and organize the results of the great intellectual and spiritual discoveries. Because the seventeenth century lacks the feverish excitement of the earlier Renaissance-Reformation and the later epoch of Enlightenment-Revolution, it is frequently ignored by students and unfairly criticized by historians and theologians. One hears, for example, the assertion that the scholars of the seventeenth century "dulled the edge" of the Renaissance, and that the Orthodox theologians of the time "froze" the living quality of the Reformation Gospel into formalistic, scholastic categories. In point of fact, these criticisms can be sustained only by using extreme cases as examples; the truth of the matter is that the seventeenth century constituted a magnificent summing up of the whole Classical-Christian tradition. During the seventeenth century attempts were made to bring together the great insights and discoveries of all the periods of Western history which we have discussed, and to organize them into a coherent whole.

In terms of historiography, this effort manifested itself in the rise of modern librarianship and the gathering, organization, and publication of vast collections of historical source materials. In France, Gabriel Naudé wrote the first systematic treatise on library administration, entitled, Advice on Establishing a Library (1627), and Louis Jacob de Saint-Charles, a close friend of Naudé, produced in 1644 the first book-length, universal history of libraries (Treatise on the Finest Libraries, Public and Private, Which Have Existed and Which Exist Today in the World).[82] These publications reflected a growing interest in collecting and arranging both the literary remains of antiquity and the scholarly interpretations of the past which are constantly being written in the present. As the reader will discover from Volume Two of the present series, the library serves as the historian's laboratory; without it he would be lost, and for the indispensable aid it gives him today he must forever be thankful to the men of the seventeenth century who first made it a vital tool in scholarly endeavor.

Collections of historical source materials were produced especially by Roman Catholic historians and antiquarians. The Bollandist Fathers, a society of Jesuit scholars, published the stupendous Acta Sanctorum, an attempt to bring together all of the reputable information on the saints of the church. The

Benedictine monks of St. Maur edited texts and produced numerous source collections; the shining lights among the Maurists were Jean Mabillon, who specialized in the mediaeval history of the Latin church, and Bernard de Montfaucon, who concentrated on the history of the Greek church in the Middle Ages.[83] But it was not only Roman Catholics who carried out the great tasks of systematic historiography, as the magnificent History of Lutheranism by Veit Ludwig von Seckendorf evidences; in this gigantic work the author utilized documentary sources which had been neglected by others and which are to-day made available largely through his own book.[84] Moreover, as Karl Holl has pointed out, Roman Catholic scholarship of the time owed far more to Protestantism than it realized:

> Whoever has learned the intellectual history of seventeenth-century France not only from the manuals, but also senses something of the connection of scientific work with the ecclesiastical questions that were prominent at the time, will also know that only the aggravation of opposition, the necessity of discussion with equal - or victorious - Reformed adversaries, coerced the Catholic side also into a strictness of procedure, which, taking its beginning from theology, became a part of a common intellectual possession.[85]

By the end of the seventeenth century, there were clear indications that "Old Western Man" was being moved from stage center to the wings. New ideologies presented themselves even before the century closed, and their depersonalized, materialistic orientation could not have been other than antithetical to historical scholarship as well as to the Classical-Christian tradition. The eminent philosopher Descartes (1596-1650), though preceding the Age of Reason in point of time, well stated its fundamental antipathy to historical studies when he wrote in his Discourse on Method:

> I believed that I had already given sufficient time to languages, and likewise to the reading of the writings of the ancients, to their histories and fables. For to hold converse with those of other ages and to travel, are almost the same thing. It is useful to know something of the manners of different nations, that we may be enabled to form a more correct judgment regarding our own, and be prevented from thinking that everything contrary to our customs is ridiculous and irrational, - a conclusion usually come to by those whose experience has been limited to their own country. On the other hand, when too much time is occupied in travelling,

we become strangers to our native country; and the over
curious in the customs of the past are generally ignorant of
those of the present. Besides, fictitious narratives lead us
to imagine the possibility of many events that are impossible; and even the most faithful histories, if they do not wholly misrepresent matters, or exaggerate their importance to
render the account of them more worthy of perusal, omit, at
least, almost always the meanest and least striking of the
attendant circumstances; hence it happens that the remainder does not represent the truth, and that such as regulate
their conduct by examples drawn from this source, are apt
to fall into the extravagances of the knight-errants of ro-
mance, and to entertain projects that exceed their powers.[86]

How would historians reply to these objections which cut to the
very heart of their activity? The history of history from 1700
to the present day is a record of their answers.

NOTES

1. On "Scientism" (the Religion of Science), see below Pt. II,
   chap. iii, sec. 2; the "Enlightenment" or "Age of Reason"
   is discussed briefly in chap. iv of the present Part.

2. Cf. the following remarks by a prominent bibliographical
   historian: "Explanations for the disappearance of bibliographies of bibliographies around 1700 are readily found.
   Even a casual reading of the subject indexes to Labbé or
   Teissier [seventeenth-century bibliographies of bibli-
   ographies] reveals few themes to attract eighteenth-century
   scholars, who were studying theological, political, economic, historical, literary, and scientific problems in new
   ways. . . . The changes in the intellectual climate around
   1700 are too varied and numerous to discuss here. It is
   enough to note that they included the disappearance of bibliographies of bibliographies from the list of scholarly
   tools" (Archer Taylor, A History of Bibliographies of Bibliographies [New Brunswick, N. Y.: Scarecrow Press,
   1955], pp. 45-46).

3. The term is C. S. Lewis's. "C. S. Lewis . . . regards
   European history up to the nineteenth century as part of the
   history of 'Old Western Man,' with no significant break at
   the Renaissance; the break for him has come with modern
   industrial and technological civilization, and for him

therefore the main function of literary as of historical study is to make contact with that great tradition which for the first time since ancient classical times has been broken, with the breach widening daily" (David Daiches, The Present Age in British Literature [Bloomington: Indiana University Press, 1958], p. 144). Note that Lewis places the cultural cleavage at the beginning of the nineteenth century; we place it a century earlier because only then is the "Age of Reason" seen in its true light as a bedfellow of Scientism and a prime contributor to the modern dilemma.

4. It is worth pointing out that modern Western science is essentially a-historical; that is, it is concerned with experiment in the present and prediction of the future through the discovery of general laws, not with the record of past human activity.

5. Baldoon Dhingra, "Conception indienne de l'histoire," Synthèses, XIII (1958), 77-81.

6. These points concerning the Chinese view of history were made by Joseph R. Levenson of the University of California (Berkeley) in the session on "Determinants of Western Civilization" at the 75th Annual Meeting of the American Historical Association, December 28, 1960. Mr. Levenson quite correctly noted that this a-historical attitude on the part of Chinese culture made it easy for the Chinese to shift from their traditional absolutes to the new Marxist absolute.

7. Ulrich von Wilamowitz-Moellendorff, Greek Historical Writing and Apollo, trans. Gilbert Murray (Oxford: Clarendon Press, 1908), pp. 5-6. Unfortunately this great classicist does not recognize the importance of ancient Hebrew historical writing.

8. Paul Schubert, "The Twentieth-Century West and the Ancient Near East," in The Idea of History in the Ancient Near East, ed. Robert C. Dentan ("American Oriental Series," Vol. 38; New Haven: Yale University Press, 1955), pp. 337-38.

9. Wilamowitz-Moellendorff, op. cit., p. 5.

10. James Westfall Thompson, A History of Historical Writing (2 vols.; New York: Macmillan, 1942), I, 21.

11. Mircea Eliade, The Myth of the Eternal Return, trans. Willard R. Trask ("Bollingen Series," No. 46; New York: Pantheon Books, 1954).

12. Plato, Politicus, 269c ff. Cf. Arnold J. Toynbee, Greek Historical Thought from Homer to the Age of Heraclius (New York: New American Library Mentor Books, 1952), pp. 129 ff.

13. Cf. Henri Puech, "La Gnose et le temps," Eranos Jahrbuch, XX (1951), 57-113.

14. Polybius, History, Bk. XXXVIII, secs. 21-22.

15. Eliade, op. cit., p. 123.

16. Edith Hamilton, The Greek Way to Western Civilization (New York: New American Library Mentor Books, 1948), p. 102.

17. Eliade, loc. cit.

18. Readers who wish to consult the works of the great Classical historians referred to here are advised to acquaint themselves with the Loeb Classical Library (published by William Heinemann in London, and Harvard University Press in Cambridge, Massachusetts), which provides Greek or Latin texts with facing English translations.

19. Thompson, op. cit., I, 29.

20. This was made especially clear in "The Secret of Freedom," Archibald Macleish's television drama of a few years ago; in it, the "Periclean" claim that the secret of freedom is Courage was shown to have powerful relevance for Western man in the present era of nuclear tension and totalitarian agression.

21. In Freud's Moses and Monotheism, the founder of psychoanalysis realigns historical fact concerning Moses to fit his analytic theorizing; but more about this in the next chapter. It is especially suggestive in this connection that

C. N. Cochrane (Thucydides and the Science of History) argues that the dominant influence on Thucydides was Hippocratic medicine, which gave a psychological emphasis to his historical scholarship.

22. Polybius, History, XII, 25b.

23. J. H. Westcott (ed.), Livy (Boston: Allyn and Bacon, 1924), p. xx.

24. Cf. R. B. Steele, "The Historical Attitude of Livy," American Journal of Philology, XXV (1904), 15-44.

25. Thompson, op. cit., I, 84-85.

26. The Annals served as an introduction to the Histories; taken together, the two works treat the imperial line from A.D. 14 to 96. The Annals is generally considered Tacitus' masterpiece.

27. William Francis Allen (ed.), Tacitus: The Annals (Boston: Ginn, 1890), p. xxxiii.

28. The term "substantiality" is taken from R. G. Collingwood (The Idea of History [New York: Oxford University Press' Galaxy Books, 1956], pp. 42-45). We do not agree with Collingwood, however, when he asserts that the "humanistic" emphasis of Classical historiography is its chief merit; and we feel that his over-all evaluation of Classical historical writing is far too negative.

29. See Mt. 27:51 and Heb. 10:19-20.

30. "Christus Tiberio imperitante per procuratorem Pontium Pilatum supplicio adfectus erat" (Annals, XV, 44; Tacitus wrote this about A.D. 115). See C. R. Haines, Heathen Contact with Christianity during Its First Century and a Half; Being All References to Christianity Recorded in Pagan Writings during That Period (Cambridge, England: Deighton, Bell, 1923), pp. 48-49 and passim.

31. The Hebrew word for "create" in Gen. 1:1 is bara. As the great systematic theologian Augustus H. Strong said, "If bara does not signify absolute creation, no word exists in the Hebrew language that can express this idea." Cf.

Heb. 11:3: "By faith we understand that the world was created by the word of God, so that what is seen was made out of things which do not appear."

32. The "suffering servant" passage in Isaiah 53 is far too individualistic in its emphasis to be applied to the Hebrew nation as a whole.

33. Karl Löwith, Meaning in History (Chicago: University of Chicago Press' Phoenix Books, 1957), p. 182.

34. We do not employ the diagrammatic scheme popularized by Oscar Cullmann (Christ and Time, trans. Floyd V. Filson [Philadelphia: Westminster Press, 1950], pp. 82, 115-18, and passim) in which the Christ-event constitutes a midpoint from which past and future are viewed:

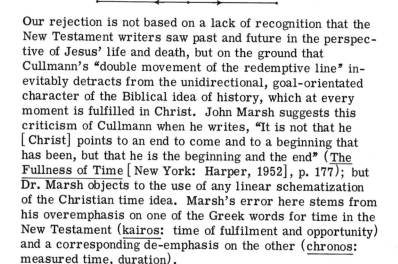

Our rejection is not based on a lack of recognition that the New Testament writers saw past and future in the perspective of Jesus' life and death, but on the ground that Cullmann's "double movement of the redemptive line" inevitably detracts from the unidirectional, goal-orientated character of the Biblical idea of history, which at every moment is fulfilled in Christ. John Marsh suggests this criticism of Cullmann when he writes, "It is not that he [Christ] points to an end to come and to a beginning that has been, but that he is the beginning and the end" (The Fullness of Time [New York: Harper, 1952], p. 177); but Dr. Marsh objects to the use of any linear schematization of the Christian time idea. Marsh's error here stems from his overemphasis on one of the Greek words for time in the New Testament (kairos: time of fulfilment and opportunity) and a corresponding de-emphasis on the other (chronos: measured time, duration).

35. "What must be insisted is that the very spirit of progress takes its form and depends for its origin on the Judaeo-Christian idea of history" (George P. Grant, Philosophy in the Mass Age [Vancouver: Copp Clark, 1959], p. 49).

36. G. Ernest Wright, The Old Testament against Its Environment ("Studies in Biblical Theology," No. 2; London: SCM Press, 1950), p. 110.

37. See Exodus 12.

38. I Cor. 5:7.

39. The most ambitious attempt along this line is Thorlief Boman's Hebrew Thought Compared with Greek, trans. Jules L. Moreau (London: SCM Press, 1960).

40. James Barr, The Semantics of Biblical Language (London: Oxford University Press, 1961). In a paper delivered at the University of Toronto on May 15, 1962, Barr explicitly stated that in his opinion the philological difficulties of the Biblical theology movement stem in large part from its unconscious agreement with Barth's absolute rejection of natural revelation and his depreciation of the cultural ties between Biblical and non-Biblical worlds of thought. (We shall have more to say about Barthian Neo-Orthodoxy in chap. v.)

41. Eric Voegelin, Order and History, I (Baton Rouge: Louisiana State University Press, 1956), 139-42. The same general point is made by Otto J. Baab (The Theology of the Old Testament [New York: Abingdon, 1949], pp. 175-58), but the value of Baab's analysis is severely limited by a blind and outmoded acceptance of the Graf-Kuenen-Wellhausen documentary theory of Pentateuchal origins.

42. Christian worship has always centered on the rite of the Lord's Supper, which Jesus commanded to be done "often, in remembrance of Me"; Brilioth well expresses this historical aspect of the early Christian worship service when he writes: "The fundamental difference between the heathen mysteries and the Christian [is] that while in the cult-legends of Isis, Attis or Mithra, not even the best will in the world could find a grain of historical truth, the Christian mysteries commemorate the historical facts of a human life whose essential actuality no sober critic can doubt" (Yngve Brilioth, Eucharistic Faith & Practice, Evangelical & Catholic, trans. A. G. Hebert [London: S.P.C.K., 1930], p. 34). Concerning the cyclical-historical nature of the church year, we have Horn's accurate depictation: "The major events of the life of our Lord pass in review perennially in the first half of the church year, keeping the Christian community in perpetual remembrance of 'all that our Lord hath done for our sakes.' The second

half of the church year relates the profound implications of our Lord's incarnation, life, death and resurrection to the life in time of the Christian and of the Christian community" (Edward T. Horn, III, The Christian Year [Philadelphia: Muhlenberg Press, 1957], p. 8).

43. The Greek word appears in Eph. 1:10. See also Rom. 5:12 ff. and my article "Some Comments on Paul's Use of Genesis in His Epistle to the Romans," Evangelical Theological Society Bulletin, IV (April, 1961), 4-11.

44. Irenaeus, Adversus haereses, III, xviii, 1; III, xxii, 3; V, xvi, 3; V, xviii, 3. Cf. J. L. Neve and O. W. Heick, A History of Christian Thought (2 vols.; Philadelphia: Muhlenberg Press, 1946), I, 80-81. For the historical conceptions of other Patristic writers, see R. L. P. Milburn, Early Christian Interpretations of History; the Bampton Lectures of 1952 (London: Adam and Charles Black, 1954).

45. Simone Weil, Intimations of Christianity among the Ancient Greeks, ed. and trans. E. C. Geissbuhler (Boston: Beacon Press, 1958). Two older works which are almost forgotten today deserve to be carefully studied in this connection: B. F. Cocker, Christianity and Greek Philosophy; or, the Relation between Spontaneous and Reflective Thought in Greece and the Positive Teaching of Christ and His Apostles (New York: Harper, 1870); and Edward Hicks, Traces of Greek Philosophy and Roman Law in the New Testament (London: S.P.C.K., 1896).

46. Acts 17:28; the whole of Paul's Areopagus address should be read for the setting of this remark. The frequently-repeated assertion that in I Cor. 1:17 ff. Paul later confessed that he had preached "worldly wisdom" instead of the Gospel at Athens is pure supposition and should be disregarded.

47. Acts 14:17.

48. Jn. 12:20-21. The Apostle John himself made every effort to present Christ in terms that the Greeks of his day would understand; in the opening chapter of his Gospel he uses the word Logos for Jesus, thereby creating common ground with those who were acquainted with the powerful and ancient logos tradition in Greek philosophical speculation.

49. Thompson, op. cit., I, 137.

50. A point well made by E. L. Allen in his Guide Book to
Western Thought (London: English Universities Press,
1957), pp. 74-77.

51. Augustine, Civitas Dei, XIV, 28.

52. Cf. Gordon H. Clark, A Christian View of Men and Things
(Grand Rapids, Michigan: Eerdmans, 1952), pp. 85-88.

53. This criticism has been made most forcefully by Anders
Nygren, in his Agape and Eros, trans. Philip S. Watson
(Philadelphia: Westminster Press, 1953), pp. 449-562.
We shall have occasion to discuss Nygren's epochal work
in another chapter.

54. Löwith, op. cit., pp. 170-71.

55. William C. Beaver, The Science of Biology (4th ed.; St.
Louis: C. V. Mosby, 1952), pp. 442, 740-42.

56. This great work may be consulted in the Loeb Classical
Library. Bede is rightly called "the father of English
history."

57. On Joachim, see Paul Fournier, Études sur Joachim de
Flore (Paris, 1909). The common periodization used by
mediaeval historians was based upon the Four World Empires prophesied in the Book of Daniel (Daniel 7); on this
prophecy and its relation to Daniel's precise time prediction of the birth of Jesus the Messiah, see Sir Robert
Anderson's remarkable work, The Coming Prince
(Glasgow: Pickering & Inglis, n.d.).

58. Collingwood, op. cit., p. 53.

59. See James Westfall Thompson, The Medieval Library, reprinted with a supplement by Blanche B. Boyer (New York:
Hafner, 1957).

60. This interpretation of the Renaissance and the Reformation
will be presented in context in Volumes IV and V of this
series.

61. John Addington Symonds, Renaissance in Italy (2 vols.; New York: Modern Library, n.d.), I, 12-13.

62. On Valla, see John Edwin Sandys, A History of Classical Scholarship, II (reprint ed.; New York: Hafner, 1958), 66-70.

63. Collingwood, op. cit., p. 57.

64. Cellini's Autobiography is published by the Modern Library.

65. Myron P. Gilmore, The World of Humanism, 1453-1517 (New York: Harper, 1952), p. 201.

66. See the Introduction to Erwin Panofsky's Studies in Iconology; Humanistic Themes in the Art of the Renaissance (New York, 1939).

67. Gilmore, op. cit., p. 236.

68. Jesse H. Shera, Historians, Books, and Libraries (Cleveland: Western Reserve University Press, 1953), p. 35.

69. Thompson, History of Historical Writing, I, 529, On Chytraeus, see the editorial introduction to my translation of Chytraeus on Sacrifice (St. Louis: Concordia, 1962).

70. See my article, "Luther and Libraries," The Library Quarterly, XXXII (April, 1962), 133-47.

71. Eph. 2:8-9.

72. For an excellent expansion of the points to follow, see Peter Brunner, "The Secret of History," in Luther in the 20th Century ("Martin Luther Lectures," Vol. 5; Decorah, Iowa: Luther College Press, 1961), pp. 11-25.

73. Luther - and the other Reformers as well - believed in the ontological existence of evil; this is unfortunately not true of the current Neo-Orthodox theology represented by Karl Barth, as was made evident by the discussion between Barth and the conservative theologian Edward John Carnell at the University of Chicago Barth Lectures on April 26, 1962. (More about Barthian Neo-Orthodoxy in chap. v.) With regard to the God-permitted activity of Satan in the present

age, cf. my short story, "God's Devil," in Chiaroscuro, IV (1961), 20-28.

74. The "orders" have been given particularly trenchant modern expression by Emil Brunner; see in Pt. Two my essay, "A Critical Examination of Emil Brunner's The Divine Imperative, Bk. III."

75. Peter Brunner, Luther in the 20th Century, pp. 23-24.

76. Heinrich Bornkamm, Luther's World of Thought, trans. Martin H. Bertram (St. Louis: Concordia, 1958), pp. 216-17; cf. Bornkamm's Gott und die Geschichte nach Luther (Lünenburg: Heliand, 1947). See also Theodore G. Tappert, "The Theologian and the Study of History," in The Mature Luther ("Martin Luther Lectures," Vol. 3; Decorah, Iowa: Luther College Press, 1959), pp. 21-38.

77. E. Harris Harbison, The Christian Scholar in the Age of the Reformation (New York: Scribner, 1956), pp. 153, 161.

78. Calvin, Institutes, I, xvi, 3.

79. Ibid., IV, xx, 30-31.

80. Limitations of space forbid us from discussing the particular historiographical emphases of the Anabaptists of the Reformation period. Readers interested in this subject are advised to consult Ethelbert Stauffer, "The Anabaptist Theology of Martyrdom," Mennonite Quarterly Review, XIX (July, 1945), 179-214; Robert Friedmann, "The Doctrine of the Two Worlds," in Guy F. Hershberger (ed.), The Recovery of the Anabaptist Vision; A Sixtieth Anniversary Tribute to Harold S. Bender (Scottdale, Pa.: Herald Press, 1957), pp. 105-118; and Ronald J. Sider, "The Political Theory and Philosophy of History of a Radical Reformer: An Analysis of Bernhardt Rothmann's Van erdesscher unnde tytliker Gewalt" (unpublished honours B.A. thesis, Department of History, Waterloo Lutheran University, 1962).

81. In my editorial introduction to "The Libraries of France at the Ascendancy of Mazarin: Louis Jacob's Traicté des plus belles bibliothèques, Part Two, in English Translation,

with Introduction and Notes" (Ph.D. dissertation, University of Chicago, 1962).

82. I have translated and edited the primary-source section of Jacob's work; see the preceding note. Naudé's book is available in an English translation edited by Archer Taylor (Berkeley: University of California Press, 1950).

83. On the Bollandists and Maurists, see Thompson, History of Historical Writing, II, chap. xxxvii.

84. See Lewis W. Spitz, "Veit Ludwig von Seckendorf: Statesman and Scholar," Concordia Theological Monthly, XVI (1945), 672-84.

85. Karl Holl, The Cultural Significance of the Reformation, trans. Hertz and Lichtblau (New York: Meridian Living Age Books, 1959), pp. 120-21.

86. René Descartes, A Discourse on Method, trans. John Veitch ("Everyman's Library," No. 570; London: J. M. Dent, 1912), pp. 6-7. Lucien Lévy-Bruhl writes: "The Cartesians' attitude to history . . . was the immediate consequence of their uncompromising definition of truth, which excluded whatever was not rationally evident. . . . There is in the Cartesian mind a kind of natural distrust, almost an antipathy, for history" ("The Cartesian Spirit and History," in Klibansky and Paton [eds.], Philosophy & History; Essays Presented to Ernst Cassirer [Oxford: Clarendon Press, 1936], pp. 195-96).

CHAPTER FOUR

MODERN HISTORICAL THOUGHT

Descartes had leveled two fundamental criticisms against the historian's work: historical narratives do not provide trustworthy accounts of the past, and they lack sufficient utilitarian value to aid present-day living. Obviously the second criticism depends upon the first, and we are led to ask why Descartes became convinced that historical studies lacked reliability. What caused him to couple history with fable and to argue that accounts of the past omit vital information and "lead us to imagine the possibility of many events that are impossible"? The answer lies in Descartes' conviction that if certainty is to be found, it will be discovered not in the variegated realm of human experience, but in the absolute realm of mathematics and philosophy. Descartes was the true father of the eighteenth-century "Age of Reason," in which pure rationality was elevated above the flux of human life and the alleged superstitions of revealed religion. Highly symbolic of the epoch which Descartes ushered in was the rededication, during the French Revolution, of Notre Dame Cathedral to the goddess Reason.[1]

History during the Age of Reason

Rationalists of the eighteenth century usually passed history by; their interests lay elsewhere - in philosophical speculation, mathematical calculation, and scientific experimentation. Those scholars of the time whose native concern for people could not be this easily sublimated into impersonal channels found historical studies either a challenge or a frustration.

Voltaire, the prince of skeptics, published his first historical work at the age of thirty-seven and then (significantly) devoted the next twenty years of his life to natural philosophy and poetry; but finally he came back to historical studies and through them achieved a reputation among his contemporaries as the greatest living historian. Voltaire's intellectual father in the subject of history was Bolingbroke, who popularized the aphorism that "history is philosophy teaching by examples" - a view particularly congenial to the Age of Reason. Here "one detects the peculiarly optimistic and delusive belief of the age, that enlightened reason is the sovereign instrument for remedying the ills of humanity. Men are everywhere the same, was the argument; therefore give reason a chance, set it face to face with the tableau of history, let it assimilate the principles embodied in this tableau, and inevitably it will proceed to institute a more rational order."[2] This naïve belief on Voltaire's part led "to a curious sameness in his presentation of events,"[3] to a dogmatic belief in the invariable course of nature,[4] and to a continual vilification of the part played by religion in history. For Voltaire, history constituted a challenge; he would use its numerous instances of human superstition and irrationality to teach men how to act in accord with reason. "Abolish the study of history," he argued, "and you will probably see new Saint Bartholomew's days in France and new Cromwells in England."[5]

The most profound thinker to be influenced by the eighteenth-century "Enlightenment" was a philosopher who is often studied in the context of the nineteenth century. However, the outlook of Immanuel Kant "was singularly unhistorical, and he remained in this as in other respects a typical product of the Enlightenment rather than a forerunner of the Romantic Age which was shortly to follow."[6] Though Kant was a philosopher and not an historian, he must be included in any discussion of eighteenth-century historiography, for on the basis of the rationalist world-view he went far beyond Voltaire and asserted that "the history of the human race, viewed as a whole, may be regarded as the realization of a hidden plan of nature to bring about a political constitution, internally, and, for this purpose, also externally perfect, as the only state in which all the capacities implanted by her in mankind can be fully developed."[7] Kant, in other words, held that history is a rational process - that Reason actually provides the plan and the goal of history. On the surface this does not appear to be the case always and everywhere, Kant admits, but in reality man's "unsociableness" - his "envious jealousy and vanity" and "unsatiable desire of possession or even of power" - turns man from "idleness and inactive contentment" to "further development of his natural capacities."[8] Kant's view suffers from two serious objections: it does not take evil seriously, for it employs the argument that the end justifies the means (in actuality, the means employed always alters the character of the end, so that if an evil means is used, the end becomes evil); and it attempts to say something substantial about the plot of history without investigating the data of historical experience. These objections are sufficient to destroy Kant's proposed philosophy of history, but the importance of his endeavor cannot be denied; he projected what many would attempt after him: the creation of a philosophy of history on the basis of pure reason.

Edward Gibbon shared with Voltaire and Kant an Enlightenment confidence in rationality, but in his case the result was frustration. Gibbon's huge Decline and Fall of the Roman Empire (which everyone refers to as if he had read it but almost no one has!) is a literary masterpiece and an enduring monument of historical research, but its author concluded that he was setting down "little more than the register of the crimes, follies and misfortunes of mankind."[9] Why did Gibbon experience this profound melancholia? Chiefly because he saw in the Fall of Rome the triumph of Christian superstition and barbarism over the rational civilization of Classical times. This view of the past was widely shared by eighteenth-century scholars who were imbued with the rational spirit. Most of them were too realistic to treat history as Voltaire and Kant did; the majority agreed with Gibbon's negative judgment - and consequently turned their attention to the present, where they thought they could discern a new age of rational enlightenment being ushered in.

Descartes had criticized historical studies for their irrationality and lack of certainty; for him and for most intellectuals of the Age of Reason certainty was identified with rationality, and rationality with philosophy, mathematics, and science. The only scholar of this period who clearly saw the central fallacy in Descartes' approach was an obscure Italian philologian by the name of Giambattista Vico, whose great work, The New Science, did not receive its due recognition for almost two centuries, and was not translated into English until 1948. In The New Science Vico argued the seemingly paradoxical proposition that "philosophy contemplates reason, whence comes knowledge of the true; philology [i.e., historical studies in general] observes that of which human choice is author, whence comes consciousness of the certain."[10] Vico here distinguishes the provinces of philosophy and history according to the different kinds of knowledge they impart. Philosophy (and here Vico would include mathematics and science) deals with abstract truth, but not with experiential reality, for it studies what is external to man himself. History, on the other hand, deals in realities, for it describes what men themselves experience and create - though it never arrives at universal and eternal principles because human creations are fallible and the records of the past are only imperfectly preserved.[11] Vico shrewdly saw that philosophy and "reason" should not be pitted against historical studies, but that in reality the two fields are complementary; and his analysis of the problem of historical and philosophical truth not unnaturally had vital ramifications for the defense of the Christian faith against rationalist critics.[12] Moreover, within a Christian framework (and few of Vico's intellectual contemporaries could appreciate his retention of this framework), Vico found a place for a cyclical view of human history. Basing his analysis on "the three ages which the Egyptians handed down to us," he sets forth the following epochs:

> (1) The age of gods, in which the gentiles believed they lived under divine governments and everything was commanded them by auspices and oracles, which are the oldest institutions in profane history. (2) The age of heroes, in which they reigned everywhere in aristocratic commonwealths, on account of a certain superiority of nature which they held themselves to have over the plebs. (3) The age of men, in which all men recognized themselves as equal in human nature, and therefore there were established first the popular commonwealths and then the monarchies, both of which are forms of human government.[13]

After moving through these divine (theocratic), heroic (mythological), and human (civil) stages, "the whole course (corso) begins anew from a new barbarism in a recurrence (ricorso) which is, at the same time, a resurgence. Such a recurrence has already occurred once, after the fall of Rome, in the creative return of barbaric times in the Middle Ages."[14] Vico's conception of the corsi and recorsi of the nations is not simply cyclical, nor is it purely linear; Caponigri describes it accurately and beautifully as "contrapuntal."[15] And in the final analysis this counterpoint is played by Providence, working immanently in the affairs of men. Each human corso falls short of its goal, and the subsequent ricorso is a judgment which, by producing a new corso, creates a higher tribunal wherein the human case is reviewed. "The highest court of justice is, however, providential history as a whole,"[16] and the concept of Providence is "the supreme principle of the 'New Science.'"[17] Through historical judgments God works in the city of man; to Augustine's city of God, Vico added human history as a direct sphere of God's activity. But in presenting this profoundly theologic world-view, Vico was, if any man has ever been, "one born out of due time."[18]

The Nineteenth Century

In the century preceding our own, historians and philosophers of history attempted in various ways to counter the negative view of history expressed by Descartes and accepted by most intellectuals during the Age of Reason. Five major attempts can be distinguished: the philosophical attempt (Hegel), the scientific attempt (Positivism), the economic attempt (Marx), the literary attempt (Macaulay and Carlyle), and the realistic attempt (Burckhardt and Acton). We shall discuss each of these in turn.[19]

The most obvious way of disarming Cartesian critics was not to try to "beat 'em" but to "join 'em." Descartes had argued that historical study lacked the certainty of philosophy and the preciseness of science. Vico had seen that such a comparison was invidious; but in the nineteenth century many thinkers came to believe that history ought to be able to stand comparison with philosophy, with science, or with both, and that Descartes' fault was that he did not recognize the essentially philosophical or scientific character of history.

The great German philosopher Hegel argued that "world history is a rational process,"[20] and that it moves in dialectical fashion through four great "world-historical" epochs (Oriental, Greek, Roman, and Germanic) towards the goal of freedom. In this process, each nation's hour strikes but once, and then it serves as the vehicle of the world spirit of reason and makes its specific contribution to the history of mankind; and great men play their unique roles at crucial junctures - roles which cannot be judged as "good" or "bad" by ordinary moral standards. Hegel's philosophy of history can be (and has been) severely criticized on many counts: it errs (as did Kant's) in purporting to deduce historical substance and goal from reason itself; it accepts the Four Empires periodization without committing itself to a belief in the revelatory character of the Book of Daniel where the conception is presented;[21] it suffers from Hegel's Germanic point-of-view; and its doctrine of the crucial hours of the nations and its meta-ethical evaluation of great men in history can easily be employed to justify national imperialism and unprincipled actions by individuals.

These difficulties in Hegel's system should not, however, obscure its one great merit: the notion of the dialectic and the application of it to history. By dialectic, Hegel meant the

70

tendency both in life and in thought for a position to spawn its own opposite, and for these two extremes to be succeeded by a compromise which partakes of some elements of both of them.[22] Expressed in a diagrammatic way,

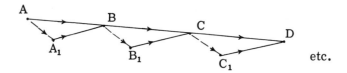

A, the original idea or event (the "thesis") produces its opposite, A_1 (the "antithesis"); out of these develops a "synthesis" of the two (B), which constitutes a new thesis. This new thesis is opposed by a new antithesis (B_1), and from them a new synthesis (C) arises, and the refining process moves on and on. Numerous historical examples of dialectic movement will suggest themselves; one illustration is the history of France before, during, and after the French Revolution. The absolute, authoritarian monarchy of the Old Régime can be considered a thesis to which the near anarchy and libertarianism of the Revolutionary period arose as an antithesis; out of both extremes eventually developed a republican form of government which adopted certain elements of both extremes. It is important to realize that the Hegelian dialectic is really a formal principle which neither discloses the goal of a process nor places any value judgment upon it; the dialectic can describe a continual refinement of evil as well as a continual refinement of good. Indeed, one of the chief errors made by Hegel himself lay in his conviction that the historical dialectic is moving toward the specific goal of freedom; in actuality, the dialectic never requires such a conclusion. Moreover, though Hegel saw reason as the motivating force of the dialectic process in history, the dialectic need not center on ideas. We shall soon see that it is the very flexibility of the dialectic concept that has made it so useful to historians and philosophers whether they have held Hegel's idealistic presuppositions or not.

Hegel attempted to show the rational, philosophical significance of history; the Positivists made every effort to demonstrate the scientific respectability of historical study. Descartes had argued that history could not produce the certain results that modern man demanded; the Positivists admitted that historical studies had seldom produced the kind of certainty desired, but they argued that this was the fault not of the subject, but of those who had practiced it with insufficient exactness, rigor, and method. The nineteenth century in many ways marked the flowering of the scientific world-view (Darwin's Origin of Species was published in 1859), and it was felt by many that history could climb on the scientific bandwagon and thereby forever silence the negative criticisms expressed by intellectuals of the Enlightenment. Who were the Positivists? For the most part they were practicing historians who had become dissatisfied with the uncritical and inexact historical work of others. Barthold Georg Niebuhr wrote in the Preface to the second edition of his History of Rome:

> At the end of the last century [the eighteenth] . . . men became dissatisfied with superficialities, with vague, meaningless words. But the work of destructive criticism which had pleased the preceding age was no longer adequate. Like our forefathers we sought certain, positive knowledge; but we wanted true knowledge, not the illusory knowledge which had been overthrown.[23]

Henry Thomas Buckle maintained that history could be made a scientific discipline if historians would only admit that human social activity conforms to universal laws just as physical phenomena do, and that by statistical method the regularity of human conduct can be discovered. In his History of Civilization in England he argued that "the great truth that the actions of men, being guided by their antecedents, are in reality never inconsistent, but, however capricious they may appear, only form part of one vast scheme of universal order . . . is at once the key and the basis of history."[24] In taking this position, Buckle was much influenced by Auguste Comte, a French philosopher trained in mathematics, who invented the term "sociology" and has been called the "apostle of Positivism"; Comte asserted that only the methods of the empirical sciences yield truth, and that history marks the three-stage progress of mankind from the low level of theology through the more advanced level of metaphysics (philosophical concern with ultimates) to the highest and only satisfactory level: science.[25] The German philosopher and historian of ideas Wilhelm Dilthey, who argued for analytic psychology as a base for philosophy and thoroughly mistrusted metaphysics, fell back on "the positivistic view that the only way in which the universal (the proper object of knowledge) can be known is by means of natural science or a science constructed on naturalistic principles."[26] The greatest historian of the nineteenth century - he is called the "Nestor of historians" - also maintained a positivistic approach in historiography. This was Leopold von Ranke, who wrote over sixty volumes, the best known of which is probably his History of the Popes. His method was strictly scientific; he concentrated on "the purest, most immediate documents" and on rigorous criticism of source materials (Quellenkritik). Ranke maintained that history (which should always be viewed as universal history) must be written "wie es eigentlich gewesen" (as it actually happened),[27] and his entire career testified to his belief that such historicism (Historismus) is an attainable goal.

What evaluation should be placed upon nineteenth-century historical Positivism? In its more attractive varieties (e.g., Ranke) it deserves high praise for having set rigorous standards for historical investigations, and for improving greatly the quality of historical research. But on the negative side, the attempt to turn history into a science on a par with physics or chemistry was doomed to failure. A contemporary critic of both Ranke and Buckle saw this clearly; he was Johann Gustav Droysen, the author of a fourteen-volume history of Prussian policy from the Middle Ages to the Seven Years' War. In his Principles of History Droysen wrote:

> History is Humanity's knowledge of itself, its certainty about itself. It is not "the light and the truth," but a search therefor, a sermon thereupon, a consecration thereto. It is like John the Baptist, "not that Light but sent to bear witness of that Light."[28]

The Positivists made the mistake of believing that historical studies could attain the same degree of objectivity as scientific studies, and therefore that proper investigation must yield universally acceptable historical interpretations; and when this did not happen - when, for example, reputable historians arrived at divergent views - Positivists could offer no other explanation than stupidity or intransigeance. Thus one positivistic historian would frequently vilify another for not agreeing with him. The real difficulty was not in the sincerity or scholarship of the historians, but in their lack of recognition of the point we made in our first chapter: that a historian's views of human nature and significance stem from his "sovereign decision" - from his general religio-philosophical beliefs - and that these views always precede and influence his historical studies.[29] Different philosophies of life have always, and will always, produce different interpretations of history. The Positivists did not recognize this, and spoke as if one could enter on historical work with complete objectivity - with the imaginary mental tabula rasa (blank slate) of John Locke. In its extreme form (Comte and Buckle), Positivism made the further mistake of assuming that past and present human actions could be reduced to laws which would allow the future to be predicted. Here Positivism misunderstood the unique, free, and gloriously unpredictable character of human beings. This error has been decisively pointed up and refuted by Karl Popper, who correctly argues that from a purely human standpoint, "if there is such a thing as growing human knowledge, then we cannot anticipate today what we shall know only tomorrow," and bases this on a strictly logical proof that "no scientific predictor - whether a human scientist or a calculating machine - can possibly predict, by scientific methods, its own future results."[30] The current relevance of Popper's argument is made especially evident by the dedication of his classic, The Poverty of Historicism:

> In memory of the countless men and women
> of all creeds or nations or races
> who fell victims to the fascist and communist belief in
> Inexorable Laws of Historical Destiny.

The impact of this dedication stems particularly from the fact that the most influential of all historical Positivists has been Karl Marx.

Marx and his co-worker Friedrich Engels derived from Hegel an understanding of the dialectic process (and thus an appreciation of philosophical history), and shared with the Positivists the conviction that history follows inexorable natural laws, which, if understood, would allow the future to be predicted (scientific history). However, in taking over Hegel's dialectic, Marx boasted that he "stood it on its head." For Hegel the dialectic represented the action of the world-spirit of rationality in the historical process, but for Marx such a metaphysic was completely unrealistic. Marx had been greatly influenced by the German materialist philosopher Ludwig Feuerbach, who believed that "der Mensch ist, was er isst" (man is what he eats), and consequently he saw materialistic (or more specifically, economic) factors as the determinants of the dialectic. Instead of thought determining nature, Marx maintained that nature determines thought. Marx built his economic theory of surplus value on this materialistic conception of the dialectic, and became convinced that class struggle, revolutionary action, and, ultimately, a classless society, are the inevitable products of the dialectic action.[31] In applying this philosophy to history, Marx recognized four major stages of development: "In broad outline we can designate the

Asiatic, the ancient, the feudal, and the modern bourgeois modes of production as progressive epochs on the economic formation of society";[32] the bourgeois-capitalist phase he regarded as the precursor of the millenial classless society.

Marx's philosophy of history, though accepted with religious veneration by large numbers of people in the world today, falls to the ground on many counts. Its dogmatic materialism is really an unrecognized metaphysic which does not bear up under scrutiny, as my essay in Part Two of the present work demonstrates. The previously-mentioned criticisms of Positivism apply as fully to Marx as to any of the nineteenth-century advocates of historicism. Moreover, "even if we assume that all history is a history of class struggles, no scientific analysis could ever infer from this that class struggle is the essential factor that 'determines' all the rest."[33] Historical events since Marx's day have belied his prophecy that only revolution against capitalism will satisfy the proletariat; labor unions and governmental anti-trust and anti-monopolistic legislation have given workers such a high standard of living in the West that good television reception is closer to their hearts than a forceful overthrow of society! Finally, Marx held a very ambiguous view of human nature, in that he saw men as evil exploiters of one another, and yet capable of an idyllic, classless existence once a suitable economic environment was provided. The present state of the U.S.S.R. is an excellent evidence that human nature requires the continuing restraint of government, and that a Marxist state, far from "winnowing away," shows great rigidity and a powerful tendency to fall under the control of a "new class" - not a temporary "dictatorship of the proletariat" but a permanent dictatorship of bureaucratic totalitarians.[34]

The nineteenth century was an age of positivistic science, but it was also an age of literary romanticism. While Ranke's scholarship gave history new status in scientific circles and Marx's thunderings gave it a new role in the political arena, novelists and popular historians were justifying history to the average man. The historical novels of Sir Walter Scott, though they have often been censured as misleading by dryasdust Positivists, enjoyed such popularity that Trevelyan said that they taught Europe its history.[35] Macaulay, the author of a five-volume History of England from the Accession of James II which enjoyed enormous popularity,[36] held in common with the Positivists a materialistic, pragmatic perspective (he found both Greek philosophy and the Christian faith deficient because, unlike Bacon's empiricism, they had not "extinguished

diseases" or "increased the fertility of the soil"), and his belief in Progress was extremely naïve (his satisfaction with the
England of his day blinded him to the wretched lot of the English industrial proletariat); moreover, he was far too "cocksure" in his historical judgments.[37] But at the same time he
exhibited a prodigious memory (he could, for example, recite
the whole of Paradise Lost), and, more important, an ability to
make facts live. He saw what the Positivists did not, that
"history begins in novel and ends in essay" and that "no picture
and no history can present us with the whole truth: but those
are the best pictures and the best histories which exhibit such
parts of the truth as most nearly produce the effect of the
whole."[38] Carlyle, with his cult of personality and stress on
the great man in history, has been characterized as the first of
the Heroic Vitalists, prefiguring "the highbrow fascism" of
"the professors of Hitler's Germany."[39] Yet his emphasis on
biography provided a good antidote to the impersonal, "causal"
history of the Positivists, and his works vibrated with such life
that he became one of the most popular historians of his day.
Both Carlyle and his disciple and biographer James Anthony
Froude have rightly been criticized by professional historians
for permitting their biases to warp accurate depiction of the
past, but Carlyle's weaknesses do not lessen the force of his
argument against the historicists: "The Artist in History may
be distinguished from the Artisan in History; for here, as in all
other provinces, there are Artists and Artisans; men who labour mechanically in a department, without eye for the Whole,
not feeling that there is a Whole; and men who inform and en-
noble the humblest department with an Idea of the Whole, and
habitually know that only in the Whole is the Partial to be truly
discerned."[40]

In spite of their numerous differences, the nineteenth-
century Hegelians, Positivists, and Marxists, as well as their
romanticist critics, suffered from one common error of the
time, inherited from the Enlightenment: dogmatic optimism
with regard to human nature. The romantics idealized man in
the past, and the Hegelians, Positivists, and Marxists believed
that rational, scientific, or revolutionary progress was solving
man's problems in the present and would create an ideal society for him in the future. Two major historians of the last
century did not share this common belief, however. They were
Jakob Burckhardt, the author of an enduring classic, The Civilization of the Renaissance in Italy, and Lord Acton, the editor
of the original Cambridge Modern History. Burckhardt had the
"power of penetrating to the soul of an epoch"; for him, "the

76

inner life was much more interesting than the outer world of forms and institutions which he valued chiefly as supplying favourable conditions for its expression."[41] He rejected Hegel's theodicy, the Positivists' claim that history is an objective science, all attempts to find cyclical patterns in history, and the evolutionary progressivism of his day. "Instead of dividing history up into periods in the conventional way . . . Burckhardt analyzed each epoch in terms of its peculiar equilibrium of the several typical interests of humanity."[42] This concern with the psychology of ages and peoples made him a true realist - unwilling to gloss over the evil tendencies in human nature. This was commendable, but since at the same time Burckhardt could receive no consolation in the liberal, watered-down, humanistic religion of his century, he was left with little of what Professor Kantonen calls "the Christian hope."[43]

> However creative great upheavals and destructions may turn out to be, evil remains evil, Burckhardt maintains, and we cannot fathom the economy of the world's history. If there is anything to be learned from the study of history, it is a sober insight into our real situation: struggle and suffering, short glories and long miseries, wars and intermittent periods of peace.[44]

Only in the cultural continuity of the Western tradition did Burckhardt find solace; and yet even this paled before his prophetic vision of the totalitarian state to come. In 1871 he wrote presageful words:

> I have a premonition, which sounds like utter folly and yet which positively will not leave me: the military state must become one great factory. . . . Long voluntary subjection under individual Führers and usurpers is in prospect. . . . Authority will again raise its head in the pleasant twentieth century, and a terrible head.[45]

During the last forty years of his life, Burckhardt published nothing;[46] a major reason for this was almost certainly his growing discouragement with unredeemed human nature. A similar disenchantment seems to have prevented the great Roman Catholic historian Acton from completing his projected "History of Liberty." Early in his career he was a voracious book collector and reader (while in his 'teens he read through the Biographie universelle in fifty-five volumes!), and so much influenced by Macaulay's perspective and temperament that the adjective "cocksure" has been applied to him as well.[47] He remained intellectually arrogant and judgmental all his life, and the evils of the human situation appeared more and more evident to him as time went on. He believed passionately in liberty, but found his early enthusiasm for the French Revolution unjustified.[48] Because he could not be certain that liberty was growing in the world, he found it impossible to write his "History of Liberty."[49]

> Acton's voice is that of Ecclesiastes: "There is nothing new under the sun." It is the voice of Schopenhauer. It is, with some reservation, also the voice of Burckhardt, who saw history's "constant" in "suffering, striving and acting man, as he is, always was, and will be." . . . If Acton is placed amongst his contemporaries, then in this respect he belongs amongst the anti-Hegelian nineteenth-century pessimists.[50]

His religion was (as has been the case for so many Roman Catholics) one of Law more than one of Gospel, and though he saw evil clearly, he did not see God's redemption with equal clarity. Thus he became one of the most satirical historians of all time. For him, history was "an iconoclast," and he could write: "The feet of many men, valued by divines, crumble to pieces in the contact with history"; "People rather like themselves - not better in proportion to greatness but worse"; "History undermines respect . . . shows up horrors, errors, follies, crimes of the ablest and the best."[51]

To Acton and to Burckhardt we owe a realistic appraisal of human character over against the optimistic liberalism of the time, and a recognition that history can aid greatly in providing man with an unflattering but true portrait of himself. Unhappily, however, neither historian applied the dynamic Christian message to the human situation. Acton was limited by a moralistic Catholicism, and Burckhardt, like the Neo-Orthodox Protestant theologians of the twentieth century,[52] lacked the courage to bring the Gospel into the arena of secular life and into intimate contact with the perennial problems of historical interpretation. Both saw man as man; but neither saw God as God - as the Lord of history - as the One who gives meaning to all historical events. Neither provided the nineteenth-century with the Christian philosophy of history it so badly needed.

The Contemporary Scene

The twentieth century inherited the central historiographical dispute of the nineteenth century: whether history should be regarded primarily as a science or as an art. It is this problem which has especially occupied secular historians of our own day. But at the same time a new dimension has appeared in the historiographical scene: a serious attempt to relate theology to the historian's task. The remainder of this chapter will be devoted to a survey of the most important secular approaches to history commanding attention today; in the next chapter we shall consider evidences of the new religious interest in historiographical thinking and try to understand why such a concern has manifested itself in this "post-Christian" age.

Secular Scientific Historians

The desire to find meaning in history even though the God of traditional religion appears dead has provided impetus for a number of allegedly scientific analyses of man's past. Lord Acton's successor as Regius Professor of Modern History at Cambridge, J. B. Bury (d. 1927), served as a link between the Positivism of the nineteenth century and the rationalistic historicizing of our own time. In his Cambridge inaugural lecture of 1902, significantly entitled, "The Science of History," Bury maintained that the past could be understood by the application of rigorous and rational scientific method, and that the key to history is man's upward progress by means of ever-increasing fascination with his own humanity:

> There is no passage, perhaps, in the works of the Greek tragedians so instructive for the historical student as that song in the Antigone of Sophocles, in which we seem to surprise the first amazed meditation of man when it was borne in upon him by a sudden startling illumination, how strange it is that he should be what he is and should have wrought all that he has wrought - should have wrought out, among other things, the city-state. He had suddenly, as it were, waked up to realize that he himself was the wonder of the world. "None is more wonderful than man." That intense expression of a new detached wondering interest in man, as an object of curiosity, gives us the clue to the inspiration of Herodotus and the birth of history. More than two thousand years later human self-consciousness has taken another step, and the "sons of flesh" have grasped the notion of their upward development through immense cycles of time. This idea has recreated history. Girded with new strength she has definitely come out from among her old associates, moral philosophy and rhetoric; she has come out into a place of liberty; and has begun to enter into closer relations

with the sciences which deal objectively with the facts of the universe.[53]

As we shall see, Trevelyan later made mincemeat of this epitomal example of narcissistic humanism; and Bury himself was so affected by "man's inhumanity to man" during World War I that late in life he lost faith in establishing absolute causal patterns in history, and came to emphasize "contingency" - simple chance - in human affairs. But he remains the prototype of the happy humanistic historicist of the early twentieth century.

Marxist historiography in this century has continued to be bound by the positivistic dialectical materialism of its founder. However, it has suffered even further immobilization as a result of the pressures of state policy. Prior to the Russian Revolution of 1917, Marxism was no more than a philosophical option; after 1917 it became the official philosophy of a state, and since then its interpreters have been compelled to understand it according to the prevailing views of those in power. This has meant the frequent rewriting of history, as we indicated by example in chapter one. Under Stalin, M. N. Pokrovsky (d. 1932), whose five-volume History of Russia had been highly praised by Lenin, was denounced as an enemy of the state.[54] This event marked the establishment of a peculiarly Stalinist interpretation of Marx, which held, inter alia, that personality (not just economic force) has a vital independent role to play in history; that the state need not "winnow away" into the classless society; and that "since all roads lead to Communism, all those who take the part of the Soviet Union are historically in the right."[55] However, in 1956 Stalin received posthumous purging for his "cult of personality," and Pokrovsky has again been placed in a favorable light by the Russian historical journals. A recent Western article on "Bulgarian Historiography, 1942-1958" concludes with remarks of wide applicability: "It is quite obvious that, short of radical change in the political climate, the role Bulgarian historians can safely and conscientiously play is that of Geschichtssammler [collectors of historical material] rather than that of Geschichtsschreiber [writers of history]. The experience with the shifting party line in regard to Tito, which cost quite a few Communists their lives and careers, should serve both as a warning and as a pretext to historians to resist being used as tools of politics."[56] Let us hope that Communist historians will resist this pressure more energetically than they have in the past, and come to see that the shifting party line is in reality one of the best arguments against every form of

Marxist Positivism, for such shifts illustrate Burckhardt's contention that "history is the record of what one age finds worthy of note in another." But we must not be too quick to anathematize the Marxist historian who clings so tenaciously to his Faith; he is a true son of our secular century, and his materialist creed, unlike most atheisms, gives him what he so fervently desires: a meaning for history.

The twentieth century has been called "the age of analysis,"[57] and the wide influence of psychoanalytic theory is probably the best reason for so designating it. Certainly psychoanalysis is one of the most important manifestations of a general twentieth-century preoccupation with subjectivity and the inner life.[58] We are not concerned here with the validity of psychoanalytic theory per se,[59] but with the conviction of many that such theorizing provides a scientific key for the interpretation of history. In the most general terms, psychoanalytic theory "is based on the hypothesis that all maladjustments originate from the conflicts that a child has toward his parents."[60] Freud, Adler, and Jung differed chiefly in their emphasis on the root element in emotional conflicts; for Freud, "sexuality in its various aspects is the central problem,"[61] for Adler, the basic issue is pride (compensation for inferiority feelings),[62] and for Jung it is adjustment to the archetypes of the collective unconscious which color and condition man's emotional life.[63]

The precedent for applying psychoanalytic theory to history was given by Freud himself in his book, Moses and Monotheism,[64] a work which plays fast and loose with the historic Moses and attempts to "explain" him by forcing him and his religious beliefs into the predetermined categories of the analytic method. Before the appearance of this work, Albert Schweitzer had shown[65] (albeit from his humanistic point of view) that great dangers attended psychiatric studies of the central figure of the Bible, Jesus; but this offered no deterrent to Freud or to his disciples.[66] Since Freud's day, numerous key historical persons have been put, so to speak, on the analytic couch, in an effort to gain scientific knowledge of their "real" motivations and a "real" insight into their time. A good example is Feldman's psychoanalytic treatment of Benjamin Franklin, in which his thunderbolt experiments leading to the development of the lightning rod are related to the "windbreak" (the expulsion of flatus or intestinal gas from his anus), and in which it is asserted that his "venture into the science of odors (osphresiology) forms a proper climax to the lifelong efforts of Franklin to control his own anal-erotic drives."[67]

The lack of data on Franklin's early anal conflicts (if any!)
gave Feldman no pause; he makes the extraordinary statements: "If Franklin's family had preserved the facts of his
education in rectal cleanliness there would be no need for psychoanalysis to prove the main point of this inquiry. Logic will
have to supply what the biographers miss."[68] Similar, if less
dramatic, psychoanalytic attempts to solve personality problems of historical figures - in spite of the paucity of documents
on their childhood experiences - were made at a session of the
Seventy-Fifth Annual Meeting of the American Historical Association in 1960.[69] Even the best recent psychoanalytic study of
a historical character, Young Man Luther, by Erikson, contains
numerous examples of involved interpretation on the basis of
the sketchiest childhood data.[70]

All of these applications of psychoanalysis to history can be
criticized on three counts. First, even from the standpoint of
orthodox psychoanalysis - from Freud's own presuppositions -
they are questionable, for two years of daily analytic sessions
at a minimum[71] are normally required to uncover the personality conflicts of a living person; how then can we expect to arrive at satisfactory conclusions concerning the unconscious
motivations of those long dead? Secondly, psychoanalytical interpreters do not recognize that their theories are not purely
scientific, but are based upon many philosophical presuppositions;[72] and yet they are so positivistic in regard to their approach that they are eager "to supply what the biographers
miss." As soon as a historian begins for any reason to engage
in such supplementation of the historical records, he ceases to
be a historian and becomes no more than a litterateur. Thirdly, psychoanalytic historiography errs as does all Positivism
in forcing human beings into preconceived categories, thereby
destroying their uniqueness. Individuals become types - grist
for the analytic mill - rather than unique personalities to be
studied for their own sake. Psychoanalytic historicism assumes that it has the key to understanding all human character;
but historical man stands above this human system as he does
above every other monistic effort to classify him. Moses,
Luther, Franklin, and the Christ still elude the analytic couch,
and will always elude it.

The two most ambitious twentieth-century attempts to provide secular scientific conceptualizations of human history
have been made by Oswald Spengler and Arnold Toynbee.
Spengler (d. 1922), in his classic, The Decline of the West,
argues that history moves in cyclical patterns, and that self-
contained human cultures follow a life cycle similar to that of

living organisms and nature.[73] Thus a culture develops from barbarism to a civilized classical period, and finally stagnates, decays, and dies in a new barbarism of hyper-commercialism. Instead of employing the periodization of ancient, mediaeval, and modern history, Spengler speaks of four cycles: Indian, Arabian, Antique, and Western (beginning about A.D. 900), which go through the phases of spring, summer, autumn, and winter. "Spengler discovers no enduring progress, no guiding spirit, no ultimate goal, merely an endless repetition of approximately similar experiences."[74] Spengler was so certain of the scientific character of his interpretation that he claimed it possible to predict the future of our civilization on the basis of its present position (thus his book title), and he made the astounding statement in his Preface to his first edition: "I am convinced that it is not merely a question of writing one out of several possible and merely logically justifiable philosophies, but of writing the philosophy of our time, one that is to some extent a natural philosophy and is dimly presaged by all. This may be said without presumption."[75]

Although Spengler's predictions of Western decline seem to be especially well fulfilled in the First World War, the Second World War, the Korean War, and the current "cold war," we must not blind ourselves to the serious fallacies in his work. He assumes that systems of relations (cultures) created by organic beings must have the same life cycles as those beings; but this is by no means necessary (philosophies created by men are also systems of relations, and they obviously do not absorb analogous life cycles - though in many cases it is perhaps unfortunate that they don't!). His attempt to predict the future is subject to Popper's devastating critique mentioned previously. Spengler suffers from numerous unrecognized value judgments (e.g., "instinct is favored as opposed to understanding, the life of the soil as opposed to the life of the city, faith and reverence for tradition as opposed to rational calculation and self-interest"[76]); and why should these values be accepted rather than a host of others? Finally,

Spengler's book is loaded with a mass of historical learning, but even this is constantly deformed and perverted to fit his thesis. To take one example out of many, he maintains that as part of its fundamental character the classical or Graeco-Roman culture lacked all sense of time, cared nothing for the past or the future, and therefore (unlike the Egyptian, which had a keen time-sense) did not build tombs for its dead. He seems to have forgotten that in Rome orchestral concerts are held every week in the mausoleum of

83

Augustus; that the tomb of Hadrian was for centuries the
fortress of the Popes; and that for miles and miles outside
the city the ancient roads are lined with the vastest collection of tombs in the whole world. Even the positivistic
thinkers of the nineteenth century, in their misguided attempts to reduce history to a science, went no farther in the
reckless and unscrupulous falsification of facts.[77]

The most influential living philosopher of history[78] is by all
odds Arnold Toynbee, author of the massive work, A Study of
History.[79] The title of his book should be observed closely, for
it indicates a fundamental difference between his approach and
Spengler's: Toynbee is presenting, not "the philosophy of our
time," but "a study" of world history; in this sense he rejects
the pretentions of absolutistic Positivism. In a discussion with
Pieter Geyl, Toynbee stated:

> I should never dream of claiming that my particular inter-
> pretation is the only one possible. There are, I am sure,
> many different alternative ways of analyzing history, each
> of which is true in itself and illuminating as far as it goes,
> just as, in dissecting an organism, you can throw light on its
> nature by laying bare either the skeleton or the muscles or
> the nerves or the circulation of the blood. No single one of
> these dissections tells the whole truth, but each of them re-
> veals a genuine facet of it. I should be well-content if it
> turned out that I had laid bare one genuine facet of history,
> and even then, I should measure my success by the speed
> with which my own work in my own line was put out of date
> by further work by other people in the same field.[80]

Toynbee, then, is not a Positivist, but he is a scientific historian, in that he searches for general laws which can give meaning
to and assist in the understanding of the historical process. To
what conclusions does he come? He has stated[81] that the "two
keys" to his interpretation of history are Civilizations and Religions. By "civilizations" Toynbee means "the smallest intelligible fields of historical study," i.e., "whole societies and not
arbitrarily insulated fragments of them like the nation-states
of the modern West."[82] He isolates 34 civilizations (including
13 "independent" civilizations, 15 "satellite" civilizations and
6 "abortive" civilizations),[83] each of which is distinguished by
a dominant motif (e.g., "Sinic" - roughly equivalent to Chinese
- characterized by deep respect for family tradition). These
civilizations are analyzed in an attempt to determine their patterns of cultural genesis, growth, and breakdown; and Toynbee
presents his "challenge-and-response" theory to explain why

so many of them have died. In essence, this theory holds that no civilization dies because of determinist necessity, but because of inadequate response on its own part to the challenges facing it; Western civilization, for example, now faces the challenge of nuclear war, and our response to this challenge can mean the difference between life or death for our society. Here Toynbee introduces Aristotle's principle of the Golden Mean,[84] and states that a challenge of the greatest stimulating power will be neither too severe (so as to discourage response) nor too mild (so as to present no vital issue); it must strike the mean to elicit maximum response. Toynbee's second "key," which receives increasing emphasis in the later volumes of A Study of History, is Religion;[85] its significance lies in the fact that it provides the only creative way to transform society and move beyond a collapsing culture. Therefore Toynbee can say that "the societies of the species called civilizations will have fulfilled their function when once they have brought a mature higher religion to birth,"[86] and can express the hope that, with the higher religions acting as "chrysalises," there will arise a "future oecumenical civilization, starting in a Western framework and on a Western basis, but progressively drawing contributions from the living non-Western civilizations embraced in it."[87] Toynbee refuses to believe that any one of the four living "higher religions" (Buddhism, Christianity, Islam, and Hinduism) have "a monopoly of truth and salvation"; he holds "a belief in the relative truth and relative saving-power of all the higher religions alike."[88] Christianity has a special role to play in the world of today because it is the dominant faith of Western civilization, but this does not mean that it is true while other religions are false, or that it will necessarily remain the most advanced human religious expression.

Toynbee's philosophy of history has been the subject of an amazing number and variety of critiques, and this is one of the best proofs of the importance of his work. However, it must be said that the great majority of evaluations of A Study of History have been negative. We could not possibly include here all of the critics' arguments, and the following is intended as no more than a summary of several of the more damning evaluations: (1) As Toynbee himself admits, he has used Hellenic civilization (his particular historical specialty) as a model or pattern for the interpretation of other civilizations; but there is no compelling reason why Hellenic civilization should serve as the model, and, indeed, it is so inappropriate for dealing with certain other civilizations that Toynbee is led to pervert historical data by forcing them into foreign categories.[89] (2) Toynbee frequently chooses his examples to fit his a priori theories, rather than modifying his theories to accord with the facts.[90] (3) Because of his interest in obtaining a general, synoptic view of human history in the large, his treatment of particular historical problems is often superficial and misleading.[91] (4) Toynbee's work evidences "creeping determinism," illustrated by his "hardening of the categories," i.e., "a tendency in the later volumes to treat as established laws what were earlier stated merely summatively or, at any rate, tentatively."[92] Insofar as he moves toward determinism, Toynbee is subject to criticisms leveled against Positivism earlier. (5) "Toynbee still believes that the idea of 'challenge and response' constitutes a magical key to the why and how of human creativity. But is it not, after all, little more than a formal principle, like Hegel's dialectic, which cannot provide us with a canon of interpretation?"[93] (6) Toynbee's view of religion is eclectic and syncretic, and as such does violence to the historical uniqueness and particularistic claims of Christianity.[94] The core of Christianity lies in its historical particularity, and Toynbee's neo-Mahayana Buddhist spirituality thus opposes the very essence of the Christian message.[95]

Toynbee's desire to find pattern and meaning in history without benefit of revelation and without acceptance of Spenglerian fatalism is also reflected in the latest attempt at a comprehensive view of world history: The Evolution of Civilizations (1961) by Carroll Quigley, a teacher at the Georgetown School of Foreign Service (Washington, D.C.). Quigley tells us that he "came into history from a primary concern with mathematics and science,"[96] and he stresses again and again that history is a "social science" in which the "scientific method of observation, formulation of hypotheses, and testing" can and should always be applied.[97] He begins by attempting to gain a profile of human nature through an analysis of "the range of human potentialities or human needs" and arrives at six basic human concerns: intellectual, religious, social, economic, political, and military.[98] Quigley then moves to a discussion of "groups, societies, and civilizations." Here lies the author's real interest, for "civilization is an object that can be studied in a scientific way just as a quartz crystal can be studied."[99] He argues as follows:

> The social sciences are usually concerned with groups of persons rather than with individual persons. The behavior of individuals, being free, is unpredictable. There is more hope of success when we deal with the activities of aggregates of persons because in such aggregates the

unpredictable behaviors of individuals tend to cancel each other out and become submerged in the behavior of the group as a whole. While the behavior of such a group may not be predictable, it is less free to change and can, accordingly, be extrapolated in a way that individual behavior does not allow. . . . We must, like the student of crystals, examine in a comparative way a large number of examples - even, ideally, all the examples available. . . . The "laws" of historical change described in this book seem to me to fit the observed cases at least as closely as most of the theories of natural science. Most of the laws I shall mention apply, without exception, or with only slight, explicable divergencies, to all the cases I know. They are then, it would seem to me, as worthy of consideration as the scientific laws on the formation of crystals.[100]

By the application of his scientific principles, Quigley arrives at sixteen civilizations,[101] each of which manifests the six basic human concerns mentioned above and passes through seven stages: Mixture (of two or more cultures), Gestation, Expansion, Conflict, Universal Empire, Decay, and Invasion.[102] However, when he discusses Western civilization, Quigley confesses that the seven stages cannot be used in their pure form because the future of our civilization is "not yet settled" and the Western culture is "exceptional" in that no culture has ever exceeded it "in power and extent."[103] Thus Quigley discusses the history of the West in terms of "a series of at least three successive pulsating movements of expansion," each of which "has been followed by an Age of Crisis, but in two, and probably in all three, of these crises the organization of expansion has been circumvented or reformed sufficiently to provide a new instrument of expansion and accordingly a new period in Stage 3."[104] The result is three periods of Western expansion (970-1270, 1420-1650, and 1730-1929), each followed by an epoch of Conflict.

This analysis of history, modeled at many points on Toynbee's, suffers from at least three serious defects. First, Quigley's "quartz crystal" analogy is highly misleading. Human beings - regardless of the density of some of their heads - are not quartz, and the statistical attempt to predict or generalize concerning human behavior offers the historian little help, for (as Hegel and Carlyle pointed out) great individuals at crucial junctures in history often set the world's course, and there is no way of anticipating their appearance or successfully categorizing them after they have appeared. The uniqueness of human personality is the consideration which vitiates all purely "scientific" attempts to understand history.[105] Secondly, Quigley does not seem to realize that historical records are infinitely diverse, and therefore one cannot choose "random samples" as is done in the case of crystal analysis. In historical investigation, the documents and events studied always reflect the presuppositions of the investigator (as we demonstrated in chapter one); thus purely "objective" history is an impossibility. Quigley is largely unaware of his own presuppositions, but at many points in his book they are painfully evident (e.g., his designation of the religious history of the West from 1300 to 1550 as a period of "Confusion"[106]). Thirdly, his assumption that Western civilization is "exceptional," but all other civilizations can be characterized by a growth-to-decay pattern, seems to manifest his own thoroughly Westernized, school-of-foreign-service point-of-view and his lack of sufficiently exacting knowledge concerning the history of non-Western cultures.

Secular Relativistic Historians

The unwillingness of Toynbee or Quigley to state a thoroughgoing historical Positivism, even though they both obviously desire to treat history as objectively as possible, well indicates the effect of anti-positivistic argument in the twentieth century. Many historians have become thoroughly disenchanted with "scientific" attempts to explain history, and instead have argued that history should be viewed more as an "art" than as a science, that no over-all pattern in history is discernible, and that historians who try to find such a pattern are wasting their time.[107]

Twentieth-century opposition to history as pure science was heralded by the appearance in 1903 of a refutation of J. B. Bury's inaugural lecture, "The Science of History," to which reference has been made earlier in this chapter. The refutation, entitled "Clio, a Muse," was written by George Macaulay Trevelyan, the grand-nephew of Macaulay. Trevelyan did not deny that the historian must use scientific method ("the accumulation of facts and the sifting of evidence"), but he did deny that history could arrive at universal, scientific laws concerning human action and that it could provide a utilitarian guide for human conduct. "The functions of physical science are mainly two," he wrote. "Direct utility in practical fields; and in more intellectual fields the deduction of laws of 'cause and effect.' Now history can perform neither of these functions." For Trevelyan the true value of history is not scientific but "educational": "it can educate the minds of men by causing them to reflect on the past."[108] Shortly before his retirement he expressed this conviction in a particularly striking way:

> How wonderful a thing it is to look back into the past as it actually was, to get a glimpse through the curtain of old night into some brilliantly lighted scene of living men and women, not mere creatures of fiction and imagination, but warmblooded realities even as we are. In the matter of reality, there is no difference between past and present; every moment a portion of our prosaic present drops off and is swallowed up into the poetic past. The motive of history is at bottom poetic.[109]

Trevelyan's appreciation of such eminent English literary historians as Macaulay and Carlyle has caused him to place great stress on the artistic presentation of historical material. Indeed, "recent English historiography has produced no one to equal him as a stylist, no one who could make the past come to life so meaningfully and so vividly."[110]

Trevelyan's opposition to history as science also characterized the historical philosophy of Charles A. Beard (d. 1948) and Carl Becker (d. 1945).[111] Beard has been viewed by many as little more than an economic determinist, and his economic interpretation of American history, which is still represented in some U. S. school texts, is certainly an extreme position.[112] However, Beard "did not confine his analysis to economic interpretation,"[113] and although on occasion he used the phrase "theory of economic determinism" in a favorable way, he was no Positivist. In his paper "That Noble Dream" Beard demonstrated that "Historicism is not and never has been accepted everywhere as the official creed of the American Historical Association," and set out an eleven-point argument to show that Ranke's position is untenable.[114] If history could not be an exact science, what then was its function? Beard had answered that question to his own satisfaction as early as 1907 when he had collaborated with James Harvey Robinson in a two-volume text, The Development of Modern Europe; "in this text, both writers took up the pragmatic idea that history should justify itself by its usefulness for the present."[115] Later Beard summed up his pragmatic philosophy of historical writing by speaking of "the magic of thought projected into the forum of practice."[116]

Carl Becker, though primarily a historian of ideas rather than an economic historian,[117] likewise opposed historical scientism with a pragmatic philosophy. Against the Positivists he wrote: "However accurately we may determine the 'facts' of history, the facts themselves and our interpretation will be seen in a different perspective or less vivid lights as mankind moves into the unknown future."[118] Becker's pragmatism is illustrated by his expression of regret that "a hundred years of expert historical research did nothing to prevent the World War, the most futile exhibition of unreason, take it all in all, ever made by civilized society."[119] Beard and Becker are to be praised for providing incisive refutations of historical Positivism and for creating "among their fellow historians an interest in, even an enthusiasm for, the study of that most 'neglected of provinces,' the philosophy of history";[120] but certainly their pragmatic approach to historiography merely begs the question with regard to the nature of historical truth. As with the philosophical pragmatism of C. S. Peirce, the psychological pragmatism of William James, and the educational pragmatism of John Dewey, this historical pragmatism creates more problems than it solves.[121]

Relativistic historians such as Beard were profoundly influenced by the Italian philosopher-historian Benedetto Croce (d. 1952). As early as 1893 - when he was only twenty-seven - Croce wrote an essay whose title clearly indicated his opposition to the idea of history as science: La storia ridotta sotto il concetto generale dell'arte (History Subsumed under the Concept of Art).[122] Here Croce argued that since science is knowledge of the general and art is knowledge of the particular, history should be viewed as a species of art rather than of science; history differs from art in the wide sense only in that history narrates what happened, whereas art represents what might happen.[123] Like Bergson, Croce came to regard physical science as providing useful, but arbitrary concepts; unlike Bergson, however, he believed that the reality which the scientist manipulates conceptually is history, not immediate inner experience. Thus to Croce, history provides the data with which science works, and it is absurd to speak of history as if it were one of the sciences. Croce sees the historian's task artistically - as reliving the past in imagination. He uses as an example the chronicle of a monk of Monte Cassino, where one reads: "1001. Beatus Dominicus migravit ad Christum"; this will remain no more than chronicle unless we can turn it into the history it was originally by weeping over the death of the departed Dominic as the writer did.[124]

To Croce the average historian is a mere chronicler, for facts only become history when they have passed through the crucible of an individual mind. We talk glibly of cause and effect, but no historian can forecast the future, since history never repeats itself. The annals of civilisation record the instinctive and unceasing struggle of man to escape from the limitations of barbarism, and the yardstick of progress is the increasing possibility of self-realisation. Here Croce changes from the critic to the prophet, and a warmer note comes into his voice.[125]

This "warmer note" is Liberty, and Croce, who sees no trace of a Divine hand in history, considers liberty to be the only truly meaningful element in man's story.[126] Thus when in his History of Europe in the Nineteenth Century he depicts the failure of liberals to create a social life consistent with their ideals, the story becomes a high tragedy of Sophoclean proportions.[127] However, Croce's belief in liberty must, on his own ground, remain no more than a prophet's impassioned appeal; for the relativism of his position keeps even liberty from attaining the status of an absolute.

Croce's stress on reliving the past is also found in the historical philosophy of R. G. Collingwood (d. 1943), whose posthumous Idea of History has been cited at several places in the present work. The conviction that historical thinking is at root the re-enactment of past experience set Collingwood squarely against all forms of historical Positivism; "for this reason the systems of Spengler and Toynbee were as unacceptable in his eyes as those of Comte and Marx, whatever differences in detail there might be between them: all such projects were infested with 'naturalism,' with the mistaken prejudice that the only true knowledge is scientific knowledge, the only true forms of explanation those which exhibit particular occurrences as instances of laws."[128] Let us hear Collingwood himself describe the essential nature of the historian's work over against that of the natural scientist:

When a scientist asks "Why did that piece of litmus paper turn pink?" he means "On what kinds of occasions do pieces of litmus paper turn pink?" When an historian asks "Why did Brutus stab Caesar?" he means "What did Brutus think, which made him decide to stab Caesar?" The cause of the event, for him, means the thought in the mind of the person by whose agency the event came about: and this is not something other than the event, it is inside of the event itself. . . . All history is the history of thought. But how does the historian discern the thoughts which he is trying to discover? There is only one way in which it can be done: by re-thinking them in his own mind. . . . This re-enactment. . . is not a passive surrender to the spell of another's mind; it is a labour of active and therefore critical thinking. The historian not only re-enacts past thought, he re-enacts it in the context of his own knowledge and therefore, in re-enacting it, criticizes it, forms his own judgement of its value, corrects whatever errors he can discern in it. . . . All thinking is critical thinking; the thought which re-enacts past thoughts, therefore, criticizes them in re-enacting them.[129]

Collingwood is quite correct in pointing out that historical thinking ought not to be subsumed under scientific thinking, but his own idealist theory is also subject to criticism. As Walsh says, "The process of putting oneself in another's place is itself susceptible of further analysis," for in the act of interpreting historical evidence to find what men of the past were thinking and why they thought it "we make at least implicit reference to general truths."[130] Collingwood is not sufficiently aware that the historian in the process of critically re-enacting the past - of forming "his own judgement of its value," must constantly bring his own presuppositions of value to bear upon the historical data. Collingwood rightly warned against applying the a prioris of scientism to the historian's task, but he offered no satisfactory substitute philosophy to undergird historical analysis.

Another historian of recent times who opposed the claims of "scientific" historiography was the eminent Dutch scholar Johan Huizinga (d. 1945). Although he was certainly not a methodological skeptic, Huizinga trenchantly argued "that history is pre-eminently an inexact science, that its concept of causality is extremely defective, that it resists the formulation of laws,"[131] and on more than one occasion he defended the thesis that "the concept of evolution is of little utility in the study of history, and frequently has a disturbing, obstructive influence."[132] Huizinga thus distinguishes the approach of the historian from that of the sociologist or social scientist:

The sociologist, etc., deals with his material as if the outcome were given in the known facts: he simply searches for the way in which the result was already determined in the facts. The historian, on the other hand, must always maintain towards his subject an indeterminist point of view. He must constantly put himself at a point in the past at which the known factors still seem to permit different outcomes. If he speaks of Salamis, then it must be as if the Persians might still win; if he speaks of the coup d'état of Brumaire, then it must remain to be seen if Bonaparte will be ignominiously repulsed. Only by continually recognizing that possibilities are unlimited can the historian do justice to the fulness of life.[133]

Huizinga's stress on "the fulness of life" reminds one of Jakob Burckhardt, with whom he has often been compared. Huizinga's greatest work, The Waning of the Middle Ages,[134] successfully captures the spirit of society in northern Europe (especially Burgundy) as the magnificent edifice of mediaeval civilization was crumbling; it does for northern Europe what Burckhardt's Civilization of the Renaissance in Italy did for the Renaissance culture of southern Europe, for both studies are artistic portraits depicting in cross-section the life of the time. "The Waning of the Middle Ages may be likened to a vast canvas which, like the great altarpieces of the brothers Van Eyck, contains a prodigious variety of detail, and yet does not detract from the main central theme of the picture."[135] Huizinga explicitly sets forth this philosophy of history when he writes: "A dramatic interpretation based on a morphology of human society would probably in the final analysis provide the most balanced definition for expressing the nature of history, as long as it places special emphasis upon its unsystematic, descriptive character and upon the necessity of seeing its object in action."[136] Because Huizinga views the historian's proper work as total morphological understanding, he considers the "re-experiencing" approach of Croce and Collingwood to be "merely one part of historical understanding." The central aim of the historian must not be simply to evoke re-experiencing of the past, but to construct contexts and to design forms whereby past reality can be comprehended. "History creates comprehensibility primarily by arranging facts meaningfully."[137]

What shall we say of Huizinga's approach? He deserves high praise for his efforts to prevent history from being absorbed in scientific sociology, and for his concern to present the historian as delineator of comprehensive morphologies of past cultures. However, he neglects to provide the historian with what he must have in order to create morphologies: valid criteria and sound value judgments. Huizinga recognizes that the needed values will not automatically arise from the cultures being studied, for he asserts that the historian "must organize historical phenomena according to the categories with which his Weltanschauung [world view], his intellect, his culture provide him."[138] But surely one cannot leave it at that, for cultural values vary from time to time and place to place, and must themselves be judged. Otherwise, to take an obvious example, the Marxist historians are justified in their revisionist activities! But no secular philosophy of history - Huizinga's included - can provide the necessary external criteria for value judgment, since these philosophies are themselves totally within the historical flux.

The last secular relativistic historian we shall discuss is Raymond Aron, who is well-known to his fellow countrymen in France because of his activities as a political journalist and commentator. In spite of Aron's position as professor of sociology at the Sorbonne, he is by no means a sociologizing historian; characteristically, his influential Introduction to the Philosophy of History carries the subtitle, "An Essay on the Limits of Historical Objectivity."[139] These limits are very radically set; as a reviewer points out, Aron introduces into historiography "a radical relativism, holding that the historian can neither understand the events and productions of history nor explain them causally and arrange them in developmental series without bringing to them an interpretive scheme that is not found in the historical subject matter itself."[140] The essence of Aron's position can be seen in the following statements from his paper delivered at the Hayden Colloquium on Scientific Concept and Method:

> The historian does not become scientific by de-personalizing himself but by submitting his personality to the rigors of criticism and the standards of proof. He never offers a definitive image of the past but, sometimes, he offers definitively one valid image of it. . . . Historical unity is not experienced, but constructed. . . . In the place of a history which tends always toward one meaning, one should put the presentation of a struggle between relatively autonomous forces whose outcome is not decided in advance. The image of conflict seems to me preferable to the image of a river. . . . The meaning of the history of an activity is bound to the essential nature of that activity. The meaning of "total" history is the meaning which we attach to human existence and to the succession of forms that it takes through time. Is man in search of something - salvation of the soul, the truth in nature or in himself? Or is he merely a beast of prey, fated to remain such, gratuitously and vainly creating cultures, all unique, and all doomed to die? . . . The historical experience does not give an answer; rather the experience which we draw from the past is prescribed by an implicit answer which we carry in us before we question those who have been.[141]

How then is the historian to arrive at his philosophy of history among "the plurality of systems of interpretation"[142] available ? Aron's answer is that of the atheistic philosophical existentialist Jean-Paul Sartre: "You're free, choose, that is, invent. . . . There are no omens in the world."[143] It is Aron's conviction that the only way for the individual to "overcome the relativity of history" is "by the absolute of decision," and that such decision affirms "the power of man, who creates himself by judging his environment, and by choosing himself."[144]

Raymond Aron serves as an appropriate conclusion to this chapter on modern historical thought. At the beginning of the modern secular era Descartes questioned the legitimacy of historical study, and practicing historians as well as philosophers of history from that day to this have attempted to meet his objections. In the main, the answers have been of two kinds: history is philosophically or scientifically meaningful; and history is meaningful artistically, but not scientifically or philosophically. The great scientific historians have produced remarkable and awe-inspiring systems of historical explanation to prove their contention, but, as we have discovered, none of these systems has been able to stand up under rigorous criticism. Historical relativism, on the other hand, offers no satisfactory alternative approach; in Aron, we particularly see the debility of this position when carried to its logical conclusion, for decision itself becomes an absolute, my choice becomes as good as yours among "the plurality of systems of interpretation," and each individual historian becomes his own god of history. It is clear that both the scientific historians and the relativistic historians are correct and in error at the same time: the scientific historian is right that history demands a meaningful explanation, but he errs when he claims that secular philosophy or science can provide that explanation; and the relativistic historian is right in pointing out that scientific explanations of history are unsuccessful, but he makes the mistake of concluding that no definitive explanation is needed and one "sovereign decision" is as good as another. Does any path out of this labyrinth exist ? This is the crux question, and it carries us - not just semantically - to a Cross.

NOTES

1. This occurred on November 9, 1793. A veiled woman representing Reason was brought before the Convention, and Chaumette orated: "Mortals, cease to tremble before the powerless thunders of a God whom your fears have created.

Henceforth, acknowledge no divinity but Reason. I offer you its noblest and purest image; if you must have idols, sacrifice only to such as this." The veiled woman turned out to be Madame Maillard of the opera, and at Notre Dame she was elevated on the altar and received the adoration of those present.

2. J. B. Black, The Art of History: A Study of Four Great Historians of the Eighteenth Century (London: Methuen, 1926), p. 33.

3. Ibid., p. 56.

4. "Refusons notre créance à tout historien ancien et moderne qui nous rapporte des choses contraires à la nature et à la trempe du coeur humain" (Voltaire's Préface to his Charles XII).

5. "Anéantissez l'étude de l'histoire, vous verrez peut-être des St. Barthélemy en France et des Cromwells en Angleterre." This characteristic remark appears in Voltaire's "De l'utilité de l'histoire"; the English translation in the text is by Jacques Barzun and is contained in Fritz Stern (ed.), The Varieties of History from Voltaire to the Present (New York: Meridian Books, 1956), p. 45.

6. W. H. Walsh, Philosophy of History: An Introduction (New York: Harper Torchbooks, 1960), p. 122.

7. This is Kant's eighth proposition in his "Idea of a Universal History from a Cosmopolitan Point of View"; the translation by W. Hastie is reprinted in Patrick Gardiner (ed.), Theories of History (Glencoe, Illinois: Free Press, 1959), p. 30.

8. Ibid., p. 26.

9. Edward Gibbon, The History of the Decline and Fall of the Roman Empire, ed. J. B. Bury (7 vols.; London, 1897-1900), I, 77. An excellent abridgment of Gibbon's work is published in paperback in the Viking Portable Library.

10. The New Science, par. 138. Bergin and Fisch translated Vico's work in 1948 and Cornell University Press published the translation. In 1961 a revised (but abridged) edition

was issued in paperback by Doubleday in the Anchor Books series. This revision should be used in preference to the 1948 edition, but the paragraphs omitted in the revision must be consulted in the earlier edition.

11. Sometimes Vico seems to reverse his distinction between history as more certain and philosophy as more true; for example, he identifies verum (the true) with factum (the created), and argues that history provides us with real truth, for it records what men have themselves created. However, Vico is not contradicting himself; in both cases he is saying that whereas philosophy yields abstract certainty and formal truth, history offers mankind concrete certainty and experiential truth.

12. See below, Pt. II, my essay entitled, "Vico and the Christian Faith."

13. The New Science, par. 31.

14. Karl Löwith, Meaning in History (Chicago: University of Chicago Press' Phoenix Books, 1957), p. 132.

15. A. Robert Caponigri, Time and Idea; the Theory of History in Giambattista Vico (London: Routledge and Kegan Paul, 1953), p. 119.

16. Löwith, op. cit., p. 133. On pp. 125-27 Löwith correctly argues that Benedetto Croce, in his great interpretative study of Vico (The Philosophy of Giambattista Vico, trans. R. G. Collingwood [London: Howard Latimer, 1913]), does not do justice to Vico's belief in Providence; Croce's humanism blinded him to the importance of the theistic in Vico's thought.

17. Caponigri, op. cit., p. 142.

18. A more sympathetic (but less defensible) picture of eighteenth-century historiography than we have provided here is given by Ernst Cassirer (The Philosophy of the Enlightenment, trans. Koelln and Pettegrove [Princeton: Princeton University Press, 1951], chap. v, pp. 197-233); Cassirer's rationalistic presuppositions are evident from his three-sentence summary dismissal of Vico's New Science as "destined to remove rationalism from

historiography" and as "based rather on the logic of phantasy than on the logic of clear and distinct ideas" (p. 209).

19. The finest treatment of nineteenth-century historiography is G. P. Gooch, History and Historians in the Nineteenth Century (2d ed.; London: Longmans, Green, 1952). The five-fold categorization employed in our presentation is original, however; it does not derive from Gooch.

20. ". . . dass es also auch in der Weltgeschichte vernünftig zugegangen sei" (Lectures on the Philosophy of History). On Hegel's philosophy of history, note especially Jean Hyppolite, Introduction à la philosophie de l'histoire de Hegel (Paris: Marcel Rivière, 1948).

21. That this was the source of Hegel's four empires has been pointed out by R. G. Collingwood (The Idea of History [New York: Oxford University Press' Galaxy Books, 1956], p. 57, n. 2).

22. The reader should carefully distinguish Hegel's use of the term "dialectic" from its use in mediaeval (or modern) scholasticism, where it designates the branch of logic that teaches the art of disputation and rational debate.

23. Translated by Fritz Stern and included in Stern, op. cit., p. 51.

24. Quoted in Gardiner, op. cit., p. 118.

25. See ibid., pp. 73-82, for important extracts expressing Comte's philosophy of history and of society.

26. Collingwood, op. cit., pp. 173-74. Dilthey was in many ways a forerunner of positivistic psychoanalytical historiography, which we shall discuss later on in this chapter.

27. Ranke's famous statement appears in the Preface to the first edition of his Histories of the Latin and Germanic Nations from 1494 to 1514.

28. Johann Gustav Droysen, Outline of the Principles of History, trans. E. Benjamin Andrews (Boston, 1893), p. 49, par. 86. It should be noted that Collingwood (op. cit., pp. 165-66)

treats Droysen shabbily and fails to recognize his importance in the history of historical thought.

29. Walsh (op. cit., pp. 100-108) discusses the following "factors making for disagreement among historians": personal bias, group prejudice, conflicting theories of historical interpretation, and underlying philosophical conflicts.

30. Karl R. Popper, The Poverty of Historicism (2d ed.; London: Routledge & Kegan Paul, 1960), p. x. Other recent critiques of Positivism and historicism are: Isaiah Berlin, Historical Inevitability ("Auguste Comte Memorial Trust Lecture," No. 1; London: Oxford University Press, 1954); Ludwig von Mises, Theory and History; an Interpretation of Social and Economic Evolution (New Haven: Yale University Press, 1957); Felix Morley (ed.), Essays on Individuality (Philadelphia: University of Pennsylvania Press, 1958).

31. For a detailed overview and critique of Marx's system on the basis of primary sources, see Pt. II, my essay entitled, "The Importance of a Materialistic Metaphysic to Marxist Thought and an Examination of Its Truth Value."

32. This statement appears in Marx's Preface to A Contribution to the Critique of Political Economy. Orthodox Marxist historians usually interpret historical events a priori in terms of these categories; thus the U. S. Civil War is regarded as a victory of the bourgeois-capitalist phase (represented by the industrialized North) over the older feudal phase (represented by the agrarian, slave-holding South). For a good general presentation of the Marxist philosophy of history over against misinterpretations of it, see Georgi Plekhanov, Essays in Historical Materialism (New York: International Publishers, 1940).

33. Löwith, op. cit., p. 43.

34. See Milovan D(j)ilas, The New Class; an Analysis of the Communist System (New York: Prager, 1957).

35. George Macaulay Trevelyan, Clio, a Muse and Other Essays (2d ed.; New York, 1930), pp. 165-66.

36. "He was the first English writer to make history

universally interesting. A traveller in Australia recorded
that the three works he found on every squatter's shelf were
the Bible, Shakespeare and the 'Essays.' The inscription
on his monument in the chapel of his old college, Ita scripsit
ut vera fictis libentius legerentur, is the simple truth"
(Gooch, op. cit., pp. 279-80).

37. See Pieter Geyl's article, "Macaulay in His Essays," in
    Geyl's Debates with Historians (London: B. T. Batsford,
    1955), pp. 19-34.

38. Lord Macaulay, "History," Miscellaneous Works, ed. Lady
    Trevelyan, I (New York, 1880), pp. 153 ff. This essay was
    written by Macaulay when he was only twenty-eight, and ap-
    peared first in the Edinburgh Review.

39. Eric Russell Bentley, A Century of Hero Worship; a Study
    of the Idea of Heroism in Carlyle and Nietzsche with Notes
    on Other Hero-Worshipers of Modern Times (Philadelphia:
    J. B. Lippincott, 1944), p. 77. Geyl (op. cit., p. 51) holds
    that Bentley's work provides "the most comprehensive and
    satisfactory view" of Carlyle.

40. Thomas Carlyle, "On History," Critical and Miscellaneous
    Essays, II (New York, 1900), pp. 83 ff.

41. Gooch, op. cit., p. 533.

42. James Hastings Nichols, in his editorial introduction to
    Burckhardt's Force and Freedom; an Interpretation of
    History (New York: Meridian Books, 1955), p. 55. Nichols
    correctly warns that Burckhardt's philosophy of history
    "has been almost perversely misunderstood by . . .
    Benedetto Croce . . . . Thus is repeated the legend of
    Burckhardt the irresponsible but delightful Epicurean. Al-
    most the exact contrary is the case" (p. 46).

43. T. A. Kantonen, The Christian Hope (Philadelphia:
    Muhlenberg Press, 1954).

44. Löwith, op. cit., p. 25.

45. Jakob Burckhardt, Briefe, ed. F. Kaphahn (Leipzig, 1935),
    correspondence with F. von Preen.

46. Many of his lecture notes of these years have been made available, however; both his Force and Freedom and his Judgements on History and Historians (trans. Harry Zohn [London: George Allen & Unwin, 1959]) consist of lecture materials left unpublished at his death.

47. Herbert Butterfield, "Acton: His Training, Methods and Intellectual System," in A. O. Sarkissian (ed.), Studies in Diplomatic History and Historiography in Honour of G. P. Gooch (London: Longmans, 1961), pp. 170, 172. See also Butterfield's Man on His Past (Boston: Beacon Press, 1960), passim, where Acton and Ranke are discussed and compared in detail.

48. Lionel Kochan, Acton on History (London: Andre Deutsch, 1954), p. 125. Acton lauded the American Revolution, but Kochan notes how in this case he inconsistently "located the ideal in the real," and suggests that his "support of the American Revolution is more of a tribute to his heart than to his head" (p. 151).

49. A point well made by Gertrude Himmelfarb (author of Lord Acton, 1952) in her address on Acton at the Seventy-Sixth Annual Meeting of the American Historical Association, December 28, 1961.

50. Kochan, op. cit., p. 110. Notwithstanding this strong statement, Kochan overstresses the progressive in Acton's thought.

51. These quotations from Acton's unpublished notes (Add. MSS. 4981, 5011, 5641) are transcribed ibid., pp. 134-35.

52. Burckhardt has been compared favorably with modern Neo-Orthodox theologians by Löwith, op. cit., p. 32.

53. J. B. Bury, "The Science of History," Selected Essays, ed. Harold Temperley (Cambridge: Cambridge University Press, 1930), pp. 3 ff.

54. See Klaus Mehnert, Stalin versus Marx; the Stalinist Historical Doctrine (London: Allen and Unwin, 1952). Extracts from Pokrovsky are included in Stern, op. cit., pp. 330-41.

55. Khvostov, "Stalin's Foreign Policy," Voprossy Istorii, 1950, no. 1, p. 38.

56. Marin Pundeff, "Bulgarian Historiography, 1942-1958," American Historical Review, LXVI (April, 1961), 693.

57. In the Mentor series of philosophy anthologies, the twentieth-century volume carries this title.

58. For an indication of the dangers inherent in this approach to reality, see my article "Ascension Perspective," The Cresset, XXIV (May, 1961), 17-19; and cf. in Pt. II of the present work the essay on "Constructive Religious Empiricism: An Analysis and Criticism."

59. On the negative side, see Andrew Salter, The Case against Psychoanalysis (New York: Henry Holt, 1952). Salter argues that therapy should concentrate on emotional reconditioning of the patient as an adult ("conditioned reflex therapy") rather than attempt to solve his problems through "transference" of repressed childhood conflicts.

60. E. G. Boring, H. S. Langfeld, and H. P. Weld, Foundations of Psychology (New York: John Wiley, 1948), p. 541.

61. Gardner Murphy, Historical Introduction to Modern Psychology (rev. ed.; New York: Harcourt, Brace, 1950), p. 330.

62. Ibid., pp. 336 ff.

63. Jung's position has closer affinity to Christian doctrine than Freud's or Adler's, for it has been able largely to free itself from reductionist biologism (Freud) and social determinism (Adler). (In saying this, I take a position opposite to that of my former teacher, Dr. Aarne Siirala of Järvenpää, Finland, for whom, however, I retain the highest respect.) See Jung's Modern Man in Search of a Soul, now published in paperback by Harcourt, Brace in its Harvest Books series; and the outstanding analysis of Jung by an eminent Roman Catholic scholar, Raymond Hostie's Religion and the Psychology of Jung, trans. G. R. Lamb (New York: Sheed & Ward, 1957). I have pointed up a relation between Jung's conceptual structure and the Christian mythological writing of C. S. Lewis in my paper, "The

Chronicles of Narnia and the Adolescent Reader," Religious Education, LIV (September-October, 1959), 418-28. If more space were at our disposal, we would say something at this point concerning the particular psychoanalytic approaches of such other modern analysts as Karen Horney, who has influenced the great Protestant theologian Paul Tillich; readers interested in these rewarding by-ways are encouraged to pursue them via R. Monroe's Schools of Psychoanalytic Thought.

64. Available in the Vintage Books paperback series published by Alfred A. Knopf. Freud followed the same general approach in his Leonardo da Vinci: A Study in Psychosexuality (issued in Modern Library Paperbacks), with the same disregard for the canons of historical method. In recent years, however, Freud has had the tables turned on him: he has been the subject of posthumous probing by his biographer Ernest Jones (The Life and Work of Sigmund Freud [3 vols.; New York: Basic Books, 1953-1957]), and by the prominent analyst Erich Fromm (Sigmund Freud's Mission; an Analysis of His Personality and Influence ["World Perspectives," Vol. 21; New York: Harper, 1959]).

65. In Schweitzer's M.D. dissertation, published in English as The Psychiatric Study of Jesus; Exposition and Criticism, trans. Charles R. Joy (Boston: Beacon Press Paperbacks, 1958).

66. It is of considerable interest that the writer of the Foreword to the English edition of Schweitzer's thesis, Dr. Winfred Overholser, a past president of the American Psychiatric Association, makes clear that psychiatry is unwilling even today to give up medical analysis of Jesus: "One may disagree with Schweitzer on one or two minor points. He takes for granted that the failure of Jesus to develop ideas of injury and persecution rules out the possibility of a paranoid psychosis. This is not necessarily true; some paranoids manifest ideas of grandeur almost entirely, and we find patients whose grandeur is very largely of a religious nature, such as their belief that they are directly instructed by God to convert the world or perform miracles. Again, he offers as evidence of freedom from paranoia the fact that Jesus modifies his views as to his missions [sic!]. Some paranoids substantially modify

their delusions in accordance with their view of environmental factors, and may indeed appear to reason logically concerning events of interest to them -- logically, that is, if one grants their premises" (ibid., p. 15).

67. A. Bronson Feldman, "Ben Franklin - Thunder Master," Psychoanalysis, V (Summer, 1957), 53.

68. Ibid., p. 35.

69. I refer to the session on "Personality and Biography in American History," in which William Willcox dealt with "Sir Henry Clinton and the Problem of Unconscious Motivation," and David Donald discussed "The Quest for Motives" in regard to Charles Sumner, a leader of the radical Reconstruction program after the U. S. Civil War.

70. E. g., beatings received by Luther from his father and schoolteacher; such severity was common practice in the sixteenth century, but not every child became a Luther! Erik H. Erikson's Young Man Luther: A Study in Psychoanalysis and History (New York: W. W. Norton, 1958) is favorably reviewed by Donald B. Meyer in History and Theory; Studies in the Philosophy of History, I (1961), 291-97.

71. There is some question as to whether Freud did not come to view analysis as "interminable": "Not only the patient's analysis but that of the analyst himself has ceased to be a terminable and become an interminable task" (Freud, Collected Papers, V [London: Hogarth Press, 1950], 353).

72. "We have already seen that psychotherapy did, in fact, develop in an atmosphere conditioned by the reductive naturalism and secularism of the nineteenth century. Freud claimed that all philosophic systems are equally uncertain and Jones appears to have believed that all the basic issues could be settled 'quite empirically'! . . . They already had a philosophic outlook which had come to be taken so for granted that all contrary philosophical possibilities were ignored, by not being seen as possibilities at all!" (Albert C. Outler, Psychotherapy and the Christian Message [New York: Harper, 1954], p. 60 [italics Outler's] and passim).

73. The Spenglerean cycle-patterns are well set out in

diagrammatic form by Edwin Franden Dakin, Cycles in History ("Foundation Reprints," No. 7; Riverside, Connecticut: Foundation for the Study of Cycles, 1948).

74. Gooch, op. cit., p. xxxv.

75. Oswald Spengler, The Decline of the West: Form and Actuality, trans. C. F. Atkinson (New York: Alfred A. Knopf, 1926), p. xv. Spengler frequently claimed that he was not employing the methods of the natural sciences, and that there is no such thing as absolute truth; but it is clear that in practice he operates with positivistic presuppositions.

76. Gardiner, op. cit., p. 188. It is instructive to contrast with Spengler's antipathy to the metropolis Lewis Mumford's The City in History (New York: Harcourt, Brace & World, 1961).

77. Collingwood, op. cit., pp. 182-83.

78. Walsh argues that Toynbee should not be termed a "historian," for his interests are not those of practicing historical investigators (op. cit., pp. 167-68). This is a doubtful argument, for it could be maintained that practicing historians would more truly fulfil their function if they demonstrated live concern for the issues Toynbee raises.

79. Available in both a two-volume and a one-volume abridgment, as well as in the original twelve-volume set. The twelve volumes can now be purchased in an inexpensive paperbound edition.

80. Toynbee, in Geyl, Toynbee, and Sorokin, The Pattern of the Past: Can We Determine It? (Boston: Beacon Press, 1949), pp. 81-82. The same debate is reprinted in Gardiner, op. cit., pp. 307-19.

81. In a National Broadcasting Company "Wisdom Series" film discussion with Christopher Wright, teaching fellow at Harvard University; the film is distributed by Encyclopaedia Britannica Films, Inc.

82. Toynbee, Civilization on Trial (London: Oxford University Press, 1948), chap. i.

83. Toynbee, A Study of History, XII (Reconsiderations) (London: Oxford University Press, 1961), 546-61. This represents Toynbee's latest position. "In the course of the first ten volumes of this book I arrived at a list of twenty-three full-blown civilizations, four that were arrested at an early stage in their growth, and five that were abortive" (p. 546).

84. This frequently misunderstood concept is well explained by C. S. Lewis in his Pilgrim's Regress; an Allegorical Apology for Christianity, Reason and Romanticism (London: Bles, 1950), pp. 86-87.

85. So strong is this emphasis that Geyl titles his critique of Vols. VII-X of A Study of History, "Toynbee the Prophet" (Geyl, Debates with Historians, pp. 158-78).

86. Toynbee, Civilization on Trial, p. 236.

87. Toynbee, A Study of History, XII, 559. Toynbee makes it clear in his "reconsiderations," however, that he has come to believe that "religion is an end in itself," not just a means to an end (p. 94, n. 1).

88. Ibid., p. 99. Cf. his emotively-charged statement: "The writer of this Study will venture to express his personal belief that the four higher religions that were alive in the age in which he was living were four variations on a single theme, and that, if all the four components of this heavenly music of the spheres could be audible on Earth simultaneously, and with equal clarity, to one pair of human ears, the happy hearer would find himself listening, not to a discord, but to a harmony" (A Study of History, VII [London: Oxford University Press, 1954], 428). However, he admits that "as far into the future as we can see ahead" he does "not expect that they will agree to make a merger of their different doctrines, practices, and institutions, in which their common spiritual treasure is diversely presented" (A Study of History, XII, 100, n. 1).

89. This is pointed out particularly well by the experts in the history of Islam, Russia, etc. who have contributed to The Intent of Toynbee's History, ed. Edward T. Gargan (Chicago: Loyola University Press, 1961).

90. See Geyl's critique, "Toynbee Once More: Empiricism or Apriorism ?," in Geyl's Debates with Historians, pp. 144-57.

91. To take a single but typical example: Gilmore, in discussing European history from 1453 to 1517, shows that "Latin Christendom, far from being the least likely candidate for expansion [Toynbee's view], emerges as the candidate most likely to succeed" (Myron P. Gilmore, The World of Humanism [New York: Harper, 1952], p. 34).

92. William Dray, "Toynbee's Search for Historical Laws," History and Theory, I (1960), 49; F. H. Underhill, "The Toynbee of the 1950's," Canadian Historical Review, XXXVI (September, 1955), 227.

93. Gerhard Masur, Review of A Study of History, Vol. XII, in American Historical Review, LXVII (October, 1961), 79.

94. Jn. 14:6 (Jesus speaking): "I am the way, and the truth, and the life; no one comes to the Father, but by Me." Acts 4:12 (referring to Jesus): "There is no salvation in anyone else at all, for there is no other name under heaven granted to men, by which we may receive salvation." To disregard these testimonies of Jesus and of the primitive church concerning the uniqueness and finality of Christianity is to do no less than abrogate one's position as a historian.

95. See Will Herberg, "Arnold Toynbee - Historian or Religious Prophet ?," Queen's Quarterly, LXIV (1957), 421-33. Herberg also takes Toynbee to task, as have so many others, on his negative evaluation of Judaism.

96. Carroll Quigley, The Evolution of Civilizations (New York: Macmillan, 1961), p. x.

97. Ibid., p. 12.

98. Ibid., p. 18.

99. Ibid., p. 38.

100. Ibid., pp. 2, 25, 38.

101. "With careful study it would be possible to distinguish approximately eight more civilizations divided about equally

between the Near East and the Far East. We refrain from attempting to do this because the facts are not clear and any conclusions would be disputable" (ibid., p. 35).

102. "These divisions are largely arbitrary and subjective and could be made in any convenient number of stages. We shall divide the process into seven stages, since this permits us to relate our divisions conveniently to the process of rise and fall" (ibid., p. 79).

103. Ibid., pp. 210-11.

104. Ibid., p. 211.

105. Quigley is so interested in large units, and so little interested in individual uniqueness, that he can say in his only reference to Canada: "Canada can be understood only as part of the larger system. . . . Canada can only be understood as a political group within Western culture" (ibid., p. 29).

106. Ibid., p. 248.

107. At least one relativist, however, has argued that there is a need for deterministic social theories of the highest standard - so that the refutations of them will carry the greatest possible weight (see A. Donegan, "Social Science and Historical Antinomianism," Revue internationale de philosophie, XLII [1957], 448).

108. Trevelyan, op. cit.

109. Trevelyan, "History and the Reader," in his An Autobiography and Other Essays (London, 1949), p. 60.

110. Henry R. Winkler, "George Macaulay Trevelyan," in S. William Halperin (ed.), Some 20th-Century Historians (Chicago: University of Chicago Press, 1961), p. 54.

111. See Cushing Strout, The Pragmatic Revolt in American History: Carl Becker and Charles Beard (New Haven: Yale University Press, 1958).

112. Note, for example, the critique of Beard's An Economic Interpretation of the Constitution of the United States by

Robert E. Brown (Charles Beard and the Constitution [Princeton, 1956]).

113. Harvey Wish, The American Historian: A Social-Intellectual History of the Writing of the American Past (New York: Oxford University Press, 1960), p. 292.

114. Charles A. Beard, "That Noble Dream," American Historical Review, XLI (October, 1935), 74-87. It should be noted that Beard (like Popper) uses the term "historicism" as an equivalent for historical Positivism; however, since the publication in 1936 of Meinecke's Die Entstehung des Historismus, the word has often been employed to denote a historical relativism that reduces all absolute laws and values to phenomena appearing in time.

115. Wish, op. cit., p. 268.

116. Charles A. Beard, The Discussion of Human Affairs (1936), quoted in Beard's The Economic Basis of Politics and Related Writings, ed. William Beard (New York: Vintage Books, 1957), p. 18.

117. See especially Becker's classic, The Heavenly City of the Eighteenth Century Philosophers (11th ed.; New Haven, 1955). Cf. Raymond O. Rockwood (ed.), Carl Becker's Heavenly City Revisited (Ithaca, New York: Cornell University Press, 1958).

118. Carl L. Becker, "Everyman His Own Historian," American Historical Review, XXXVII (January, 1932), 236.

119. Carl L. Becker, "What Are Historical Facts?," in his Detachment and the Writing of History: Essays and Letters, ed. Phil L. Snyder (Ithaca, New York: Cornell University Press, 1958), p. 63. Here Becker speaks of World War I! In the perspective of a second world holocaust far more terrible than the first, we can see how naïve Becker's statement really is and how difficult it is to say anything meaningful about these wars apart from a doctrine of sin and a recognition of the existence of the demonic.

120. John C. Rule, Review of The Pragmatic Revolt in

American History by Cushing Strout, in History and Theory, I (1961), 219.

121. See in Pt. II my essay, "A Critique of William James' Varieties of Religious Experience," for a discussion of the chief fallacies in pragmatism.

122. This essay was reprinted in Croce's Primi Saggi (Bari, 1919).

123. In his essay Croce did not answer the vital question of how the historian distinguishes between what happened and what did not - between the real and the unreal. Later he did try to answer it, and in doing so argued that the distinction is not made by appeal to a philosophy external to history, but by the actual nature of the historical task; he maintained, in other words, that philosophy is actually contained in history and can be defined simply as the methodology of history. As Gardiner notes (op. cit., p. 226), "such a characterization of historical thinking would not seem to be particularly illuminating." Cf. Guido Calogero, "On the So-Called Identity of History and Philosophy," in Klibansky and Paton (eds.), Philosophy & History; Essays Presented to Ernst Cassirer (Oxford: Clarendon Press, 1936), pp. 35-52.

124. See the selections from Croce's History - Its Theory and Practice, trans. Douglas Ainslie (New York: Harrap, 1921), quoted in Gardiner, op. cit., pp. 230-32. Unfortunately, this valuable emphasis on reliving the past is weakened in Croce by his making it contingent upon the interests of the present. When he writes (ibid., pp. 227-28) that the accounts of the Mithradatic War "for me at the present moment are without interest, and therefore for me at the present moment those histories are not histories" and that "they have been or will be histories in those that have thought or will think them, and in me too when I have thought or shall think them, re-elaborating them according to my spiritual needs," he is subject to two criticisms: (1) He makes the past relative to the present and, typical of the non-Christian, considers the egocentric interests of the historian central instead of demanding that the historian be regenerated so that he can take an interest in the past for its sake; and (2) He makes the character of historical records relative to the user of them, and thereby

110

reduces their objective significance (this is the error of the Neo-Orthodox interpreters of the Bible, who refuse to say that the Bible is objectively the word of God, but instead argue that the Scripture becomes God's word only when it enters a receptive heart).

125. Gooch, op. cit., p. xxxvi.

126. See Croce's History As the Story of Liberty, trans. Sylvia Sprigge (New York: Meridian Books, 1955).

127. A point well made by Hayden V. White in his paper on Croce delivered at the Seventy-Sixth Annual Meeting of the American Historical Association, December 28, 1961.

128. Gardiner, op. cit., p. 250.

129. Collingwood, op. cit., pp. 214-16.

130. Walsh, op. cit., p. 58. On pp. 68-69 Walsh also questions Collingwood's skeptical view that there are no "eternal" truths concerning human nature because human nature is continually changing; Walsh notes quite correctly that, taken to its logical conclusion, such a view would prohibit any understanding of the literature of the past.

131. Johan Huizinga, "De historische Idee," in his Verzamelde Werken, VII (Haarlem, 1950), 134 ff. Translation in Stern, op. cit., pp. 290 ff.

132. Johan Huizinga, "De taak der cultuurgeschiedenis," in his Verzamelde Werken, VII, 35 ff. Translated by Holmes and Van Marle as "The Task of Cultural History" in Huizinga's Men and Ideas; History, the Middle Ages, the Renaissance (New York: Meridian Books, 1959), p. 29.

133. Huizinga, in Stern, op. cit., p. 292.

134. Available in Doubleday's Anchor Books paperback series.

135. Bert F. Hoselitz, in his Introduction to Huizinga's Men and Ideas, p. 12.

136. Huizinga, in Stern, op. cit., p. 293.

111

137. Huizinga, Men and Ideas, p. 55. Huizinga's morphological approach is shared by Jacques Barzun, who speaks of total cultural history in much the same terms. Barzun concluded a 1954 paper on "Cultural History: A Synthesis" with these words: "Intelligibility being his [the cultural historian's] goal, he cannot escape the effort to understand; he cannot ask somebody else to explain nor shut his eyes and count. It is insight, after the count has shown a preponderance of old-fashioned dwellings, that makes him say the dominant architecture of New York is modern. The rest is footnotes" (quoted in Stern, op. cit., p. 402).

138. Huizinga, in Stern, op. cit., p. 292.

139. Aron's Introduction, though published originally in 1938, did not appear in English translation until 1961; the English translation by George J. Irwin (London: Weidenfeld and Nicolson) unfortunately leaves much to be desired.

140. Lloyd R. Sorenson, Review of Introduction to the Philosophy of History by Raymond Aron, in American Historical Review, LXVII (January, 1962), 372. Aron's relativism is especially evident in his "Owl of Minerva" address on the unpredictability of the future; see Raymond Aron (ed.), L'histoire et ses interprétations: Entretiens autour de Arnold Toynbee ("École Pratique des Hautes Études-Sorbonne. VIᵉ Section: Sciences économiques et sociales. Congrès et colloques," No. 3; Paris: Mouton, 1961), pp. 152-62.

141. Raymond Aron, "Evidence and Inference in History," in Daniel Lerner (ed.), Evidence and Inference (Glencoe, Illinois: Free Press, 1959), pp. 29, 36, 44, 46.

142. Aron, Introduction to the Philosophy of History, pp. 86 ff.

143. Jean-Paul Sartre, Existentialism and Human Emotions ("The Wisdom Library"; New York: Philosophical Library, 1957), p. 28. Modern philosophical existentialism is rather well defined by Webster as "an introspective humanism or theory of man which expresses the individual's intense awareness of his contingency and freedom; a theory which states that the existence of the individual precedes his essence, and which stresses the individual's responsibility for making himself what he is." Both

philosophical existentialism and Christian existentialism (more about the latter in the next chapter) have their roots in the teachings of the nineteenth-century Danish philosopher-theologian Søren Kierkegaard.

144. Aron, Introduction to the Philosophy of History, p. 334.

CHAPTER FIVE

THE CHRISTIAN ANSWER

In a widely influential book dealing with the current ideological milieu, we read:

> Today the real Christian creed, viewed in the broad, scarcely survives as a vitally creative force. The peoples of the West, as they live out their lives - and this takes into account the majority of those who call themselves Christians - in their thinking and behavior have ceased to pay the least attention to Christiantiy's idea of God and the hereafter, or the Christian notions of sin and grace . . . . We, the inheritors of Western culture, live in the midst of all kinds of testimonials and memories of Christianity, as will many generations to come, and this circumstance still leaves a characteristic mark on our lives. Yet, in this same connection, the bulk of people who busy themselves professionally with the appreciation and evaluation of these Christian memorials are not motivated in truth by religious zeal, but by a mere philological or esthetic interest.[1]

The author of this description of our "post-Christian" age gives, by and large, an accurate portrait. However, he assumes that the mid-twentieth century situation is to be plotted on a rising curve of secularism, whereas there is good reason to hold that the present high level of secularism is the vertex of a parabolic curve which is now moving into the descendant. The failure of secularistic world-views to cope with the complexity of modern life on all levels is bringing about a renewal of interest in the point of view of Old Western Man. This revival of Christian concern is nowhere more evident than in historical studies, as a recent writer in the Yale Review indicated: "I venture to suggest that there is developing in our society a revived theory of history, transcending strict doctrinal barriers, which takes into account - indeed, gives first consideration to - religious knowledge and traditional belief and classical theories as means to the proper understanding of history . . . . Yes, the climate of opinion among historians is altering mightily."[2] In this chapter we shall first consider several of the most prominent theological attempts to alter the current climate of historical opinion; this will lead us to the central problem of the validity of the Christian position; and we will conclude by summarizing the essential principles of historical interpretation which follow from acceptance of the Christian world-view.

Recent Theologies of History

Current <u>Roman Catholic</u> historiography provides an appropriate beginning point for our discussion, since in this area as in others Roman thought displays more homogeneity than does Protestant theology. The recognized master of present-day Roman Catholic historiography is the prolific English historian <u>Christopher Dawson</u>. Dawson argues that all secular philosophies of history are inadequate and misleading because they offer no remedy for diseased human nature, and he presents the redemptive work of Christ through the Church as the only solid basis of historical progress.

Christianity creates the motive power - spiritual will - on which all true progress must ultimately rest. Without this spiritual foundation, all progress in knowledge or wealth only extends the range of human suffering, and the possibilities of social disorder. All the great movements, which have built up modern secular civilisation, have been more or less vitiated by this defect. Whether we look at the Italy of the Renaissance, the England of the Industrial Revolution, or the Germany of the last forty years, we see in each case that the progress and wealth which are founded on individual or national selfishness lead to destruction and suffering. A civilisation which recognises its own limitations, and bows before the kingdom of the spirit, even though it be weak and immature like European civilisation during the Dark Ages, has more true life in it than the victorious material civilisation of our own age. . . . Civilisation after civilisation in the past has stagnated and fallen into ruin, because it is tainted at the source, in the spiritual will which lies behind the outward show of things. The only final escape for humanity from this heartbreaking circle of false starts and frustrated hopes is through the conquest of the world by charity - the coming of the Kingdom of God. . . . The Christian faith alone has measured how deep is the need of humanity and how great is the possibility of restoration.[3]

115

A similar emphasis is present in the writings of the Jesuit theologian <u>M. C. D'Arcy</u>, who centers attention on the incarnation of Christ.[4] Because of the historical fact that God became man, "the fleeting values of time and history are rescued from oblivion."[5] God's act in Christ gave meaning to the historical process, and through the Church Christ "continues in the world and in history."[6] Both Dawson and D'Arcy suffer from two characteristic difficulties in Roman theology: its Biblically unsupportable claim that the Roman Church is the extension of Christ's incarnation in time;[7] and its inadequate doctrine of sin, which claims that man can be made holy through the sacraments. A further difficulty becomes evident in <u>Jacques Maritain's</u> <u>On the Philosophy of History</u>,[8] where the noted scholastic philosopher gives "final proof, if any were needed, that a Thomist is not really interested in the problem of history at all. Maritain is interested in Being, not in Becoming."[9] The abstract, philosophical approach in Maritain's book confirms his statements made some years earlier: "I am not much interested . . . in any new turn or new historic orientation toward religion. What is of interest, from the point of view of faith, are . . . events which, by their very nature, do not take place in 'history,' but in what Berdyaev called 'metahistory.'"[10] Most Roman Catholic theologians are so conditioned to think in terms of the eternal, rational categories of Aristotelian scholasticism that they find little of interest in the "becomingness" of history. However, such Roman Catholic writers as Dawson and D'Arcy have performed a valuable service by emphasizing that the Christian faith claims to find genuine meaning in history, and that it bases its claim on the incarnation of Jesus Christ.

Twentieth-century <u>Protestant</u> interpretations of history reflect the theological trends of the last several decades: the modernism of the pre-World War I period, the Neo-Orthodoxy of the 1920's and 1930's, the Christian existentialism of the 1940's, and the recent attempts by individual thinkers to break new theological ground.[11] It will be helpful to think of these positions schematically as representing a decrease followed by an increase in scope of historical interpretation.

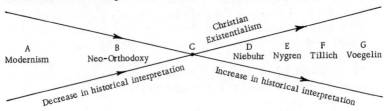

"Modernism" or theological "liberalism" was an optimistic theology which stressed human ability to bring about "God's kingdom on earth" through social action and cultural improvement (the "social gospel"). It derived from the teachings of the nineteenth-century German theologians Schleiermacher and Ritschl, and was popularized in the Western hemisphere by such well-known churchmen as Walter Rauschenbusch (d. 1918) and Harry Emerson Fosdick. Orthodox theologians of the 1920's pointed out that modernism deviated radically from Reformation Christianity, which had always stressed personal redemption from sin through Christ's death on the Cross as a necessary grounding for social action, and which had viewed "God's kingdom" not as the sphere of human social action, but as the sphere of God's sovereignty and ultimate triumph through the Second Coming of Christ.[12] But the liberals argued that the twentieth century had ushered in a new era of human progress and cultural renewal, that the Bible must be read in the light of evolutionary modern science, and that the essence of Christianity was not doctrine but ethics.

Such a philosophy of religion gave rise to works on the meaning of history which ambitiously attempted to interpret all human history in terms of spiritual progress or in terms of ethical imperatives. A prime advocate of the "progress" approach was Shailer Mathews (d. 1941), who maintained that "the conviction thrust upon us by history [is] that the Christian religion is in accord with the tendency of human progress";[13] a more careful statement of the same position is presented by the eminent church historian Kenneth Scott Latourette: "The Christian understanding of history does not necessarily deny progress. . . . As the centuries pass the evidence is accumulating that, measured by his effect on history, Jesus is the most influential life ever lived on this planet. That influence appears to be mounting."[14] The moralistic interpretation of history appears in the work of Sherwood Eddy, whose publishers refer to him as the "most fearless and colorful exponent of the social gospel in this generation"; Eddy sets forth a fourfold "criterion for the appraisal of history": justice, brotherhood, liberty, and love, and asserts that "in so far as we fulfill these conditions, we have peace on earth; when they are grossly violated we have war, revolution, and incessant strife."[15]

Theological thought in recent years has pointed up the high degree of naïveté in these "social gospel" approaches: the liberal emphasis on progress does not sufficiently recognize the depravity of man and his devolutional tendencies, and the

117

modernist stress on ethical values neglects the central Biblical teaching that morality cannot be divorced from regeneration - that only if a man is reborn through Christ will he have the power to follow good moral advice when he hears it. However, even in such an emasculated variety as modernism, Christian philosophy of history has more strength than most secular historiography: it can speak of historical progress in relation to "the most influential Life ever lived on this planet," and it can interpret history in the light of ethical imperatives which claim eternal validity.

The decades immediately prior to the first World War were bathed in an illusory glow of optimism and evolutionary progress; the French psychologist Émile Coué (d. 1926) gave the era its motto with his formula, "Day by day, in every way, I am getting better and better." World War I burst the bubble of this naïveté by revealing man as the same self-seeking egoist he had been throughout recorded history, and Protestant Neo-Orthodoxy reflected this new realism. Unlike modernism, Neo-Orthodoxy took as axiomatic the Biblical teaching concerning man's depravity and his absolute need to depend on Christ's sacrificial death for human sin. Neo-Orthodoxy saw ultimate historical meaning only in the act of God in Christ, not in man's attempts to better himself or his society. History has meaning - but the meaning is a transcendent one actualized only in Jesus Christ. One must not make the grievous error of modernism and identify God's Kingdom with man's accomplishments. Thus the Swiss Reformed theologian Karl Barth, who ushered in Neo-Orthodoxy with his epochal Commentary on Romans in 1919, writes in his Church Dogmatics:

> The verdict that all have sinned [Rom. 5:12] certainly implies a verdict on that which is human history apart from the will and word and work of God . . . and a knowledge of the sin and guilt of man in the light of the word of grace of God implies a knowledge that this history is, in fact, grounded and determined by the pride of man. . . . The history of the world which God made in Jesus Christ, and with a view to him, cannot cease to have its center and goal in him. But in the light of this goal and center God cannot say Yes but only No to its corruption. . . . What is the obviously outstanding feature of world history? . . . [It] is the all-conquering monotony - the monotony of the pride in which man has obviously always lived to his own detriment and that of his neighbor, from hoary antiquity and through the ebb and flow of his later progress and recession both as a whole and in detail, the pride in which he still lives . . . and

> will most certainly continue to do so till the end of time. . . .
> History . . . constantly re-enacts the little scene in the Garden of Eden.[16]

This passage from Barth clearly indicates both the strength and the weakness of Neo-Orthodox historical interpretation: on the positive side, a re-emphasis upon God's transcendent sovereignty over history and the centrality of the Christ-act in history; on the negative side, a narrowing of historical interest to the point where the human drama becomes "all-conquering monotony."[17]

Emil Brunner, like Barth a Swiss Reformed theologian and a chief founder of Neo-Orthodoxy, has a wider conception of God's activity in history than does Barth,[18] but his general position is much the same. Brunner writes in the Epilogue to his Gifford Lectures on Christianity and Civilisation:

> The first and main concern of the Christian can never be civilisation and culture. His main concern is his relation to God in Jesus Christ. . . . The gospel of Jesus Christ is the revelation of [man's] destiny beyond and above historical life. . . . This Christian faith therefore cuts across all forms of historical life with their different forms of civilisation, good and bad. It is not identical with any of them and none of them can ever be thought of as its adequate expression. All the differences between forms of civilised and cultural life are relative, whilst their distance from the eternal kingdom of God is absolute. . . . Christians . . . stand on a rock which no historical changes can move. . . . The Christian Church knows that no progress in the sphere of civilisation and culture can reach that goal of history beyond history, and that no setbacks, not even the complete destruction of civilised life, can deflect history from that ultimate goal which is beyond itself. . . . God wants us to be in this world and to do our best in humanising and personalising its life. But we can render this service only when we know that this is not our primary but only our secondary task, as we keep ourselves free from all illusions of universal progress and of despair in sight of general degeneration and dissolution.[19]

Here, as with Barth, we have a conception of historical meaning in the Cross and in final Judgment which accords well with the Biblical view of history sketched in an earlier chapter. History has meaning because of what God did in Jesus Christ and what He will do at Christ's Second Coming; this provides historiographical "rock." But the general activity of man in history seems to hold little more interest for Brunner than for Barth. Neo-Orthodoxy has rightly stressed that man must "seek first the Kingdom of God," but it has said little of man's multifarious activity through the centuries. Historical interpretation is here narrowed to the interpretation of the events of salvation-history (Heilsgeschichte).

Protestant historiography in the twentieth century underwent even more stringent narrowing in the work of the recently retired professor of New Testament at the University of Marburg, Germany, Rudolf Bultmann, who has combined the rationalistic Biblical criticism of the modernists with an existentialism having much in common with that of Aron.[20] Bultmann begins with a radical "demythologizing" of the Biblical records, on the ground that in our scientific age it is absurd to believe that miracles such as the Virgin Birth and the physical resurrection of Jesus ever occurred historically. Having dispensed with what he considers to be a Gnostic myth of the theophany of God, he concentrates attention on what he believes to be the true meaning of the Gospel accounts - the coming of God into the human personality in every age. This advent of God in the heart is "lifted out of all temporal limitations" and "continues to take place in any present moment both in the proclaiming word and in the sacraments."[21] No longer should we speak of the meaning of history in terms of Christ's historical First Coming or His ultimately decisive ("eschatological") appearance at the end of time; these myths merely represent His perpetual advent in judgment and grace within the personality of man. Redemption did not occur at a single point of time; it occurs "in any present moment." Eschatology is continually "realized"; it should not be regarded as "futuristic." Christian philosophy of history narrows to the psychology of individual existential experience. Bultmann thus concludes his Gifford Lectures:

> The meaning of history lies always in the present, and when the present is conceived as the eschatological present by Christian faith the meaning of history is realised. Man who complains: "I cannot see meaning in history, and therefore my life, interwoven in history, is meaningless," is to be admonished: do not look around yourself into universal history, you must look into your own personal history. Always in your present lies the meaning in history, and you cannot see it as a spectator, but only in your responsible decisions. In every moment slumbers the possibility of being the eschatological moment. You must awaken it.[22]

Bultmann's position is subject to a number of very serious criticisms. Philosophically, it is evident that he presupposes the impossibility of miracles and uses the term "myth" to cover those elements in the Biblical records which do not accord with his own naturalistic world-view. But such an approach confuses the scientific method with the so-called Religion of Science, and assumes a Newtonian view of absolute natural law which is foreign to twentieth-century Einsteinian-relativistic science.[23] Theologically, like Albert Schweitzer in The Quest of the Historical Jesus, Bultmann unwittingly tears the center out of the Christian faith by claiming that Jesus erred in believing that His death would usher in the Kingdom of God and the eschatological end of the age.[24] The anti-Christian philosopher Walter Kaufmann quite logically argues: "If first-rate scholars like Rudolf Bultmann and Albert Schweitzer are right that Jesus was mistaken about the central tenet and premise of his message, why should not this undermine our confidence in his authority?"[25] Moreover, "for Bultmann the name 'Jesus Christ' represents not a personal living reality of God's saving revelation in the sphere of history but merely a concept, an ideogram, a symbol or a principle for the event of contemporary preaching."[26]

Historiographically, Bultmann makes Aron's mistake: he narrows historical meaning to the point of personal decision, thus absolutizing subjective experience and relativizing everything else in the historical process. Such existential subjectivizing is, to be sure, a fundamental characteristic of our uprooted contemporary culture; existentialism is the intellectual counterpart of artistic abstractionism and social beatnikism, for all of these movements retreat into subjective personal experience after losing all confidence in objective reality. But the prevalence of this approach to life should not blind us to its dangers - chief of which are solipsistic separation from all reality and demonic egocentrism. Bultmann makes a valiant attempt to avoid these pitfalls by characterizing the true existential experience in Christian terms, and he deserves praise for underscoring the Christian claim which we set forth in Chapter Two, that only personal experience of Christ can free a man from himself so as to permit him to understand the past. But since the demythologization of the Bible leaves us with no more than a shadow-Christ, it is next to impossible to describe the nature of the Christ-experience or distinguish true experience from false. Bultmann's existential historiography is superior to Aron's because he sees the necessity of giving specific Christian content to the experience; however, once the demythologizing process is begun, where is it to stop? Bultmann demythologized the historic Christ; what if the next step is to demythologize the existential experience of Christ - leaving nothing but subjective religiosity? Since Bultmann's existentialism cannot stand up against such a criticism, it provides a very unsubstantial basis for Christian philosophy of history, in spite of its laudable emphasis on the transforming character of Christian salvation.[27]

The narrowing of Protestant historical interpretation from society in general (modernism) to the Christ-act (Neo-Orthodoxy) to the subjective experience of Christ (Bultmann) has been arrested in recent years through the work of four outstanding intellectuals: Niebuhr, Nygren, Tillich, and Voegelin, all of whom have been influenced in varying degrees by Neo-Orthodoxy and Christian existentialism, but who have gone beyond these positions to create more adequate philosophies of history. Reinhold Niebuhr has been termed "the most important living American theologian."[28] Recently retired from a professorship at Union Theological Seminary in New York, Niebuhr has made a tremendous impact on the scholarly and general public through his writings on theology, history, political theory, and social action. He began his ministry as a confident liberal, but soon saw modernism's weaknesses and assimilated many of the insights of Neo-Orthodoxy. However, Niebuhr went beyond Barth by giving reason an especially vital place in his theology. "Niebuhr believes that the insights of revelation can be applied, by reason, to explain and understand the contradictory aspects of reality. Reason cannot of itself prove the truth of revelation, but, given the revelation, reason can show that it gives a more adequate picture of reality than any alternative."[29]

This stress on rationally comparing the Christian faith with other alternatives leads Niebuhr not unnaturally to interest himself in the understanding of general human history. He affirms that history is too complex and too full of mystery to permit our finding a single pattern of explanation for it, as Marx or Toynbee claims to find; but history does have a unity, and that unity rests in God's sovereignty over the historical process.[30] Niebuhr asserts that the reality of human sin and evil keeps history from ever producing its own means of salvation; but salvation has come about in history through the act of God in Christ.[31] "The Christian faith," he writes, "begins with, and is founded upon, the affirmation that the life, death, and resurrection of Christ represent an event in history, in and through which a disclosure of the whole meaning of history

122

occurs."[32] What does the Christ-event disclose? Its proclamation of man's sin and God's forgiving love gives a key for
evaluating all acts in history. Through the Christ-act one can
see the symbolic and revelatory quality of all acts.[33] On the
basis of the Christian doctrine that man is a creature of nature
and spirit, of necessity and freedom, Niebuhr points up the
polar character of all human history; men always shuttle between poles, such as faith and reason, principle and practice,
spontaneity and ritual, idealism and realism, utopianism and
cynicism, and this-worldliness and other-worldliness.[34] Because man is a sinner, history must be viewed ironically: "One
of the pathetic aspects of human history is that the instruments
of judgment which it uses to destroy particular vices must belong to the same category of the vice to be able to destroy
it."[35] Niebuhr utilizes this approach magnificently in his Irony
of American History, where he states such ironies as the fact
that the United States felt most confident when it was young and
weak, and feels most impotent now that it is very strong.[36] It
is Niebuhr's conviction that the recognition of historical irony
should lead man to an awareness of his true nature, and thus to
contrition.[37] Niebuhr writes:

> The whole drama of human history is under the scrutiny of a
> divine judge who laughs at human pretensions without being
> hostile to human aspirations. The laughter at the preten-
> sions is the divine judgment. The judgment is transmuted
> into mercy if it results in abating the pretensions and in
> prompting men to a contrite recognition of the vanity of
> their imagination.[38]

Two criticisms will be directed against Niebuhr's approach:
First, though he broadens Christian philosophy of history well
beyond existentialism through the presentation of several profound interpretative principles, he does not go far enough; his
unwillingness to concede that single patterns of history can be
valid prevents him from seeking more comprehensive historical explanations. Secondly, like modernism, Neo-Orthodoxy,
and Bultmannian existentialism, Niebuhr lacks a solid Biblical
foundation for his theological and historiographical assertions.
He says at one point: "Since myth is forced to state a paradoxical aspect of reality in terms of concepts connoting historical sequence, it always leads to historical illusions. Jesus, not
less than Paul, was not free of these illusions."[39] Even the
religious naturalist Henry Nelson Wieman gags at such an approach:

Niebuhr claims to base his faith upon the Bible and calls it

Biblical faith. But a careful examination shows that he corrects the Bible according to his own convictions. . . .
Niebuhr may be right and the Bible wrong, but I should like to hear what Jesus and Paul had to say in their own defense before pronouncing Niebuhr right and Jesus and Paul mistaken about the Christian faith.[40]

Wieman correctly shows that Niebuhr uses the epistemological criterion of pragmatic utility rather than Biblical authority;[41] fortunately, on most occasions Niebuhr's pragmatism is sufficiently immersed in the Biblical world of thought to yield reliable Christian philosophy of history.

Anders Nygren, formerly professor at the University of Lund, Sweden, and now bishop of Lund, is one of the foremost representatives of the so-called "Lundensian movement" in theology.[42] This movement is often regarded as a Swedish - or Lutheran - equivalent of the Swiss Reformed-Calvinist Neo-Orthodoxy of Barth and Brunner. However, as Nygren's philosophy of history makes clear, there are important differences. In his great work Agape and Eros Nygren begins not with the Christ-act as do the Neo-Orthodox, but with the isolation of a "fundamental motif," i.e., a "basic idea," a "driving power," which gives to the subject matter under discussion "its character as a whole and communicates to all its parts their special content and colour."[43] By the use of this characteristically Lundensian technique of "motif research" (Motivforsking), Nygren isolates two basic concepts of love in Western history: Eros, a self-centered love which seeks an object in order to gain something from it; and Agape, a self-giving love which seeks an object in order to bestow something upon it.[44] Nygren contrasts the two ideas of love in the following tabular summary:[45]

Eros is acquisitive desire and longing.	Agape is sacrificial giving.
Eros is an upward movement.	Agape comes down.
Eros is man's way to God.	Agape is God's way to man.
Eros is man's effort: it assumes that man's salvation is his own work.	Agape is God's grace: salvation is the work of Divine love.
Eros is egocentric love, a form of self-assertion of the highest, noblest, sublimest kind.	Agape is unselfish love, it "seeketh not its own," it gives itself away.

Eros seeks to gain its life, a life divine, immortalised.	Agape lives the life of God, therefore dares to "lose it."
Eros is the will to get and possess which depends on want and need.	Agape is freedom in giving, which depends on wealth and plenty.
Eros is primarily man's love; God is the object of Eros. Even when it is attributed to God, Eros is patterned on human love.	Agape is primarily God's love; "God is Agape." Even when it is attributed to man, Agape is patterned on Divine love.
Eros is determined by the quality, the beauty and worth, of its object; it is not spontaneous, but "evoked," "motivated."	Agape is sovereign in relation to its object, and is directed to both "the evil and the good"; it is spontaneous, "overflowing," "unmotivated."
Eros recognises value in its object--and loves it.	Agape loves--and creates value in its object.

After isolating these two motifs, Nygren discusses the history of Western thought from the ancient Greeks to the Protestant Reformation in terms of the opposition and interaction of these two love-ideas. The ancient Greek philosophers presented an Eros concept of love, as typified by Aristotle's god (the "prime mover") who spent his time thinking of himself (since there was nothing higher to think of), and by the Platonic and Neo-Platonic urge to seek God in order to acquire the greatest benefits for oneself. In contrast, the New Testament presents an Agape concept of love, for the Christian God is Agape[46] and by His very nature gives Himself for His lost creatures through His incarnation and death on the Cross; as the Apostle tells us: "Even for a just man one of us would hardly die, though perhaps for a good man one might actually brave death; but Christ died for us while we were yet sinners, and that is God's own proof of His love [Agape] towards us."[47] The mediaeval period was a time when Agape and Eros - though fundamentally opposed to each other - were blended in an uneasy synthesis (Nygren calls it the Caritas-synthesis).[48] The one chiefly responsible for introducing an amalgam of Eros and Agape was St. Augustine, who had been a Neo-Platonist before he was converted to Christianity, and brought many Neo-Platonic ideas into the Christian faith with him. Though both Eros and Agape co-exist in the Middle Ages, Eros has the stronger hold; this can be seen in the religious life of the mediaeval church, where, although lip service was always given to the self-giving love of God who provided the church and its sacraments, the real emphasis was on man's <u>use</u> of the church's techniques of self-help, sacraments, and mysticism to climb up to God and acquire benefits from Him.[49]   The mediaeval synthesis was broken by the Renaissance (which, in reviving classical antiquity, reasserted pure Eros) and by the Reformation (which attempted a return to the New Testament Gospel of God's free, Agape-motivated grace). We can diagram Nygren's interpretation thusly:

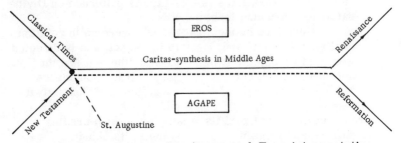

Nygren does not carry his Agape-and-Eros interpretation beyond the period of Renaissance and Reformation, but he does provide a striking Christian philosophy for much of Western history. His motif technique gives him a wider historical perspective than is found in Neo-Orthodoxy, and he goes beyond Niebuhr in setting forth a definite schema for understanding epochs in Western history. Several negative points with regard to Nygren's approach must, however, be raised as well. First, in common with other Lundensians such as Gustaf Aulén, Nygren does not begin with the necessary formal principle of an authoritative Bible; this lack of a specific criterion for judging the truth-value of motifs leaves his approach without solid foundation. Secondly, Nygren, like Aulén, commits the logical sin of "cross-classification" by attempting to juggle two fundamental bases of division: theological truth and historical coherence. Unfortunately, what is historically coherent is not necessarily the theologically true; but without a clean-cut epistemological starting-point (the authoritative Scriptures) such confusion is almost inevitable.[50]   Thirdly, Nygren assumes that the Eros-idea is utterly foreign to the Christian faith properly understood; however, if one begins from a Biblical standpoint, one finds that sinners inevitably seek God for selfish reasons, and that such seeking is not to be condemned <u>per se</u>, but is to be fulfilled and transformed through contact with Christ. Significantly, when Greeks came seeking Jesus,[51] He did not reject their seeking, though, as sinners, they could not have come with selfless motives. Eros becomes deadly

126

only when it is elevated to a position of honor within the Christian faith (as it was in mediaeval theology); to reject all Eros-motivated seeking of God is to reject all seeking for Him, since "there is none that doeth good, no, not one."[52] Lastly, as I have shown elsewhere, Nygren's technique of "motif research" too easily categorizes epochs and the individuals living in those epochs; actually, both Agape and Eros are present throughout Western history (and God's Agape was at work even in the Renaissance!).[53] Notwithstanding these negative criticisms, we must commend Nygren for giving us an interpretative scheme for Western history which utilizes one of the most central themes of Biblical religion - God's love in Christ.

Niebuhr and Nygren have been strongly influenced by Neo-Orthodoxy and have gone beyond it; Paul Tillich of Harvard, often called the "theologian's theologian" because of the profundity and breadth of his thought, has in a comparable way utilized and improved upon existentialism.

> In 1924-25 existentialist philosopher Heidegger, New Testament scholar Bultmann, and philosophical theologian Tillich were colleagues at the University of Marburg. All three have had a marked interrelated influence on twentieth century thought and all three have utilized the now well-known existentialist approach to the "human predicament." . . . Since 1925, however, Tillich (in contrast to both Heidegger and Bultmann) has been developing an ontological interpretation of theology that centers in the Being of God and requires man's participation in the New Being manifest in the Christ.[54]

Like the existentialists, Tillich speaks much of "decision" and of "ultimate concern." But his stress is not so much on the human act of commitment (existentialism) as on the true source and object of the commitment (ontology). Tillich sees man's greatest danger as that of idolatry - commitment to false gods. Since we so frequently anthropomorphize God in the terms we apply to Him, and thereby bring Him down to our level where we can treat Him as an idol, Tillich insists on referring to God as "Being itself," i.e., not just another being, but the Being which enables all else to be.[55] Tillich conceives man's basic problem as a split between his "essence" (what God intended him to be) and his "existence" (what he actually is); in Christ we see this dichotomy mended, and thus we can speak of Christ as the "New Being."[56] Christ manifests the essential nature of Being, which is love; and Tillich conceives of love primarily as Eros, self-realization; in His death for the sins of the world, Christ died for the self-realization of love in Himself and in the many.[57] The Christ-event serves as the key to understanding the creative participation of Being itself in existence throughout history.[58]

This concept of the New Being means that, for Tillich, history is in its essence the history of salvation (Heilsgeschichte): the continuous transforming action of the New Being. The New Being is not, as in Barthian theology, the Logos, limited to one particular, unique Christ-event; but, as the power of being, is the essence of all history. Heilsgeschichte, the history of salvation, is not a super-historical reality. Nor is it, in the Hegelian sense, the history of "the idea." It is the essence of history as such. For Tillich, a separation between a holy and a profane history is impossible. The concrete history in which we stand is the continuous conflict between the New Being, as the creative power, and the deformations and perversions of the new, which Tillich calls the "demonic."[59]

Thus Tillich broadens Christian historical interpretation beyond both Bultmannian existentialism and Barthian Neo-Orthodoxy; all history - not merely existential experience or the events of salvation history - must be seen as the province of divine action.[60]

Moreover, like Niebuhr (but in a more comprehensive way) Tillich develops specific interpretative principles to aid in understanding history. Two of these are particularly noteworthy: his heteronomy-autonomy-theonomy concept, and his kairos principle. By "heteronomy" Tillich means the imposition of law upon man from outside himself; by "autonomy," man's attempt to make his own laws and determine his own fate; and by "theonomy," the rule of God's law, which calls man to be what he was meant to be.[61]

As Tillich looks back over history he finds that different historical periods have been characterized by one or the other of these forms. The early Middle Ages and the early Reformation were periods of theonomy when the ultimate depth of life, God, shone through everything. Religion is a natural expression of life in the theonomous period. There is no division of life into sacred and secular, for all life is seen in its relation to the divine. . . . In theonomous periods men do not feel split; instead they feel whole, centered, and at home in the universe. When a theonomous period loses its power, it normally sinks into heteronomy. When the religious life is no longer that which comes naturally, the religious authorities try to force men to be religious. . . .

Thus the late Middle Ages and the later period of the Reformation both developed heteronomies. . . . Religious persecution became common. The reaction to a heteronomous period is often a period of autonomy. The Renaissance reacted autonomously to the late Middle Ages, and Rationalism, in the eighteenth century, reacted to the heteronomous orthodoxy of later Protestantism. . . . The autonomous period throws aside all external rule. It sets up principles such as "Art for art's sake," "Business is business," and "One man's religion is as good as another's." Although Tillich applauds the reassertion of autonomy against heteronomy, he finds that the autonomous period cannot satisfy the deeper needs of man. It leaves him without any depth or cohesion in life. . . . When an autonomous period breaks down, as it is doing today, it may go in one of two directions. . . . Secular heteronomies arise in the form of totalitarian states, whether Nazi or Communist, offering men . . . "escape from freedom." The other alternative is that a new theonomy may arise. Men on the borderline of despair may, instead of abandoning their freedom, find the wholeness, meaning, and depth of life in God. . . . Theonomy is expressed for Tillich in the essential principle of Protestantism. . . . Because of its understanding of grace, Protestantism represents the eternally necessary protest against everything that is set up to take the place of God.[62]

The kairos concept is derived by Tillich from the New Testament, where this Greek word is usually translated "fullness of time," i.e., a significant moment of time, especially the time of Christ's coming. Tillich employs the word in the broad sense, but always against the background of the Christ-event. He writes: "Kairos, which first [in Classical Greek] was used as meaning 'right time' in the sense of good timing, and which secondly was used as meaning the one right time, the fulfillment of time in the appearance of the Christ, is now used to signify a category of a prophetic interpretation of the 'signs of the time' and of history universal."[63] Tillich believes that in our present kairos situation we have a responsibility and opportunity to create a new theonomous era; and that to do this and to understand past history rightly, we must, as "historical realists," reach "the ultimate ground of meaning of a historical situation and through it of being itself."[64] We may schematize Tillich's historical interpretation thus:

Early Middle Ages	Later Middle Ages	Renaissance	Early Reformation	Later Reformation	Enlightenment	Theonomy—?
Theonomy	Heteronomy	Autonomy	Theonomy	Heteronomy	Autonomy	Today's Kairos / Heteronomy—?

Several legitimate negative criticisms can be directed against Tillich. (1) He accepts Bultmannian demythologizing in principle, though it is only fair to add that he does not go to the lengths of Bultmann in applying it.[65] (2) Tillich's use of the expression "Being itself" for God does not really eliminate theological anthropomorphism. Any assertion about God will necessarily be anthropomorphic, since "no man hath seen God at any time"; when we use the expression "Being itself," we fill it with human content just as we do any traditional expression. Since all our statements about God will be anthropomorphic, the question is not how to avoid anthropomorphism, but how to find legitimate anthropomorphic predicates for God. Is it not best to let the revelation of God in Christ and in the Scriptures be the source of terminology? Even the anti-Christian philosopher Kaufmann sees this terminological problem when he writes: "Tillich's 'being-itself' is neither the God of Abraham, Isaac, and Jacob nor the God of Jesus and Paul, of Matthew and Luke, of the martyrs and Reformers, or of the vast majority of religious people today."[66] (3) The vagueness, ambiguity, and philosophical abstraction in Tillich's conceptual framework make his system hospitable to world-views diametrically opposed to the Christian faith, such as Buddhism;[67] this certainly says something negative, if only on a semantic level, concerning Tillich's approach per se. (4) By denying the historical truth of the Genesis account of man's Fall,[68] and applying his presupposition that "existence cannot be derived from essence," Tillich identifies Creation and Fall; he asserts that "actualized creation and estranged existence are identical."[69] But this logically makes God the author of sin and removes any real hope of a non-tragic "new heaven and new earth."[70] (5) As comparison with Nygren indicates quite clearly, Tillich's self-realization Eros-idea of love does not do justice to the unique self-giving Agape concept of the New Testament. Whereas Nygren erred by not seeing that Eros is a legitimate attempt on the part of man to seek God and that it becomes evil only if it is made an end in itself, Tillich errs by identifying this Eros-idea with God Himself (or, as Tillich would say, Being itself). Nygren, influenced by Neo-Orthodoxy, concentrates on the history of salvation, where Agape reigns;[71] Tillich, desperately desiring to see God's hand in all of history, goes too far in the other direction and introduces Eros into the very nature of God.[72] Leibrecht makes this point decisively - yet also sympathetically - when he writes:

> Tillich's theology does not originate in the appreciation of love as God's condescension and forgiveness. . . . Is not the domination of the eros motive in Tillich's thought the reason why tragedy is conquered by love, but never overcome? We feel the immense intellectual effort and power behind Tillich's attempt to unite the love of Apollo, of Dionysius, and of Christ. The tensions between Tillich's concepts are evident; here also lies his greatness. . . . Tillich stands with those who have sincerely tried to attain an abiding synthesis, in which the split between Greek wisdom and Christian faith is overcome.[73]

Tillich's system indeed reflects greatness; the negative criticisms just stated must not obscure his powerful contributions to modern Christian philosophy of history - specifically, his concept of the New Being, which offers the historian the opportunity for personal transformation, thereby opening up the real possibility of understanding the past for its own sake; his kairos concept, which provides a criterion for historical significance; and his heteronomy-autonomy-theonomy conceptualization of Western history.

Writing of Tillich in 1952, James Luther Adams said: "Whatever one may think of Tillich's interpretation of history as a whole or of this or that detail, one must grant that the interpretation is the most elaborate and substantial one that has been worked out in the history of Protestant philosophical theology."[74] This statement may yet hold for philosophical theology per se, but since 1956 the statement has needed revision with respect to Protestant historiography in general. For in that year was published Volume One of a projected six-volume history of Western civilization which "may do more to effect a general revision of learned opinion than any other historical production of this century."[75] The work here referred to is Order and History by Eric Voegelin, a German political scientist now holding the Boyd professorship of government at Louisiana State University, who describes himself both as a Lutheran[76] and as a "pre-Reformation Christian."

Voegelin's philosophy of history starts from presuppositions which he presents without apology but which are anathema to most thinkers in this post-Christian age.[77]   He is, first of all, concerned not with the history of mankind taken by itself, but the history of man as related to a transcendent, metaphysical realm - to "the truth of being beyond the world." Significantly, he employs as a prefatory quotation to each volume of his work Augustine's assertion: "In consideratione creaturarum non est vana et peritura curiositas exercenda, sed gradus ad immortalia et semper manentia faciendus" (In examining created things, one should not exercise a vain and perishing curiosity, but ascend toward the immortal and the everlasting).[78] Voegelin affirms the existence of God and the necessity of relation to Him; his definition of philosophical inquiry makes this clear: "Philosophy is the love of being through love of divine Being as the source of its order."[79]   Against Toynbee's syncretism of "higher religions" and dream of "ecumenical civilization" based upon them, Voegelin argues particularistically:

> There is no such thing as a non-Western philosophy of history.   For a philosophy of history can arise only where mankind has become historical through existence in the present under God. . . . Only the Judaeo-Christian response to revelation has achieved historical consciousness.   The program of a universal history valid for all men, when it is thought through, can mean only one of two things: the destruction of Western historical form, and the reduction of Western societies to a compact form of order in which the differentiations of truth through philosophy and revelation are forgotten; or, an assimilation of the societies, in which the leap in being has not broken the cosmological order as thoroughly as in the West, to existence in Western historical form.[80]

Moreover, Voegelin isolates himself from a wide range of philosophical and scientific "isms" of our day which have strongly influenced many of the historiographies already discussed; he calls these isms "ideological mortgages" and lists them as follows:

> I am speaking of the pervasive climate of opinion in which a critical study of society and history was practically impossible because the varieties of nationalism, of progressivist and positivist, of liberal and socialist, of Marxian and Freudian ideologies, the neo-Kantian methodologies in imitation of the natural sciences, scientistic ideologies such as biologism and psychologism, the Victorian fashion of

132

agnosticism and the more recent fashions of existentialism and theologism prevented with social effectiveness not only the use of critical standards but even the acquisition of the knowledge necessary for their formation.[81]

What, in essence, is Voegelin's philosophy of history? It will perhaps be best understood by a statement of his central thesis, followed by an explanation of his concepts of evil (Metastasis and Gnosis) and salvation, and a brief summary of his interpretation of the course of Western history.

His major thesis is that every society must create for itself a system of order so as to give meaning "in terms of ends divine and human" to its existence. To create such a system a society must search for symbolic forms that will adequately express its conception of the order of being. No single system expresses the "true order" although, viewed historically, the various orders and their respective symbolisms form a series "intelligibly connected with one another as advances towards, or recessions from, an adequate symbolization of truth concerning the order of being." Each advance, moreover, involves a "leap in being" that "brings God and man into their mutual presence" and raises man's existence to a new level. The true order of being is ultimately rooted in a transcendent God and although finite man can never grasp the whole of it, a study of the history of order enables us to see the broad patterns which emerge from man's struggle to express in his own terms the ultimate nature of reality.[82]

For Voegelin, "human nature is constant,"[83] and therefore "the problem of order is the same for all men at all times."[84] This means that all individuals and societies are subject to the same basic temptation: flight from the reality of existence under God. This evil appears in two forms: Metastasis, "the will to transform reality into something which by essence it is not, . . . the rebellion against the nature of things as ordained by God";[85] and its modern development, Gnosis, the conviction that "the Christian idea of supernatural perfection through Grace in death [should be] immanentized to become the idea of perfection of mankind in history through individual and collective human action."[86] Against all metastatic and gnostic flights from reality stands the Christian Gospel:

In the letters of St. Paul, especially in the Epistle to the Romans, we find for the first time a profound understanding of the mutual involvement of man in the advance of mankind toward truth and of mankind in the truth of everyman's existence. The Law of Israel and the Jews is for St. Paul not a mere past now superceded by Faith, but the very condition for the extension of divine grace through Christ. For grace is extended to the sinner; only when man is conscious of his existence in the untruth of sin, only when he is aware of his death, is he on the way toward the life; and this consciousness of death in sin is awakened when man finds himself unable to fulfill the law. . . . "So the Law has been our schoolmaster (paidagogos) on our way to Christ, so that we might be made upright (justified) through faith . . . " (Gal. 3:24-25). The climax of revelation, the entrance of God into history through the sacrificial assumption of human form, is followed by a sudden luminosity of man's spiritual life.[87]

From the standpoint just described Voegelin interprets the history of Western civilization. He begins with the ancient Near East in general and with Israel in particular.

In contrast to the cosmological symbolism of the quest for meaningful order in the ancient Near Eastern empires, Israel is portrayed as having experienced a "leap in being" into "existence in the presence under God." This was the historical form, and "history is the Exodus from civilizations." Search in space no longer revealed the divine presence. Paradigmatic narrative replaced cosmomythology. Meaningful order was found in the immediate presence of transcendent being, not in consubstantial identity of microcosmic with macrocosmic order. . . . Israel could commit spiritual suicide by backsliding into the Sheol of civilizations. Or living toward the transcendent she could loose security and space for mundane existence. At this impasse, kingship and law filled a vacuum in the original symbolism; while in the line of those who continued to make the Exodus from civilizations followed those who prepared "the Exodus of Israel from itself," the emigration from its own concrete order.[88]

Hellenic society made a similar, but independent, "leap in being"; in this case the leap was from the symbolism of myth to the symbolic form of philosophy. Unlike Barthian Neo-Orthodoxy, Voegelin regards both Jerusalem and Athens as the proper backdrop for the Christian city of God.

The philosophy of order and history is a Western symbolism because Western society has received its historical form through Christianity. And the Patres of early Christianity could create the symbolism because they could draw on the resources of Israel and Hellas when they articulated their own mode of existence. As Clement of Alexandria formulated it: "To the barbarians [i.e., the non-gentiles; the Jews] God has given the Law and the Prophets; to the Hellenes he has given philosophy; so that the ears of both might be prepared to hear the Gospel." And on the same relation in retrospect: "To us he gave the New Testament; those of the Judaeans and Hellenes are the Old ones." The scriptures of both Israel and Hellas are the Old Testaments of Christianity. The origin and historical structure of Western order were better understood by the men who created the form than by their late successors who live in it without remembering the conditions of tenancy.[89]

In Christianity, "metastatic symbols were transformed into the eschatological events beyond history, so that the order of the world regained its autonomy. . . . Throughout the Middle Ages, the Church was occupied with the struggle against heresies of a metastatic complexion; and with the Reformation this underground stream has come to the surface again in a massive flood - first, in the left wing of the sectarian movements and then in the secular political creed movements which purport to exact the metastasis by revolutionary action."[90] In the modern national states, Voegelin sees such Gnosis elevated to the position of a "symbolic form of order,"[91] and here he thinks especially of Hitlerian fascism which drove him from his homeland, and Soviet communism. Modern theology has contributed to this dire state of affairs, and is itself riddled with Gnosticism; the following trenchant criticism by Voegelin will provide a fitting conclusion to our brief exposition of his philosophy: "When the scientia Dei, which includes God's foreknowledge of man's eternal destiny, was immanentized into man's foreknowledge of his destiny, the foundation was laid for separate churches of the elect down to the contemporary degeneration into civic clubs for socially compatible families."[92]

In Voegelin's Order and History we undoubtedly have, as one reviewer put it, "the most important historical work of our century, not to be ignored by anyone seriously concerned with our time of troubles."[93] Order and History successfully avoids most of the pitfalls we have encountered in other philosophies of history, both secular and Christian, and it clearly sees the central demonic temptation of our time: the attempt to create God in man's own image - in the image of his political, social, and religious theories and projects. Voegelin calls upon us to use all our efforts to "repress Gnostic corruption and restore the forces of civilization."[94] As Luther cried to his age, so Voegelin cries to ours: "Let God be God!"

It would not be in place to engage in negative criticism of Voegelin's system when his work is still to be completed and when all evaluation of it suffers from attenuated historical perspective. However, one serious problem does need to be mentioned, and it will serve as a transition into our next section, dealing with the "Validation of the Christian View." Voegelin, though rejecting orthodox Graf-Kuenen-Wellhausen documentary criticism of the Old Testament,[95] takes a very loose view of Biblical inspiration. The book of Judges contains material which is "partly monotonous, partly amusing";[96] the prophet Isaiah suffers from Metastasis and incipient Gnosis;[97] Metastasis and Gnosis have been "absorbed into the symbolism of Christianity itself through the Old Testament as well as through the Revelation of St. John";[98] and "the Pauline method of historical interpretation is defective."[99] It is clear that Voegelin does not consciously use the Scriptural revelation as the source of his philosophy of history; rather, he uses selected material from the Bible to illustrate an independently formulated philosophy.

What, then, is the actual source of Voegelin's system? He apparently believes that his system is rationally self-evident, for, as noted previously, he presents it "usually without argument or defense." In asserting the constancy of human nature, for example, we have found him stating that "the very idea of a history of mankind presupposes it." I have shown elsewhere[100] that a religio-philosophical system based on pure rationality is indefensible; here I wish only to illustrate the difficulties Voegelin encounters when he attempts to present his (essentially very Christian) system to non-Christians on the basis of pure rationality.

On July 17, 1958, at a colloquium where the great philosophers of history of our time met to debate on the topics (but not the text) of Toynbee's A Study of History, Voegelin presented his transcendent theme that our age is suffering from metastatic Gnosis: "The great dream of man today - in the West as well as in the East - is simultaneously to 'evangelize' the whole of humanity and to organize a terrestrial Empire along political lines."[101] Lucien Goldmann, a leading French Marxist scholar, then proceeded to show that Voegelin's position was without adequate foundation. The following are typical verbal exchanges in the debate:[102]

Goldmann. - Mr. Voegelin regards the appearance of messianisms as a kind of regression or decadence or departure from "reality." I should like to know the basis of such a value judgment. For, in a word, one could regard the messianic attitude as "natural" and, conversely, the idea of transcendence as a decadent phenomenon.

Voegelin. - I believe that my analysis is founded on objective criteria. I have defined "reason" as the maximum distinction between realms of being. Cannot one say, in the most objective fashion, that from the moment one gives up this distinction between immanence and transcendence, one is regressing?

Goldmann. - Perhaps, but on condition that one first proves that several realms of being actually exist and that the transcendent is not simply an illusion.

Voegelin. - Historically, there is an experience of transcendence.

Goldmann. - There have been in history thousands of experiences which critical analysis has afterwards reduced to the level of illusions. When you yourself speak of what you call a Gnosis, you perform reductions of this kind. Socialistic messianism reflects a kind of religious experience but a non-transcendental experience. Why should you take exception to it a priori when it is as much a historical fact as the others?

Voegelin. - For an epistemological reason which seems to me entirely valid: because it is a derivative type of experience, not an original experience.

Goldmann. - But right there I discern what I called a value judgment. Why isn't non-transcendental messianism the original form of religious experience, with the transcendental messianisms being merely the degenerate forms? Religion doesn't need to be connected with the idea of the supernatural.

In this verbal skirmish it must be admitted that Voegelin comes off second best. He is unable to demonstrate the existence of a transcendental realm of being (God's kingdom), and therefore he has no ground for asserting that modern Gnosis is a degeneration, or, indeed, an evil of any kind.[103] "Professor Voegelin's work of historical reconstruction is intended to redeem us" from "denial of the divine guidance which is the source of all order in personality and in society";[104] granted, but what if there is in fact no divine guidance because there is no divine Guide? We have presented a host of recent theological attempts to answer the basic questions of philosophy of history; now we must ask the most fundamental question of all:

How can we know that Christian theology and Christian interpretation of history are true?

The Validation of the Christian World-View

At one point in the Cerisy-la-Salle colloquium on philosophy of history, Raymond Aron states a position which is widely held today:

> If I am a rationalist, I am a rationalist who . . . recognizes the specific character of different spiritual universes. . . . Belief in the transcendent, even if I do not agree with it myself, seems to me to be a human activity of a particular type with a significance I can perceive. But when belief touches on matters within the jurisdiction of empirical study and sociological analysis, I am convinced that it presents an entirely different aspect, and its falsity is easily demonstrated simply because it deals with values inaccessible to science.[105]

To many non-Christian historians and philosophers of history, the classic and contemporary Christian interpretations of history have great appeal, but are ultimately disregarded because they are believed to rest on "values inaccessible to science." The Christian faith may provide attractive and powerfully meaningful solutions to the perennial problems of historical analysis, but of what use are they if they rest on an undemonstrable foundation?

It is the conviction of the present writer that the Christian world-view is in fact "accessible to science" and rests upon an objective foundation which will stand up under the most exacting criticism. In essays comprising the second part of this book I have analyzed the various methods of acquiring truth,[106] and have pointed up the deficiencies in such methods as subjective empiricism and pragmatism.[107] In an essay on the Petrine theory of papal supremacy, I have shown that the objective-empirical argument for the authority of the Roman Church is insupportable historically.[108] On what, then, does the case for Christianity rest? It rests, as the apostles well knew,[109] on the objective, historical truth of the resurrection of Jesus Christ from the dead. Since the historical and philosophical demonstration appears in Part Two of this book, we need only set forth the argument in outline here:

1. On the basis of accepted principles of textual and historical analysis, the Gospel records are found to be

trustworthy historical documents - primary source evidence for the life of Christ.[110]

2. In these records, Jesus exercises divine prerogatives and claims to be God in human flesh;[111] and He rests His claims on His forthcoming resurrection.[112]

3. In all four Gospels, Christ's bodily resurrection is described in minute detail; Christ's resurrection evidences His deity.[113]

4. The fact of the resurrection cannot be discounted on a priori, philosophical grounds; miracles are impossible only if one so defines them - but such definition rules out proper historical investigation.[114]

5. If Christ is God, then He speaks the truth[115] concerning the absolute divine authority of the Old Testament[116] and of the soon-to-be-written New Testament;[117] concerning His death for the sins of the world;[118] and concerning the nature of man and of history.

6. It follows from the preceding that all Biblical assertions bearing on philosophy of history are to be regarded as revealed truth, and that all human attempts at historical interpretation are to be judged for truth-value on the basis of harmony with Scriptural revelation.

Two cautions need to be stated with reference to this demonstration. First, the argument is not a rational proof in the sense of a demonstration in pure mathematics or formal logic; rather, it is an empirical argument based upon the application of historical method to an allegedly objective event. Thus it provides no more than probable evidence for the truth of the Christian world-view. Paul Tillich is quite right when he says with reference to the resurrection: "Historical research can never give more than a probable answer";[119] he is wrong, however, when he concludes from this that the historical argument is inadequate. Probability argumentation is employed constantly by historians in their work, and must be relied upon if historical research is to have any meaning at all.[120] Huizinga's comments on historical scepticism are appropriate here:

The strongest argument against historical scepticism . . . is this: the man who doubts the possibility of correct historical evidence and tradition cannot then accept his own evidence, judgment, combination and interpretation. He cannot limit his doubt to his historical criticism, but is required to let it operate on his own life. He discovers at once that he not only lacks conclusive evidence in all sorts of aspects of his own life that he had quite taken for granted, but also that there is no evidence whatever. In short, he finds himself forced to accept a general philosophical scepticism along with his historical scepticism. And general philosophical scepticism is a nice intellectual game, but one cannot live by it.[121]

The purpose of the resurrection argument is not to "force" anyone into the Christian faith; any forced intellectualization of the Christian religion is completely inconsistent with the nature of Christianity. The argument is intended, rather, to give solid objective ground for testing the Christian faith experientially. How is the test made? By confronting, with no more than "suspension of disbelief," the Christ of the Scriptures; for "faith comes by hearing and hearing by the word of God" and (said Christ) "whoever has the will to do the will of God shall know whether my teaching comes from God or is merely my own."[122] The Scriptural Gospel is ultimately self-attesting, but the honest inquirer needs objective ground for trying it, since there are a welter of conflicting religious options and one can become psychologically jaded through indiscriminate trials of religious belief. Only the Christian world-view offers objective ground for testing it experientially; therefore Christ deserves to be given first opportunity to make His claims known to the human heart.

A second caution with reference to the resurrection argument is that it is not intended to exclude other varieties of Christian apologetics. Acknowledgment is made of such capable defenses of the Christian faith as those of Pascal, Urquhart, C. S. Lewis, and Edward John Carnell,[123] but it is believed that the resurrection argument has the two-fold advantage of being the prime apologetic employed by the early church,[124] and of being the fundament on which, ultimately, all other defenses rest.[125]

Let us now consider several objections which have been, or can be, raised with regard to the resurrection apologetic. (1) "You begin with the presuppositions of historical method and an implicit interest in the Christian faith. What right have you to such assumptions? Why not begin with the investigation of some other religion through the use of some other methodology?" We begin with an examination of the Christian faith because it is the only religion which purports to offer external, objective evidence of its validity. All other religions appeal to inner experience without any means of objective validation.

140

What is needed (to put it crassly) is a means of distinguishing true religious experience (that is to say, religious experience of the truth) from gastric disturbance! We accept the canons of historical method (i.e., scientific method as applied to historical phenomena) because such heuristic presuppositions assume as little as possible and provide for the objective discovery of as much as possible. Kant conclusively showed that all arguments and systems begin with presuppositions; but this does not mean that all presuppositions are equally desirable. It is better to begin, as we have, with presuppositions of method (which will yield truth) rather than with presuppositions of substantive content (which assume a body of truth already). In our modern world we have found that the presuppositions of empirical method best fulfil this condition; but note that we are operating only with the presuppositions of scientific method, not with the rationalistic assumptions of Scientism ("the Religion of Science").[126]

(2) "You can never reach the divine by investigating the human. No amount of historical study of the life of Jesus will yield more than a picture of a very remarkable man." This argument rests on the rationalistic presupposition that God could not become man. But how do we know this unless we examine the historical evidence in support of Jesus' claim to be God in human flesh? We must begin with the historical data, not rule them out by metaphysical speculation. If Jesus did rise from the dead, then He is in a better position to explain how this happened than anyone else, and, as we have seen, He pointed to it as the prime evidence of the truth of His claims. Moreover, if Jesus was not God as He claimed, then He was either a maniac or a charlatan - and these possibilities are completely inconsistent with His exemplary life and moral teachings. In an honest, unprejudiced encounter with the man Jesus, one finds himself face to face also with the divine Christ. There is no other alternative if one employs the canons of historical evidence to the Gospel records, for they declare unequivocally that "the Word was God . . . and the Word was made flesh."[127]

(3) "The resurrection cannot be used as an argument for the truth of Christianity because it was not a public event." We have already shown that the apostles, who are the earliest witnesses to the resurrection, testified to it in their preaching as a public event. The Apostle Paul is especially at pains to declare the objective, public character of Christ's resurrection: "First and foremost, I handed on to you the facts which had been imparted to me: that Christ died for our sins, in

141

accordance with the Scriptures; that He was buried; that He was raised to life on the third day, according to the Scriptures; and that He appeared to Peter, and afterwards to the Twelve. Then he appeared to over five hundred of our brothers at once, most of whom are still alive. . . ."[128]

(4) "The resurrection should not be viewed as an historical event. It is trans-historical - an eschatological, not a temporal, occurrence." This argument, frequently reiterated by Bultmannian existentialists, is stated in a particularly audacious way in a recent work by Carl Michalson:

> The eschatological event of the resurrection is not an answer to the question "how" but to the question "why." The resurrection, that is, does not pertain to a picture of the world but to one's self-understanding. As Bultmann has said to Barth in a private letter, the weakness of our time, indeed of the last two centuries, has been the effort to relate Christianity to an objective world-view without self-understanding. I was reminded of this problem one evening when I heard my wife ask my children, "Would you like to hear the story of how Jesus was born?" I interrupted with a stricture from Bultmann. I said, "But my dear, the thing to be known about the birth of Jesus is not how but why he was born." My wife replied with an innocence which remains the plague of the theologian, "I was only going to read what the Bible says!" The Bible undeniably hints how Jesus was born and comes very close to telling how Jesus was raised from the dead. It is as if the birth of Jesus were the genetic consequence of the wedding of God with Israel and as if the resurrection of Jesus were a cosmographic vindication of realities immanent in the life and ministry of Jesus. Is this not the misleading thing about the Gospels which a reading of the Epistles helps to correct? . . . The demythologizing of the resurrection is the task of a kerygmatic historiography.[129]

In actuality, "the weakness of our time" is manifest in the very kind of reasoning Michalson employs: complete disregard of the historical claims of the Gospel records with regard to the objectivity of the resurrection, and the substitution of Bultmann's metaphysical speculations for Biblical and historical truth. Michalson's wife has proved herself twice the theologian that her husband is, for she clearly recognizes that the Christian faith begins in historical record, not in existentialistic subjectivizing. A recent article in The American Scholar has well pointed up the debility of the "trans-historical" approach:

In the Bible there is set forth on many, many pages the conviction that God is revealed in history. The Bible knows
nothing of trans-history, and, indeed, the very idea is one
hundred and eighty degrees removed from what the Bible
says. It is the shabbiest kind of learning that dares to call
trans-history biblical. And since the word is mongrel, for
trans is Latin and history is Greek, a supposedly better
term, metahistory, is offered. It too is not biblical. Is
trans-history or metahistory an explanation, or is it an
evasion? . . . . Does the modern theologian enter the arena
of the intellectual combat with the secular historian? Is he
grappling with a genuine issue, and setting it into a convincing array of ideas and propositions? Or does he simply
abandon the field to his adversary? In my judgment the
modern theologian is guilty of evasion. And, I would add,
the theologian is at this point throwing away even the bare
possibility of communicating with the layman, for to most
of us the word history has had a particular import; the word
trans-history seems to me to be more a barrier to, than a
vehicle of, communication.[130]

As we have pointed out earlier in this chapter, the Bultmannian
trans-historical approach is utterly unbiblical and unverifiable,
and his demythologization of the Bible is self-contradictory and
wholly inconsistent with the essence of the historic Christian
faith.

(5) "Historical truths are insufficient as a foundation for
faith [because of] their relative degree of certainty. Even the
facts most definitely ascertained possess but relative certainty,
while the very nature of faith requires absolute certainty for its
foundation. . . . Only the apriori has apodictic certainty."[131]
But how do we choose among a priori positions? Each religion
has its own a prioris, and many of the most fundamental tenets
contradict those of other faiths. Without an objective criterion,
one is at a loss to make a meaningful choice among a prioris.
The resurrection provides a basis in historical probability for
trying the Christian faith. Granted, the basis is only one of
probability, not of certainty, but probability is the sole ground
on which finite human beings can make any decisions. Only
deductive logic and pure mathematics provide "apodictic certainty," and they do so because they stem from self-evident
formal axioms (e.g., the tautology, if A then A) involving no
matter of fact. The moment we enter the realm of fact, we
must depend on probability; this may be unfortunate, but it is
unavoidable, and since it does not keep us from making

decisions in non-religious matters, it should not immobilize us when religious commitment is involved.

(6) "Christianity should be preached, not defended." But there is no such thing as preaching Christianity without defending it. The apostles knew this, as their preaching evidences; and the church has known this throughout history. To preach the Gospel is to present it to a world in which innumerable religions are clammering for adherents, and in which numerous misconceptions and false ideologies make it exceedingly difficult for many people even to give the Christian faith a fair and impartial hearing. It is the responsibility of the Christian to "be ready always to give an answer to every man that asks him a reason of the hope that is in him."[132] Not to do this is to disregard the apostolic example of being "all things to all men that I might by all means save some."[133] The non-Christian will want to know, and has a right to know, why he should listen to Christian preaching; the resurrection provides the best reason for his listening very closely.

(7) "Your position is biblicistic - it treats the Bible as a propositional source of information on philosophy of history. Instead of stressing the Bible as the word of God, you should view it as containing the word of God. Christ the living Word should be emphasized, not the Bible as the written word. Indeed, what is really important is not the biblicistic Jesus of history, but the Christ of faith." In actuality, our approach is "biblicistic" only to the degree that the Bible itself is "biblicistic," for we are taking the same attitude toward the Bible that Jesus Himself took; as we have shown, Jesus regarded the Bible as fully authoritative, and if He is God as He claimed and as He evidenced by His resurrection, what right have we to take any other attitude toward the Bible than the one He took?[134] As to our "propositional" treatment of Biblical statements, it should be recognized (but seldom is) that all literary and historical communication occurs by way of propositions; one cannot even argue against the use of propositions without using propositions to do so![135] The Bible is not primarily a book for eliciting emotional feelings; it is first and foremost God's objective revelation of Himself - of His nature, His plan of salvation, and His will for mankind. The "word of God" is, in the most ultimate sense, Christ Himself, but in a wider sense it refers to the Gospel about Christ, and to the entire Bible, which testifies of Him. The Reformers fully recognized that the canonical Scriptures as a whole are the word of God, for in their entirety they testify of the living Word.[136] We know nothing of the living Word (Christ) apart from the written word

(the Bible), and to set them against each other is to oppose the real Christ (the Christ of the Gospels) with a Christ created in our own presuppositional or cultural image. If our "Christ of faith" deviates at all from the Biblical "Jesus of history," then to the extent of that deviation, we also lose the genuine Christ of faith.[137] As one of the greatest Christian historians of our time, Herbert Butterfield, has put it: "It would be a dangerous error to imagine that the characteristics of an historical religion would be maintained if the Christ of the theologians were divorced from the Jesus of history."[138]

Principles of Christian Historical Interpretation

Having provided objective evidence for the validity of the Christian world-view, let us now summarize the fundamental Scriptural principles of historiography. Many of these principles have been touched on in discussing the Biblical idea of history in an earlier chapter and in dealing with contemporary theologies of history in this chapter; but it will be useful to provide an organized summation here. We shall distinguish ten principles in all, and these will be divided into four groups: Metaphysical (principles one, two, and three), Ethical (principles four and five), Anthropological (principles six, seven, and eight), and Redemptive (principles nine and ten). In order to show the specific practical application of these principles, we shall indicate their relevance to the historian's understanding of his own work and to his interpretation of typical historical events (in the latter case the French Revolution will be taken as a random example).

Metaphysical Principles

(1) The entire historical process is meaningful, for it is the result of God's creative activity and has been hallowed by God's appearance in human flesh in the person of Christ and by His death for the sins of the whole world. This truth provides the Christian historian with his charter for historical work, since it assures him that every event in the world's history is worth investigating. Unlike the non-Christian historian who must fall back on aesthetic or antiquarian motivations, the Christian historian takes his cue from Christ's words: "Are not five sparrows sold for two farthings, and not one of them is forgotten before God? . . . Ye are of more value than many sparrows."[139] With reference to a particular historical event such as the French Revolution, the Christian historian must give it the

benefit of his full intellectual powers; he has no right to disregard it or deemphasize it because it does not happen to strike his fancy or appeal to his personal tastes. If to God the Revolution and the people who fought and died in it are of "more value than many sparrows," then they must be regarded in that same way by the Christian historian.

(2) The decisive event ("Kairos") in the history of mankind is the act of God in Jesus Christ, and the ultimate criterion of historical significance for other events ("kairoi") - all of which are unique - lies in their relation to the Christ-act. The events of the French Revolution must be treated as unique, not forced into a predetermined mold (contrast Toynbee's use of Greek civilization as a model for other civilizations, and the psychoanalytic historians' use of Freudian theories as categories for historical data). In evaluating the Revolution by the great Kairos, the Christian historian will probably conclude that in spite of the many positive results of the Revolution,[140] in the long run it contributed to what Voegelin calls metastatic Gnosis: the decline of the Christian faith in Europe through the substitution of human reason and immanent values for reliance upon God's transcending grace in Word and Sacrament.[141]

(3) Final judgment on the historical process rests in the hands of God, not of men, and will be made manifest on the last day, when all history is brought to a close with the return of Christ. Because the final evaluation of all historical events rests with God and not with man, and because the final judgment will take place at the end of time, not within time,[142] the Christian historian does not presume to make categorical judgments himself, and is more concerned with understanding than with pontificating. He has been assured that "there is nothing covered that shall not be revealed, neither hid that shall not be known" and that "whatsoever ye have spoken in darkness shall be heard in the light, and that which ye have spoken in the ear in closets shall be proclaimed upon the housetops";[143] in the confidence of God's final judgment he does not need to play demigod by way of his personal judgments. "Once battles are over," writes Herbert Butterfield, "the human race becomes in a certain sense one again; and just as Christianity tries to bind it together in love, so the role of the technical historian is that of a reconciling mind that seeks to comprehend. Taking things retrospectively and recollecting in tranquillity, the historian works over the past to cover the conflicts with understanding, and explains the unlikenesses between men and makes us sensible of their terrible predicaments; until at the finish - when all is as remote as the tale of Troy - we are able at last perhaps

146

to be a little sorry for everybody."[144] In the interpretation of
the French Revolution, such Christian humility will be directed
to making men "sensible of the terrible predicament" both of
those of the Old Régime, who wept at the fall of the monarchy,
and of the revolutionaries, who in their own way "went out, not
knowing whither they went, seeking a better city."

Ethical Principles

(4) There exists in the universe an absolute moral law (revealed in the Holy Scriptures and fulfilled in Christ) and an absolute ethical ideal (the Agape-love of God incarnated in
Christ). The Christian historian, by willingly subjecting himself to the Biblical moral law and ethical ideal, imposes upon
himself an absolute standard of truth; knowing that lying is of
the devil,[145] he will not consciously bend the historical facts
of an event such as the French Revolution to fit his theories,
nor will he make his case by the clever omission of facts which
do not fit his hypotheses.[146] The morality of the Bible also
provides the Christian historian with absolute standards for the
evaluation of historical events. "He will not bleach the moral
color out of history by steeping it in corrosive skepticism";[147]
at the same time he will not fall into the naïve error expressed
in the popular aphorism, Tout comprendre, c'est tout pardonner.
Unlike the secular historian, he will not be compelled to use the
relative and changing ethical standards of his own age (or of
past ages) in the general evaluation of historical acts; in reference to the French Revolution, he can condemn the bloody ex-
cesses of certain phases of the Revolution on the basis of moral
standards which remain true for all men of all times, whether
they recognize them or not.

Furthermore, an absolute morality and an absolute ethical
ideal provide the Christian historian with something desperately needed by, but unavailable to, the non-Christian historian: a
criterion of progress. Optimistic secular historians such as
E. H. Carr may assert that history is no longer history if its
meaning depends on "some extra-historical and super-rational
power" and that "history properly so-called can be written only
by those who find and accept a sense of direction in history itself; the belief that we have come from somewhere is closely
linked with the belief that we are going somewhere";[148] but
without the revelation of the Super-historical in time one has
no absolute criterion whatever for determining where we have
come from or where we should be going.[149] In evaluating the
French Revolution, the Christian historian, unlike his secular

counterpart, has solid ground for claiming that - notwithstanding the appearance of many evils - progress did take place in respect to "a liberty henceforth guaranteed by constitutional government," "equality before the law," "the assertion that a people has the right to dispose of itself and cannot be annexed to another without its own adherence freely expressed," and the dream of the Revolutionaries "that all peoples would emulate their example."[150]

(5) Truth in the most real sense is to be identified with personality, not with impersonal factors or forces. The Christian holds a concrete (not abstract), personal (not impersonal) idea of truth, for Christ identified truth with Himself.[151] Thus the historian who is a Christian will be unafraid to inject his own personality into his writings; he will not make the mistake of the "scientific" historians who attempt the impossible task of writing completely impersonal history. Moreover, he will resist the temptation to which positivistic historiography has succumbed: the reduction of human history to a product of "trends" and "forces." In treating the French Revolution, he will make every effort to understand and appreciate the work of each individual involved in the struggle; and he will oppose all attempts of Marxist historians (to take one obvious example) who would explain the Revolution simply in terms of competitive means of production. "One of the most dangerous things in life is to subordinate human personality to production, to the state, even to civilisation itself, to anything but the glory of God."[152]

Anthropological Principles

(6) Human nature is constant. We noted that Voegelin unsuccessfully argues on purely rational grounds for the constancy of human nature; divine revelation, however, gives us absolute assurance that man's essential nature does not change.[153] Thus the Christian historian has the assurance that a common ground exists between himself and the men of past ages whom he studies; he can confidently interpret the motives of a Louis XVI, a Marie Antoinette, or a Robespierre in terms of the common humanity which he shares with them and which is described in the pages of Holy Writ. It should be noted that apart from Biblical testimony in this matter, no historian can possibly be sure that human nature is stable enough to allow for analogous reasoning from the historian's own present to the dim and distant past. Thus the non-Christian historian is unable even to justify his own field of study philosophically!

Furthermore, the constancy of human nature permits the

Christian historian to seek patterns in human history; as Koheleth says: "that which hath been is now, and that which is to be hath already been."[154] It is on this solid ground that such Christian philosophers of history as Tillich have been able to set forth schemas describing recurring epochs of human activity. No secularistic patterns, on the other hand, have more than the most tenuous philosophical justification, for the secularist can never be sufficiently sure of human nature to know that "that which is to be hath already been." We noted earlier the dilemma of present-day secular historiography: scientific historians see the need of finding patterns in the past and yet cannot justify their patterns, and relativistic historians point up the errors of their scientific counterparts but refuse to admit the need of comprehensive historical interpretations. Here again, only the Christian view has the answer: interpretive patterns are both legitimate and desirable, for they reflect the constancy of man's nature as revealed by God's word.

(7) Fallen human nature is sinful, i.e., self-centered, and this self-centeredness extends to all human activities in every age. The Bible presents man as fallen from an original state of grace as a result of a volitional choice of self over God, and even the Christian is not exempt from this evil egocentrism.[155] Luther well described sinful man as incurvatus in se, "curved in upon himself"; and the Christian historian will recognize that this curvature applies also to him, for he is simul justus et peccator (simultaneously a sinner and a man justified by God's grace) and therefore not infallible in his historical work. The Christian historian will be the last one to say or to imply (as Spengler seemed to do in the preface to his Decline of the West), "When I speak, let no dog bark!" In confronting the past, the Christian historian will not attempt to gloss over or whitewash the numerous evidences of man's inhumanity to man. He will, for example, treat Marie Antoinette's remark, "The people want bread; let them eat cake," as another indication of the callous insensitivity of men in power toward those who are beneath them; he will apply Acton's Scripturally-grounded axiom, "Power corrupts, and absolute power corrupts absolutely." Unlike many liberal, optimistic, progressivistic historical interpreters of our own day, he will see man not as moving to higher and higher levels of ethical achievement, but as always equidistant from eternity and in the same need of God's forgiving act upon the Cross. Butterfield illustrates this point well:

> During the war it was put to a British ambassador that after the destruction of Germany Russia would become a similar

149

menace to Europe if she found herself in a position to behave over a large area with impunity. The answer given on behalf of this country was that such apprehensions were unjustified, Russia would not disappoint us, for we believed that her intentions were friendly and good. Such an attitude to morality - such a neglect of a whole tradition of maxims in regard to this question - was not Christian in any sense of the word but belongs to a heresy black as the old Manichaean heresy. . . . It is essential not to have faith in human nature. Such faith is a recent heresy and a very disastrous one.[156]

(8) Because all human decisions are made in a sin-impregnated human environment, all decisions must be evaluated historically in terms of the lesser of two or more evils. The realistic Christian conception of man's nature carries with it a realistic evaluation of human actions both in the past and in our own day. The presence of sin in an act does not in itself damn that act historically, for no act is performed without involving sins of commission or of omission.[157] The Christian historian will always compare an act with its existential alternatives before arriving at a judgment, and his judgment will never be absolutely white or absolutely black, for the former is possible only in heaven, and the latter only in hell. As Niebuhr has so effectively emphasized, the Christian historian is the most realistic interpreter of the past, for he recognizes its grey character. Thus in viewing the French Revolution, the Christian historian will weigh the revolutionaries' sins of bloodshed and paganism against the alternative sin of condoning a corrupt and lecherous Old Régime of vested interest and oppression. For the historian who is a Christian, there are no "easy answers"; whatever his other failings, superficiality is unlikely to be one of them.

Redemptive Principles

(9) To God, history is "totum simul" - an eternal present - and in the sacrificial death of Christ on the Cross His love goes out to all men of all ages. God's love binds together the entire human race, past, present, and future. The great contemporary English writer Charles Williams (d. 1945) expressed this central Christian truth beautifully in his concept of the City, where the already-dead and the yet-unborn "coinhere" with us in perpetual redemptive love. The motto of the City is "Your life and death are with your neighbor," and this refers to our relations with people of the past as well as with those of the present. At one point in his great poem Taliessin Through Logres,

Williams describes the rescue of the Roman epic poet Vergil from damnation; this is accomplished by the redemptive love of Christians, who through the ages have themselves been upheld by the truth and beauty of his poetry:

Virgil fell from the edge of the world. . . .
The air rushed up; he fell
into despair, into air's other. . . .
Unborn pieties lived.
Out of the infinity of time to that moment's infinity
they lived, they rushed, they dived below him, they rose
to close with his fall; all, while man is, that could
live, and would, by his hexameters, found
there the ground of their power, and their power's use.
Others he saved; himself he could not save.
In that hour they came; more and faster, they sped
to their dead master; they sought him to save
from the spectral grave and the endless falling,
who had heard, for their own instruction, the sound
     of his calling.
There was intervention, suspension, the net of their
     loves. . . .
Virgil was fathered of his friends.
He lived in their ends.
He was set on the marble of exchange.[158]

This great principle of universal substitution and exchange impels the Christian historian to save from oblivion and misjudgment those who historically could not save themselves; and the universal perspective of God's grace keeps the Christian from writing partisan histories which label certain nations, races, or classes as "inferior" or "degenerate" as compared with others or with his own. In reference to the French Revolution, the Christian historian will not distort those momentous events to fit a "French" viewpoint, or an "English" viewpoint, or any other parochial viewpoint; and he will be especially conscious of his responsibility to "save from the spectral grave and the endless falling" those dramatis personae who have been neglected or misunderstood by other historians. To the Christian, "all local histories are really one history";[159] and since "God so loved the world that He gave His only begotten Son that whosoever believeth in Him should not perish but have everlasting life,"[160] the Christian historian will be vitally concerned with all the "whosoevers" of time past, and will do all that he can to set them in universal perspective and provide them with historical immortality.

(10) Redemption from self-centeredness takes place in the presence of Christ, and is available to anyone who puts his trust in Him. "Turning to the Jews who had believed Him, Jesus said, 'If you dwell within the revelation I have brought, you are indeed My disciples; you shall know the truth, and the truth will set you free.' They replied, 'We are Abraham's descendants; we have never been in slavery to any man. What do you mean by saying, "You will become free men"?' 'In very truth I tell you,' said Jesus, 'that everyone who commits sin is a slave. The slave has no permanent standing in the household, but the son belongs to it for ever. If then the Son sets you free, you will indeed be free.'"[161] The secular historian likewise claims that he has never been in slavery to any man. But the brutal fact is that he is in slavery - to himself - to his cultural ideals, his aesthetic tastes, his prejudices, his desire for fame. Christ's death on the Cross provides the only way out of this slavery, for Christ - who was both omnipotent God and representative Man - took all our sins and inadequacies upon Himself, and by "that blessed exchange" expiated them, conquering the whole host of evil powers arrayed against us. God continually offers this greatest of all gifts to men, and if a person will do no more than recognize his need and accept the proffered gift, he can personally experience manumission and the opportunity to know the truth. The Christian historian, having been freed from slavery to himself, is able to enter into the lives of men of the past and find the historical truths that so frequently escape secularists blinded by the self. "In the fulness of time," Scripture says, "God sent forth His Son";[162] when the historian lets Christ into his heart, time's fulness becomes a reality for him as well.

APPENDIX TO CHAPTER FIVE
OTTO PIPER'S NEGATIVE CRITIQUE OF BULTMANN[163]

"In a new and original manner the concept of myth was applied to the New Testament, when Professor Rudolf Bultmann, of the University of Marburg, Germany, published his famous article on 'Neues Testament und Mythologie,' in 1941. The radical manner in which he stated the problem called forth a heated debate in Germany, and the issue soon became central in New Testament interpretation.

"Bultmann points out that for the student of the Gospels a serious difficulty lies in the question, What relevancy for our life of faith can we assign to the Gospel stories, given the fact that to the modern scholar they appear as the work

152

of the early church? Lessing, Schleiermacher, Strauss, and Wilhelm Herrmann had already indicated the problem and offered various and sagacious solutions. But Bultmann finds them unsatisfactory, because they all assume in principle that the Gospel records are historically reliable. He thinks that Form Criticism has proved conclusively that the historical nucleus of the evangelical narratives is concealed by the religious interpretation which the early church gave to the life of Jesus. Hence not only the miracle stories of the gospels but the gospels in their totality are declared to be myths, i.e., the description of a theophany. In that respect they are but one of the many modifications of the gnostic myth of the descent of the heavenly redeemer and his return to God. To the modern man reared in the scientific tradition of our age, not only the belief in miracles and heavenly beings is unacceptable, but also the whole frame of reference of that christological myth, as e.g., the belief in heaven and hell, the Old and the New Aeon, the return of Christ, and in general the idea of a god who tampers with the laws of nature.

"Yet despite these stringent criticisms of the Gospels, Bultmann is not willing to give up Christianity altogether. Rather, by adopting an existentialistic interpretation of the Christian faith, for which he is indebted to Kierkegaard, Barth, and Martin Heidegger, he suggests a 'demythologization' of the Gospels. Holding that Paul and John had already overcome in principle the mythical world view of the Palestinian church, he contends that the true objective of the gospel message never was to describe supernatural events taking place in space and time but rather that under the mythical garb the gospel story was intended to announce God's coming to man's soul, or self, and the radical change thus accomplished in a person's 'existence.' When the gospel story is proclaimed, the individual thereby becomes aware of the misery of his 'existence,' viz., that his self is enslaved by the powers of this world, such as worry, sin, and death, and thus unable to live a life truly his own. Inasmuch as the same story calls forth belief in its truthfulness, however, the self is delivered from that tyranny and enabled to live a new life of true spontaneity. That change of 'existence' is considered as an act of divine grace, and according to Bultmann it is identical with what the New Testament calls redemption. Yet that result is accomplished by means of the hearing of the gospel story rather than by any activity of the man Jesus.

"Bultmann's critics have granted him that he has rightly emphasized aspects of the Christian faith which, particularly in Continental Protestantism, had been badly neglected, e.g., the operation of the Holy Spirit in the genesis of faith, the experiential character of faith, the soteriological aspect of biblical history, and the need of something more than belief in the merely 'historical Jesus.' But there is also wide agreement that his 'existentialistic' interpretation of the gospel is untenable both for historical and theological reasons. First of all, it is pointed out that in his view of gnosticism, Bultmann reads modern ideas into that movement. It is a matter of record that in the history of human thought it was by Christianity that the ancient concept of the soul was transformed into that of the self. Furthermore, Bultmann's contention that the New Testament message is a myth created by the early church fails to explain how historically it was possible that immediately after Jesus' death the primitive church should have applied such an interpretation to his life, unless both his personality and his work had already provided sufficient evidence to his followers for the fact that he was the Messiah and the Son of God promised in the Jewish prophetic writings.

"Moreover, the 'demythologization' of the gospel story does violence to the message of the New Testament. By denying the Incarnation and ascribing to Jesus but an incidental role in the formation of the gospel, Bultmann ignores the particular emphasis all the New Testament writers place upon the necessity of a divine redemption through the agency of an individual man. Similarly, Bultmann's individualistic interpretation of faith leaves no room for the central role which according to the New Testament the church plays in the execution of the saving purpose of God. Finally, his disdain of eschatology demands that the believer consider his religious experience as the only gift God wants to impart to him, and robs him of the hope of a new heaven and a new earth, and of a life everlasting in communion with the Lord. In other words, the biblical belief in the creation of this world is perverted into a Manichean disregard for the whole universe except the self."

NOTES

1. Gerhard Szczesny, The Future of Unbelief (New York: George Braziller, 1961), quoted in Crane Brinton (ed.), The Fate of Man (New York: George Braziller, 1961), p. 23.

2. Russell Kirk, Review of Order and History, Vol. I, by Eric Voegelin, in Yale Review, n.s. XLVI (1957), 471.

3. Christopher Dawson, Enquiries into Religion and Culture (London: Sheed & Ward, 1933), pp. 343, 345. Cf. also his Religion and Culture; Gifford Lectures Delivered in the University of Edinburgh in the Year 1947 (London: Sheed & Ward, 1948). For a valuable discussion of Dawson's theology of history, see John J. Mulloy's "Continuity and Development in Christopher Dawson's Thought," in Mulloy's superb anthology of Dawson's writings: The Dynamics of World History (New York: New American Library Mentor Omega Books, 1962), pp. 403-57.

4. In theological circles D'Arcy is known particularly for his book The Mind and Heart of Love, in which Nygren's Agape and Eros is criticized; we shall speak of Nygren's work later in the present chapter.

5. M. C. D'Arcy, The Sense of History, Secular and Sacred (London: Faber and Faber, 1959), p. 272. This book is published in the United States under the title, The Meaning and Matter of History. A stimulating review of it by E. Harris Harbison appears in History and Theory, I (1960), 86-89.

6. D'Arcy, The Sense of History, p. 244.

7. See Pt. II, my essay entitled, "The Petrine Theory Evaluated by Philology and Logic."

8. Jacques Maritain, On the Philosophy of History, ed. Joseph W. Evans (New York: Scribner, 1957).

9. E. Harris Harbison, Review of On the Philosophy of History by Jacques Maritain, in The Christian Scholar, XLI (December, 1958), 620. Maritain's labors in the field of Christian philosophy have been of great consequence, but his work in the historical area has not done him credit; his Three Reformers, for example, is a perfect illustration of the harm which can result when a philosopher without proper historical training attempts to write history.

10. Jacques Maritain, in Partisan Review, XVII (1950), 233 ff.

11. For helpful summaries of these theological trends, see Arnold S. Nash (ed.), Protestant Thought in the Twentieth Century: Whence & Whither? (New York: Macmillan, 1951); Daniel Day Williams, What Present-Day Theologians Are Thinking (New York: Harper, 1952); William Hordern, A Layman's Guide to Protestant Theology (New York: Macmillan, 1955); and (especially) the current issues of the fortnightly, Christianity Today.

12. The best critiques of modernism during its heyday were written by the Presbyterian New Testament scholar J. Gresham Machen (d. 1937); such works as his Christianity and Liberalism (1923), What Is Faith? (1925) and The Virgin Birth of Christ (2d ed., 1932) are still well worth reading.

13. Shailer Mathews, The Spiritual Interpretation of History (4th ed.; Cambridge, Mass: Harvard University Press, 1920), p. 216.

14. American Historical Review, LIV (January, 1949), 272 ff. Similar affirmations appear in Latourette's recent article, "Protestantism's Amazing Vitality," Christianity Today, VI (March 2, 1962), 3-5. See also Latourette's monumental History of the Expansion of Christianity (7 vols., 1937-1945).

15. Sherwood Eddy, God in History (New York: Association Press [of the Y.M.C.A.], 1947), pp. 17 ff.

16. Karl Barth, Church Dogmatics, IV, Pt. 1 (New York: Scribner, 1957), 505-508.

17. Barth's anti- and meta-historical tendencies are pointed up by Walter Köhler in his Historie und Metahistorie in der Kirchengeschichte (1930). Cf. the following statements by Robert P. Lightner: "Barth's terms for understanding history are 'historiographic' and 'unhistoriographic.' The unhistoriographic aspect relates primarily to creation and means that it is not to be understood in creaturely terms. History which stands in an indirect relation to God is called historiographic, i.e., man. All of this simply means that records may be true, but if the event stands in a direct relation to God, it is beyond history, i.e., Adam. Brunner, another neo-orthodox leader, uses the term primal history to explain his view. This he contrasts to real history. For

him then, there is an history behind history. The one operates on the plane of faith; the other on the plane of sight.
Before the monuments become understandable and credible
records appear, everything is in the realm of primal history and the plane of faith. The creation and fall, for example, would appear in this area. . . . More emphasis is
placed upon the faith of historical happenings than upon the
fact of those happenings. Take for example, the creation of
the first man called Adam, his position in a garden called
Eden, his relation to a woman called Eve - these are all
denied as factual. The faith of these things ? Yes. The fact
of them ? No" (Neo-evangelicalism [Findlay, Ohio:
Dunham, (1961)], p. 117). I have drawn attention to other
serious weaknesses in Neo-Orthodoxy in my articles "Ascension Perspective," The Cresset: A Review of Literature, the Arts, and Public Affairs, XXIV (May, 1961), 17-
19 (cf. an abstract entitled, "Neo-Orthodoxy Scored by
ULCA Professor," in The Lutheran Witness, Pt. 1, LXXX
[June 13, 1961], 23), and "Can We Recover the Christian
Devotional Life ?," Christianity Today, V (September 25,
1961), 3-6 (cf. my debate with Professor Paul Ramsey of
Princeton in Christianity Today, VI [November 10, 1961],
21-23).

18. Brunner, unlike Barth, holds that there is a valid "natural
    theology," i.e., that all created things objectively bear the
    divine stamp upon them, and that revelatory faith makes
    this apparent rather than brings it about. Also, as is evi-
    dent from my "Critical Examination of Emil Brunner's
    The Divine Imperative, Book III" (see Pt. Two of the pres-
    ent work), Brunner places great stress on the "orders of
    creation" - the divinely-established structures governing
    all human life. Brunner's position is superior to Barth's in
    these respects in that it takes more seriously such Biblical
    statements as Rom. 1:20, and in that it emphasizes not only
    God's redemptive work on the Cross but also his creative
    "common grace" in the affairs of men throughout history.

19. Emil Brunner, Christianity and Civilisation; Gifford Lec-
    tures Delivered at the University of St. Andrews (2 vols.;
    London: Nisbet, 1948-1949), II, 140-41. For a balanced
    evaluation of Brunner, see Paul K. Jewett, Emil Brunner:
    An Introduction to the Man and His Thought (Chicago: Inter-
    Varsity Press, 1961).

20. Because of Bultmann's great influence at the present time, it has been thought desirable to provide the reader with a more detailed analysis and critique of his approach than space would allow in the body of this chapter. The reader should therefore turn at this point to the appendix to this chapter, where Otto Piper's analysis of Bultmann's thought is quoted in extenso.

21. Rudolf Bultmann, Theology of the New Testament, trans. Kendrick Grobel, I (New York: Scribner, 1951), 303.

22. Rudolf Bultmann, The Presence of Eternity: History and Eschatology; the Gifford Lectures 1955 (New York: Harper, 1957), p. 155 (italics Bultmann's).

23. See my discussion of the problem of miracles in sec. 4 of my essay, "Constructive Religious Empiricism: An Analysis and Criticism" (included in Pt. II of the present work).

24. "Of course, Jesus was mistaken in thinking that the world was destined soon to come to an end" (Rudolf Bultmann, Primitive Christianity in Its Contemporary Setting, trans. R. H. Fuller [New York: Meridian Living Age Books, 1956], p. 92). "All attempts to escape the admission that Jesus had a conception of the kingdom of God and its impending arrival which remained unfulfilled and cannot be taken over by us mean trespasses against truthfulness" (Albert Schweitzer, "Die Idee des Reiches Gottes," Schweizerische theologische Umschau, XXIII (February, 1953), 19. Cf. Schweitzer's oft-quoted statements in The Quest of the Historical Jesus: "In the knowledge that he is the coming son of man, Jesus lays hold of the wheel of the world to set it moving on that last revolution which is to bring all ordinary history to a close. It refuses to turn, and he throws himself upon it. Then it does turn and crushes him." On December 8, 1961 Time magazine announced (p. 41) that Schweitzer "had accepted honored membership in Unitarian ranks."

25. Walter Kaufmann, Critique of Religion and Philosophy (New York: Harper, 1958), p. 153. The fact of the matter is that Jesus never claimed that His death would mean the immediate end of the world; He claimed that He would immediately send the Holy Spirit after His ascension, and

that His second advent would ultimately terminate human history.

26. Walter Künneth [professor of systematic theology in Erlangen University, Germany], "Dare We Follow Bultmann?," Christianity Today, VI (October 13, 1961), 28. Other decisive theological critiques of Bultmann are Philip E. Hughes, Scripture and Myth; an Examination of Rudolf Bultmann's Plea for Demythologization (London: Tyndale Press, 1956); Paul Althaus, Fact and Faith in the Kerygma of Today, trans. David Cairns (Philadelphia: Muhlenberg Press, 1959); and Fritz Rienecker, "The Cross and Demythologizing," Christianity Today, VI (March 16, 1962), 9-12. The Neo-Orthodox also show some tendencies toward de-historicizing Jesus, but not to the same extent. Barth has stated that behind the New Testament picture of Christ one can see only a rather unexceptional "Rabbi of Nazareth" (Karl Barth, The Doctrine of the Word of God [Edinburgh: T. & T. Clark, 1936], p. 188), and Brunner has said that the Deity of Christ "as such does not enter into the sphere of history at all" (Emil Brunner, The Mediator [Philadelphia: Westminster Press, 1947], p. 343 n.). To such assertions the best reply is the straightforward Johannine claim concerning Christ: "Our theme is the Word of Life. This life was made visible; we have seen it and bear our testimony; we here declare to you the eternal life which dwelt with the Father and was made visible to us" (I Jn. 1:1-2).

27. Even in the presentation of Christian existential experience Bultmann should not be accorded the highest honors; these should go to his nineteenth-century forerunner Kierkegaard, whose Fear and Trembling and Sickness unto Death (available in Doubleday Anchor Books paperback series) remain the classic expressions of man's despair apart from God and the reality of existential encounter with Him. The recent attempt by Robert Scharlemann to rehabilitate Bultmann by way of Luther's theological approach is to be commended more for its ingenuity than for its validity; in his article, "Shadow on the Tomb," in Dialog, I (Spring, 1962), 22-29, Scharlemann argues that in Bultmann "one sees in unmistakable outlines the shadow of Luther," for just as Luther saw the inadequacy of man's moral efforts toward salvation, so Bultmann sees the inadequacy of man's intellectual efforts to provide a solid Biblical and historical basis for the Christian faith. The parallel is, of course,

fallacious and "constructed" (cf. the old saw: What does an elephant and a tube of toothpaste have in common? Answer: Neither one can ride a bicycle). Whereas Luther turned from moral guilt to confidence in the objective facts of Christ's death for his sin and resurrection for his justification, Bultmann turns from his intellectual doubts to subjective anthropological salvation - a direct about-face from the objective Gospel Luther proclaimed.

28. Hordern, op. cit., p. 145.

29. Ibid., p. 151.

30. Reinhold Niebuhr, Faith and History; A Comparison of Christian and Modern Views of History (New York: Scribner, 1949), pp. 102 ff.

31. Ibid., chaps. v, vi, viii.

32. Ibid., p. 26.

33. Especially noteworthy is his treatment of the coronation of Elizabeth II: "Coronation Afterthoughts," Christian Century, LXX (July 1, 1953), 771-72.

34. These and many other polarities in Niebuhr's thought are set out by Robert E. Fitch, "Reinhold Niebuhr's Philosophy of History," in Kegley and Bretall (eds.), Reinhold Niebuhr: His Religious, Social, and Political Thought ("Library of Living Theology," Vol. 2; New York: Macmillan, 1956), pp. 299-300.

35. Reinhold Niebuhr, Reflections on the End of an Era (New York: Scribner, 1934), p. 94.

36. Reinhold Niebuhr, The Irony of American History (New York: Scribner, 1952), chap. iv and passim.

37. Ibid., pp. 156, 168-69.

38. Ibid., p. 155. On Niebuhr's philosophy of history, see also Gordon Harland, The Thought of Reinhold Niebuhr (New York: Oxford University Press, 1960), pp. 85 ff.; and Georgette Paul Vignaux, La théologie de l'histoire chez Reinhold Niebuhr (Neuchâtel: Delachaux & Niestle, 1957).

39. Reinhold Niebuhr, An Interpretation of Christian Ethics (New York: Harper, 1935), p. 57.

40. Henry Nelson Wieman, "A Religious Naturalist Looks at Reinhold Niebuhr," in Kegley and Bretall, op. cit., pp. 339-40.

41. For my refutation of the pragmatist epistemology, see below, Pt. II, my essay, "A Critique of William James' Varieties of Religious Experience."

42. On the Lundensian movement, see Nels F. S. Ferré, Swedish Contributions to Modern Theology, with Special Reference to Lundensian Thought (New York: Harper, 1939).

43. Anders Nygren, Agape and Eros, trans. Philip S. Watson (Philadelphia: Westminster Press, 1953), p. 35. For the publication history of this seminal work, see my article "Eros and Agape in the Thought of Giovanni Pico della Mirandola," Concordia Theological Monthly, XXXII (December, 1961), 733.

44. Nygren also deals with a third love motif which he calls the Nomos (Gk., "law") type (Nygren, op. cit., pp. 254-288, 335-348, and passim); however, since this is a subsidiary motif, we shall not discuss it here. Eros and Agape, like Nomos, are Greek words. Eros is the most common classical Greek word for love; it does not appear in the New Testament. Agape is the characteristic New Testament word for God's love.

45. Ibid., p. 210.

46. I John 4:8-9: "God is love [Agape]; and His love was disclosed to us in this, that He sent His only Son into this world to bring us life." Cf. John 3:16, and the great Agape chapter of the New Testament, I Cor. 13.

47. Romans 5:7-8.

48. Caritas is a common mediaeval-Latin word for love; our word "charity" derives from it. Caritas was frequently used to translate the New Testament word Agape, but, unlike Agape, it acquired a "works-righteousness" (Eros) connotation along with its Agape-idea.

49. Cf. Roland H. Bainton, The Reformation of the Sixteenth Century (Boston: Beacon Press, 1952), pp. 28 ff.

50. I have made these first two points with greater fulness in my "Short Critique of Gustaf Aulén's Christus Victor," printed as an appendix in my Chytraeus on Sacrifice (St. Louis: Concordia Publishing House, 1962).

51. John 12:20 ff.

52. Rom. 3:12; quoted by Paul from Ps. 14:1, 3 and 53:1. It seems clear that Nygren's radical rejection of all Eros-motivation is a heritage of the Barthian rejection of common grace and natural revelation. In reality, God uses man's Eros-selfishness - man's desire for his own salvation - to bring him into contact with His great act of Agape-love in Christ. Augustine (for all his faults) recognized this when he wrote, "Plato made me know the true God, Jesus Christ showed me the way to Him."

53. Montgomery, Concordia Theological Monthly, XXXII, 733-46. In this article I show on the basis of previously un-analyzed sources that one of the greatest Renaissance humanists, Pico of Mirandola, moved from Eros to Agape during the last years of his life (particularly as a result of the evangelical witness of Savonarola).

54. William W. Paul, "Bultmann, Tillich, and the American Response," Christianity Today, VI (December 8, 1961), 22.

55. Tillich has frequently shocked the uninitiated by asserting that he does not believe that God exists. What he means is that he does not want to think of God in terms of the category of existence, for this is just another way of our treating God as someone like us. God is the transcendent ground and depth of everything, not simply another existent thing. "The being of God cannot be understood as the existence of a being alongside others or above others" (Paul Tillich, Systematic Theology, I [Chicago: University of Chicago Press, 1951], 235 ff.).

56. See Tillich's Systematic Theology, II (Chicago: University of Chicago Press, 1957), 29 ff. The third volume of the Systematic Theology is still in preparation.

57. Tillich has most fully developed his concept of love in <u>Love, Power, and Justice</u> (New York: Oxford University Press, 1954).

58. "My Christology and Dogmatics were determined by the interpretation of the cross of Christ as the event of history in which divine judgment over the world becomes concrete and manifest" (Tillich, <u>The Interpretation of History</u>, trans. Rasetzki and Talmey [New York: Scribner, 1936], p. 32). When Tillich wrote <u>The Interpretation of History</u> he was still in Germany (he later came to America because of his opposition to the Hitler regime).

59. Walter Leibrecht, "The Life and Mind of Paul Tillich," in Leibrecht (ed.), <u>Religion and Culture; Essays in Honor of Paul Tillich</u> (New York: Harper, 1959), p. 21.

60. This same concern for the world at large is evident in Tillich's "principle of correlation" - that in every age theology is to answer those questions actually posed by the culture and life of the time (<u>Systematic Theology</u>, I, 3 ff.).

61. See Tillich's <u>The Interpretation of History</u>, pp. 22 ff. The three terms derive from the Greek; heteronomy = "law of another," autonomy = "law to oneself," theonomy = "divine law."

62. Hordern, <u>op. cit.</u>, pp. 169-73. With the last sentence of this quotation, cf. Tillich's <u>Protestantisches Prinzip und proletarische Situation</u> (Bonn: Cohen, 1931), and <u>The Protestant Era</u> (Chicago: University of Chicago Press, 1948).

63. Paul Tillich, "Kairos," in Halverson and Cohen (eds.), <u>A Handbook of Christian Theology</u> (New York: Meridian Living Age Books, 1958), pp. 196-97.

64. Tillich, quoted by Leibrecht, <u>op. cit.</u>, p. 14.

65. Tillich's position on the historicity of the Christ-event is much more positive than Bultmann's; see A. T. Mollegen's "Christology and Biblical Criticism in Tillich," in Kegley and Bretall (eds.), <u>The Theology of Paul Tillich</u> ("Library of Living Theology," Vol. 1; New York: Macmillan, 1952), pp. 230-45, and Tillich's <u>imprimatur</u> on Mollegen's

interpretation, pp. 347-48. However, one finds on occasion in Tillich such Bultmannish assertions as, "It is the certainty of one's own victory over the death of existential estrangement which creates the certainty of the Resurrection of the Christ as event and symbol" (Systematic Theology, II, 155); surely this is a clear case of putting the existential cart before the historical horse! When Tillich does engage in demythologizing, he rationalizes and delimits it by asserting that it is justified if it helps people to confront the real offense in Christianity - the offense of the Cross; and, in any case, he prefers to speak of "deliteralizing" rather than demythologizing (ibid., pp. 152, 164).

66. Kaufmann, op. cit., p. 140.

67. See Yoshinori Takeuchi, "Buddhism and Existentialism," in Leibrecht, op. cit., pp. 291-318.

68. Adam and Eve can be both historical and typical; see my articles, "The Cause and Cure of Sin," Resource, III (February, 1962), 2-4; and "Some Comments on Paul's Use of Genesis in His Epistle to the Romans," Evangelical Theological Society Bulletin, IV (April, 1961), 4-11.

69. Tillich, Systematic Theology, II, 44.

70. This criticism has been well stated by Reinhold Niebuhr in his "Biblical Thought and Ontological Speculation in Tillich's Theology," in Kegley and Bretall (eds.), The Theology of Paul Tillich, pp. 215-27.

71. For evidence of Agape in the canonical and apocryphal Old Testament, see my paper "Wisdom as Gift," Interpretation, XVI (January, 1962), 43-57.

72. It will be noted that Tillich is here condemned by his own "principle of correlation," for instead of finding the solution to the legitimate Eros problem in revelational Agape, he tries to make the problem supply its own solution and identifies that solution with revelation itself. Of course Tillich's emphasis on love as self-realization has made him very popular with psychiatrists and psychoanalysts (such as the late Karen Horney); but this has only compounded the difficulty, for the analysts of all people need to see that God's regenerating love in salvation is qualitatively

164

different from all human self-realization. Tillich is quite right that Christianity provides true fulfilment of personality, but he only pours oil on the fire when he describes this as Eros self-realizing itself.

73. Leibrecht, op. cit., pp. 26-27.

74. James Luther Adams, "Tillich's Interpretation of History," in Kegley and Bretall (eds.), The Theology of Paul Tillich, p. 308.

75. Russell Kirk, Yale Review, n.s. XLVI, 471.

76. In his biographical sketch in Who's Who in America.

77. "Many philosophers (the reviewer included) will undoubtedly be repelled by Voegelin's pontifical way of presenting his main thesis, usually without argument or defense" (Robert Ammerman, Review of Order and History, Vols. II and III, in Philosophy and Phenomenological Research, XIX [1958-1959], 540).

78. The current resistance to transcendental philosophy of history was well evidenced at a recent symposium of prominent philosophers of history, where "Voegelin's metaphysical thesis led to a combined intellectual assault on the speaker" (George H. Nadel, Review of L'histoire et ses interprétations: Entretiens autour de Arnold Toynbee, in American Historical Review, LXVII [January, 1962], 374).

79. Eric Voegelin, Order and History (6 vols.; Baton Rouge: Louisiana State University Press, 1956-date), I, xiv.

80. Ibid., II, 22.

81. Ibid., I, xii.

82. Ammerman, Philosophy and Phenomenological Research, XIX, 539.

83. "Human nature is constant in spite of its unfolding, in the history of mankind, from compact to differentiated order: the discernible stages of increasing truth of existence are not caused by 'changes in the nature of man' that would disrupt the unity of mankind and dissolve it into a series of

different species. The very idea of a history of mankind presupposes that constancy of nature" (Voegelin, op. cit., II, 5).

84. Ibid., p. 6.

85. Ibid., I, 453.

86. Ibid., III, 278.

87. Ibid., II, 10-11.

88. Paul Ramsey, Review of Order and History, Vol. I, in Philosophy and Phenomenological Research, XVIII (1957-1958), 407.

89. Voegelin, op. cit., II, 23-24.

90. Ibid., I, 454.

91. Ibid., p. x.

92. Ibid., III, 278.

93. Russell Kirk, Yale Review, n.s. XLVI, 469.

94. See the concluding paragraph of Voegelin's The New Science of Politics (Chicago: University of Chicago Press, 1952). The quoted sentiment "was denounced as illiberal in a scholarly journal, by a well-known professor of political science - apparently on the premise that all notions are equally estimable, including ideological corruption of the Nazi and Communist varieties. And a young lion of political science, addressing a convention of his colleagues, made it one of his claims to fame that he had not read 'The New Science' and did not intend to, because it seemed to be all about 'someone called Saint Joachim of Flora,' and therefore irrelevant to political science. Mr. Voegelin has his work cut out for him when he attempts to reason with minds of this cast; yet I think that he may prevail" (Kirk, Yale Review, n.s. XLVI, 472-73).

95. Voegelin, Order and History, I, 152-55.

96. Ibid., p. 141.

97. Ibid., pp. 451-53. Voegelin acknowledges his debt to Bultmann in this regard (pp. 452-53, n. 6).

98. Ibid., p. 454.

99. Ibid., II, 12.

100. Montgomery, "The Apologetic Approach of Muhammad Ali and Its Implications for Christian Apologetics," Muslim World; A Quarterly Journal of Islamic Study and of Christian Interpretation among Moslems, LI (April, 1961), 111-22 (cf. author's "Corrigendum" in the July, 1961 Muslim World).

101. Voegelin, in Raymond Aron (ed.), L'histoire et ses interprétations: Entretiens autour de Arnold Toynbee, Centre culturel international de Cerisy-la-Salle, 10-19 Juillet 1958 ("École Pratique des Hautes Études-Sorbonne. VIᵉ Section: Sciences économiques et sociales. Congrès et colloques, No. 3"; Paris: Mouton, 1961), p. 135. The text of this exceedingly important colloquium has thus far been published only in French; the translations given above are my own.

102. Ibid., pp. 138-39. The succeeding argument has been somewhat condensed (without ellipses) for the sake of brevity and ease in comprehension. The reader who is able to handle French is encouraged to peruse the entire debate (pp. 133-51).

103. Goldmann, by a similar epistemological critique, also shows that Voegelin cannot defend, on the basis of pure rationality, his basic conviction that human nature is constant (ibid., pp. 143-45).

104. Kirk, Yale Review, n.s. XLVI, 476.

105. Aron, L'histoire et ses interprétations, pp. 164-65.

106. See the essay, "Constructive Religious Empiricism: An Analysis and Criticism." For a tabular summary of epistemological methods as applied to the validation of religions, and a demonstration of fallacies in the rationalistic and subjective-empirical methods, see my previously-cited article in Muslim World, LI, 111-22.

107. See the essay, "A Critique of William James' Varieties of Religious Experience."

108. See the paper, "The Petrine Theory Evaluated by Philology and Logic" (in Pt. II).

109. "If Christ was not raised, then our gospel is null and void, and so is your faith" (I Cor. 15:14). Throughout the book of Acts, the apostolic preaching again and again centers the truth of the Christian faith on the historical fact of the resurrection of Christ. Cf. Walter Künneth, "The Easter Message As the Essence of Theology," Dialog, I (Spring, 1962), 16-21.

110. See Mr. Barnes' essay, "The Dependability and Value of the Extant Gospel Manuscripts" (in Pt. II); also see the best available monograph on the subject, F. F. Bruce [Rylands Professor of Biblical Criticism and Exegesis in the University of Manchester, England], The New Testament Documents: Are They Reliable? (5th rev. ed.; London: Inter-Varsity Fellowship, 1960). Bruce's work is available in paperback for 3s. 6d. (50 cents) from Inter-Varsity Fellowship, 39 Bedford Square, London WCl, England, and is highly recommended for purchase. Cf. also E. C. Blackman's inaugural lecture as Professor of New Testament Literature and Exegesis in Emmanuel College, Toronto, printed in part as "Jesus Christ Yesterday: The Historical Basis of the Christian Faith," Canadian Journal of Theology, VII (April, 1961), 118-27.

111. In Mark 2:1-12 Jesus forgives sins; in such passages as Matt. 11:27; 16:13-17; John 10:30; 12:45; 14:6-10, Jesus states His divine relation to God the Father. It is also of great significance that the Gospel writers apply to Jesus the ascription Kyrios ("Lord") which in the Greek translation of the Old Testament (the Septuagint) had been used as an equivalent of Adonai and Yahweh, the Hebrew designations for God Himself. On the matter of Jesus' deity as presented in the Gospels, see William Childs Robinson (ed.), Who Say Ye That I Am? Six Theses on the Deity of Christ (Grand Rapids, Michigan: Eerdmans, 1949).

112. John 2:18-22: "The Jews challenged Jesus: 'What sign,' they asked, 'can you show us as authority for your action?' 'Destroy this temple,' Jesus replied, 'and in three days I

will raise it again.' . . . The temple He was speaking of
was His body. After His resurrection His disciples re-
called what He had said, and they believed the Scripture
and the words that Jesus had spoken."

113. See the section "Christus Victor" in my essay, "The Importance of a Materialistic Metaphysic to Marxist Thought
and an Examination of Its Truth Value." Note also Wilbur
M. Smith's classic, The Supernaturalness of Christ
(Boston: W. A. Wilde, 1940); T. C. Hammond, Reasoning
Faith (London: Inter-Varsity Fellowship, 1943), Pt. III;
and Frank Morison, Who Moved the Stone ? (London:
Faber and Faber, 1944). The most decisive recent argument in support of the historicity of Christ's resurrection
is provided by Professor Ethelbert Stauffer of Erlangen
University, in his book, Jesus and His Story, trans.
Richard and Clara Winston (New York: Knopf, 1960). The
following is a useful summary of Stauffer's position: "By
means of inference and the combination of Jewish and
Hellenistic material, Stauffer seeks to verify the Gospel
tradition in a new way. Applying to the resurrection narratives his method of establishing certainty where friend
and foe agree, he gathers support for the narrative of the
empty tomb in the witness of the church and the rumor circulated by the Sanhedrin, as well as in the marble tablet
from Nazareth. . . . Stauffer first states that there has
never been a Christian tradition about Jesus or a message
of the resurrection without a witness to the empty tomb.
Although the apostles' preaching in Jerusalem encountered
bitterest opposition, no one opposed their witness to the
empty tomb, not even the Sanhedrin which circulated the
rumor of the disciples' theft. Stauffer continues by saying
that Justin Martyr [ca. 100-166] mentions an official cir-
cular of the Sanhedrin which further perpetuates the rumor
and that Tertullian [ca. 150-ca. 230] is also aware of such
a rumor as well as of the rumor presupposed in the Gospel
of John (viz., that the gardener removed Jesus' body).
Further commenting that both these tales are contained in
the Jewish Toledoth Jeshu, Stauffer infers from Matthew
28:12 ff. that the rumor of the theft was also intended for
Roman ears and refers to Tertullian's description of a report made by Pilate to Tiberius concerning the empty tomb
and the authorities' assertion that Jesus' body was stolen
by his disciples. Noting that his sources thus far are of
Christian origin, Stauffer refers to Eusebius' [ca. 280-

339] mention of certain 'pagan records' from which the existence of non-Christian witnesses to Pilate's report may be inferred. Unfortunately, adds Stauffer, such records have been lost, though they undoubtedly shared with their enemies the presupposition that Pilate reported to Caesar concerning the case of Jesus of Nazareth. Stauffer finds justification for his inferences in an inscription from Nazareth, published in 1930, which contains an abbreviated report of an imperial edict against grave-robbing and desecration. In all probability, Stauffer concludes, an imperial reply to Pilate's report concerning Jesus, the empty tomb and the rumor circulated by the Jews underlay this inscription. Turning next to the christophanies, Stauffer contends that the protepiphany to Peter is attested to by his friends as well as by his foes within the Christian community, adding that without such an appearance of Jesus to Peter the latter's position in the primitive church would be historically unintelligible" (Roy A. Harrisville, "Resurrection and Historical Method," Dialog, I [Spring, 1962], 32-33). Harrisville's characterization of Stauffer's approach as positivistic, and his consequent rejection of it, is based on a lamentable confusion of "historical method" with "historical positivism" (or "historicism"). One can apply accepted historical method to the resurrection accounts without being a positivist, just as one can apply scientific method to a problem without accepting the presuppositions of "scientism" (the "religion of science"). (We shall have more to say about these distinctions later.)

114. Stauffer says in reference to the powerful historical evidence for the resurrection: "What do we do [as historians] when we experience surprises which run counter to all our expectations, perhaps all our convictions and even our period's whole understanding of truth? We say as one great historian used to say in such instances: 'It is surely possible.' And why not? For the critical historian nothing is impossible" (op. cit., p. 17). See the section "Hume and the Objective Empirical Approach to Religious Truth" in my essay, "Constructive Religious Empiricism: An Analysis and Criticism" (in Pt. II). Important monographs dealing with the subject of miracle are: C. S. Lewis, Miracles (New York: Macmillan, 1947 [available for 50 cents in Collins Fontana Books paperback series]); and Edward John Carnell, An Introduction to Christian Apologetics; a Philosophic Defense of the Trinitarian-Theistic

<u>Faith</u> (Grand Rapids, Michigan: Eerdmans, 1948), chaps. xiv-xv.

115. John 14:6 (Jesus speaking): "I am the way; I am the truth and I am life; no one comes to the Father except by Me."

116. Jesus considered the Old Testament fully reliable, as is seen from Matt. 5:17-19 ("So long as heaven and earth endure, not a letter, not a stroke, will disappear from the Law until all that must happen has happened") and from John 10:34-35 ("Is it not written in your own Law, 'I said: You are gods'? . . . Scripture cannot be broken"). In the second passage Jesus makes clear that He considers the entire Old Testament authoritative, for He uses the word "Law" not in the restricted sense of the Pentateuch (the first five books of the Old Testament) but in a general sense (his quotation is from Psalm 82:6). B. B. Warfield is quite correct when he writes of Jesus' arguments with his Jewish opponents: "Everywhere, to Him and to them alike, an appeal to Scripture is an appeal to an indefectible authority whose determination is final; both He and they make their appeal indifferently to every part of Scripture, to every element in Scripture, to its most incidental clauses as well as to its most fundamental principles, and to the very form of its expression" (B. B. Warfield, <u>The Inspiration and Authority of the Bible</u>, ed. Samuel G. Craig [Philadelphia: Presbyterian and Reformed Publishing Co., 1948], p. 140; Warfield's book is the greatest work in the English language on this subject). See also Carl F. H. Henry (ed.), <u>Revelation and the Bible</u> (Grand Rapids, Michigan: Baker Book House, 1958); John R. Lavik, <u>The Bible Is the Word of God</u> (Minneapolis: Augsburg, 1959); Hermann Sasse, "The Inspiration of Holy Scripture," <u>Christianity Today</u>, VI (March 16, 1962), 3-5; and H. Daniel Friberg, "The Locus of God's Speaking," <u>Christian Century</u>, LXXIX (April 11, 1962), 455-57.

117. Jesus told His apostles that He would send the Holy Spirit to them and that the Holy Spirit would "guide them into all the truth," "teach them everything," and "call to mind all that He had told them" (John 14:26-27; 16:12-15; cf. Acts 1:21-26). As for the Pauline writings, the book of Acts (written by the same author as the Gospel according to Luke) makes clear that Paul was accepted as an apostle and that his doctrine was in conformity with that of the

original apostles to whom Jesus spoke the above words; moreover, in II Pet. 3:15, Paul's epistles are treated as Scripture along with the Old Testament. The apostles claim divine authority for their writings (see, e.g., I Cor. 14:37) - and in fact regard the Old Testament as "God-breathed" (Gk., theopneustos, II Tim. 3:16). The early church considered authorship as the prime criterion in collecting the books of the New Testament; books written by apostles, or writings by close associates of apostles (the latter were able to be checked for truth-value by apostles - e.g., Mark by Peter, Luke by Paul) could safely be regarded as authoritative Scripture.

118. Mt. 20:28; Mark 10:45 (Jesus speaking): "The Son of man came not to be ministered unto, but to minister, and to give His life a ransom [Gk., lutron] for many."

119. Tillich, Systematic Theology, II, 155.

120. This was well shown by Richard Whately (Historic Doubts Relative to Napoleon Buonaparte [12th ed.; London: J. W. Parker, 1855]), who proved that if the same historical scepticism frequently applied to the life of Christ were applied to the life of Napoleon, the result would be complete historiographical chaos and absurdity.

121. Johan Huizinga, "De Historische Idee," in his Verzamelde Werken, VII (Haarlem, 1950), 134 ff.; quoted in translation in Fritz Stern (ed.), The Varieties of History (New York: Meridian Books, 1956), p. 302. Cf. Burtt's parallel assertion for the realm of empirical science: "There is simply no science possible of the realm of sensible phenomena unless the trustworthiness of our immediate perception of spatial directions and relations be taken for granted. . . . To substitute for [the] thoroughly empirical process of the improvement and social correction of the senses a speculative apriorism that flatly contradicts the immediate testimony of sense and places its objects in spatial relations wholly different from those in which they are sensed, can only lead, if carried out to its logical conclusion, to the complete confusion and mystification of science" (E. A. Burtt, The Metaphysical Foundations of Modern Physical Science [rev. ed.; Garden City, N. Y.: Doubleday Anchor Books, 1955], pp. 318-19).

122. Rom. 10:17; John 7:17.

123. See Pascal's Pensées (available in many editions, e.g., in the Everyman's Library); John Urquhart, The Wonders of Prophecy (Harrisburg, Pa.: Christian Publications [1925]); C. S. Lewis, Mere Christianity (New York: Macmillan, 1958) and The Pilgrim's Regress (London: Bles, 1950); Edward John Carnell, An Introduction to Christian Apologetics (op. cit.) and A Philosophy of the Christian Religion (Grand Rapids, Michigan: Eerdmans, 1952).

124. "In the proclamation of the apostles the argument from prophecy and the argument from miracle coincided and culminated in the resurrection of Jesus. This was the supreme messianic sign, the greatest demonstration of the power of God, and it was at the same time the conclusive fulfilment of those prophecies which pointed to the Messiah. Not only so, but it was something to which the apostles could bear direct testimony. 'This Jesus God raised up, and of that we all are witnesses' (Acts ii. 32)" (F. F. Bruce, The Apostolic Defense of the Gospel; Christian Apologetic in the New Testament [London: Inter-Varsity Fellowship, 1959], p. 12).

125. See my previously-cited article in Muslim World, LI, 111-22.

126. For this distinction, see below (Pt. II), my essay, "Constructive Religious Empiricism: An Analysis and Criticism," sec. 2. Cf. also R. E. D. Clark, Scientific Rationalism and Christian Faith; with particular reference to the writings of Prof. J. B. S. Haldane & Dr. J. S. Huxley (London: Inter-Varsity Fellowship, 1945).

127. John 1:1-14. The argument that this passage does not assert Jesus' deity because the Greek definite article is not used before the word "God" in reference to Jesus has been refuted by E. C. Colwell in his paper, "A Definite Rule for the Use of the Article in the Greek New Testament," Journal of Biblical Literature, LII (1933), 12-21. The climax of John's Gospel occurs in 20:28 when "doubting Thomas" is confronted by the resurrected Christ who shows him the nailprints in His hands and the wound in His side; Thomas replies, "My Lord and my God" (Gk., ho kyrios mou kai ho

theos mou). The latter passage is also one of the best
evidences of the physical (not merely spiritual) nature of
Christ's resurrection.

128. I Cor. 15:3-6. Harrisville (in Dialog, I [Spring, 1962],
35-36) argues as follows against the position we are presenting: "To this interpretation, however, such passages
as Matthew 28:17 give the lie: 'And when they saw him
they worshiped him; but some doubted.' . . . Jesus did not
represent himself to his disciples in such a manner that
they needed only to open their eyes in order to be convinced of his rising. . . . That willingness to enter into fellowship which denoted their walk with the earthly Jesus
must now denote the disciples' 'sight' of their resurrected
Lord. . . . Further, the witnesses to the resurrection consisted solely of those who were with him in the way. . . .
And finally, the question concerning its visual aspects is
never put to the resurrection by the texts. Though Jesus'
appearing is indeed emphasized, there is nowhere any attempt to describe his corporeality, to say nothing of an attempt to describe the event of the resurrection itself.
From this it is clear that the category of the empirical is
totally unsuitable for approaching the nature of the Easter
narratives." The fallacious character of this argument
can be seen from the following points: (1) The resurrection narratives take the utmost pains to demonstrate the
empirical, corporeal nature of Christ's resurrection.
Luke 24:36-43: "As they [the disciples] were talking, . . .
there He was, standing among them. Startled and terrified,
they thought they were seeing a ghost. But He said, 'Why
are you so perturbed? Why do questionings arise in your
minds? Look at My hands and feet. It is I myself. Touch
Me and see; no ghost has flesh and bones as you can see
that I have.' They were still unconvinced, still wondering,
for it seemed too good to be true. So He asked them, 'Have
you anything here to eat?' They offered Him a piece of
fish they had cooked, which He took and ate before their
eyes." (2) It is true that all the recorded appearances of
Jesus after His resurrection and before His ascension are
to "brethren," but this does not mean that prior belief was
a condition for seeing the risen Christ. This is patent
from the "doubting Thomas" incident, where Thomas first
says, "Unless I see the mark of the nails on His hands, unless I put my finger into the place where the nails were,
and my hand into His side, I will not believe it"; a week

174

later Jesus appears to Thomas and says, "Reach your finger here: see My hands; reach your hand here and put it into My side; be unbelieving no longer, but believe"; and Thomas replies, "My Lord and my God" (John 20:24-29). Moreover, it should be noted that Jesus' post-ascension appearance to Paul on the Damascus road - an appearance which Paul includes with Jesus' resurrection appearances (I Cor. 15:4-8) - occurred while Paul was still an unbeliever, and was in fact the immediate cause of his conversion to Christianity. The conclusion to be drawn from Jesus' appearances only to believers or to potential believers is not that the resurrection should not be treated empirically, but that Jesus - both before and after His resurrection - does not "cast pearls before swine," i.e., does not manifest Himself to those whose minds are irrevocably closed against Him - to those who are totally unwilling to bridge by faith the gap between historical probability and experiential certainty.

129. Carl Michalson, The Hinge of History; an Existential Approach to the Christian Faith (New York: Scribner, 1959), pp. 198, 212.

130. Samuel Sandmel [President of the Society of Biblical Literature and Exegesis], "The Evasions of Modern Theology," The American Scholar [published by the Phi Beta Kappa academic honorary society], XXX (Summer, 1961), 377.

131. Anders Nygren, Religiöst apriori, pp. 15-16; quoted in Ferré, op. cit. [see note 42], p. 55.

132. I Pet. 3:15.

133. I Cor. 9:22.

134. The so-called "kenosis" argument that Jesus accomodated Himself to human error in this matter is insupportable, for if this were the case, then one would have to give specific reasons why the accomodation did not extend to all of Jesus' words. Such accomodation would remove meaning from everything Jesus said, and would leave us with no criterion for the interpretation of His teachings. One must assume, in all historical and literary study, that a person means what he says unless there is contextual reason to

think otherwise (cf. Aristotle, De arte poetica, 1460b-1461b). On the matter of alleged Biblical "contradictions," see the best modern refutation by one of the leading Hellenistic Greek lexicographers of our time, W. Arndt's Does the Bible Contradict Itself? (5th rev. ed.; St. Louis: Concordia Publishing House, 1955 [available in paperback]). Classical treatments of the subject include Andreas Althamer, Conciliationes locorum scripturae, qui specie tenus inter se pugnare videntur, centuriae duae (Wittenberg: Lehman, 1582), and Thomas Hartwell Horne, An Introduction to the Critical Study and Knowledge of the Holy Scriptures, II (7th ed.; London: Cadell, 1834), Pt. 2, Bk. 2, chap. vii, 564-630. Cf. also H. E. Guillebaud, Some Moral Difficulties of the Bible (London: Inter-Varsity Fellowship, 1949). I myself have never encountered an alleged contradiction in the Bible which could not be cleared up by the use of the original languages of the Scriptures and/or by the use of accepted principles of literary and historical interpretation.

135. Barr is quite correct when he writes in his epochal Semantics of Biblical Language: "Modern biblical theology in its fear and dislike of the 'proposition' as the basis of religious truth has often simply adopted in its place the smaller linguistic unit of the word, and has then been forced to overload the word with meaning in order to relate it to the 'inner world of thought'" (James Barr, The Semantics of Biblical Language [London: Oxford University Press, 1961], p. 246).

136. See John F. Walvoord (ed.), Inspiration and Interpretation (Grand Rapids, Michigan: Eerdmans, 1957); A. Skevington Wood, Luther's Principles of Biblical Interpretation (London: Tyndale Press, 1960); and my review of Luther and the Bible by Willem Jan Kooiman, in Christianity Today, VI (February 16, 1962), 498.

137. For a refutation of the erroneous view presented by Emil Brunner and Joseph Sittler, see note 14 to my essay, "A Critical Examination of Emil Brunner's The Divine Imperative, Book III" (in Pt. Two).

138. Herbert Butterfield, Christianity and History (London: Collins Fontana Books, 1957), p. 168. On Butterfield, see Harold T. Parker, "Herbert Butterfield," in S. William

Halperin (ed.), Some 20th-Century Historians; Essays on Eminent Europeans (Chicago: University of Chicago Press, 1961), pp. 75-101.

139. Luke 12:6-7.

140. For a balanced summary of the positive contributions, see John Hall Stewart, A Documentary Survey of the French Revolution (New York: Macmillan, 1951), pp. 785 ff.

141. "By 1799 . . . although France remained nominally a Catholic country, the forces of secularism were fast making themselves felt - two outstanding examples of which tendency were the establishment of civil marriage and the legalization of divorce" (ibid., p. 789).

142. On the Last Judgment, see especially Karl Heim, Jesus the World's Perfecter; the Atonement and the Renewal of the World, trans. D. H. van Daalen (Edinburgh: Oliver and Boyd, 1959), Pt. III.

143. Luke 12:2-3.

144. Butterfield, op. cit., p. 122.

145. See John 8:44 and Acts 5:1-11.

146. For examples of how secular historians and history textbook writers have engaged in such perversions, see E. H. Dance, History the Betrayer: A Study in Bias (London: Hutchinson, 1960).

147. E. Harris Harbison, "History," in Hoxie N. Fairchild (ed.), Religious Perspectives in College Teaching (New York: Ronald Press, 1952), p. 94.

148. E. H. Carr, What Is History? The George Macaulay Trevelyan Lectures Delivered in the University of Cambridge, January - March 1961 (London: Macmillan, 1961), pp. 126-27. In his review of this work, Boyd C. Shafer highly commends it as "the best recent book in English on the nature of historical study," but singles out its great philosophical weakness: the absence of any demonstrable criterion of progress. Shafer writes: "Carr is persuasive. As one reads him, one agrees, quickly and easily. Later,

in sober aftermath, one asks, what 'sense,' what 'direction,' whose 'sense of direction' [for the historical process]? That of Marx or Wells? of Hitler or Churchill? Gandhi or Toynbee? Mao Tse-tung or Khrushchev? Nehru or Kennedy? or that of the enlightened, liberal, hopeful professor at Trinity College [i.e., Carr himself]? If, as Carr believes, the definable nineteenth-century goal of progress no longer fashions a key to the past, will the 'evolving ends' of Carr's future unlock doors?" (Boyd C. Shafer, Review of What Is History?, in American Historical Review, LXVII [April, 1962], 676-77).

149. The same problem of lack of absolute criteria for progress is evident in Robert L. Heilbroner's The Future As History (New York: Harper, 1960), pp. 193-209.

150. Georges Lefebvre, The Coming of the French Revolution, trans. R. R. Palmer (Princeton: Princeton University Press, 1947), pp. 209-210.

151. John 14:6.

152. Butterfield, op. cit., p. 91.

153. See, for example, Gen. 1:26-27; Ps. 8:4-8; Ecclesiastes, passim; Rom. 10:12; Heb. 2:6-8.

154. Eccl. 3:15; cf. 1:9; 6:10.

155. See my article, "The Cause and Cure of Sin," Resource, III (February, 1962), 2-4.

156. Butterfield, op. cit., pp. 65-66.

157. See Gen. 6:5; Ps. 53:3; Rom. 3:23; I John 1:8.

158. Charles Williams, Taliessin Through Logres (London: Oxford University Press, 1938), pp. 31-32. On Williams and his work, see Anne Ridler's critical introduction to her edition of Williams' The Image of the City and Other Essays (London: Oxford University Press, 1958), and John Heath-Stubbs, Charles Williams ("Writers and Their Work," No. 63; London: Longmans, Green, for the British Council and the National Book League, 1955).

159. Harbison, "History," in Fairchild, op. cit., pp. 86-87.

160. John 3:16.

161. John 8:31-36.

162. Gal. 4:4.

163. Otto A. Piper, "Myth in the New Testament," in L. A. Loetscher (ed.), Twentieth Century Encyclopedia of Religious Knowledge; An Extension of the New Schaff-Herzog Encyclopedia (2 vols.; Grand Rapids, Michigan: Baker Book House, 1955), II, 780-81.

AFTERWORD

In his debate with Pieter Geyl, Professor Toynbee presents the following cogent argument:

> Historians who genuinely believe they have no general ideas about history are, I would suggest to them, simply ignorant of the workings of their own minds, and such willful ignorance is, isn't it, really unpardonable. The intellectual worker who refuses to let himself become aware of the working ideas with which he is operating seems to me to be about as great a criminal as the motorist who first closes his eyes and then steps on the gas. To leave oneself and one's public at the mercy of any fool ideas if they happen to have taken possession of one's unconscious, is surely the height of intellectual irresponsibility.[1]

In the preceding chapters we have attempted to describe the general ideas about history which have influenced the course of Western historical writing. We have also attempted to analyze the weaknesses of secular historiographies and to provide a solid philosophy of history rooted in the historic Christian faith.

The importance of this endeavor should not be underestimated. All secular philosophies of history have built into them an insuperable difficulty: they are unable to stand off from the course of history so as to see it in its entirety. All attempts to reach absolutes by analyzing the human situation from within are doomed to failure because the human situation is in constant flux. As the pre-Socratic philosopher Heraclitus is supposed to have said, "You could not step twice in the same rivers; for other and yet other waters are ever flowing on."[2] No one can "sit in a house by the side of the road and watch the world go by"; everyone is caught up in the flux of human life, and there is no naturalistic resting place within human history from which one can gain a universal, absolute perspective on man's life. Christianity is the only answer to this basic human predicament, for it claims, and by the resurrection backs up its claim, that there is a God and that He entered human history and revealed its essential nature. Since Christ was

Himself the creator of history,[3] He was not subject to our limited perspective; and thus His assertions concerning the Scriptures and concerning the nature of man and history have absolute validity.

If we would have a sound philosophy of history, then, our "sovereign decision" (again to use Butterfield's phrase which we employed in the Foreword) must be a decision for Jesus Christ. Christ has not given us all the historiographical answers (the best seminars on the subject will be given in heaven!), but He has provided us with the only reliable answers there are. On the half-title sheet to Part One of this book, Plato and C. S. Lewis are quoted: Plato, whose myth of the Cave so well sums up the human predicament; and C. S. Lewis, whose Pilgrim discovers that he must remain with Father History "till the morning." All of us must do this in our pilgrimages to the eternal City, but, thank God, eternity once entered time, and history has been forever hallowed by that Advent. The words of the great French historian Jules Michelet have more truth than even he realized: "L'histoire c'est une résurrection."[4]

NOTES

1. Arnold Toynbee, in Geyl, Toynbee, and Sorokin, The Pattern of the Past: Can We Determine it? (Boston: Beacon Press, 1949), pp. 91-92.

2. Milton C. Nahm (ed.), Selections from Early Greek Philosophy (3d ed.; New York: Appleton-Century-Crofts, 1947), p. 91.

3. "All things were made by Him, and without Him was not any thing made that was made" (John 1:3).

4. These words were inscribed on Michelet's grave.

PART TWO

CRITICAL AND EPISTEMOLOGICAL ESSAYS

"What is truth ?"

- Pontius Pilate (John 18:38)

"I am the Truth."

- Jesus Christ (John 14:6)

PREFATORY NOTE

The essays comprising the second part of this book are included for the clarification, expansion, and support of positions taken in Part One. Their relevance to the preceding chapters is indicated by specific references to them in the notes at the end of chapters in Part One. The essays to follow may be read independently of Part One, however, and each essay can be perused by itself without reference to the others if the reader so desires.

No attempt has been made to conform the bibliographical style of these essays to the uniform style employed in Part One, and different styles will be observed in the several essays. In Part Two, the subject matter of each essay has been allowed to determine its format and bibliographical dress.

1. VICO AND THE CHRISTIAN FAITH

I. INTRODUCTION AND STATEMENT OF THESIS

The Subject for Discussion

The connection between religion and any type of intellectual enterprise is a strong one. "The cleavage which divides intellectual from spiritual life is probably the most ominous defect of modern civilization. 'High religion and intellectual enterprise belong together,' says Professor Robert L. Calhoun. 'Each gains from close association with the other. The two in conjunction, but neither one by itself, can move with hope toward more effective conquest of the chaos that again and again threatens to engulf human living.'"[1] Religion probably has a closer connection with philosophy than with any other field of intellectual activity. It is almost a truism to state that theological problems have held a very prominent place in the thinking of the great Western philosophers. Plato and Aristotle immediately come to mind in this respect, but one might as equally well consider Locke, Berkeley, Hume, Kant, Hegel, Dewey, and a host of others too numerous to mention here, to see the truth of this statement. This close connection between religion and philosophy is nowhere more evident than in the work of Giovanni Battista Vico (1668-1744), the Italian jurist and philosopher.[2]

In this paper an attempt will be made both to point up the fallacies in the prevailing view of the religious element in Vico's philosophy, and to suggest a more realistic connection between Vico's religious beliefs and the whole of his philosophical structure. A modified and clear picture of the religious in Vico will necessarily result in some modification and clarification of the accepted picture of his total Weltanschauung, and the latter will then be seen to have definite significance for Christian philosophy.

The Prevailing Opinion of Vico's Philosophy

Early Views of Vico's Philosophy. Immediately following

187

the discovery of Vico in the 19th century[3] "those who took the trouble to read him for themselves did not so much learn from him as recognize in him what was already their own, and acknowledge him as the great forerunner of doctrines and causes to which they were already committed."[4] Vico was considered to be the anticipator and discoverer of the historical method;[5] the first thinker to advocate the union of philology (history) and philosophy;[6] the founder of true metaphysics;[7] one whose thinking appealed to the leaders of the Broad Church movement;[8] a forerunner of Fascism;[9] the first observer of the class struggle which plays so important a part in Marxist theory;[10] a defensor fidei of orthodox Catholic Christianity;[11] etc., etc. However, as extreme views have often been tempered by further study and more adequate information, scholars have gradually come to feel that no one of the above evaluations of Vico is entirely adequate.[12]

The View of Vico's Philosophy Widely Held at the Present Time. At the present time Vico's so-called Historical Theory, which attempts to unite philology (i.e., history) and philosophy, is considered to be the most important and significant aspect of his thinking. C. E. Vaughan says: "It was his [Vico's] mission to recall political theory to the concrete abstractions; those very abstractions against which it was his main purpose to protest."[13] The other evaluations of Vico which we have cited above are now considered inadequate,[14] and the view that Vico had any particular relationship to Christianity is felt to do special violence to the facts. Robert Flint maintains that Vico "made no attempt . . . to found his system on Christianity, and he derived from Christianity little of the material which he employed in the construction of his system."[15] Benedetto Croce argues that Vico's "apologetic for an harmonization of sacred history remains in him a mere episode, which it is possible to ignore."[16]

My Opinion of the View of Vico's Philosophy Widely Held Today. I am in favor, on the whole, of the emphasis which has been placed on Vico as discoverer and anticipator of the historical method and as the first thinker specifically to state the necessity of a union of history and philosophy in the quest for truth. Statements such as the following are almost self-evident to students of Vico:

> Alike in methods and results, it is manifest that he [Vico] stands at the opposite pole from the writers of his own day and of the century before him. Where they are abstract, he is concrete. Where they deal in fictions, he appeals to history. Where they draw an impassable line between politics

and morals, he conceived of man's nature as one organic growth in which politics and morals, reason and imagination, law and poetry, are all inseparably intertwined, all blended in one indissoluble whole. Finally, where they are material- ist and utilitarian, he is defiantly religious and idealist. Here, therefore, if anywhere, we have a new departure. The contrast between him and his predecessors could hardly have been greater.[17]

The latter [Vico] fused philosophy and philology, idealism and empiricism, Plato and Bacon, Christian universalism and Machiavellian individualism, the affirmation of high ethical norms and the consideration of pragmatical histori- cal developments.[18]

Vico fused the doctrine of interests, as it stands out in Machiavelli, with the doctrine of reason, as set forth by Grotius; and lifted the contradiction which separated history (practice) and philosophy (theory).[19]

However, I feel that at the same time scholars have deserv- edly lauded Vico's Historical Theory, they have, in reacting against the Catholic attempt to bring Vico completely into the fold, gone to the extreme of ignoring the religious element in him; as has often happened before, the pendulum has not been stopped in the middle of its course, but has been allowed to con- tinue to an opposite extreme.[20] As Flint puts it, "Excessive laudation is apt to evoke excessive depreciation."[21] I believe that the religious side of Vico's philosophy has not been given the consideration that it deserves, and that the relation of his philosophical thinking to his religious beliefs and to the Chris- tian faith has not been made clear as yet.

II. A CRITIQUE OF THE PREVAILING OPINION OF VICO'S RELIGIOUS PHILOSOPHY

The Present-Day View of Vico's Religious Beliefs and the Evidence for It

Religion in Vico. The very nature of Vico's writings has prevented scholars from maintaining that Vico was non- Christian in his beliefs. Almost all present-day commentators on Vico see him as one who accepted the Christian dogma as a matter of course. Such passages as the following abound in all Vico's works:

Furono tre le spezie delle ragioni. La prima, divina, di cui

Iddio solamente s'intende, e tanto ne sanno gli uomini
quanto è stato loro rivelato: agli ebrei prima e poi
a'cristiani, per interni parlari, alle menti, perché voci d'un
Dio tutto mente; ma con parlari esterni, cosi da'profeti,
come da Gesú Cristo agli appostoli, e da questi palesati alla
Chiesa.[22]

In Europa, dove dappertutto si celebra le religion cristiana
(ch'insegna un'idea di Dio infinitamente pura e perfetta e
comanda la caritá inverso tutto il gener umano), vi sono
delle grandi monarchie ne'lor costumi umanissime.[23]

Having admitted that Vico accepted the main tenets of the
Catholic faith, scholars have relegated his religious beliefs to
the most insignificant position possible. According to present-
day critics, Vico attempted to construe orthodox Catholicism to
fit his philosophical structure, but came off badly in the process. Vaughan, in describing Vico's picture of primitive man
in a state of nature, sees "the pathetic efforts of the author to
square his fancies with the records of Scripture."[24]   To these
scholars of Vico, his Historical Theory--the most significant
aspect of his thought--stands upon its own feet, entirely independent of his religious beliefs which, as a matter of fact, hamper one's understanding of it as they hampered his formulation
of it.[25]   Students of Vico believe, furthermore, that he did not
clearly see the relationship between his religious beliefs and
his philosophical thinking--that he did not realize the contradictions which existed between them.[26]

The Evidence for the Above View. The view of Vico's religious beliefs which has been given in the preceding paragraph
has been supported by five principal arguments. (1) There are
innumerable examples in Vico's writings where he has perverted Scripture to support his theories.[27]   (2) Prominent in
Vico's Historical Theory is the evolutionary development of
man; such evolution is in no sense consistent with the degeneration pictured in the early chapters of the book of Genesis.[28]
(3) Vico was the forerunner of the so-called "higher critical"
approach to history and literature, which has been instrumental
in showing the inspiration of the Christian Scriptures to be a
myth.[29]   (4) Vico's God is immanent, not transcendent, and
this is not the God of orthodox Christianity. On the one hand,
we see from paragraphs 141-146 of La Scienza Nuova that Vico
believed in a Providence which through a "common sense"
guides nations everywhere to pass through the same course of
development.[30]   On the other hand, it is evident that to Vico
God operates in an eternal world--one which passes through

endless <u>corsi</u> and <u>ricorsi</u>, and which does not come into existence through <u>ex nihilo</u> creation.[31] (5) Vico's relativistic view
of natural law which follows from and is integrally connected
with his Historical Theory is not at all the orthodox Christian
conception of an absolute natural law.[32]

Evaluation of the Evidence upon which the Present-Day View of Vico's Religious Philosophy Is Built

As indicated above, I do not believe that the present-day
view of the religious in Vico is adequate. Now an attempt will
be made to show the fallacies in the arguments given to support this view.

(1) Although many strong statements have been made by
scholars to the effect that Vico perverted Scripture to support
his arguments, I am certain that a careful reading of those
passages in <u>La Scienza Nuova</u>[33] where Vico refers to sacred
history will conclusively demonstrate that virtually no "perversion" exists, and that which does is unintentional.[34] One must
look in an unprejudiced manner at Vico's use of Scripture to
support his theories; many critics, such as Croce, have distorted Vico by looking at him through the dark glass of their
own negative view of the Bible.[35] We know that Vico had contact with the writings of St. Augustine,[36] and Augustine warned:

> When they [unbelievers] find one belonging to the Christian
> body, falling into error on a subject with which they them-
> selves are thoroughly conversant, and when they see him
> moreover enforcing his groundless opinion by the authority
> of our Sacred Books, how are they likely to put trust in these
> Books about the resurrection of the dead, and the hope of
> eternal life, and the kingdom of heaven, having already come
> to regard them as fallacious about those things they had
> themselves learned from observation, or from unquestion-
> able evidence ?[37]

(2) That Vico was in no sense a non-Christian evolutionist
may be easily seen. It is true that Vico pictured primitive man
as evolving from a barbaric state, but this barbaric state was
a direct result of the Fall of Man described in Genesis. In <u>La
Scienza Nuova</u> Vico talks about "il primo principio della
cristiana religione ch'è Adamo intiero, qual dovette nell'idea
ottima essere stato criato da Dio."[38] Furthermore, there are
many Christians who believe in the main tenets of the Faith and
yet believe that God works through evolution--that the Biblical
account in the early chapters of Genesis is to be interpreted

191

allegorically. Vico believed that the evolution of ma.. which took place after the Fall was brought about and guided by God; Luis M. Ravagnan says: "Será genuina instancia religiosa aquella que, sin desvirtuar el sentimiento originario, ofrezea en su evolución el complemento y referencia racional a un Dios único, base y fundamento supremo de todo cuanto existe."[39]

(3) Any one who maintains that Vico was the forerunner of the present-day destructive critics of Scripture, is not clear concerning the two meanings of the term "higher criticism." It is true that Vico believed in viewing literature in light of its historical background, but it is even more clear that he was not a precursor of the so-called "higher critic" school of Biblical interpretation - a school which, in the words of one Christian apologist, "does not prove the Bible wrong, but assumes that it is in error from the beginning." Even the most cursory reading of La Scienza Nuova will show that Vico believed in the complete trustworthiness of the Bible and would never have advocated literary and historical destruction of it.[40]

(4) The Christian view of God is both a transcendent and an immanent one; God is not only Father and Son, but also Holy Spirit, who in this latter capacity dwells in the hearts of men.[41] A belief in a God who works through secondary causes is not non-Christian as long as this mode of action is not believed to be His only one. Gianturco says: "The root of De Maistre's idea . . . presupposes the concept that God acts only through causae secundae,"[42] but this logically exclusive statement was never made by Vico.[43] That Vico did believe that the world was created ex nihilo has been proved by Berry;[44] that his corsi and ricorsi do not imply identical repetition in history from eternity has been shown by Flint[45] and by Croce.[46]

(5) I shall discuss below the relation of Vico's conception of natural law to the Christian faith.

The above discussion has shown the inadequacy of the evidence presented by those who believe that Vico did not clearly think through the mutual relationship between the religious and the other aspects of his thought. Let us therefore pass on to the more positive phase of this discussion: the evidence which would indicate that Vico's powerful mind saw the relationship of his religious beliefs to his philosophical structure and to Christianity much more clearly than his critics have seen it.

III. VICO'S PHILOSOPHICAL THOUGHT AND ITS RELATION TO HIS RELIGIOUS BELIEFS AND TO CHRISTIANITY

Preliminary Considerations

There are several considerations of a positive nature which indicate that the religious element in Vico is not inconsequential, that it did not hamper his formulation of the other aspects of his thought, and that he did clearly think through the relationship between religion and his over-all philosophical orientation. (1) Vico's stature as a thinker makes it very doubtful that he would not have carefully considered the mutual relationship between his philosophical structure and religious beliefs.[47] (2) Renown orthodox Christians of his day attested to the soundness of his thinking on religion and philosophy. Typical were the famous Protestant thinker Jean Le Clerc,[48] and Cardinal Corsini of the Catholic church, who later became Pope Clement XII.[49] (3) Vico had an ecclesiastical education; during it he studied church doctrine most assiduously;[50] like the scholastics his studies emphasized the relation of religious to secular philosophy.[51] (4) Throughout all his writings Vico stated that his whole philosophical structure was based upon the premise of the Christian God.[52] (5) In La Scienza Nuova and his other writings Vico emphasizes again and again the harmony of the Scriptures and secular sources.[53] (6) The clarity of Vico's thinking concerning the relation of Revelation and the Church to his philosophical thought is made evident by his own statements.[54]

Let us now consider Vico's philosophical structure.

Exposition of Vico's Philosophical Thought

Theory of Knowledge. In De Antiquissima Italorum Sapientia Vico states his criterion of knowledge, that the true is identical with the created:

> Latinis verum, et factum reciprocantur, seu, ut Scholarum vulgus loquitur, convertuntur. . . . Verum . . . ipsum factum; ac proinde in Deo esse primum verum, quia Deus primus Factor. . . .
> Cum igitur scientia humana nata sit ex mentis nostrae vicio, nempe summa eius brevitate, qua extra res omnes est, et qua quae noscere affectat non continet, et quia non continet, vera quae studet non operatur; eae certissimae sunt, quae originis vicium luunt et operatione scientiae

divinae similes evadunt, utpote in quibus verum et factum convertantur. Atque ex his, quae sunt hactenus dissertata, omnino colligere licet, veri criterium ac regulam ipsum esse fecisse.[55]

From this criterion of truth it follows that history--or as Vico termed it, "philology"--is the most true of the sciences. Croce says: "What was the history of man but a product of man himself? . . . The truth of the constructive principles of history then comes not from the validity of the clear and distinct idea, but from the indissoluble connection of the subject and object of knowledge."[56] However, history and those other sciences which deal with corporeal matter have less certainty than those which do not, such as philosophy and logic. Vico says: "Cumque humana scientia abstractione sit, iccirco scientiae minus certae, prout aliae aliis magis in materia corpulenta immerguntur."[57] The situation exists that what is most true is least certain.[58] Truth is limited to our observations at any given time, and any historical a priori is inconsistent with this principle.[59]

Historical Theory. The essence of Vico's Historical Theory is the elevation of history to its proper place among the sciences, and the bringing about of its union with philosophy.[60] In man's quest for knowledge, history--having much truth but little certainty--must be combined with philosophy, which has much certainty but little truth.[61] Philosophy is still the queen of the sciences, but without the facts of history it can impart little truth.[62] Furthermore, the study of history is its own end; there are no inflexible laws governing the course of history which can be known by man--only God knows the future.[63]

Natural Law. Vico did not view natural law as an absolute structure imposed upon the universe by God.[64] In contrast to the thinkers of his time who were "under the spell of the tremendous advance of physical science in the seventeenth century,"[65] Vico saw natural law as an historical development-- not stationary, but progressive.[66] God's plan for the running of the universe is known in its entirety only by God himself, and what knowledge man acquires of this plan is gained by constantly observing the world in which the Creator has placed him. Miguel Ángel Virasoro says in commenting about Vico's view of natural law:

> Verdadero es sólo aquello que ha sido realizado por el sujeto cognoscente. Por eso, para la inteligencia finita del hombre sólo puede llegar a ser comprendido el mundo de lo histórico, desde que la historia es una producción inmanente

del hombre; y el mundo de la culture o del espíritu que es
su producción transcendente. En cambio la naturaleza es
para nuestro entendimiento un libro cerrado cuyas páginas
sólo pueden ser recorridas por las manos de su creador.[67]

We have seen above that although history is man's best method
of acquiring truth (since he is the maker of it), it does not have
a high degree of certainty because there is always the possibility of discovering new data which may cause the destruction
or revision of even the most hallowed theories. Likewise
knowledge of natural law, since it is derived from historical observation, is continually to be revised and corrected in light of
new facts, and is not to be regarded as static or able to be
known with certainty by man. In his conception of natural law
Vico "puts the sciences in their place by swallowing them up in
history, and anticipates the later view that the true philosophy
of science is simply its history."[68]

The Harmonious Relation of Vico's Historical Theory to His Religious Beliefs and to Christianity

At this point I shall endeavor to show that the two cardinal
points of Vico's philosophy--his Historical Theory and his conception of natural law--demonstrate conclusively that he did in
fact understand the relationship of his philosophical structure
to his religious beliefs and to Christianity.

As has been said earlier in this paper, Vico maintained
rightly that virtually every philosopher preceding and contemporary with him had rejected history and had relied upon abstract reasoning in formulating his Weltanschauung.[69] Vico
realized that such philosophizing was inconsistent with the
Christian faith; in the chapter "Nova scientia tentatur" of his
Universal Law he wrote: "Itaque philologiae studium a . . .
praestantissimis philosophis, si communi christiani nominis,
non privatae philosophorum gloriae studuissent, . . . erat
protrudendum."[70] Christianity is an historical religion, i.e.,
the metaphysical concepts which lie at its core rely for their
validity upon the truth (actual occurrence) of certain events
purported to have happened historically.[71] Thus any theory of
knowledge, to be consistent with Christianity, on the one hand
must not reject or refuse to emphasize history as a means of
discovering truth, and on the other hand must give precedence
to metaphysics over history (since Christian theology is a deductive system--a pyramidal structure based upon belief in the
existence of the God who creates history and reveals Himself
in the Scriptures).[72] Vico's Historical Theory embodies these

two principles; it advocates the union of philology with philosophy, as we have seen above, but it gives precedence to the latter over the former.[73] This correspondence was in no sense accidental; Vico was cognizant of the fact that more than a few philosophers had, because of their low opinion of history as a science, declared any historical religion to be below the level of rationality,[74] and he realized that his Historical Theory was a theory of knowledge which harmonized with the theological position of orthodox Christianity.[75]

The Harmonious Relation of Vico's Conception of Natural Law to His Religious Beliefs and to Christianity

Catholicism--and the whole of orthodox Christianity--believes in a God who is not beneath or on a par with natural law, but who is the Creator and Sustainer of it.[76] As such He can interpose in the natural scheme of things whenever He wills to do so, and has done so upon occasion.[77] Thus the rigorous, inflexible, absolute, Newtonian conception of natural law--a law never suspended even by God Himself--is Platonic rather than Christian. The skeptics of the Enlightenment saw the contradiction between these two views of natural law and branded the miraculous in Christianity irrational. As noted above, Vico conceived natural law as a description of reality--not as an absolutely rigorous structure which could be discovered in its entirety by man. To Vico natural law is never static, but is revised as new facts of experience are recognized historically. Croce describes Vico's cosmology as "dynamic" in opposition to "the mechanicism of contemporary philosophy" and then goes on to say, "Look where we will among his works, we shall never find a materialistic Vico."[78] Vico's conception of natural law of course permits the miraculous, for any event with sufficient historical attestation must be considered when men attempt to describe the structure of natural law, rather than ruled out a priori--as miraculous events have been--by a preconceived appeal to an absolutely regular framework of law in the universe.[79] To those who maintain that Vico's historical view of natural law is inconsistent with Christian belief, one can reply that had Vico held the opposite, absolutistic view of natural law, he would then truly have exhibited inconsistency, for he would have expressed belief in a non-miraculous Christianity. William Ernest Hocking has stated what he believes to be "the dilemma for the modern mind in the idea of God," and little thought will convince us that Vico's conception of natural law offers the only adequate solution for it:

196

(1) God must not intrude in the causal sequences which concern the natural sciences. Neither the observer in the laboratory nor the maker of hypotheses must be called on to refer any effect to his activity.

(2) God must act. It is a persuasion of our time amounting to a fundamental insight that whatever is real is active: if God were not active, we could not think him real.[80]

The above discussion has shown that the prevailing view of the religious element in Vico's philosophy, is clearly incorrect. Vico was not one to overlook such an important problem as that concerned with the relationship between his religious faith and his philosophical thinking; he developed an Historical Theory and a conception of natural law which were in every sense Christian.

Vico's Importance to Christianity

Although Vico's importance to Christianity has been virtually unrecognized[81] (except in the publications of certain Catholic writers who have gone to extremes in attempting to make him support their particular opinions), the arguments of many present-day Christian apologists show clearly an indebtedness to Vico's Historical Theory and conception of natural law. Dr. Edward John Carnell, professor of apologetics at Fuller Theological Seminary;[82] C. S. Lewis, professor of Mediaeval and Renaissance English at Cambridge University and author of numerous books on Christianity;[83] Martin J. Scott, S. J., Roman Catholic apologist;[84] and T. C. Hammond, the British philosopher and writer,[85] are but a few of the many Christian scholars whose arguments for the Faith follow the Vician pattern.

The recently recognized principle of indeterminacy in physics[86] has vindicated in the realm of the exact sciences Vico's conception of an indeterminate natural law. Arthur H. Compton says:

Now, Heisenberg tells us, science must abandon its cherished law of causality. His case has been made so convincing that I should consider it more likely that the principle of the conservation of energy or the second law of thermodynamics would be found faulty than we should return to a system of strict causality.[87]

During the present century there has been a definite trend among philosophers and scientists towards giving history the status which Vico saw that it deserved, and towards viewing natural law as a description of reality--subject to modifications--rather than as an absolute structure which may be known in its entirety by man.[88]

It does not seem an exaggeration to say that Vico's historical approach to reality is gaining wide support and acceptance, and that due to it Christianity has been given a powerful epistemological basis--one which has made it possible for the Christian faith to stand with its head high in the present-day philosophical and scientific realm. Vico may be compared with St. Augustine, who achieved a Platonic understanding of the Christian Revelation when the philosophy of Plato was considered the perfect type of rational knowledge; with St. Anselm of Canterbury, who achieved a purely logical demonstration of the revealed truths of Christianity (the "ontological proof") at a time when syllogistic reasoning was thought to offer the only sure path to absolute verification; with Roger Bacon, who achieved a mathematical and experimental understanding of Christianity when these two methods of acquiring truth were believed to provide the essence of rational proof.[89]

NOTES

(Numbers refer to pages, except in the case of La Scienza Nuova (N. S.), where they refer to paragraphs. An author's last name only is given in referring to his work--see Bibliography for title, publisher, date, etc. of any citation.)

1. Greene, 3.

2. A brief but excellent general article on Vico's life and thought appears in the Encyclopaedia Britannica, 13th ed., Vol. 28, pp. 23-25.

3. Autobiography (Introduction), 75: "The decisive event for Vico's European reputation in the nineteenth century was Michelet's discovery of the New Science in 1824." Ibid., 20: "If . . . Vico's influence was not as immediate and palpable in the one case as Galileo's in the other, that was not because his break with the past was less decisive, but because the prestige of Italian culture had sharply declined in the intervening century, and the lead had passed to France and England." Flint, 3: "In his own age, indeed, he was not appreciated. But in the latter half of the eighteenth century the best spirits of Italy adopted and elaborated various of his leading principles. In the nineteenth century the most

renowned of Italian philosophers--Gioberti, Mamiani, and
other distinguished men--have rejoiced to enroll themselves
under his flag. He has been a powerful living force in the
great Italian awakening which this age has witnessed." The
entire first part (pp. 1-44) of Berry's thesis discusses
"The Obscurity of Vico's Writings" and the reasons for this
obscurity; q.v.

4. Autobiography (Introduction), 61. Berry, x: "Above all
   things Vico's thought should be kept his thought. Too frequently his writings have been used as a sounding board to
   echo his commentators' own thoughts. His terminology has
   served as a convenient expression for ideas quite different
   from his own."

5. Flint, 44: "The works on jurisprudence showed that the
   phenomena of law could only be understood when studied in
   their historical connections. They brought to light the principles of what is called the historical method, and applied
   them with considerable success to explain the development
   of legislation."

6. Autobiography, 138, 154.

7. Flint, 80, 81: "Very different estimates have been formed
   of the worth of Vico's metaphysical treatise. Not a few
   Italian authors of this century [19th] have assigned to it an
   altogether extravagant value. They have described it as a
   singularly profound and precious work,--one of epochmaking
   importance, in which were laid for the first time the foundations of the only modern philosophy which can combine and
   reconcile idealism and realism, and displace and overcome
   rationalism, empiricism, and scepticism."

8. Autobiography (Introduction), 84: "Coleridge's influence,
   reinforced by Michelet's, was responsible for much of the
   interest in Vico on the part of English writers in the second
   and third quarters of the nineteenth century. The two
   groups to whom he most appealed were the leaders of the
   Broad Church movement on the one hand, and the positivists and 'rationalists' on the other."

9. Autobiography (Introduction), 67: "More recently, Vico
   has been restored to good Catholic standing and has

unhappily again become a political symbol; he and Mazzini are 'the two greatest forerunners of Fascism.'"

10. <u>Autobiography</u> (Introduction), 104-107 (section entitled, "In the Marxist Tradition").

11. <u>Autobiography</u>, 155, 207.

12. E.g., over against the Roman Catholic apologist view of Vico, Flint remarks: "He [Vico] supposed that philosophy and Christianity were not antagonistic but accordant" (p. 69).

13. Vaughan, 236. See also <u>Autobiography</u> (Introduction), 46.

14. For example: Concerning Vico as the founder of the true metaphysics Flint says (82): "His real greatness in the sphere of historical philosophy, his opposition to foreign modes of thought, and the general character and tendencies of his own positive principles, have led to his being honoured as the most Italian of Italian philosophers, and to a strong desire on the part of many Italian authors not only to have Vico on their side, but to find the profoundest wisdom in passages of his writings where the ordinary, and especially the foreign intellect, can perceive little or none. The wish to discover in him the founder of the true metaphysics has been, to a large extent, the father of the thought that he was so." Concerning the fallacy involved in treating Vico as a forerunner of Marxist doctrine, one can point out that (a) Vico saw no cataclysmic resolution of class conflict as do the Marxists, (b) Vico is no longer much mentioned by Communist writers.

15. Flint, 69.

16. Croce, 149.

17. Vaughan, 211, 212.

18. Gianturco, 101.

19. Cattaneo, <u>Opere edite ed inedite</u>.

20. My criticism of the present-day opinions of Vico should be considered in light of the fact that Vico remained virtually unknown until the nineteenth century (see note 3), and that

the first English translations of Vico's New Science and
Autobiography appeared only a few years ago. It is almost
always found necessary to modify or restate early interpretations of the philosophy of a thinker; perspective is one of
the prime requisites for valid criticism.

21. Flint, 82. Ironically, Flint's own estimate of Vico's philosophy lies at this new extreme; see p. 70. See also Autobiography (Introduction), 40-44.

22. N. S., 947, 948. Paragraphing is identical in Nicolini's
Italian edition and Bergin and Fisch's English translation of
La Scienza Nuova, where the above passage is rendered as
follows: "There were three kinds of reason [or right:
divine reason, reason of state, natural reason]. The first is
divine and understood only by God; men know of it only what
has been revealed to them. To the Hebrews first and then to
the Christians, this has been by internal speech to their
minds as the proper expression of a God all mind; but [also]
by external speech through the prophets and through Jesus
Christ to the Apostles, by whom it was declared to the
Church."

23. "In Europe, where the Christian religion is everywhere pro-
fessed, inculcating an infinitely pure and perfect idea of God
and commanding charity to all mankind, there are great
monarchies most humane in their customs" (N. S., 1092);
see also 31, 51, 167, 168, 1047. Cf. Autobiography, 155;
Autobiography (Introduction), 49; Croce, 21.

24. Vaughan, 213.

25. Autobiography (Introduction), 44: "It is not possible to
trace with any assurance the precise steps by which Vico
moved toward a resolution of the conflict between his
Catholic piety and his eminently secular if not heretical
philosophy."

26. Croce, 94.

27. Croce, 146-148.

28. Frank Bryon Jevons says concerning the Genesis account of
man's origin (An Introduction to the History of Religion,
p. 7): "Some writers argue that Genesis may be literally

true, but it never says that religion was revealed. But it seems to me that the account in Genesis could never have been written except by one who believed (1) that monotheism was the original religion, (2) that there never was a time in the history of man when he was without religion, (3) that the revelation of God to man's consciousness was immediate, direct, and carried conviction with it." Contrast Vaughan's paraphrased description of Vico's evolving civilization (212-227), and his philosophical discussion of the same (241-245).

29. Vaughan, 206; Flint, 167; Autobiography (Introduction), 56-59, 84.

30. Flint, 199; Vaughan, 246.

31. Flint, 225.

32. Vaughan, 210, 211. For a summary of the above points of criticism, see Autobiography (Introduction), 63.

33. N. S., 13, 16, 62, 95, 256, 299-301, 373, 542, 548, 555, 557, 658; Vaughan, 212-227.

34. Croce, 152, 153: "Careless, headstrong and confused in detail; cautious, logical and penetrative in essentials; he exposes his flank or rather his whole body to the attacks of the most miserable and mechanical pedant, and overawes and inspires respect in every critic and historian however great."

35. Croce, 148, 149: "One certainly feels in all this something of an effort, a will to see or not to see: a kind of self-interruption and stimulation to belief. It is not infrequent among cultured and scientifically educated believers."

36. Autobiography (Introduction), 44; Autobiography, 119.

37. Augustine, De Genesi ad Litteram, Lib. i, Cap. xix, n. 39. (Quoted from Modern Science and Christian Faith, pp. 72, 73.)

38. N. S., 310 (". . . the first principle of the Christian religion, which is Adam before the fall, in the ideal perfection in

.which he must have been created by God"). Cf. Flint, 200, 203; Autobiography, 122.

39. Ravagnan, "Religión y Poesía en Juan Bautista Vico", Vico y Herder, 221. In his article "Significación sociológica de la ley de la evolución en Vico" (ibid., 164), Alfredo Poviña says: "La ley de evolución supone así, por un lado, la existencia de la Providencia divina que gobierna las cosas humanas." See Vaughan, 209, 245, 246; Flint, 206. Berry entitles Ch. XIX of his thesis (pp. 118-123), "The Second Beginning of History," q.v.

40. N. S., 54, 62, 95, 126, 165, 166, 171, 172, 222, 223, 256, 296-298, 299-301, 308, 313, 363, 371-373, 396, 401, 481, 526, 527, 530.

41. I Corinthians 3:16--"Know ye not that ye are the temple of God, and that the Spirit of God dwelleth in you?"; 6:19-- "What? know ye not that your body is the temple of the Holy Ghost which is in you, which ye have of God, and ye are not your own?" See also John 14:17; I Corinthians 14:25.

42. Gianturco, 47.

43. Croce, 143: "Vico's thought was limited by the idea of transcendence."

44. Berry, 112: "He [Vico] . . . accepted the Christian tradition of the origin of the world by creation in time ex nihilo. Here, as usual, he appears as a dualist and a Christian." The reader is referred to the chapter (XVIII: "The Eternity of the World") from which this quotation has been taken (pp. 112-117 of Berry's thesis).

45. Flint, 227, 228: "He [Vico] avowed firm faith in a Providence ever seeking what is best; he strongly maintained the freedom of the human will both in relation to divine grace and to divine law; he believed in the perpetuity, the coming triumphs, and the surpassing excellence of Christianity; he saw in history the grandest of all vindications of the ways of God. How could he, then, adopt a view which would warrant us to sum up the teachings of all history in these lines of the poet?--

'There is the moral of all human tales,
    'Tis but the same rehearsal of the past:

First freedom, and then glory--when that fails,
Wealth, vice, corruption, barbarism at last,
And history with all her volumes vast
Hath but one page.'

I do not think that he adopted any such dreary view. He held that ancient Egypt, Greece, and Rome alike passed through a cycle of three stages, but he nowhere represented these three histories as precisely alike. He fully recognized that each nation had its own individuality; that the events and the personages of one nation were not repetitions of those of another, but had each a special character of its own. Why suppose, then, that he fancied the histories of modern Italy, Germany, and Spain had been or were to be, mere repetitions of those of ancient nations ? I can find no warrant for ascribing to him so absurd an opinion. He deemed feudalism sufficiently like the heroic age of Greece to be accounted a second heroic age, but he was not ignorant that these two ages had great differences. He thought Dante might be regarded as another Homer, but he did not imagine that all that he had affirmed about Homer he could reaffirm about Dante. He held that the ethnic religions arose, flourished, and decayed, but also that Christianity as a revealed religion was not subject to this law. It must be admitted that he has not spoken clearly or hopefully regarding the future; but that does not justify the common representation that he believed the future would be a mere dull plagiarism of the past, without any new disclosures of the glory of God and of the capacities of man. If he had supposed that the future would merely rehearse the past, he would naturally have had no hesitation in anticipating what it would utter. His whole attitude towards the future seems irreconcilable with the notion that he imagined it would be the transcript of a page which had been already written. His belief in cycles of ricorsi was, indeed, inconsistent with a belief in continuous progress in a straight line, but not with advance on the whole, not with a gradually ascending spiral movement; and still less did it imply that any cycle was perfectly like another, and that history merely repeated itself."

46. Croce, 131, 132: "Nor is the Vician law of reflux necessarily opposed, as has often been thought, to the conception of social progress. It would be so opposed if instead of being a law of mere uniformity it were one of identity, in agreement with the idea of an unending cyclical repetition of single individual facts which have been adopted by certain

extravagant minds of both ancient and modern times. The reflux of history, the eternal cycle of the mind, can and must be conceived, even if Vico does not so express it, as not merely diverse in its uniform movements, but as perpetually increasing in richness, and outgrowing itself, so that the new period of sense is in reality enriched by all the intellect and all the development that preceded it, and the same is true of the new period of the imagination or of the developed mind. The return of barbarism in the Middle Ages was in some respects uniform with ancient barbarism; but is must not for that reason be considered as identical with it, since it contains in itself Christianity, which summarizes and transcends ancient thought."

47. Statements to the effect that Vico was a thinker of the highest caliber are legion. See for example: Vaughan, 207, 208, 240, 250; Autobiography (Introduction), vii, 20; Flint, 2.

48. Autobiography, 164, 165.

49. Autobiography, 173, 198.

50. Autobiography, 119.

51. Thompson and Johnson, 706: "The method of reconciling contradictions, eliminating errors, and bringing the whole into line with God's purpose for the universe, confided to the Scriptures and the Church, was the application of Aristotelian logic as worked out by the logicians of the eleventh and early twelfth centuries. In earlier times scholars had a little Aristotle to apply to a limited store of learning. Now they had all Aristotle's logic to apply to a large new body of Greek and Arabic science and philosophy. It was a vast and difficult task that they were attempting, whose magnitude would stagger the most courageous mind and has compelled scholars of later times to dismiss it as impossible. Whereas the contemporary scholar is driven to confine himself willy-nilly to one subject, and to a limited field within that subject, the medieval scholar took all knowledge as his province, and must prepare himself to answer all questions. Since most of the new knowledge came from Aristotle, the new task was to a large extent to Christianize Aristotle. But since much of it came from Plato through Neo-Platonism, which was inherent in much of Arabic philosophy, it was necessary to bring the mysticism of Neo-

Platonism into accord with the intellectualism of Aristotle. And since some of it came from mystic theology of the Byzantines, this had to be harmonized with western theology. All this the scholastic philosophers did." Sabine, 247: "The church wisely relied less on prohibition than on reconstruction, and there is no better evidence of the intellectual virility of medieval Christianity than the rapidity with which Aristotle was not merely received but made the cornerstone of Roman Catholic philosophy."

52. Vico had the God of Christianity in mind as he wrote the Synopsis at the beginning of the first New Science (Autobiography, 49), and as he wrote the Introduction and conclusion to the second New Science (N. S., 42, 1110-1112). See also N. S., 334 and 179 and Autobiography, 145. Cf.: Croce, 4, 86, 135, 249; Flint, 46, 68, 100, 102, 103; Gianturco, 118; Berry, 113.

53. See note 40.

54. See Berry, 14; and cf. note 12.

55. De Antiquissima Sapientia, in Opere scientifiche latine, p. 89; and Opere I, ed. by Gentile and Nicolini, p. 136.

56. Croce, 23.

57. De Antiquissima Sapientia, in Opere I, p. 136; see also Autobiography (Introduction), 38.

58. Flint, 88-93, 102; Croce, 4; Jacinto J. Cúccaro, "La Teoría de Conocimiento en la Filosofía de J. B. Vico", Vico y Herder, 13, 14.

59. Flint, 94: "Truth and knowledge are for Vico coextensive and convertible terms. What is true to us is all that we know. What we know is all that is true to us. There is no human truth outside of human knowledge, just as there is no divine truth outside of divine knowledge. There is no unknown truth. If there were, there would be unmade or ungenerated truth, and the criterion would not apply. The truth is what is known; to be known it must be made; the knowing and the making of truth are inseparable. It obviously follows from this view that truth and knowledge, so far as man is concerned, must be confined within very

narrow limits. And we have seen that Vico does assign to them very narrow limits. We must not infer from this, however, that he rejects as untrue or unknown, in any other sense than his own, what lies beyond these limits, and is designated in ordinary language as truth and knowledge."

60. Vico's Historical Theory was in direct antithesis to the method of Descartes; see Croce, 2; Autobiography (Introduction), 40, 29.

61. Flint, 144, 145: "The distinction between truth and certainty in the doctrine of the criterion has already been shown to have led not unnaturally, even although not strictly logically, to the recognition of the necessity of combining reason and authority, philosophy and philology, and so the devising of an historical method applicable to the study of the law." Flint, 96: "Science, instead of presupposing the separation of truths from certainties, aims in all its departments at knowing truth with certainty." See also Flint, 97, 190; Autobiography (Introduction), 40.

62. Croce, 16: "Like Bacon he [Vico] held that the syllogism and sorites produce nothing new, and only repeat what was already contained in their premises." Vaughan, 208, 209: "What is it, Vico asks, that has made the political philosophy of the moderns--and of the ancients too, with hardly an exception--so barren as speculation and, in its practical consequences, so dangerous and subversive ? It is that the method adopted has almost always been not concrete, but abstract; not historical, but dogmatic: a barefaced transference of the ideas and conditions of the present into the utterly alien world, the wholly different conditions of a remote, but still not irrecoverable, past . . . . Each of them in turn has striven to impose his own system--abstract, arbitrary, one-sided--upon the flesh and blood of history and reality: to clip down the 'wild nature' of primitive man--so diverse, so 'ferocious', so incalculable--to the single type which, by a long process of abstraction, he has chosen for his own academical ideal. To one, the moving principle is pleasure; to another, blind self-mortification; to another, blind force; to another utility of self-interest. And this principle is asserted to the exclusion of all others; nay, in those remote ages it is assumed to have operated after precisely the same fashion as we have persuaded ourselves that it does in ours. What is more, all these

principles are alike in ignoring what is, in fact, the most important principle of all--the impulse of religious awe, which is at once the deepest and most human impulse in the heart of man, and without which there could be no such thing as human society at all. All alike therefore have flouted the most vital elements of man's nature; all alike have trampled the roots of humanity under foot. And this is as true of the Stoics as it is of Epicurus: as true of Spinoza or Grotius as it is of Hobbes or Bayle."

63. Croce, 128: "On the whole it is probable that the difficulty of determining Vico's opinion as to the fate of contemporary society is due to the fact that he had really no settled conviction on the subject." See also Berry, Ch. XXIII ("The Future"), 152-155.

64. Vaughan, 210, 211: "That there is a law of nature, Diritto natural delle Genti, is, he [Vico] holds, absolutely certain. It is, however, a law entirely different from that assumed by the philosophers. Like all laws which apply to living creatures, above all to their spiritual being, it is not stationary, but progressive: a law varying with the stage of growth reached by a given community or nation, not a law the same always, everywhere and for all. . . . Vico . . . lays his denial of natural law, in the absolute sense, at the foundation of his whole argument. Indeed, this denial was implicit in his very adoption of the historical method; as, conversely, any resort to the historical method would have been impossible without it."

65. Autobiography (Introduction), 55.

66. Flint, 141.

67. Virasoro, "Juan Bautista Vico y el problema del saber histórico," Vico y Herder, p. 43. See also Croce, 241.

68. Autobiography (Introduction), 60.

69. Autobiography (Introduction), 11; see also our note 62; Vaughan, 211, 212, 204.

70. De Antiquissima Sapientia, in Opere scientifiche latine, 497. See also De Antiquissima Sapientia, in Opere I, ed. by

Gentile and Nicolini, p. 140. Cf. the concluding paragraphs of <u>La Scienza Nuova</u> (1110-1112).

71. The prime illustration of the historical nature of the Christian faith is that the Christian doctrine of the Incarnation of God in Christ depends for its validity upon the historical fact that a man by the name of Jesus lived in Palestine two thousand years ago, died on a Roman cross, and was actually raised from the dead.

72. Sabine says this concerning the theological viewpoint of Thomas Aquinas, one of the greatest Christian philosophers of all time: "The picture which Thomas drew of nature conformed exactly to his plan of knowledge. The universe forms a hierarchy reaching from God at its summit down to the lowest being" (p. 248; see Sabine's entire discussion on St. Thomas, pp. 247-257). Cornelius Van Til, the brilliant Calvinist theologian, argues: "Fundamental to every thing orthodox is the presupposition of the antecedent self-existence of God and of His infallible revelation of Himself to man in the Bible" (p. 1; see entire work for a picture of the Christian deductive philosophy developed according to its pyramidal structure).

73. Vaughan, 250, 251:
"In his [Vico's] own mind, the two strains, the ideal and the historical, were inseparable. The facts were to be interpreted in the light of the idea, and had no value apart from the idea; the idea had no reality except as embodied in the facts and discoverable through the facts. This was at once the foundation and the coping-stone of his whole theory, at once the deepest and the most fruitful thought by which it was inspired.

"That, however, is not to say that he held, or even attempted to hold, the balance absolutely equal. The very nature of the relation between the two elements--between the idea and the fact, between the principle and its outward expression--made it impossible that he should. Accordingly, when at the end of his Introduction he pauses to tell us in what spirit he would wish his work to be read, it is not . . . the historical, but . . . the mind, the vital truths, the metaphysical propositions which have the first word and the last. . . . 'The reader,' he says, 'must put off his whole bodily nature (corpolenza) and all that pure reason draws from his bodily nature. He must for the time being lay

imagination to rest and put memory to sleep; because, if
these faculties are awake, the mind can never bring itself to
that state of pure intelligence, uncumbered with any definite
form, without which this Science can never be understood.'
Here we have the inner mind of the writer concerning the
scope and method of his book: his conviction that the historical element in his work was subordinate to the philosophical." See also Berry, 47; Croce, 6.

74. Vico called the Averroists "impious" (Autobiography, 129),
and Gilson has shown (pp. 42-65) that Averroës and the
European followers of his doctrines, the Latin Averroists,
relegated historical religion to a position below that of
philosophy because history deals with probabilities and cannot provide the flawless dialectical demonstrations required by the philosophers.

75. N. S., 1094: "Per fini anco umani, ella è la cristiana la
migliore di tutte le religioni del mondo, perché unisce una
sapienza comandata con la ragionata, in forza della più
scelta dottrina de' filosofi e della più colta erudizion de'
filologi" (i.e.: "Even for human ends, the Christian religion is the best in the world, because it unites a wisdom of
[revealed] authority with that of reason, basing the latter
on the choicest doctrine of the philosophers and the most
cultivated erudition of the philologists"). Cf. Autobiography,
130, 155, 173.

76. Job 42:2--"I know that thou canst do every thing, and that no
thought can be withholden from thee." Psalm 115:3--"But
our God is in the heavens: He hath done whatsoever He hath
pleased." Isaiah 43:13--"Yea, before the day was I am He;
and there is none that can deliver out of my hand; I will
work, and who shall let it?" Matthew 19:26--"But Jesus be-
held them, and said unto them, With men this is impossible;
but with God all things are possible." Luke 1:37--"For with
God nothing shall be impossible."

77. Typical Biblical examples of God's intervention in the ordinary course of nature are: The dividing of the Red Sea in
order that the children of Israel might pass through to
safety (Exodus 14:21-31); Manna from heaven (Exodus 16:
14-35); the destruction of the walls of Jericho (Joshua
6:6-20); Elijah's translation to heaven (II Kings 2:11);
Christ's walking on the sea (Matthew 14:25); Christ's

resurrection from the dead (concluding chapters of the four Gospels).

78. Croce, 142.

79. It should be emphasized that a historical approach to natural law does not rule out the possibility of there being an absolute natural law--any more than an inductive argument rules out the possibility of absolute truth. The historical approach to natural law simply says that we cannot know for certain whether an absolute natural law does exist, and that, if it does, we cannot ever comprehend it in its entirety. This approach, of course, makes meaningful the concept of a God who has the power to intervene in the ordinary course of events in the universe when He wills to do so.

80. William Ernest Hocking, Science and the Idea of God.

81. There is no mention of Vico's importance to Christianity in the long section entitled, "Vico's Reputation and Influence," Autobiography (Introduction), pp. 61-107.

82. Carnell, 251, 252: "The Christian defines nature as what God does with His creation, and a natural law as but a mathematically exact description upon the part of man of how God has elected to order His creation. For the Christian there are no 'absolute natural laws,' but only the mind of God. From man's point of view it is 'will.' Here the Christian world-view conflicts sharply with the scientific method. Almighty God, not absolute impersonal law, is the power behind all phenomena. . . . On the Christian hypothesis, therefore, laws, being but descriptions of what happens in nature, cannot be thought of as excluding the possibility of miracles; for miracles, if they actually happened, rather than breaking the laws of nature, make up part of the data which the scientist must reckon with in his original plotting of the laws of nature." See the entire chapter from which this quotation was taken (Ch. XIV: "The Problem of Miracles and Natural Law," pp. 243-260).

83. Read C. S. Lewis' work entitled, Miracles--A Preliminary Study, for many examples of arguments based upon a Vician conception of natural law.

84. Scott, 21: "Man is entitled to use all the reason he

211

possesses, in order to examine and weigh the evidence for credibility in Christ's claims. The evidence is something that can be studied and weighed as any other fact of history. In Christ's case the evidence is the deeds He performed which were possible to Divine power alone. His deeds were of two kinds--miracles and prophecies. They are recorded in the Gospels. The Gospels are admitted, even by rationalists, to be the most genuine and authentic documents of history. If we reject the Gospels as historical records, there is no document of antiquity which can stand, for none is better nor as well attested as the Gospels."

85. See Hammond, Reasoning Faith.

86. Planck, 142: "According to the law of causation as expressed in the equations of classical dynamics, we can tell where a moving particle or system of particles may be located at any given future moment if we know their location and velocity now and the conditions under which the motion takes place. In this way it was made possible for classical dynamics to reckon beforehand all natural processes in their individual behavior and thus to predict the effect from the cause." Berndtson, 18-20: "Recent physical inquiry has uncovered evidences of what some observers call uncertainty, and others indeterminacy. The phenomena yielding the evidence are such as these: the apparently undetermined transit of an electron from one circle in the atom to another, which has induced the comparison of the electron's movement with the choice of a human being; the uncertainty as to which of two photo-electric cells will be entered by a single photon, although the ascertainable conditions are identical; the problem of ascertaining the position and velocity of a particle in wave mechanics. . . . Two problems arise: whether to the admitted uncertainty in our knowledge there corresponds a real indeterminateness in the physical world of any present moment, and whether the relation of the physical world at any given moment is likewise indeterminate with respect to any other moment. . . . The factors whose determinateness is at issue are the velocity and position of the moving particle. It is held by some philosophic writers that the uncertainty regarding these factors is a function not of their ontological status, but of our methods of knowing them. . . . As against this inconclusive view, Planck and other writers hold that the difficulty in the ascertainment of position and momentum are inherent in the

212

real situation, at a level independent of measurement." See entire section "Indeterminism in Physics and Its Applications," pp. 17-30 of Berndtson's work.

87. Compton, 23.

88. Theodore M. Greene, professor of philosophy at Yale University: "The 'vertical' scope of philosophy can . . . be described as an orientation to 'ultimates', if 'ultimate' is defined not as an unconditioned Absolute, but as the limit of man's most penetrating insight at any given point in his cultural evolution . . . . I have used the term 'ultimate' in order to avoid the suggestion that philosophy can ever achieve absolute knowledge or absolute certainty. Reality itself can properly be said to be absolutely what it is, and its innermost and irreducible essence might be referred to as the Absolute with a capital A. Since the philosopher is continuously trying to discover what reality is in itself, he is in this sense searching for the Absolute. But unless we believe, as some philosophers do, in the possibility of indubitable human insights into the nature of this Absolute, we must insist on the partiality and fallibility of all human knowledge, and we must brand any claim to complete adequacy or certainty of comprehension as the fallacy of 'misplaced absoluteness.' This fallacy is incurred in all dogmatism, whether secular or religious; hence such dogmatism is fundamentally unphilosophical. Philosophy should strive for more and more penetrating insights into the nature of reality, but with the full realization that any attainable ultimate is still humanly finite and fallible and therefore not to be identified with an inerrant knowledge of the absolute nature of reality itself" (pp. 7, 8). Planck: "How can we say that a scientific concept, to which we now ascribe an absolute character, may not at some future date show itself to have only a certain relative significance and to point to a further absolute? To that question only one answer can be given. After all I have said, and in view of the experiences through which scientific progress has passed, we must admit that in no case can we rest assured that what is absolute in science today will remain absolute for all time; . . . not only that, but we must admit as certain the truth that the absolute can never finally be grasped by the researcher. The absolute represents an ideal goal which is always ahead of us and which we can never reach. This may be a depressing thought; but we must bear with it.

We are in a position similar to that of a mountaineer who is
wandering over uncharted spaces, and never knows whether
behind the peak which he sees in front of him and which he
tries to scale, there may not be another peak, still beyond
and higher up. Yet it is the same with us as it is with him.
The value of the journey is not in the journey's end, but in
journey itself. That is to say, in the striving to reach the
goal that we are always yearning for, and drawing courage
from the fact that we are always coming nearer to it. To
bring the approach closer and closer to the truth is the aim
and effort of all science. Here we can apply the saying of
Gotthold Ephraim Lessing: 'Not the possession of truth, but
the effort in struggling to attain to it, brings joy to the researcher.' We cannot rest and sit down, lest we rust and
decay. Health is maintained only through work. And as it
is with all life so it is with science. We are always struggling from the relative to the absolute" (pp. 199, 200).

89. Gilson, Ch. I ("The Primacy of Faith"), 15-33.

BIBLIOGRAPHY

Bergin, Thomas Goddard, and Fisch, Max Harold, trans. The
ew New Science of Giambattista Vico. Ithaca, Cornell University Press, 1948. (An abridged but revised edition was
published by Doubleday Anchor Books in 1961.)

Berndtson, Carl Arthur. The Problem of Free Will in Recent
Philosophy. Chicago, University of Chicago Press, 1942.

Berry, Thomas. The Historical Theory of Giambattista Vico.
Washington, Catholic University of America Press, 1949.

Carnell, Edward John. An Introduction to Christian Apologetics.
Grand Rapids (Mich.), Wm. B. Eerdmans, 1948.

Cattaneo, Carlo. Opere edite ed inedite. Raccolte e ordinate
per cura di Agostino Bertani. Firenza, Lemonnier, 1908.

Compton, Arthur H. The Freedom of Man. New Haven, Yale
University Press, 1935.

Croce, Benedetto. Bibliografia Vichiana. Naples, Riccardo
Ricciardi, 1947. 2 vols.

_____. The Philosophy of Giambattista Vico. Trans. by R. G. Collingwood. New York, Macmillan, 1913.

Fisch, Max Harold, and Bergin, Thomas Goddard, trans. The Autobiography of Giambattista Vico. Introduction by Fisch. Ithaca, Cornell University Press, 1944.

Flint, Robert. Vico. (Philosophical Classics for English Readers.) Edinburgh and London, William Blackwood, 1884.

Gianturco, Elio. Joseph de Maistre and Giambattista Vico. New York, Columbia University Press, 1937.

Gilson, Étienne. Reason and Revelation in the Middle Ages. New York and London, Charles Scribner, 1950.

Greene, Theodore M. Religious Perspectives of College Teaching in Philosophy. New Haven (Conn.)., Edward W. Hazen Foundation.

Hammond, T. C. Reasoning Faith. London, Inter-Varsity Fellowship, 1946.

Hocking, William Ernest. Science and the Idea of God. Chapel Hill, University of North Carolina Press.

Lewis, C. S. Miracles. New York, Macmillan, 1947.

Modern Science and Christian Faith. Ed. by American Scientific Affiliation. Wheaton (Ill.), Van Kampen, 1948. (A 2d, improved edition appeared in 1950.)

Planck, Max. Where is Science Going? Trans. by James Murphy. New York, W. W. Norton, 1932.

Robinson, Wm. Childs, ed. Who Say Ye That I Am? Grand Rapids (Mich.), Wm. B. Eerdmans, 1949.

Sabine, George H. A History of Political Theory. Rev. ed. New York, Henry Holt, 1950. (A 3d edition appeared in 1961.)

Scott, Martin J. Why Catholics Believe. New York, P. J. Kenedy, 1932. (Imprimatur: Patrick Cardinal Hayes, Archbishop, New York).

Thompson, James W. and Johnson, Edgar N. An Introduction to Medieval Europe. New York, W. W. Norton, 1937.

Van Til, Cornelius. An Introduction to Systematic Theology. Philadelphia, Westminster Theological Seminary, 1949. (This is a syllabus for class purposes only, and is not to be regarded as a published book.)

Vaughan, C. E. Studies in the History of Political Philosophy before and after Rousseau. Manchester, Manchester University Press, 1939. Vol. 1 ("From Hobbes to Hume").

Vico, Giambattista. Opere. Ed. by Giovanni Gentile and Fausto Nicolini. (Scrittori d'Italia.) Bari, Laterza and Figli, 1914-1944. 8 vols.

_____. Opere scientifiche latine. Milano, Presso Santo Bravetta, 1837. Vol. 1.

Vico, Juan Bautista. Sabiduría primitiva de los Italianos. Buenos Aires, Instituto de Filosofía (La Universidad de Buenos Aires), 1939. (Spanish tr. of De Antiquissima Italorum Sapientia.)

Vico y Herder. Ensayos Conmemorativos del Segundo Centenario de la Muerte de Vico y del Nacimiento de Herder. Buenos Aires, Universidad de Buenos Aires, 1948.

2. THE IMPORTANCE OF A MATERIALISTIC METAPHYSIC TO MARXIST THOUGHT AND AN EXAMINATION OF ITS TRUTH VALUE

> When fiction rises pleasing to the eye,
> Men will believe, because they love the lie;
> But truth herself, if clouded with a frown,
> Must have some solemn proof to pass her down.
>
> - Charles Churchill, Epistle to Hogarth.

PART ONE. EXPOSITION: MATERIALISM THE BASIC PREMISE IN MARXISM

Introduction

In this paper I shall not attempt to criticize the entire Marxist structure; my analysis will be confined to a discussion of the materialist metaphysic in Marxism. While I shall find it necessary to state and briefly explain the major points of Marxist doctrine other than materialism, I shall cite them without criticism. This procedure is not to imply, of course, that these other elements in Marxism are either unimportant or above criticism, for they are neither; my reasons for discussing Marxian materialism to the exclusion of the other more well-known and perhaps more intellectually stimulating elements in Marxism, will become clear later in the paper. Suffice it to say here that I believe the analysis of Marxian materialism to be sufficient to condemn the entire system without further criticism - as interesting and intellectually stimulating as such criticism undoubtedly can be.

Materialism an Important Element in Marxist Theory

Materialism Defined. "The principles of materialism were first formulated by the Greek philosophers Leucippus and Democritus in the late fifth and early fourth century B.C."[1] These early philosophers believed that all existing things had ultimate constituents (atoms), and that all things could be reduced by scientific analysis into their material constituents.

To them, although the universe appeared to contain more than what was physical or material, in reality it did not. Democritus said:

> By convention sweet is sweet, by convention bitter is bitter, by convention hot is hot, by convention cold is cold, by convention color is color. But in reality there are only atoms and the void. That is, the objects of sense are supposed to be real and it is customary to regard them as such, but in truth they are not. Only the atoms and the void are real.[2]

In the late fourth and early third century Epicurus followed in the philosophical footsteps of Democritus. Epicurus' materialism was given an elaborate exposition by his disciple of the first century B.C., the Roman poet Lucretius. Lucretius wrote:

> The nature of mind and soul is bodily. For when it is seen to push on the limbs, to pluck the body from sleep, to change the countenance, and to guide and turn the whole man--none of which things we see can come to pass without touch, nor touch in its turn without body--must we not allow that mind and soul are formed of bodily nature? Moreover, you see that our mind suffers along with the body, and shares its feelings together in the body. If the shuddering shock of a weapon, driven within and laying bare bones and sinews, does not reach the life, yet faintness follows, and a pleasant swooning to the ground, and a turmoil of mind which comes to pass on the ground, and from time to time, as it were, a hesitating will to rise. Therefore it must needs be that the nature of the mind is bodily, since it is distressed by the blow of bodily weapons.[3]

Although Democritus and Epicurus are the materialist philosophers who interest us most here - since they intellectually stimulated Karl Marx[4] - we should note the statements of two more recent thinkers, Thomas Hobbes and Ludwig Buchner. In the Leviathan we read:

> The World, (I mean not the Earth onely, that denominates the Lovers of it Worldly men, but the Universe, that is the whole masse of all things that are) is Corporeall, that is to say, Body; and hath the dimensions of Magnitude, namely, Length, Bredth, and Depth: also every part of Body, is likewise Body, and hath the like dimensions; and consequently every part of the Universe is Body; and that which is not Body, is no part of the Universe: And because the Universe is All, that which is no part of it, is Nothing; and consequently no where.[5]

In his Force and Matter Buchner says:

> Thinking can and must be regarded as a special mode of
> general natural motion, which is as characteristic of the
> substance of the central nervous elements as the motion of
> contraction is of the muscle-substance, or the motion of
> light is of the universal ether. . . . The words mind, thought,
> sensibility, volition, life, designate no entities and no things
> real, but only properties, capacities, actions, of the living
> substance, or results of entities, which are based upon the
> material form of existence.[6]

Materialism, as defined by the above philosophers and others,
assumes two forms. The strict materialists believe that "all
that exists is body, all that occurs is motion," while the more
liberal materialists say that although extra-material things may
exist, the material universe is by far the most significant reality, and an understanding of it gives one the necessary data
for an intelligent world-view.

With this brief philosophical discussion of materialism as a
background, let us turn to the metaphysic of Marxism, as outlined by Marx and Engels.

Materialism and Marxism. The following statements of
Marx and Engels, quoted from their various works, point out
with clarity the metaphysical views of these two thinkers.

> My own dialectical method is not only different from the
> Hegelian, but is its direct opposite. For Hegel . . . the
> thinking process is the demiurge (creator) of the real world,
> and the real world is only the outward manifestation of "the
> Idea." With me, on the other hand, the ideal is nothing other
> than the material world reflected by the human mind.[7]

> In the social production of their means of existence men en-
> ter into definite necessary relations which are independent
> of their will, productive relationships which correspond to a
> definite stage of development of their material productive
> forces. The aggregate of these productive relationships
> constitutes the economic structure of society, the real basis
> on which a juridical and political superstructure arises, and
> to which definite forms of social consciousness correspond.
> The mode of production of the material means of existence
> conditions the whole process of social, political and intellec-
> tual life. It is not the consciousness of men that determines
> their existence, but, on the contrary, it is their social exist-
> ence that determines their consciousness. [8]

219

Upon the different forms of property, upon the social conditions of existence, as foundation, there is built a superstructure of diversified and characteristic sentiments, illusions, habits of thought, and outlooks on life in general. The class as a whole creates and shapes them out of its material foundation, and out of the corresponding social relationships.[9]

Life involves before everything else eating and drinking, a habitation, clothing and many other things. The first historical act is thus the production of the means to satisfy these needs, the production of material life itself. And indeed this is an historical act, a fundamental condition of all history, which to-day, as thousands of years ago, must daily and hourly be fulfilled merely in order to sustain human life. Even when the sensuous world is reduced to a minimum, to a stick as with Saint Bruno, it presupposes the action of producing the stick. The first necessity therefore in any theory of history is to observe this fundamental fact in all its significance and all its implications and to accord it its due importance.[10]

Just as Darwin discovered the law of evolution in organic nature, so Marx discovered the law of evolution in human history; he discovered the simple fact, hitherto concealed by an overgrowth of ideology, that mankind must first of all eat and drink, have shelter and clothing, before it can pursue politics, science, religion, art, etc.; and that therefore the production of the immediate material means of subsistence and consequently the degree of economic development attained by a given people or during a given epoch, form the foundation upon which the state institutions, the legal conceptions, the art and even the religious ideas of the people concerned have been evolved, and in the light of which these things must therefore be explained, instead of vice versa as had hitherto been the case.[11]

According to the materialistic conception, the determining factor in history is, in the final instance, the production and reproduction of the immediate essentials of life. This, again, is of a twofold character. On the one side, the production of the means of existence, of articles of food and clothing, dwellings, and of the tools necessary for that production; on the other side, the production of human beings themselves, the propagation of the species.[12]

Has God made the world or is the world from eternity? As this question was answered this way or that the philosophers were divided into two great camps. The one party which placed the origin of the spirit before that of nature, and therefore in the last instance accepted creation in some form or other - and this creation, is often according to the philosophers, according to Hegel for example, still more odd and impossible than in Christianity - made the camp of idealism. The others, who recognized nature as the source, belong to the various schools of materialism. Then came Feuerbach's "Wesen des Christenthums." With one blow it cut the contradiction, in that it placed materialism on the throne again without any circumlocution. Nature exists independently of all philosophies. It is the foundation upon which we, ourselves products of nature, are built. Outside man and nature nothing exists, and the higher beings which our religious phantasies have created are only the fantastic reflections of our individuality.[13]

Chemistry leads to organic life, and it has gone far enough to assure us that it alone will explain to us the dialectical transition of the organism. What Helmholtz says of the sterility of attempts to produce life artificially is pure childishness. Life is the mode of existence of protein bodies, the essential element of which consists in continual, metabolic interchange with the natural environment outside them, and which ceases with the cessation of this metabolism, bringing about the decomposition of the protein.[14]

Let us now see what the commentators say concerning the Marxian metaphysic and its importance to Marx's system as a whole.

The Metaphysic of Marxism is Materialism--is a Physic. That is, Marxism can be stated by the controversialist to be a denial of metaphysic in the sense of a study of that which is other than the material universe. There is nothing other; and that which is other is no thing, nothing. But, if by metaphysic we mean the logical discussion of the nature of being, then there is most definitely a Marxist metaphysic which affirms that this nature can dogmatically be stated to be material. Materialism is chosen because it seems to place man firmly in the arms of Nature, his mother. Marx asserts that there is a "necessary connection of materialism and communism." It offers man an explanation of his own nature and bids him look to his origins if he would consider how he should develop, instead of looking away to some other world of gods and spirits.[15]

It is the economic factor--so it is argued--above all, as that is embodied in the conditions of production, that ultimately determines all things. It governs the structure of the society in which men live. It fashions their religion; it determines their laws; it shapes their literature and their art. The spiritual is determined by the material; things are in the saddle and ride mankind.[16]

It is clear from the above array of quotations that Marx and Engels were avowed - vehemently avowed - materialists, and that both they and their commentators believe materialism to be integrally connected to the Marxian system. As to why there is this necessary connection or what precisely its nature is, we have not yet been informed; below I shall attempt to give an answer to this question. Furthermore, it is well to note that from the above quotations - and, I believe, from all of early Marxist literature, one cannot determine whether Marx and Engels were strict or liberal materialists: some statements in their writings seem to imply the former, others the latter. In order to give them the benefit of the doubt, and in order to increase the applicability of my criticism, I shall throughout this paper take the liberal or "mild" interpretation of Marxist materialism.

Demonstration that the Force and Validity of the Marxian Philosophy Does and Must Depend upon its Materialistic Metaphysic

The Essential Elements in Marxist Theory. In order to see the relationship between materialism and the Marxian system as a whole, it is necessary to understand the nature of the chief elements in the system. George Catlin has summarized these elements in his Story of the Political Philosophers, and it is his order of discussion which I shall employ here:

Together Marx and Engels, by a combination of Jewish rabbinic subtlety and German industry, built up a philosophy which in its involved consistency has no compeer since St. Thomas laid down his pen. For it the Communist Manifesto provided the Prophecy and Das Kapital provided the Torah, the Law. Here is "the Book." . . . This Marxian philosophy is a coherent whole. It is massive because revolutionary action is built upon class-war theory; the class war upon the economic theory of surplus value; this economic theory upon the economic interpretation of history; this interpretation upon the Marxo-Hegelian logic or dialectic; and this upon a materialistic metaphysic.[17]

222

Marxian materialism is not static - not mechanistic as was
the materialism of the ancients, of Hobbes, and of Condillac.
Marx condemned such materialism as not taking into account
free will and dynamic energy, and adopted Hegel's dialectic interpretation of history "with considerable changes, to be sure,
in its supposed metaphysical implications but with no important
change in the conception of it as a logical method."[18] What,
then, is the dialectic interpretation of history? Essentially
this: Every tendency when carried to the full (thesis) breeds
an opposite tendency (antithesis), which combines with the
thesis to form a new tendency (synthesis). The synthesis then
becomes a new thesis, and the dynamic process begins anew.
The conflict of two opposites never results in the complete annihilation of either; out of the conflict always emerges the synthesis which, while leaving elements of both thesis and
antithesis behind, yet embodies the truth contained in each.
Obviously, two different interpretations of these dialectic processes are possible: the emphasis may be on continuity - the
impossibility of making radical and voluntary departures from
the past; or it may be upon discontinuity - the necessity of continual break with the past. Whereas Hegel emphasized continuity in this historical "spiral that mounts as it turns," Marx
emphasized discontinuity and revolution - "the continual swing
of socialist theory between revolutionism and revisionism."[19]
A further difference between the Hegelian and Marxian dialectic
lay in metaphysical assumption: Hegel's essentially idealistic
belief that history was the progressive realization and materi-
alization of the World Spirit in time, was vehemently rejected
by Marx. Marx and Engels were dialectic materialists, not
"bourgeois" idealists:

> "In Hegel's hands," claims Marx, "dialectic underwent a
> mystification." The laws which Hegel "first developed in all
> embracing but mystical form," Engels explains, "we made it
> our aim to strip off this mystic form and to bring clearly be-
> fore the mind in their complete simplicity and universality."
> Putting the matter somewhat more picturesquely, Marx as-
> serts that "In Hegel's writings dialectic stands on its head."
> It "is upside down," Engels elucidates, "because it is sup-
> posed to be the "self-development of thought," of which the
> dialectic of facts is therefore only a reflection, whereas
> really the dialectic in our heads is only the reflection of the
> actual development which is fulfilled in the world of nature
> and of human history. . . ." "You must turn it right way up
> again," admonishes Marx, "if you want to discover the ra-
> tional kernel within the mystical shell."[20]

Despite their materialism, Marx and Engels, like Hegel, saw a truly moral necessity in the development of civilization through the dialectic process. To Hegel, the expansion of the inner forces of civilization meant a powerful and united German state; to Marx it meant the inevitable success of the proletarian revolution. Marxism has always seen the dialectic process as more than a working hypothesis; were it not a method of historical interpretation which makes prediction possible, the proletarian revolution would lose its essential inevitability.

Marx's economic interpretation of history, the third essential element in his system, may be stated very simply: the economic factor is the key to the dialectic process. To Marx and Engels, an analysis of economic trends and movements rewards the student with an understanding of the course which history will take; for the theses, antitheses, and syntheses which create the upward spiral of civilization, are economic in nature. Some writers have claimed, it is true, that Marx did not make the course of history completely dependent upon economics, but such an interpretation is refuted both by the logic of Marxism (Marx derived his Messianic view of the proletarian revolution solely from an economic interpretation of the dialectic process), and by a consideration of innumerable statements from the writings of both Marx and Engels:

> Our conception of history depends on our ability to expound the real process of production, starting out from the simple material production of life, and comprehend the form of intercourse connected with this and created by this (i.e. civil society in its various stages), as the basis of all history; further, to show it in its action as State; and so, from this starting-point, to explain the whole mass of different theoretical products and forms of consciousness, religion, philosophy, ethics, etc., etc., and trace their origins and growth, by which means, of course, the whole thing can be shown in its totality (and therefore, too, the reciprocal action of these various sides on one another) . . . . It does not explain practice from the idea but explains the formation of ideas from material practice; and accordingly it comes to the conclusion that . . . not criticism but revolution is the driving force of history, also of religion, of philosophy and all other types of theory. It shows that . . . at each stage there is found a material result: a sum of productive forces, a historically created relation of individuals to nature and to one another, which is handed down to each generation from its predecessor; a mass of productive forces, different forms of capital, and conditions, which, indeed, is modified

224

by the new generation on the one hand, but also on the other prescribes for it its special character.[21]

The materialist conception of history starts from the proposition that the production of the means to support human life and, next to production, the exchange of things produced, is the basis of all social structure; that in every society that has appeared in history, the manner in which wealth is distributed and society divided into classes or orders, is dependent upon what is produced, how it is produced, and how the products are exchanged. From this point of view the final causes of all social changes and political revolutions are to be sought, not in men's brains, not in man's better insight into eternal truth and justice, but in changes in the modes of production and exchange. They are to be sought, not in the philosophy, but in the economics of each particular epoch.[22]

The complex and highly technical theory of surplus value shows how the distribution of wealth determines the course of history. The capitalist, according to Marx, continually drives the wages of his employees down to subsistence level in order to cut his labor costs and obtain the cheapest labor. Capital, by its inherent desire for economic domination, becomes more and more concentrated: organized trusts replace small businesses, and more and more efficient machines come to be employed. Thus the worker is continually paid less for running his machine, while at the same time his machine becomes more and more productive through improvement and replacement. Since, according to Marx, in a perfect competitive system the real value of a product is the value of the labor put into it, a vast discrepancy arises between the wages which the worker receives and the real labor value of the commodities which he produces. This difference - which is appropriated or stolen by the capitalist - is what Marx termed "surplus value." Yet the capitalist is little better off than his employees: since the capital - "constant capital" - produced by his machines is only sufficient for their own repair and replacement, the capitalist experiences a falling rather than a rising profit rate as his machines increase in number and his workers decrease in number. Only surplus value is profit for the capitalist, and surplus value cannot be extorted without workers; yet the capitalist must decrease rather than increase wages in order to have money for fixed capital, without which he will fall behind in the production race. The lumbering capitalistic monster advances to its own destruction - a destruction preceded by many workers unemployed and the rest working for practically nothing; few capitalists owning tremendous factories filled with machines which yield practically no profit.

The intolerable situation described here obviously means a violent change in the existing structure of society. The dialectic process grinds to a stop with the class-war between proletariat and capitalist - a struggle which results in the final overthrow of capitalism both economically and politically. The State itself - the instrument of capitalism - "withers away," and the proletariat ceases to exist once the means of production falls into the hands of the workers.[23] After a literal "dictatorship of the proletariat" of indefinite length,[24] during which time the final vestiges of capitalism are destroyed, the golden era of the classless, socialist society is ushered in.[25] Marx asserted that the active and revolutionary opposition of the proletariat would be required in bringing the capitalistic era to a close; thus the evangelistic emphasis in the concluding section of the Communist Manifesto:

> In short, the Communists everywhere support every revolutionary movement against the existing social and political order of things. . . . The Communists disdain to conceal their views and aims. They openly declare that their ends can be attained only by the forcible overthrow of all existing social conditions. Let the ruling classes tremble at a Communist revolution. The proletarians have nothing to lose but their chains. They have a world to win. Workingmen of all countries, unite![26]

The Relation of Materialism to the Marxist Philosophy as a Whole. I have shown above through quotations that Marx, Engels, and their commentators believe materialism to have an integral connection with all of Marxist thought. Here I shall attempt precisely and rigorously to state the nature of this connection.

Two truth-functions (concepts capable of being true or false) may be related in a number of ways, the most well-known relations being equivalence and contradiction. When we say that A is equivalent to B, we mean that whenever A is true, B is true, and whenever A is false, B is false. When we say that C is contradictory to D, we mean exactly the opposite. We can set up these relations in tabular form, viz.:

A equiv. B		C contrad. D	
T	T	T	F
F	F	F	T

Other logical relations or "dependencies" between truth-functions are superimplication, subcontrariety, contrariety, and subalternation.[27] It is with the latter of these that we are concerned in this paper. Assuming that M and X are subalternates, the following table can be set up.

M	subalt.	X
T		U
F		F

where U = undecided (may be either true or false). Expressed in words, this means that if M and X are subalternates, then X is false when M is false, but X may be either true or false when M is true. Why this discussion? Because it is my contention that if M = materialism and X = the Marxian philosophy, M will be related to X as one subalternate to another.

Let us first consider what truth-value the basic elements of Marxism would have if materialism were true. Could the Marxian dialectic, the economic interpretation of history, the theory of surplus value, and the class-war theory, as outlined above, then be true? Definitely yes, for no logical contradiction exists in the relation between the various elements of the system. Could these elements be false if materialism were true? Again the answer is yes, for (1) materialism could be true, and yet it be the static materialism of Democritus, Epicurus, et al. (i.e., the dialectic could be false), (2) materialism could be true and yet materialistic factors other than the economic could be most important for the understanding of historical developments (i.e., the economic interpretation of history could be false), (3) materialism could be true and yet the theory of surplus value be invalid because of a failure to take into account government intervention in the affairs of capital, (4) materialism could be true and yet a classless society never come into being because of a fundamental antagonism in human nature.[28] Thus we see that the first condition of a subalternate relationship between M and X is fulfilled, i.e.,

M	X
T	U.

Now let us consider what truth-value the Marxian philosophy must have if materialism is false, i.e., if - taking the weak interpretation of Marxian materialism - some extra-material considerations are more important than material things in determining the course of history. Here there is a danger of jumping to a quick but false conclusion: one might maintain that, even though the economic interpretation of history would be necessarily false if materialism were false, the dialectic process, theory of surplus value, and class-war could have meaning. "After all," it might be argued, "I am certainly not a materialist, but I see thesis, antithesis, and synthesis in history; I see capital striving to reduce the wages of labor and workers striking to obtain higher wages; I can believe that a classless society will be the ultimate result of this conflict." The fallacies in this argument are (i) a lack of recognition of the pervasiveness of the materialistic metaphysic throughout the whole conceptual structure of Marxian philosophy, (ii) a lack of recognition that Marxism is a system to be believed in, a system which requires particular action on the part of its adherents. With regard to the first point, one must see that were any extra-material thing more important than the material in determining the course of history, although a dialectic process of some sort could still exist, it would no longer be a dialectic of predominantly materialistic thesis, antithesis, and synthesis - that not only the economic, but also any materialistically operated dialectic could no longer be depended upon to reveal the future; that although a surplus value theory of some sort could still exist, it would no longer be significant enough to direct the course of history; that a class-war, proletarian revolution, dictatorship of the proletariat, classless society brought about solely by materialistic causes would be rendered impossible. Secondly, one must recognize the truth of Catlin's assertion:

> It is not, however, enough to say that Marx is right on many points, that "there is much good in Marx." So there is in most writers of eminence from Mahomet to Swedenborg, including Machiavelli. The issue is whether there is enough good to justify men following him.[29]

The invalidity of the materialistic metaphysic in Marxism is sufficient to undermine the theory as a whole - is sufficient to render it untenable as a systematic philosophy of life. Elements of the doctrine could still be believed in a modified form were materialism false, but this would be far different from placing faith in the Marxian system as a world-view - as an object of faith - as a first principle upon which one's actions are to be predicated. Without the truth of materialism, Marxism could not demand that the "workingmen of all countries unite," because intellectual justification for a materialistically grounded and determined proletarian revolt and classless society would be nonexistent. Thus the second condition of a subalternate relation between materialism and the Marxist doctrine is fulfilled, i.e.,

$$\frac{M}{F} \qquad \frac{X}{F}$$

and we may assert the proposition

M subalt. X.

PART TWO.
CRITICISM: THE TRUTH-VALUE OF MATERIALISM

Method of Approach

From the valid formula (Materialism subalt. the Marxian philosophy) we can see that if the materialistic metaphysic of Marxism can be shown to be false, the Marxian system cannot rationally be held as a world-view.[30] In this section of my paper I shall attempt to demonstrate the invalidity of materialism and withal the untenability of Marxism.

Only the tautology (if A then A) can be proved true, and proof of its truth is possible only because the tautology makes no statement of fact. In the case of every theory involving statements of fact, proof is impossible, for new information may always turn up to disprove previous findings. Since this is so, all science and history - indeed all intelligent decision between alternative theories, beliefs, ideologies, must rest squarely upon probability. The rational man, when confronted with a problem of fact, must ask himself two questions: (1) What is the probable validity of the present evidence for and against the notion, (2) What is the probability of future data arising to negate the force of present evidence for or against the notion. Answers to these questions supply the only "proof" possible pro or con a theory. The remainder of this paper will consist of an attempt to answer these two questions with respect to the truth-value of materialism.

The considerations presented thus far in this paper either are not seen - or more probably are regarded as of no particular relevance by critics of Marxism. The critics are undoubtedly acquainted with the principle of subalternation as it applies to Marxism - are cognizant of the fact that if materialism can be shown to be false, the whole Marxian system will lose its force and validity; yet they make no attempt to demonstrate the invalidity of this materialistic metaphysic. The most that is generally done with the materialistic metaphysic of Marxism is to state that philosophically it cannot be dogmatically asserted - that Marx and Engels are being unphilosophical in their dogmatic assertion of it. Bertrand Russell argues that "materialism, in some sense, may be true, but it cannot be known to be so," and Catlin writes: "The question remains how we dogmatically know that the ultimate nature of being corresponds with what is generally meant by matter."[31] These criticisms are so weak that they are almost ridiculous: since nothing can be proved, since all statements of fact rely upon probability for their truth, nothing can be "known" to be true - neither materialism, nor democracy, nor the scientific method, nor the date of Napoleon's battle at Waterloo, nor the existence of the dodo bird. "Materialism cannot be known to be true": Very well, but why feel that this truism ends the discussion? Why not evaluate the probable truth or falsity of materialism - why not employ the same method of evaluation with regard to materialism as is done with every other matter of fact? To say that materialism cannot be "dogmatically" asserted is to utter an undeniable but virtually useless statement; to attempt to show in terms of probability the invalidity of materialism is to engage in a philosophical activity worthy of the name. Being agnostic about the validity of Marxian materialism will leave the Marxian structure unshaken; being bold in one's attempt to destroy its metaphysic can succeed in undermining the entire philosophy. Perhaps the unwillingness of critics to deal forceably with Marxism's first premise indicates that materialism has become a common belief not only in Soviet philosophical circles. Perhaps the essentially materialistic Anglo-American way of life has come to be reflected in the philosophical attitudes of her scholars.

My attempt at showing in terms of probability that materialism is invalid, will assume two aspects: (1) negative: a demonstration that the evidences used by Marx to support his materialist metaphysic are inadequate; (2) positive: a presentation of the evidence against materialism, i.e., a presentation of evidence to support the thesis that an extra-material entity (a) exists, (b) is more influential than the material in determining the course of history. Obviously, if I can show that it is probable that some significant extra-material entity exists, I shall make the truth of materialism - and therefore Marxism - improbable to the very degree that this extra-material entity has the probability of existing and the probability of being significant historically.

Evaluation of Marx's Evidences for Materialism

Marx often stated in violent invective his opposition to a priori ways of thinking. He condemned religion and philosophy - having a special liking for Ludwig Feuerbach's comment that "the metaphysician is a priest in disguise." Whether Marx was justified in his criticism of religion and philosophy on this ground, we shall consider in the concluding section of this paper; here we should notice that Marx at least considered himself a scientific empiricist, and claimed to derive his doctrine from the facts of science and history.

What historical and scientific evidence did Marx and Engels muster in support of their materialistic metaphysic? What evidence was sufficient to permit Engels confidently to dismiss even agnosticism as "shamefaced materialism"?[32] (1) From the physical sciences: the evidence that the planetary system and the earth itself at one time could not support life; and the clear ramification of the Second Law of Thermodynamics that life cannot remain forever in existence. (2) From the biological sciences: the evidence that life has naturally progressed from simple to complex along the evolutionary line suggested by Darwin. (3) From the social sciences: the evidence that human customs, ideologies, arts, methods of production, institutional forms, religious, ethical, and political norms and precepts have undergone enormous natural changes during the course of history. Let us evaluate these three considerations.

Marx and Engels were perfectly correct in maintaining that life cannot always have been in existence, and that Carnot's Second Law of Thermodynamics together with the Clausian formula for entropy[33] requires that life not always remain in existence. Protoplasm, the basic life-substance, can exist only under certain restricted atmospheric and thermodynamic conditions, and it has been conclusively demonstrated that these conditions were not present during all of either planetary or world history - further, that the gradual running down of the universe and lowering of the earth's temperature must eventually result in the destruction of protoplasm and therefore the extinction of life.

> The conditions for the existence of protein are infinitely more complicated than those of any other known carbon compound, because not only physical and chemical functions, but in addition nutritive and respiratory functions, enter, requiring a medium which is narrowly delimited, physically and chemically - and is it this medium that one must

suppose has maintained itself from eternity under all possible changes ?[34]

But does the impermanence of life mean that no extra-material entity can either exist or play the leading part in the universe? Certainly not. Life could conceivably have been brought into existence and be destined to eventual destruction at the hands of a supernatural entity. Of course, one would have to have independent evidence that such were the case in order to maintain this position, but the point to notice is that the impermanence of life does not per se necessitate one's accepting a materialistic metaphysic. Ironically Engels, in attempting to support his belief in the dialectic, destroyed the pan-vitalism of Liebig and Helmholtz which, if true, would have offered much the greater evidence against supernatural activity in the universe.[35]

In two letters written at almost the same time Marx explained the relationship between Darwin's theory and his own doctrine.

> During my time of trial, these last four weeks, I have read all sorts of things. Among others Darwin's book on Natural Selection. Although it is developed in the crude English style, this is the book which contains the basis in natural history for our view.[36]

> Darwin's book is very important and serves me as a basis in natural science for the class struggle in history. One has to put up with the crude English method of development, of course. Despite all deficiencies, not only is the death-blow dealt here for the first time to "teleology" in the natural sciences but their rational meaning is empirically explained.[37]

Marx saw in Darwinian evolution the gradual materialistic development of the species - a development which negated the claims of supernaturalism and idealism. But does such evolution, even if true, rule the supernatural out of existence or demonstrate that it is of little significance in the history of the race? Again we must answer in the negative. Many have believed since the publication of The Origin of Species in 1859 that the progression of life from simple to complex is the strongest evidence that an extra-material entity is at work in human history. How else, they ask, can one explain a progression towards the complex, the rational, the better? But even more significant for our argument is the ever-increasing doubt that evolution in the Darwinian sense is a valid concept at all. Of course, the theory of polygenesis[38] has a great deal of

232

truth in it, but this is a far cry from the Darwinian view - upheld by Marx - that the human being may be traced back directly to the primal one-celled animal. In 1940, Dr. Richard B. Goldschmidt, Professor of Zoology in the University of California, declared: "I cannot agree with the viewpoint of the textbooks that the problem of evolution has been solved. . . . Nowhere have the limits of the species been transgressed, and these limits are separated from the limits of the next good species by the unbridged gap, which also includes sterility. . . . This gap cannot be bridged by theoretically continuing the subspecific gradient of clime beyond its actually existing limits."[39] T. H. Morgan, Professor of Experimental Zoology at Columbia University (1904-19) and a Nobel prize-winner, wrote that "Within the period of human history we do not know of a single instance of the transformation of one species into another one. . . . It may be claimed that the theory of descent is lacking, therefore, in the most essential feature that it needs to place the theory on a scientific basis. This must be admitted."[40] The numerous objections to the evolutionary hypothesis - objections which are becoming more formidable all the time,[41] plus the big question as to why the evolutionary process, if actually taking place, has assumed an orderly and almost intelligent form, belies the Marxist claim that materialism has received confirmation from the doctrine of Darwin and his successors.

Present-day sociology and anthropology had their beginnings in Marx's time - the new sociology and anthropology which have made an effort to purge out all a prioris but one: the materialistic development of human institutions. Marx - he was far from alone in this respect - fallaciously believed that the social sciences, by overthrowing all philosophical and religious presuppositions, were overthrowing all presuppositions, and were therefore actually demonstrating the materialistic nature of human life. Marx made the serious but common error of thinking that what is assumed from the start by a discipline, is proved by that discipline. The social sciences of Marx's day, like those of ours, utilized data from a bewildering number of obscure and diversified cultures to show the transience and relativity of all human customs, ideologies and norms - whether secular or religious. From these changes in man's activities, the social scientists "induced" that human nature was also impermanent - the product of environment and not of a divine potter. Marx and Engels were only too ready to incorporate these conclusions into their thinking,[42] as the medieval scholastics whom they despised had been only too ready to accumulate passages of Plato and Aristotle which supported one or another allegorical interpretation of the sacred canon. Aside from the detrimental effects of their materialistic a priori (for example, the refusal to give proper weight to permanence and continuity in such human institutions as the Judeo-Christian tradition), the social views which Marx applauded failed to recognize what Venable so succinctly points out:

> That man's behaviour changes is obvious enough, but need this necessarily reflect in any central way upon man himself? Why, through all the vagaries that this behaviour undergoes from time to time and place to place, could not the human "essence" remain one?[43]

Sociology and anthropology do not rule out the possibility - although independent evidence would be necessary to verify it - that there is an "absolute" human nature, the product of extra-material force, and that the stability of some human institutions reflects extra-material influence. Marx's third main evidence for materialism fails as have the other two, and materialism remains a possible, but not particularly probable metaphysic.

The Evidence Against Materialism

The ineffectiveness as evidence for materialism of the data which we have just evaluated, lies in the fact that they are in reality neutral considerations - that they per se verify neither materialism nor supernaturalistic idealism. The fact that protoplasm has not been in existence forever gives evidence to the materialist that life is "not an essence but a natural development from an inorganic matrix"; the same fact proves to the believer in God that life is a fiat creation. Evolution means natural development to the materialist; it means teleology in the universe to the idealist. Thus, in terms of probability Marx and Engels give virtually no proof for the materialism which forms the basis of their philosophy. Yet, if no definitive contrary evidence exists, Engels has a perfect right to defend his meagerly supported materialism as Laplace defended his "System of the World" when Napoleon questioned the omission of God from it: "Sir," Laplace said, "I have had no reason to employ that hypothesis."[44] Obviously, if nothing has happened which can be better explained by the existence of an extra-material entity, then there is no reason to postulate the existence of one. It is my firm belief, however, that at least one datum does exist which is inexplicable without the supernaturalistic hypothesis, and a description and evaluation of this datum will comprise a good part of the remainder of this paper. I shall attempt to show, in terms of probability, that there is an historical and scientific consideration which points with a steady finger to the existence of a supernatural entity whose importance to human history surpasses that of the material. This datum of which I speak, unlike the Marxian evidences for materialism, cannot be construed to support either idealism or materialism, depending upon the a prioris of the user; it can only deliver what I believe to be a damning criticism of Marxian materialism and its subalternate, the Marxian world-view.

Christus Victor. The historical consideration which I am convinced throws the scale of probability far to the side of supernaturalism, is the man Jesus Christ - His claims and the validation which He gave for His claims. First I shall discuss the claims themselves, then the attestation which He provided for them, and lastly their ramification for this discussion.

Jesus of Nazareth - the "humble Carpenter" - made the most stupendous claims of any one who has ever lived. He claimed the following things, which if validated, would mean the annihilation of the materialist point of view:

1. That there exists a perfectly just, wise, powerful, holy, and loving personal Being;[45]
2. That He, Jesus Christ, was the human incarnation of this Being,[46] come to earth vicariously to save its inhabitants from eternal death,[47] and to reveal God to man;[48]
3. That the universe - including the earth and the human race - had been created by God,[49] that God has a continual interest in the most minute things which happen on the earth,[50] and that the termination of the present age will be brought about in God's own time and by His command;[51] in short, that the creation is in every sense teleologically and supernaturally operated.

These claims of Christ, together with substantially all the data we have concerning Him, are included in four books - the Gospels of Matthew, Mark, Luke and John. These records, which no competent scholar today maintains were written later than 50 years (Synoptics) and 65 years (John) after Christ's death,[52] contain the record of His crucifixion and Resurrection from the dead - this latter event being the one upon which He placed the most emphasis while alive, and which He considered to provide the ultimate verification for His claims.[53] We should note carefully that the dates of the Gospels remove any doubt as to their authorship by attesting their claim to have been written by Christ's contemporaries; and furthermore that since they were written while eye-witnesses of the events recorded in them were still alive, their contents could be tested at first hand for truth or error by anyone desiring to do so.

According to the Gospel records, Jesus of Nazareth was put to death by the Roman governor of Palestine during the passover celebration which took place in Jerusalem in 33 A.D. The official charge was treason against Rome (Jesus had claimed to be a King), although the Jewish religious leaders, who gave Jesus over to the Roman governor, hated Him chiefly because He had in their eyes blasphemed - claimed to be God, and to exercise divine prerogatives.[54] The city of Jerusalem was packed during the passover week, and Jesus' crucifixion was witnessed by many.[55] Upon His death, which was accompanied by an earthquake, darkness over the land, and other phenomena,[56] His body was placed in a tomb belonging to a rich man of the Jews.[57] The huge boulder at the entrance to the tomb[58] was sealed, and a Roman guard was stationed, in response to the pleas of the high-priests and rabbis, who, knowing that Jesus had said that He would rise from the dead after three days to verify His claims, desired to prevent anyone's spiriting away the body and spreading the story that Jesus had risen.[59] On the morning of the third day, however, Jesus did rise, the guard having been rendered completely ineffective through fear.[60] During the forty days following, Jesus appeared in bodily form[61] on at least eight occasions,[62] making his identity a matter of unquestioned authenticity. He charged His followers that since He had attested His claim by conquering death, that they should "go into all the world and preach the gospel to the whole creation. He who believes and is baptized will be saved; but he who does not believe will be condemned."[63] The disciples, who had been fearful and faithless before and during the events of the Passion week now boldly went forth to spread the message of salvation throughout the then-known world.[64]

Out of the first century of our era, when the Resurrection, if untrue, could have easily been disproved by anyone who took the trouble to talk with those who had been present in Jerusalem during the passover week of 33, no contrary historical evidence has come; instead, during that century the number of conversions to Christianity increased by geometric progression, the influence of the Gospel story spreading out of Jerusalem like a gigantic web. If Christ did not rise as He promised, how can we rationally explain this lack of negative evidence and number of conversions ? Furthermore, if the body of the crucified Jesus naturally left the tomb, how did it leave ? Not by its

own accord, for Jesus was unquestionably dead.[65] Not through
the efforts of the Jewish religious leaders or the Romans, for
they had placed a guard at the tomb for the express purpose of
keeping the body there.[59] Not Jesus' followers, for to perform
such an act would have been to deny the principles of truth upon
which their later lives were predicated, and which they
preached until killed for their convictions.[64] If Jesus did not
rise from the dead, what happened to His body in the city teeming with the passover crowd, a great number of whom had been
members of the mob which condemned Him and cried for Him
to be crucified?[55] The weight of historical evidence requires
us to admit the truth of the Resurrection; probability which, as
Giambattista Vico pointed out[66] and vindicated logically, is the
criterion of truth of the historian, must rule over any a priori
considerations in the making of historical judgements. Can
miracles occur ? As Vico said, history and not philosophy must
answer this question.

Conclusion. As we stated above, rational decision between
alternatives must depend upon the probable validity of present
evidence, and upon the possibility of future evidence arising to
negate the force of present evidence. I have now shown that the
evidence for the Resurrection of Jesus Christ is overwhelming
in its force, and therefore that the probable validity of His
claim to Divinity and His assurance that the universe is tele-
ological--God-directed--is likewise extremely high. It should
now be very evident to the reader that the possibility of future
evidence arising to negate the force of the now existing evidence for Christ's claims is almost too small to be entertained:
the evidence for the Resurrection involves only four documents,
whose dates of origin have been determined beyond the shadow
of a doubt. The only relevant new evidence which would be pertinent to this problem would seem to be a discovery of Christ's
remains or of documents from the first century explaining
naturalistically how a Resurrection-hoax was perpetrated; but
the possibility of such data having ever existed is virtually nil,
for almost two thousand years have taken their course without
any data of this variety having been found. Thus, whereas we
have found the evidences of Marxian materialism to be uncon-
vincing and inadequate, we have found the evidence against materialism to be extremely persuasive. As rational creatures
we must make our decision according to probability - and decide against materialism as a metaphysic, and against the
Marxian world-view which is its logical subalternate.

Obviously the discussion in this paper has not been entirely
negative: a world-view has been blasted, but another world-

view has been suggested by implication. The validity of
Christ's Resurrection, the validity of His claims to Divinity,
and the validity of His magnificent statements that He was the
Good Shepherd who had come to lay down His life for the sheep
- the truth of these considerations requires that we fall prostrate at His feet and become united with the Lord of Creation
through His Son. God came to earth "to break the power of
canceled sin, to set the pris'ner free"; and everyone has on the
one hand the opportunity to accept His great gift of eternal life,
and on the other hand the responsibility and privilege to spread
His glorious message of salvation to the ends of the earth.
Thank God that the Marxian philosophy, which advocates hate,
bloodshed, and dictatorship, and which sees the individual as an
expendable item to be sacrificed when the good of the cause demands,[67] will ultimately be conquered by the Cross.

> Lead on, O King Eternal, 'till sin's fierce war shall cease,
> And holiness shall whisper the sweet Amen of peace;
> For not with swords loud clashing, nor roll of stirring
> drums,
> But deeds of love and mercy Thy heavenly Kingdom comes.

> Lead on, O King Eternal, to lands of deepest night;
> We follow where Thou leadest as heralds of the light.
> May we to souls immortal Thy Word of life convey
> And open heaven's portal through Christ, the truth, the way.

> Lead on, O King Eternal, we follow not with fears,
> For gladness breaks like morning where'er Thy face ap-
> pears;
> Thy cross is lifted o'er us, we journey in its light;
> The crown awaits the conquest; lead on O God of might.

Epilogue: Religion Vs. Religion?

Marxism has been termed a "religion" by almost all its
critics, and has been condemned by not a few simply because of
its religious nature. George Catlin says, for example,

> I accuse Marx, by dialectical reaction, of being the own
> father of Fascism and of conflict, cause of so bitter
> miseries in this twentieth century--tantum religio potuit
> suadere malorum.[68]

Perhaps this type of criticism has been occupying the reader's
mind as he has studied my argument against Marxian materialism; perhaps he has said to himself: "If Marxism is to be rejected because it is a religion, as the critics seem to imply,

how utterly foolish it is for this fellow to attempt to invalidate Marx's doctrine by means of another religion!"

Let us see what the critics mean when they condemn Marxism as a religion. It is almost too obvious, in the first place, that these writers do not consider or condemn Marxism as a religion because of Marx or Engels' love for the supernatural: as we have shown in the early sections of this paper, Marx and Engels delivered their most hearty invective against all non-materialistic positions. Marxism is both evangelical and prophetic - are these the considerations to which the critics refer when they attack the "Marxian faith"? I do not believe so, although no one doubts the religio-prophetic elements in Marxism which have come to the surface on occasion: for example, when Engels delivered the funeral address at Marx's burial:[69]

> On the 14th of March, at a quarter of three in the afternoon, the greatest living thinker ceased to think.

> Marx was before all else a revolutionary. His real mission in life was to contribute in one way or another to the overthrow of capitalist society and of the state institutions which it had brought into being, to contribute to the liberation of the present-day proletariat, which he was the first to make conscious of its own position and its needs, of the conditions under which it could win its emancipation.

> Marx was the best hated and most calumniated man of this time. Governments, both absolutist and republican, deported him from their territories. The bourgeoisie, whether conservative or extreme democrat, vied with one another in heaping slanders upon him. All this he brushed aside as though it were cobweb, ignoring it, answering only when necessity compelled him. And now he has died--beloved, revered and mourned by millions of revolutionary fellow-workers--from the mines of Siberia to California, in all parts of Europe and America--and I make bold to say that though he may have many opponents he has hardly one personal enemy.

> His name will endure through the ages, and so also will his work!

In my opinion, when critics condemn Marxism as a religion, they mean to say that Marxism should be rejected because it tenaciously holds certain assumptions a priori - that Marxism has the dogmatic attitude of religions, and like them has rejected the non-dogmatic approach of science.

Marxists profess to reject religion in favor of science, but they cherish a belief that the external universe is evolving with reliable, if not divine, necessity in exactly the direction in which they want it to go. They do not conceive themselves as struggling to build the communist society in a world which is of its own nature indifferent to them. They conceive themselves as traveling toward that society in a world which is like a moving-stairway taking them the way they walk. Their enemies are walking the same stairway, but walking in the wrong direction. This is not a scientific, but in the most technical sense, a religious conception of the world.

Science in its mature forms casts loose from philosophy, just as earlier it cast loose from religion and magic. It contents itself on the theoretical side with specific solutions of specific problems, and on the practical side with methods of procedure for accomplishing specific things. If these solutions and methods imply some general attitude toward the universe at large, then that is conceded tentatively and with reluctance. A quick recourse to skepticism, a readiness to say 'I don't know' whenever as a simple matter of fact you do not know--is the surest mark of an advanced scientific mind, whether practical or theoretical.[70]

If these criticisms of religion are warranted, it is evident that my argument against materialism and the Marxist system needs drastic revision. Yet I am convinced that some thought on the matter will make clear that these criticisms are without force, because every world-view, whether philosophical, religious, or scientific, is necessarily based upon a premise or premises held a priori.[71] A realization that presuppositions exist in all world-views and methodologies should make clear that to condemn Marxism by calling it a religion, and to condemn religion because it is based upon a priori assumptions, is to employ a ridiculous philosophical procedure. Like all other systems, the Science which Eastman applauds is based on metaphysical assumptions, and can be condemned by the same argument Eastman uses against religion in general and Marxism in particular. Dr. Edward John Carnell argues:

The enigmatic situation in the modern world is that the scientist rejects the Christian world-view because it involves certain non-empirical, metaphysical hypotheses, while assuming for himself a truckload, each of which goes as much beyond sensory observation as does the Christian's postulate of the God Who has revealed Himself in Scripture. The Christian questions the sport of this game. Fair rules in the

contest of hypothesis-making ought to dictate that the winner
be he who can produce the best set of assumptions to account
for the totality of reality. If the Christian is disqualified
from the arena by rules which his opponent makes, it is evident that the game has been "fixed." Good sportsmanship,
to say nothing of common sense, requires that in a contest,
all participants be given the same advantages as well as the
same handicaps. Without these conditions, there is no
sport.[7][2]

Thus we are back where we started: there is nothing per se
wrong with religion, and the rational man must decide on his
world-view in terms of empirical probability. The real problem of life is not to attempt to find world-views not based on
assumptions (for there are none, nor will there ever be any),
but to evaluate the evidence presented in behalf of the most
compelling philosophical systems, and then to make a choice
among them. In this paper I have discussed at length the evidences for the basic assumptions of two such systems, Marxism
and Christianity, for the benefit of those who say with Pope:

> Farewell then, verse, and love, and ev'ry toy,
> The rhymes and rattles of the man or boy;
> What right, what true, what fit we justly call,
> Let this be all my care - for this is all.

-Imitation of the First Epistle
of the First Book of Horace.

NOTES

1. Randall and Buchler, Philosophy: An Introduction, p. 183.

2. Quoted ibid., p. 184.

3. Lucretius, De Rerum Natura, III. 161-76 (trans. Bailey).

4. "Marx's doctoral thesis at Jena, in 1841, was On the Difference between the Natural Philosophy of Democritus and Epicurus. He liked the materialist in Epicurus but disliked his
doctrine of chance, its undogmatic probabilism, its untidi-
ness. . . . He began as he ended, materialist but anti-
empiric" (Catlin, The Story of the Political Philosophers,
p. 563).

5. Leviathan, Pt. IV, Ch. 46. (Everyman edition, intro. A. D.
Lindsay, pp. 367-8.)

6. Ludwig Buchner, Force and Matter, pp. 242-3.

7. Marx, Capital (quoted in Venable, Human Nature: The Marxian View, p. 7).

8. Marx, Preface to Critique of Political Economy (quoted in Gray, The Socialist Tradition, pp. 302-3).

9. Marx, The Eighteenth Brumaire of Louis Bonaparte (in Karl Marx, Selected Works, Vol. II).

10. Marx and Engels, The German Ideology, Parts I and III, p. 16. See also ibid., pp. 7, 14-15.

11. Engels, Speech at the Graveside of Karl Marx (in Selected Works, Vol. I, p. 16).

12. Engels, The Origin of the Family, Private Property, and the State, p. 5 (Preface to the First Edition).

13. Engels, Feuerbach, The Roots of the Socialist Philosophy, pp. 58, 53. Catlin writes (op. cit., p. 563): "In 1841 Ludwig Feuerbach published a book that was to do much to "fix" Marx's thought, his Essence of Christianity--in which he maintained inter alia that the substance of the right religion was a nutritious diet, chiefly beans. . . . Feuerbach in fact is maintaining the entirely intelligible proposition [!] that hunger determined religion, not religion hunger; that the essence of Christianity is brotherly love; and that this becomes thin on an empty stomach."

14. Engels, Dialectics of Nature, pp. 157, 193-6. Cf., Engels, Anti-Duehring, pp. 113-14. Venable says (op. cit., p. 58): "Marx and Engels . . . take their stand unequivocally against all doctrines of divine creation of the first organisms on the one hand, and the pan-vitalistic alternative that was proposed by even such people as Liebig and Helmholtz on the other."

15. Ibid., pp. 570, 572.

16. Gray, op. cit., p. 305.

17. Catlin, op. cit., p. 569.

18. Sabine, A History of Political Theory, p. 637.

19. Ibid., p. 642. See the excellent discussion of Hegelian and Marxian dialectic in Sabine, Chs. XXX ("Hegel: Dialectic and Nationalism") and XXXIII ("Marx and Dialectical Materialism").

20. Venable, op. cit., p. 37. See the quotation corresponding to note 7.

21. Marx and Engels, The German Ideology, pp. 28-9.

22. Engels, at the annual conference of the German Socialists (quoted in Catlin, op. cit., pp. 578-9). See the quotations corresponding to notes 8-12.

23. "Proletariat and wealth are opposites. As such they form a whole. . . . Private property as private property, as wealth, is compelled to maintain its own existence, and therewith the existence of its opposite, the proletariat. It is the positive side of the contrast, private property satisfied with itself. The proletariat, on the other hand, is compelled as proletariat to abolish itself, and therewith to abolish private property, the opposite that has determined its own existence, that has made it into a proletariat" (Marx, The Holy Family; quoted in Catlin, op. cit., p. 593).

24. See section IV of Marx's Critique of the Gotha Programme (in Selected Works, Vol. II, pp. 576-80). Cf. with the text all footnotes.

25. On this aspect of Marxian theory, see Keith McDonald's excellent article, "Marxism: An Analysis and Criticism," HIS, Dec., 1947, pp. 6-13.

26. Marx and Engels, The Communist Manifesto (Authorized English Translation), p. 44. See all of section IV.

27. For a fuller discussion of the problem of logical dependencies between truth-functions, see Ambrose and Lazerowitz, Fundamentals of Symbolic Logic, pp. 84-91.

28. One should take care to notice that it is unimportant for our argument whether the essential elements of Marxism depend upon each other in transitivity relationships or not.

The important thing is that these elements are each the consequents of a subalternation relation of which material-ism is the antecedent. I.e., we are not concerned whether

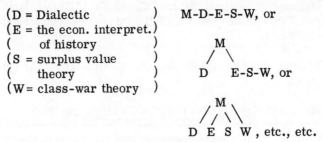

(D = Dialectic   )   M-D-E-S-W, or
(E = the econ. interpret.)
(of history   )   M
(S = surplus value   )   / \
(theory   )   D   E-S-W, or
(W= class-war theory)
                                     M
                                   / / \ \
                              D E S W , etc., etc.

Rather, we are concerned whether

M subalt. D
M subalt. E
M subalt. S
M subalt. W.

29. Catlin, op. cit., p. 587.

30. The subalternate relationship between materialism and the Marxist philosophy precludes the criticism of our method that a valid argument may have false premises but a true conclusion. This latter is true in an implication relation-ship (A → B), but not in a subalternate relationship. If two statements are subalternate, the falsity of the antecedent requires the falsity of the consequent.

31. Catlin, op. cit., p. 572. The preceding quotation from Russell appears ibid., p. 580.

32. See Engels, On Historical Materialism.

33. The Second Law of Thermodynamics states that in an iso-lated system the entropy, that is to say the amount of energy unavailable for work, tends toward a maximum, or, more simply, that heat cannot pass of its own accord from a colder to a hotter body. The Clausian formula for entropy (formulated by Clausius, a German physicist, in 1850) states that other forms of motion will ultimately be con-verted into heat, and thus will be spread out at a uniform temperature - the result being that change of all kinds will eventually come to an end.

34. Engels, <u>Dialectics of Nature</u>, pp. 194-5.

35. <u>Ibid.</u>, pp. 190-97.

36. Marx to Engels, Dec. 19, 1860; letter in Marx and Engels, <u>Correspondence 1846-1895, A Selection with Commentary and Notes</u>, p. 126. (Marx "had been nursing his wife through a severe illness.")

37. Marx to Lassalle, Jan. 16, 1861; <u>ibid.</u>, p. 125. Venable, <u>op. cit.</u>, pp. 56-7: "The phenomena of life had an origin in time, appearing on the earth when the temperature and atmosphere had become suitable, developing through long ages the various differentiations which characterize the species we find today as well as those extinct forms whose records have been left in skeletons and fossils. This evolutionary view is probably the chief theoretical source of their materialism."

38. Polygenesis - the theory that the various species of plants and animals have decended from numerous primordial ancestors rather than from one or a very few.

39. Goldschmidt, <u>The Material Basis of Evolution</u>, pp. 6, 168, 183.

40. Morgan, <u>Evolution and Adaptation</u>, p. 43.

41. See for example: Th. Graebner, <u>Evolution: An Investigation and a Criticism</u>; Anthony Standen, <u>Science is a Sacred Cow</u> (Ch. IV); American Scientific Affiliation, <u>Modern Science and Christian Faith</u>; L. T. Moore, <u>The Dogma of Evolution</u>. Cf., the prophetically accurate and long disregarded statement of Darwin's former professor, Dr. Adam Sedgwick, Woodwardian Professor of Geology in Cambridge University, written exactly one month after the publication of <u>The Origin of Species</u>: "You have deserted--after a start in that tram-road of all solid physical truth--the true method of induction, and started us in machinery as wild, I think, as Bishop Wilkin's locomotive that was to sail with us to the moon. Many of your wide conclusions are based upon assumptions which can neither be proved nor disproved; why then express them in the language and arrangement of philosophical induction?"

42. Engels, The Origin of the Family, Private Property, and the State, pp. 7-8 ("Preface to the Fourth Edition"): "Before the beginning of the 'sixties, one cannot speak of a history of the family. In this field, the science of history was still completely under the influence of the five books of Moses. The patriarchal form of the family, which was there described in greater detail than anywhere else, was not only assumed without question to be the oldest form, but it was also identified--minus its polygamy--with the bourgeois family of today, so that the family had really experienced no historical development at all." Marx, Thesis on Feuerbach, VI (in Selected Works, I, pp. 472-3): "The human essence is no abstraction inherent in each separate individual. In its reality it is the ensemble of the social relations."

43. Venable, op. cit., p. 19.

44. Engels, Dialectic of Nature, pp. 176-7.

45. See, for example, Matt. 5:44-5, 48; 6:7-13; 19:26; 22:29; Luke 6:35-6; 13:23-29; 18:27; John 3:16; 4:10, 24; 5:26; 7:18; 14:31; 15:9; 20:17. Note especially John 17. N.B. The reader is very strongly encouraged to look up and examine carefully all Bible references cited in this and the following footnotes. The Revised Standard Version has been used for Bible quotations throughout this paper.

46. Matt. 11:27: "All things have been delivered to me by my Father; and no one knows the Son except the Father, and no one knows the Father except the Son and any one to whom the Son chooses to reveal him." John 12:45: "And he who sees me sees him who sent me." John 10:30: "I and the Father are one." Matt. 16:13-17: "Now when Jesus came into the district of Caesarea Philippi, he asked his disciples, 'Who do men say that the Son of man is?' And they said, 'Some say that you are John the Baptist, others say Elijah, and others Jeremiah or one of the prophets.' He said to them, 'But who do you say that I am?' Simon Peter replied, 'You are the Christ, the Son of the living God.' And Jesus answered him, 'Blessed are you, Simon Bar-Jona! For flesh and blood has not revealed this to you, but my Father who is in heaven.'" See also Matt. 12:8; 26:63-5; Mark 2:5-7; Luke 3:21-2; 6:5; 22:66-71; John 3:13-18; 5:23; 8:58; 10:38.

47. Mark 10:45: "For the Son of man also came not to be served but to serve, and to give his life as a ransom for many." Matt. 26:26-8: "Now as they were eating, Jesus took break, and blessed, and broke it, and gave it to the disciples and said, 'Take, eat; this is my body.' And he took a cup, and when he had given thanks he gave it to them, saying, 'Drink of it, all of you; for this is my blood of the covenant, which is poured out for many for the forgiveness of sins.'" John 10:11: "I am the good shepherd. The good shepherd lays down his life for the sheep." See also Matt. 18:11; 20:28; Luke 12:50; 19:10; 22:37; John 3:14-17; 10:17-18.

48. John 14:6-11: "Jesus said to him, 'I am the way, and the truth, and the life; no one comes to the Father, but by me. If you had known me, you would have known my Father also; henceforth you know him and have seen him.' Philip said to him, 'Lord, show us the Father, and we shall be satisfied.' Jesus said to him, 'Have I been with you so long, and yet you do not know me, Philip? He who has seen me has seen the Father; how can you say, "Show us the Father"? Do you not believe that I am in the Father and the Father in me? The words that I say to you I do not speak on my own authority; but the Father who dwells in me does his works. Believe me that I am in the Father and the Father in me; or else believe me for the sake of the works themselves.'"

49. Jesus claimed in such passages as Matt. 5:17-18 that the Old Testament is the valid revelation of God. In Genesis, Chs. 1 and 2, we find the account of God's creation activity.

50. Luke 12:6-7: "Are not five sparrows sold for two pennies? And not one of them is forgotten before God. Why, even the hairs of your head are all numbered. Fear not; you are of more value than many sparrows." Cf., Matt. 10:29-31.

51. John 5:25-9: "Truly, truly, I say to you, the hour is coming, and now is, when the dead will hear the voice of the Son of God, and those who hear will live. For as the Father has life in himself, so he has granted the Son also to have life in himself, and has given him authority to execute judgment, because he is the Son of man. Do not marvel at this; for the hour is coming when all who are in the tombs will hear his voice and come forth, those who have done good, to the resurrection of life, and those who have done evil, to the

resurrection of judgment." Matt. 13: 36-43: "Then he left
the crowds and went into the house. And his disciples came
to him, saying, 'Explain to us the parable of the seeds of the
field.' He answered, 'He who sows the good seed is the Son
of man; the field is the world, and the good seed means the
sons of the kingdom; the weeds are the sons of the evil one,
and the enemy who sowed them is the devil; the harvest is
the close of the age, and the reapers are angels. Just as the
weeds are gathered and burned with fire, so will it be at the
close of the age. The Son of man will send his angels, and
they will gather out of his kingdom all causes of sin and all
evil-doers, and throw them into the furnace of fire; there
men will weep and gnash their teeth. Then the righteous
will shine like the sun in the kingdom of their Father. He
who has ears, let him hear.'" See also Matt. 7:21-3; 16:24-
7; 24; 25:31-46; 26:64; Mark 8:38; 14:62; Luke 12:35-40;
21; John 14:3.

52. With regard to the dates of the Synoptic Gospels (Matthew,
Mark, and Luke), Dr. Wilbur M. Smith, the great Christian
apologist and bibliographer, says, after surveying the
opinions of scholars who are authorities on this subject: "I
think . . . we would be safe in saying that the general consensus of opinion among the outstanding New Testament
scholars of our generation is, that all three of the synoptic
gospels were written by 80 A.D., and that none of them were
composed before, say, 55 A.D. In other words, Matthew,
Mark, and Luke . . . were all written within half a century
of our Lord's death" (The Supernaturalness of Christ, p.
39). Dr. Hugo Odeberg, Professor of New Testament Interpretation at the University of Lund, Sweden, says of the
Gospel of John: "The oldest fragment of a copy of a New
Testament Scripture which has so far been discovered is
the fragment of the Gospel of John found in 1935. This
fragment was in a group of papyrus which had been classi-
fied under the nineties of the first century A.D., and could
not be placed later than the very beginning of the second
century. But let us remember that this papyrus is only a
copy. This proves that the Gospel of John was known and
that copies of it had been spread as far as Egypt by about
A.D. 100. Clearly then, the original, the Gospel of John itself, must have been in existence before any copies of it
could be made. All theories about the Gospel which rest on
the assumption that the Gospel originally dates from some
decade in the second century, long after the death of the

Apostle John, have therefore become entirely unhistorical"
("The Authorship of St. John's Gospel," Concordia Theological Monthly, April, 1951, p. 246). How far from objective historical analysis is Engels' flippant and cynical dismissal of Matthew, Mark, Luke, and John as "the gospel
myths!" (Feuerbach, The Roots of the Socialist Philosophy,
pp. 51-2).

53. John 2:18-22: "The Jews then said to him, 'What sign have
you to show us for doing this ?' Jesus answered them,
'Destroy this temple, and in three days I will raise it up.'
The Jews then said, 'It has taken forty-six years to build
this temple, and will you raise it up in three days ?' But he
spoke of the temple of his body. When therefore he was
raised from the dead, his disciples remembered that he had
said this; and they believed the scripture and the word
which Jesus had spoken." Matt. 16:21: "From that time
Jesus began to show his disciples that he must go to Jerusalem and suffer many things from the elders and chief
priests and scribes, and be killed, and on the third day be
raised." Also see Matt. 20:17-19; 26:31-2; Mark 8:31-32a;
9:9; 14:27-8; Luke 9:22.

54. Mark 2:5-7: "And when Jesus saw their faith, he said to the
paralytic, 'My son, your sins are forgiven.' Now some of
the scribes were sitting there, questioning in their hearts,
'Why does this man speak thus ? It is blasphemy! Who can
forgive sins but God alone ?'" Mark 14:55-65: "Now the
chief priests and the whole council sought testimony against
Jesus, to put him to death; but they found none. For many
bore false witness against him, and their witness did not
agree. And some stood up and bore false witness against
him, saying, 'We heard him say, "I will destroy this temple
that is made with hands, and in three days I will build another, not made with hands." ' Yet not even so did their testimony agree. And the high priest stood up in the midst,
and asked Jesus, 'Have you no answer to make ? What is it
that these men testify against you ?' But he was silent and
made no answer. Again the high priest asked him, 'Are you
the Christ, the Son of the Blessed ?' And Jesus said, 'I am;
and you will see the Son of man sitting at the right hand of
Power, and coming with the clouds of heaven.' And the high
priest tore his mantle, and said, 'Why do we still need witnesses ? You have heard his blasphemy. What is your decision ?' And they all condemned him as deserving death.

And some began to spit on him, and to cover his face, and to strike him, saying to him, 'Prophesy!' And the guards received him with blows." Luke 23:1-5: "Then the whole company of them arose, and brought him before Pilate. And they began to accuse him, saying, 'We found this man perverting our nation, and forbidding us to give tribute to Caesar, and saying that he himself is Christ a king.' And Pilate asked him, 'Are you the King of the Jews?' And he answered him, 'You have said so.' And Pilate said to the chief priests and the multitudes, 'I find no crime in this man.' But they were urgent, saying, 'He stirs up the people, teaching throughout all Judea, from Galilee even to this place.'" John 19:6-7, 12: "Upon this Pilate sought to release him, but the Jews cried out, 'If you release this man, you are not Caesar's friend; every one who makes himself a king sets himself against Caesar.'" See also Matt. 26:63-5; Luke 22:66-71; John 10:30-33.

55. Matt. 26:47, 55: "While he was still speaking, Judas came, one of the twelve, and with him a great crowd with swords and clubs, from the chief priests and the elders of the people. At that hour Jesus said to the crowds, 'Have you come out as against a robber with swords and clubs to capture me? Day after day I sat in the temple teaching and you did not seize me.'" Matt. 27:22-5: "Pilate said to them, 'Then what shall I do with Jesus who is called Christ?' They all said, 'Let him be crucified.' And he said, 'Why, what evil has he done?' But they shouted all the more, 'Let him be crucified.' So when Pilate saw that he was gaining nothing, but rather that a riot was beginning, he took water and washed his hands before the crowd, saying, 'I am innocent of this man's blood; see to it yourselves.' And all the people answered, 'His blood be on us and on our children!'" See also Matt. 21:8-11; 27:39-43.

56. Matt. 27:45, 50-53: "Now from the sixth hour there was darkness over all the land until the ninth hour. And Jesus cried again with a loud voice and yielded up his spirit. And behold, the curtain of the temple was torn in two, from top to bottom; and the earth shook, and the rocks were split; the tombs also were opened, and many bodies of the saints who had fallen asleep were raised, and coming out of the tombs after his resurrection they went into the holy city and appeared to many."

57. Luke 23:50-53: "Now there was a man named Joseph from the Jewish town of Arimathea. He was a member of the council, a good and righteous man, who had not consented to their purpose and deed, and he was looking for the kingdom of God. This man went to Pilate and asked for the body of Jesus. Then he took it down and wrapped it in a linen shroud, and laid him in a rock-hewn tomb, where no one had ever yet been laid."

58. Matt. 27:59-60: "And Joseph took the body, and wrapped it in a clean linen shroud, and laid it in his own new tomb, which he had hewn in the rock; and he rolled a great stone to the entrance of the tomb, and departed." Mark 16:1-4: "And when the sabbath was past, Mary Magdalene, and Mary the mother of James, and Salome, bought spices, so that they might go and anoint him. And very early on the first day of the week they went to the tomb when the sun had risen. And they were saying to one another, 'Who will roll away the stone for us from the door of the tomb?' And looking up, they saw that the stone was rolled back; for it was very large."

59. Matt. 27:62-6: "Next day, that is after the day of Preparation, the chief priests and the Pharisees gathered before Pilate and said, 'Sir, we remember how that impostor said, while he was still alive, "After three days I will rise again." Therefore order the tomb to be made secure until the third day, lest his disciples go and steal him away, and tell the people, "He has risen from the dead," and the last fraud will be worse than the first.' Pilate said to them, 'You have a guard of soldiers; go, make it as secure as you can.' So they went and made the tomb secure by sealing the stone and setting a guard."

60. Matt. 28:1-10: "Now after the sabbath, toward the dawn of the first day of the week, Mary Magdalene and the other Mary went to see the tomb. And behold, there was a great earthquake; for an angel of the Lord descended from heaven and came and rolled back the stone, and sat upon it. His appearance was like lightning, and his raiment white as snow. And for fear of him the guards trembled and became like dead men. But the angel said to the women, 'Do not be afraid; for I know that you seek Jesus who was crucified. He is not here; for he has risen, as he said. Come, see the place where he lay. Then go quickly and tell his disciples

that he has risen from the dead, and behold, he is going before you to Galilee; there you will see him. Lo, I have told you.' So they departed quickly from the tomb with fear and great joy, and ran to tell his disciples. And behold, Jesus met them and said, 'Hail!' And they came up and took hold of his feet and worshiped him. Then Jesus said to them, 'Do not be afraid; go and tell my brothers to go to Galilee, and there they will see me.'"

61. Luke 24:36-43: "As they were saying this, Jesus himself stood among them. But they were startled and frightened and supposed that they saw a spirit. And he said to them, 'Why are you troubled, and why do questionings rise in your hearts? See my hands and my feet, that it is I myself; handle me, and see; for a spirit has not flesh and bones as you see that I have.' And while they still disbelieved for joy, and wondered, he said to them, 'Have you anything here to eat?' They gave him a piece of broiled fish, and he took it and ate before them." John 20:25-28: "So the other disciples told him, 'We have seen the Lord.' But he said to them, 'Unless I see in his hands the prints of the nails, and place my finger in the mark of the nails, and place my hand in his side, I will not believe.' Eight days later, his disciples were again in the house, and Thomas was with them. The doors were shut, but Jesus came and stood among them, and said, 'Peace be with you.' Then he said to Thomas, 'Put your finger here, and see my hands; and put out your hand, and place it in my side; do not be faithless, but believing.' Thomas answered him, 'My Lord and my God.'"

62. See Matt. 28; Mark 16:1-8; Luke 24; John 20, 21.

63. Mark 16:15-16 (traditional statement of the Great Commission); cf. parallel passage, Matt. 28:18-20.

64. See Luke 22:54-62.

65. John 19:32-35: "So the soldiers came and broke the legs of the first, and of the other who had been crucified with him; but when they came to Jesus and saw that he was already dead, they did not break his legs. But one of the soldiers pierced his side with a spear, and at once there came out blood and water."

66. See above, my essay, "Vico and the Christian Faith."

67. Catlin, op. cit., p. 591: "The further question is, how a regime of communist co-operation, equity and equality is to
be introduced by the inflammation of hate, not only between
capitalist and non-capitalist nations, but within the former,
and until liquidation of opponents is complete, also within
the latter. Marx temperamentally was antipathetic to the
charitable gospel of Weitling, and even (on this point) of
Feuerbach and of Owen--as well as of Marx père. He found
more satisfaction in the teaching, to which vogue had been
given by the poet Byron, sadist turned pilgrim penitent, that
there was something to be said for hate. Hate has the advantage of insuring persecution, making martyrs, inciting to
sacrifice and discipline and, hence, of being a good principle of organisation." Cf., Orwell, 1984, p. 200: "Now I will
tell you the answer to my question. It is this. The Party
seeks power entirely for its own sake. We are not interested in the good of others; we are interested solely in power.
Not wealth or luxury or long life or happiness; only power,
pure power. What pure power means you will understand
presently. We are different from all the oligarchies of the
past in that we know what we are doing. All the others,
even those who resembled ourselves, were cowards and
hypocrites. The German Nazis and the Russian Communists
came very close to us in their methods, but they never had
the courage to recognize their own motives. They pretend-
ed, perhaps they even believed, that they had seized power
unwillingly and for a limited time, and that just round the
corner there lay a paradise where human beings would be
free and equal. We are not like that. We know that no one
ever seizes power with the intention of relinquishing it.
Power is not means; it is an end. One does not establish a
dictatorship in order to safeguard a revolution; one makes
the revolution in order to establish the dictatorship. The
object of persecution is persecution. The object of torture
is torture. The object of power is power. Now do you begin to understand me?" The reader is strongly encouraged
to read the whole of this excellent novel which portrays
Marxist-Leninist philosophy carried to its logical and terri-
fying conclusion.

68. Catlin, op. cit., p. 598.

69. Engels, Speech at the Graveside of Karl Marx (in Selected
Works, I, pp. 16-18).

70. Eastman, Marxism: Is It Science, Pt. I and p. 20.

71. Carnell, An Introduction to Christian Apologetics, pp. 91-2:
"It may be asked why we make assumptions at all. Why not
stay with the facts? The answer to this is very easy indeed! We make assumptions because we must make assumptions to think at all. All knowledge is inferential and
all inferences are assumptions. Knowledge is the mind's
construction of meaning, and properly construed meaning is
truth. It is therefore useless to say, 'Stay with the facts,'
unless we mean, 'Keep your hypotheses in conformity to
facts.' Facts just are. Knowledge is inference drawn from
facts. A fact is any unit of being which is capable of bearing
meaning, but it is the meaning not the fact, which is the
knowledge."

72. Carnell, op. cit., pp. 94-5.

BIBLIOGRAPHY

Ambrose, Alice and Lazerowitz, Morris. Fundamentals of
Symbolic Logic. New York: Rinehart and Company, 1950.

American Scientific Affiliation. Modern Science and Christian
Faith. Wheaton (Ill.): Van Kampen Press, 1948. (A 2d,
improved edition appeared in 1950.)

Burtt, Edwin A. Types of Religious Philosophy. New York and
London: Harper and Brothers, 1939. (A revised edition was
published in 1951.)

Carnell, Edward J. An Introduction to Christian Apologetics.
Grand Rapids (Mich.): William B. Eerdmans Publishing
Company, 1948.

Catlin, George. The Story of the Political Philosophers. New
York and London: Whittlesey House, 1939.

Eastman, Max. Marxism: Is It Science. New York: W. W.
Norton and Company, 1940.

Engels, Friedrich. Feuerbach - The Roots of the Socialist
Philosophy. Chicago: Charles Kerr and Company, 1903.

_____. Landmarks of Scientific Socialism - (Anti-Duehring). Chicago: Charles Kerr and Company, 1907.

_____. On Historical Materialism. New York: International Publishers, 1940.

_____. The Origin of the Family, Private Property and the State. New York: International Publishers, 1942.

Goldschmidt, Richard B. The Material Basis of Evolution. New Haven: Yale University Press, 1940.

Graebner, Th. Evolution: An Investigation and a Criticism. Milwaukee: Northwestern Publishing House, 1929.

Gray, Alexander. The Socialist Tradition, Moses to Lenin. London, New York, and Toronto: Longmans, Green and Company, 1946.

Hobbes, Thomas. Leviathan. London: J. M. Dent and Sons, Ltd.; New York: E. P. Dutton and Company, Inc., 1914.

Marx, Karl. Selected Works. Prepared by the Marx-Engels-Lenin Institute, Moscow, under the editorship of V. Adoratsky. New York: International Publishers, n.d. 2 vols.

Marx, Karl and Engels, Friedrich. Correspondence 1846-1895, A Selection with Commentary and Notes. ("The only edition authorised by the Marx-Engels-Lenin Institute Moscow.") London: Martin Lawrence Ltd., 1934.

_____, _____. The Communist Manifesto. New York: International Publishers, 1948.

_____, _____. The German Ideology, Parts I and III. Ed. R. Pascal. New York: International Publishers, 1939.

McDonald, Keith. "Marxism: An Analysis and Criticism." HIS (Publication of the Inter-Varsity Christian Fellowship). Vol. 7, No. 12 (December, 1947), pp. 6-13.

Moore, L. T. The Dogma of Evolution. Princeton: Princeton University Press.

Morgan, T. H. Evolution and Adaptation. New York: The MacMillan Company, 1903.

Odeberg, Hugo. "The Authorship of St. John's Gospel." Concordia Theological Monthly. Vol. 22, No. 4 (April, 1951), p. 246.

Orwell, George, 1984. New York: The New American Library of World Literature, Inc., 1950.

Plekhanov, Georgi. The Materialist Conception of History. New York: International Publishers, 1940.

_____. The Role of the Individual in History. New York: International Publishers, 1940.

Randall, John Herman and Buchler, Justus. Philosophy: An Introduction. New York: Barnes and Noble, 1947.

Sabine, George H. A History of Political Theory. New York: Henry Holt and Company, 1937. (A 2d edition appeared in 1950, and a 3d edition in 1961.)

Smith, Wilbur. The Supernaturalness of Christ. Boston: W. A. Wilde and Company, 1940.

Standen, Anthony. Science Is a Sacred Cow. New York: E. P. Dutton and Company, Inc., 1950.

Venable, Vernon. Human Nature: The Marxian View. New York: Alfred A. Knopf, 1946.

3. CONSTRUCTIVE RELIGIOUS EMPIRICISM: AN ANALYSIS AND CRITICISM

I. THE MEANING OF CONSTRUCTIVE RELIGIOUS EMPIRICISM

Introduction and Definition

The method of approach to religious problems which Dr. Edwin A. Burtt terms "Constructive Religious Empiricism"[1] will be analyzed in this paper. Such an analysis needs no justification because Constructive Religious Empiricism not only lies at the very basis of the powerful and influential "modernist" or "liberal" movement in Protestantism, but also plays a large part in the thinking of humanists and other religious "leftists."

Although precise definitions of Constructive Religious Empiricism are seldom made, the general nature of the method may be seen from passages such as the following--the former written by John Dewey, the latter by William James:

> There are many religionists who are now dissatisfied with the older "proofs" of the existence of God, those that go by the name of ontological, cosmological and teleological. The cause of the dissatisfaction is perhaps not so much the arguments that Kant used to show the insufficiency of these alleged proofs, as it is the growing feeling that they are too formal to offer any support to religion in action. Anyway, the dissatisfaction exists. Moreover, these religionists are moved by the rise of the experimental method in other fields. What is more natural and proper, accordingly, than that they should affirm they are just as good empiricists as anybody else--indeed, as good as the scientists themselves? As the latter rely upon certain kinds of experience to prove the existence of certain kinds of objects, so the religionists rely upon a certain kind of experience to prove the existence of the object of religion, especially the supreme object, God.[2]

> As the science of optics has to be fed in the first instance, and continually verified later, by facts experienced by seeing

persons; so the science of religions would depend for its original material on facts of personal experience, and would have to square itself with personal experience through all its critical reconstructions. It could never get away from concrete life, or work in a conceptual vacuum. It would forever have to confess, as every science confesses, that the subtlety of nature flies beyond it, and that its formulas are but approximations.[3]

The above statements suggest that Constructive Religious Empiricism is a method for arriving at religious truth by empirically investigating subjective religious experience. Let us first study in detail the method described in this definition, and then evaluate it by seeing if it is capable of attaining its object.

Empirical Method Applied to Religious Experience

The chief methods of arriving at truth are four, the first two of which are commonly employed by the layman and the last two of which are the usual methods of the educated investigator. These are: common sense, authority, intuition, and empirical or scientific method.[4] Common sense, the most unsophisticated of these methods, is in reality a combination of the other three; it may be defined as the almost unconscious and certainly uncritical activity of acquiring self-evident and commonly held beliefs through experience. The authoritarian method requires that the individual relinquish his independent efforts to determine what is true or false, and transfer this function to another individual, group of individuals, or institution which seems to be in a better position to exercise it. Typical authorities are custom, tradition, revelation, consensus gentium. Intuition presupposes that truth can be known by direct insight or immediate awareness--that there are certain principles which need not be tested for error because, being self-evident, they guarantee their own truth. The intuitive approach is used both by mystics and by rationalist philosophers and theologians, the latter often deducing complex systems from principles which they hold to be intuitively true. Empirical or scientific method is a process which consists of (1) the investigation of the universe by observations, (2) the verification of these observations by others, (3) the drawing of generalizations (hypotheses) from these verified observations, (4) the verification of these hypotheses by others, etc., etc.

As the name implies, Constructive Religious Empiricism employs the empirical method in its search for truth; by doing this it separates itself from the intuitive approach and allies itself with modern science. Concerning the approach to truth of Constructive Religious Empiricism, Shailer Mathews says:[5]

Modernists endeavor to reach beliefs and their application in the same way that chemists or historians reach and apply their conclusions. They do not vote in conventions and do not enforce beliefs by discipline. Modernism has no Confession. Its theological affirmations are the formulation of results of investigation both of human needs and the Christian religion. The Dogmatist relies on conformity through group authority; the Modernist, upon inductive method and action in accord with group loyalty.

Since empiricism refers to method and not to subject matter, it is necessary to know not merely that Constructive Religious Empiricism employs empirical method, but also that it deals with subjective rather than objective data. Like psychology, Constructive Religious Empiricism empirically investigates internal, subjective experience. In this respect it is unlike history and the physical and biological sciences, which also employ empirical method, but which deal primarily with objective data.

Religion is increasingly dealt with today not in ecclesiastical or theological, but in psychological terms. Increasing numbers of people mean by religion, not first of all a true church or an orthodox system of theology, but a psychological experience.

Our real task is to achieve a religion which saves people; and such religion must be primarily an individual, psychological experience.[6]

The indispensable demand of the religio-psychological method is that the question of the truth of religion must be approached fundamentally in the light of the question of its nature. This demand seems to be purely self-evident. And looking solely at the fact itself it really is ultimately self-evident, but looked at from the point of view of the usual methods of study it is far from being self-evident.

The demand means that in dealing with the question of the truth of religion our foremost interest must be concentrated upon uncovering and making clear the basis of validity which religion itself contains. The truth of religion cannot be proved from without but it must be established from within.[7]

Constructive Religious Empiricism does not investigate all varieties of subjective experience; its interest centers upon what is today usually termed "religious experience." In his Humanism: A New Religion, Charles Francis Potter says:

> The new science of religion begins with the known phenomena, namely, the religious experience of man, and works toward the unknown. It admits that God is as yet unknown. In fact, if we are to have any science of religion at all, it must be agnostic about God. We may discover God some day, and we may not. To start with God is to beg the whole question and to place religion in the same category with alchemy and astrology.[8]

The Aim of Constructive Religious Empiricism

Criticism of a method consists in evaluating the effectiveness with which the method accomplishes its aim. It is therefore of utmost importance for us to determine the purpose of Constructive Religious Empiricism. The first point to recognize is that Constructive Religious Empiricism is not interested in religious experience for its own sake. The fact that Constructive Religious Empiricism is empirical shows us that it is concerned with formulating hypotheses and verifying them by men's religious experiences. Thus religious experiences themselves are not the sole concern of the constructive religious empiricist; their function is to provide the body of data by which he tests the truth of his hypotheses. One of the most famous constructive religious empiricists, William James, says in his Varieties of Religious Experience:

> These very lectures which I am giving are (as you will see more clearly from now onwards) a laborious attempt to extract from the privacies of religious experience some general facts which can be defined in formulas upon which everybody may agree.[9]

For two main reasons it is easy to confuse constructive religious empiricists with those who engage simply in descriptive studies of religious experience. (1) Knowing that Constructive Religious Empiricism lies at the basis of virtually all modernist thinking, some are led to the false belief that Constructive Religious Empiricism is the chief concept in the thinking of all humanists who are interested in religion. Those who do believe this, when they come upon humanists like John Dewey who are genuinely interested in religious experience, but at the same time declaim against those who would attempt by religious experience to test hypotheses concerned with metaphysical issues, think that the aim of Constructive Religious

Empiricism is to study religious experience for its own sake. A study of the following two passages from Dewey's A Common Faith will make clear the distinction between his approach and that of Constructive Religious Empiricism:

> The historic increase of the ethical and ideal content of religions suggests that the process of purification may be carried further. It indicates that further choice is imminent in which certain values and functions in experience may be selected. This possibility is what I had in mind in speaking of the difference between the religious and a religion. I am not proposing a religion, but rather the emancipating of elements and outlooks that may be called religious. For the moment we have a religion, whether that of the Sioux Indian or of Judaism or of Christianity, that moment the ideal factors in experience that may be called religious take on a load that is not inherent in them, a load of current beliefs and of institutional practices that are irrelevant to them.

> Now at present there is much talk, especially in liberal circles, of religious experience as vouching for the authenticity of certain beliefs and the desirability of certain practices, such as particular forms of prayer and worship. It is even asserted that religious experience is the ultimate basis of religion itself. The gulf between this position and that which I have taken is what I am now concerned to point out.[10]

(2) One of the reasons which constructive religious empiricists use to explain why they apply empirical method to subjective rather than objective data, is that the average layman is interested far more in the experiential than in the metaphysical aspects of religion.

> Why does a man become a Christian in the first place? Not because of his acceptance of any formal line of argumentation, but because he has been impressed with the beauty and power of the Christian spirit, individually embodied in some parent, or friend, or pastor, and socially embodied in what we call the "atmosphere" of his family, or his community, or his church. Something within him responds; and he finds the first evidence of the power of the Christian spirit in the harmony, joy, and sense of exhaustless resources which it creates within his own personality. Theological truth is primarily practical and relates in the first instance to the sphere of human values; as a representation of cosmic reality it is more or less symbolic, and much of it needs to be regarded as poetry rather than as literal truth.[11]

So much for the metaphysical attributes of God! From the point of view of practical religion, the metaphysical monster which they offer to our worship is an absolutely worthless invention of the scholarly mind.[12]

This reasoning seems on the surface to indicate that constructive religious empiricists are interested simply in descriptive studies of religious experience--that they are not interested in discovering objective religious truth through the testing of hypotheses. If men are interested solely in the experiential, why attempt to discover the metaphysical? Yet what the constructive religious empiricists who present this argument are trying to justify, is the use of subjective data--rather than objective data or metaphysical presuppositions--as the stable and basic working material for theological investigation. They do not intend their argument to restrict their method to a mere descriptive study of religious experience. Empiricism is without meaning unless hypotheses are formed and tested. Horton, whom we quoted above, says in his A Psychological Approach to Theology:

If this order of topics has the disadvantage of putting man first and God last, it has at least the merit of proceeding logically from the known to the unknown, from the empirical to the metaphysical. In the first part, where the whole point of view is practical and empirical, psychology will be taken at its face value--for it will be in its own proper field--and the whole effort will be to give science its full rights in the field of theology. One thing is sure: that when the objective element in religious experience--be it a personal God or an impersonal law, or an abstract but objectively valid ideal-- completely evaporates, and a man comes to feel himself trapped in an air-tight chamber of subjectivism, along with his own mental states, then he ceases to be religious. Especially since the rise of the psychology of religion, multitudes of people have become convinced that religion is a purely subjective phenomenon, an operation man performs upon himself; and they have accordingly ceased to be religious.

It is the perception of this rather alarming situation that is mainly responsible for the present revival of interest in religious metaphysics and epistemology, all those thorny and "impractical" problems which religious pragmatism was just congratulating itself upon having banished into the limbo of a defunct scholasticism! They have come once more to

262

the fore because it has been proved that they are very practical questions after all; for it is plain that when religion is not solidly grounded in objective reality, its pragmatic benefits fail to materialize. The quest for reality in religion, for some way of escape from the black hole of subjectivism, for genuine knowledge of God, has become the characteristic tendency of contemporary religious thought.[13]

We must further recognize that Constructive Religious Empiricism does not aim to discover general psychological information from religious experience, but rather aims to discover religious truth from religious experience. Above I delineated constructive religious empiricists from those who employ the intuitive approach, and from history and the physical and biological sciences, which deal with objective data. Now I shall distinguish Constructive Religious Empiricism from psychology. Both religious psychologists and constructive religious empiricists deal with religious experience, but the former are interested in religious experience either from the descriptive standpoint, or as a means to discovering general psychological information through the testing of psychological hypotheses. Constructive religious empiricists, however, are interested in religious experience primarily as a means to discovering religious truth--they test hypotheses concerned with religious matters by means of subjective experience.

> To say that theology is the science or the philosophy of "religious experience" may mean one of two things, according to the stress laid upon the subjective or the objective element in the concept of experience. It may mean that theology is simply the study of religious experience as a peculiar group of mental phenomena; or it may mean that theology is the attempt to erect, on the basis of such a study, a verifiable theory concerning the nature of the Object of religious experience--God. In the former case theology becomes a branch of psychology, as Professor Leuba insists it ought to; and it is easy to draw the further deduction--as he does--that the deity in whom the religious man puts his trust has a "merely subjective existence" in his own mind. In the latter case, theology becomes a branch of philosophy, aiming to interpret the nature of reality in the light of certain types of experience peculiarly rich in metaphysical insight, while corroborating and correcting its interpretations in the light of experience as a whole.[14]

Constructive Religious Empiricism desires by means of men's religious experiences to test the validity of existing claims to religious truth, accept what is verified by religious experience, reject what is not, and continue to refine religious concepts until they agree with subjective empirical evidence. Constructive Religious Empiricism desires to set religion on an empirical footing by considering as true only those religious concepts which are verified by men's religious experiences. As an illustration of the method and aim of Constructive Religious Empiricism, I quote Dr. Burtt's description of the manner in which constructive religious empiricists approach the existence of God:

> Obviously, the circumstance that God, interpreted as a metaphysical explanation, proved incapable of experiential validation, does not necessarily indicate that theism approached in this way would meet the same fate. Defining God as First Cause, we might inevitably fall into skepticism; defining him as the satisfier of a certain kind of practical need, we might find sufficient empirical evidence for his reality. Whether adequate evidence is available or not depends in large measure on our definition of the concept to be tested by it. Now, to be sure, if we are intuitionists or rationalists in our method, it is doubtless incumbent on us to take as final the particular philosophical or theological definition that that method renders axiomatic or demonstrates. But if we have adopted the tentative, hypothetical method of modern empiricism--especially if it appears plausible that the definition which baffles us does not ring true to what is most vital in the concept to the majority of religious people anyway--we seem under no obligation to remain committed to it. If the definition with which we start proves incapable of validation we may (and should, unless it seems desirable to abandon the concept entirely) redefine it by the aid of a more careful study of the experiences which appear to have given it significance to people.[15]

II. THE MERIT OF CONSTRUCTIVE RELIGIOUS EMPIRICISM--ITS EMPIRICAL APPROACH

Critique of the Methods of Acquiring Truth

Above I stated and explained the four principal methods of acquiring truth, viz.: common sense, authority, intuition, and empirical or scientific method. Let us now evaluate these methods. Common sense, since it is completely uncritical, must be rejected wherever possible by the educated investigator. The chief fallacy in the authoritarian method lies in the fact that it begs the question: how did the given authority acquire the truth it holds in the first place? Since all human authorities are fallible, they must be screened from without for truth or error. Even in the case of an alleged divine authority, it would be necessary to test by some means or another whether the authority is truly an infallible one before accepting as true all of its decrees. Thus authority must be rejected as a primary method of acquiring truth.

The intuitive method, although it has been defended vigorously by many thinkers, has at least one serious disadvantage: since the only self-evident truth is the tautology (if A then A)--which reveals no factual information whatsoever--and since no philosophies have been deduced from tautologies, all intuitive principles and systems likewise must be screened from without for their truth-value. Of course, a priori s must lie at the basis of every procedure,[16] but because of this disadvantage they should be kept to a minimum, and be as self-evident and beyond dispute as possible.

Empirical or scientific method is the truly valid way of approaching truth because it alone can accomplish to the satisfaction of all what the other methods which we have discussed cannot; not only do its results not need to be tested for error independently, but it is in itself capable of determining what authority to follow and what common sense beliefs and presuppositions to hold.

> The evidence that science accumulates is public. It is open to the scrutiny of all. If a given scientific result is to be refuted, it must be refuted by the same kind of evidence. When a biologist experiments in order to test the soundness of a biological theory, his experiments are such as could be performed and observed by all who have the requisite training and competence. If the experimental results are favorable to the theory, everyone must, in spite of extra-scientific considerations, regard the theory as more acceptable than it was previously. It is not because the biologist says so (authority); not because of any ethical or emotional reasons (faith); not because of any feelings of certainty (intuition); it is because the evidence is of the kind that compels assent.[17]

It is true that empirical method, like all other disciplines, has its presuppositions, but these a priori s are few, self-evident, and more generally agreed upon than those of any other system. Dr. Edward J. Carnell states the empirical pre-suppositions as follows:

1. Epistemology. If a law is to be meaningful, it must be true. Every successful scientist, then, must assume that knowledge is possible. . . .
2. Metaphysics. Science assumes that the universe is regular, but how can that hypothesis be made significant without a world-view which allows for regularity ? . . .
3. Ethics. All scientists know that a man must be honest before his conclusions can be trusted, but how can the empiricist show, by a laboratory experiment, that honesty is a normative affair ? Science can only describe.[18]

It might seem that since empirical method is based on intuitive premeses, even empiricism is a variety of rationalism.[19] Strictly speaking this is true, but the distinction between the two methods lies in the fact that whereas rationalists attempt to deduce their world-views from their presupposition(s), empiricists use their presuppositions only to justify investigation of the universe--this investigation providing the data for their world-view.

Because empiricism avoids the disadvantages of the other three methods of approaching truth it should be employed wherever possible. An important ramification of the scientific method should be noted at this point: nothing is certain (other than the presuppositions of empiricism and the data with which the empiricist works, by definition). Thus one must make his decisions on probability, for the conclusions of empirical method are always hypothetical (to varying degrees, of course, depending upon the strength of present evidence and the probability of relevant new evidence arising).

Constructive Religious Empiricism and Scientific Method

As pointed out above, Constructive Religious Empiricism has the great merit of having allied itself with the scientific method, and of having rejected the authoritarian and intuitive approaches to knowledge. Curtis W. Reese says:

In philosophy alleged perfect and absolute standards are being investigated. The "ideas" of Plato and the "forms" of Aristotle, together with all presuppositions and so-called self-evident truths, are subject to careful analysis. Experimental experience is the humanistic test of truth. The ideal grows out of real experience; it is consciously tested and remade in the light of new facts. With this comes an aggressive attitude towards life, replacing resignation and submission. Religion must take into account this changed way of thinking.[20]

By separating itself from the Roman Catholic approach to truth (authoritative-intuitive), Constructive Religious Empiricism rids itself of much of the conflict between "religion and science."[21] It is important to note, however, that the alignment between Constructive Religious Empiricism and Modern Science, although close, cannot be considered perfect. The presuppositions of Modern Science as a world-view (Dr. Burtt calls it the "Religion of Science") are many more than the presuppositions of empirical or scientific method, given above.

THE MAJOR DISPUTED ASSUMPTIONS OF THE RELIGION OF SCIENCE

1. Assumptions Concerning Man's Moral Situation
   a. He needs certainty to attain his highest good, whose nature is indicated by the experience of disappointed attachment.
   b. He can attain the needed certainty through the power of his own reason.
2. Assumptions Concerning Metaphysical Knowledge
   a. The ultimate criterion of truth is the clarity of direct apprehension of an object's essense.
      (1) Supplementation of human reason by supernatural revelation is therefore superfluous and irrational.
   b. The ultimate structure of the world is mathematical in its determinate order and its unconcern for human welfare.
   c. Good and evil are relative to human desire.
3. Psychological Assumptions
   a. Knowledge of the structure of the world on which we depend produces love of that which is known.
   b. Love of truth and reality is capable of indefinite growth.
   c. Such love can transform desire and emotion into harmony with itself.[22]

As can readily be seen by comparing the a prioris of the Religion of Science and those of the scientific method, the former are hospitable to the latter but the converse is not necessarily true. The fact that many Constructive Religious Empiricists refuse to accept some of the presuppositions of Modern Science, while unqualifiedly accepting those of empirical method, indicates that Constructive Religious Empiricism cannot be said to be completely allied with science.

Having given Constructive Religious Empiricism due recognition for being an empirical procedure, it is well for us to see whether the method has the further merit of being the only approach to religious truth which recognizes and evaluates mysticism. In my opinion, those who maintain that Constructive Religious Empiricism has this advantage fail to recognize two facts: (1) Mysticism in its true sense is "ineffable"--unable to be expressed in words, and therefore beyond evaluation.[23] True mysticism, as William James saw, cannot be dealt with by any empirical procedure, Constructive Religious Empiricism included:

> The handiest of the marks by which I classify a state of mind as mystical is negative. The subject of it immediately says that it defies expression, that no adequate report of its contents can be given in words. It follows from this that its quality must be directly experienced; it cannot be imparted or transferred to others. In this peculiarity mystical states are more like states of feeling than like states of intellect. No one can make clear to another who has never had a certain feeling, in what the quality or worth of it consists. One must have musical ears to know the value of a symphony; one must have been in love one's self to understand a lover's state of mind. Lacking the heart or ear, we cannot interpret the musician or the lover justly, and are even likely to consider him weakminded or absurd. The mystic finds that most of us accord to his experiences an equally incompetent treatment.[24]

(2) Mysticism is intuitive, not empirical. The mystic does not revise his "theology" in terms of the experiences of others--his religion has been revealed directly to him, and as such is final. Potter is correct when he says that the mystic "is simply a person who by meditation and concentration reaches a state of blissful assurance that he is in direct contact with reality, at one with the heart of things."[25] The intuitive nature of mysticism immediately sets it at opposite poles from all empiricism, and at least technically joins it with the Catholic and old orthodox Christian approaches, even though the latter have likewise been suspicious of mysticism due to its ineffability. Since the rationalist theologies are also based on intuitive principles, they claim an infallibility not unlike that of the mystical world-views; but since the mystic experience cannot be

described in words, harmony or disharmony between the two approaches can never be established.

III. THE IMPOTENCY OF CONSTRUCTIVE RELIGIOUS EMPIRICISM AS A METHOD FOR ACQUIRING RELIGIOUS TRUTH

We have seen that Constructive Religious Empiricism aims to discover religious truth by empirically investigating subjective religious experience, and we have given it due recognition for allying itself with the scientific method. I shall now discuss why I believe Constructive Religious Empiricism to be incapable of attaining its object, religious truth; for four main reasons (the last being the most significant) I am convinced that the empirical investigation of subjective religious experience has an almost negligible probability of yielding religious truth. I am convinced that empirical method is the proper approach to use in the search for religious knowledge, but that its application to subjective data in the hope of gaining religious truth is a blind alley necessarily marked out by and littered with a prioris. My views are the direct antithesis of James'; in the conclusion of his Varieties of Religious Experience, he says, "So long as we deal with the cosmic and the general, we deal only with the symbols of reality, but as soon as we deal with private and personal phenomena as such, we deal with realities in the completest sense of the term."[26]

As pointed out above, the validity of a method is determined by its effectiveness in attaining its desired end. Therefore, if I am right in believing that Constructive Religious Empiricism is unable to discover religious truth, we are compelled to reject it and to look elsewhere in our search for religious knowledge.

The Difficulty of Analyzing Religious Experience

In order to arrive at religious truth by an empirical analysis of religious feeling, constructive religious empiricists must be able to distinguish what is religious from what is not in subjective experience. Obviously, hypotheses concerned with religious matters can be verified only when they correspond with true religious experience. Horton says:

> An empirical account of the nature of God must begin by finding a criterion to distinguish the experience of God from other experiences. It will not do simply to analyze the object of contemplation; for not all contemplation is religious;

269

and we need a criterion to tell us which is religious and which is not.[27]

The problem of distinguishing religious from other subjective feelings involves knowing accurately the distinctive characteristics of religious experience, and there is very little evidence that at present either the constructive religious empiricist or the subjects of their analysis are in possession of this knowledge. The problem is further complicated by the fact that (1) many of the great religious figures of all faiths have maintained that at least part of their religious experiences is ineffable; (2) psychologists of some schools (Freudian, for example) have given completely naturalistic explanations for all subjective experience. This latter consideration suggests a raft of questions: Can religious experience be entirely naturalistic in origin? How could one identify the divine working through secondary causes in subjective experience, were the divine to do so? etc., etc. The problem of distinguishing the religious from the secular in subjective experience has seemed complex enough to make its solution impossible in the eyes of many thinkers, notable among whom is John Dewey:

> The adjective "religious" denotes nothing in the way of a specifiable entity, either institutional or as a system of beliefs. It does not denote anything to which one can specifically point as one can point to this and that historic religion or existing church. For it does not denote anything that can exist by itself or that can be organized into a particular and distinctive form of existence. It denotes attitudes that may be taken toward every object and every proposed end or ideal. . . . Those who hold to the notion that there is a definite kind of experience which is itself religious, by that very fact make out of it something specific, as a kind of experience that is marked off from experience as aesthetic, scientific, moral, political; from experience as companionship and friendship. But "religious" as a quality of experience signifies something that may belong to all these experiences.[28]

A further problem which confronts the constructive religious empiricist is that of determining what religious experiences will verify what hypotheses of religious truth. For example, assuming that the constructive religious empiricist is attempting to discover God's attributes, what religious experience will establish that God is love? justice? mercy? truth? This problem is likewise devoid of solution at the present time.

These problems of analyzing religious experience, although

extremely difficult, may be overcome in time. Psychology has been reasonably successful in distinguishing (with numerous marginal cases, to be sure) the psychological from the physiological; and within the psychological realm psychologists have come to study perception, motivation, learning, etc. as more or less separate disciplines. Yet, for the present, we must be cognizant of the many difficulties which confront any one who attempts to work with distinctively "religious" experience.

Constructive Religious Empiricism and the Layman

As we have seen, constructive religious empiricists, in defending their use of religious experience rather than objective data or metaphysical presuppositions as the stable and basic working material for theological investigation, argue that the layman is interested in the experiential rather than the metaphysical aspects of religion. Harry Emerson Fosdick says:

> Take such a truncated description of personal religion for what it is worth! Let it stand as merely an indication of the major fact that multiplying numbers of people, when they think of religion, mean not a church nor a system of theology, but a saving experience of inner spiritual devotion and daily spiritual power! . . . Moreover, when the modern mind hears the creeds upon which many of the churches still insist, with all the corollaries brought out by controversy and urged as indispensables of religious truth--old cosmologies, doctrines of Biblical infallibility, miracles like virgin birth or physical resurrection--the reaction is not simply incredulity, although incredulity is undoubtedly emphatic--but wonder as to what such things have to do with religion.[29]

Yet Constructive Religious Empiricism, by using experiential data to test the validity of hypotheses involving metaphysical issues, seems to feel that acquiring objective religious truth is an important function of theology. Horton remarks that since 1920

> the psychology of religion has extended its outlook from the social to the cosmic sphere; and religion is now commonly defined as a dangerous venture into the field of ultimate metaphysics, in quest of cosmic alliance and support. . . . The psychological approach to theology must necessarily take its start from the individual quest of personal development--a point of view which at once sets it in sympathy with the spirit of this restless age--but it will inevitably be led

271

out of the individual sphere into the social and cosmic spheres, in the endeavor to define the conditions that control and the resources which aid man in this quest.[30]

Apparently, constructive religious empiricists are trying to make religion not only scientific but also practical, even though they are not quite clear as to the meaning of "practical." It is my belief that the method of Constructive Religious Empiricism, contrary to the hopes of its adherents, will not provide the practical religion for which the man-on-the-street seeks.

I believe that the experiential and the metaphysical must go hand in hand in order for religion to be satisfying. (1) One's faith determines his action. Can we assume, for example, that two people, both of whom have what they believe to be "religious" experiences, but one of whom believes that a God-who-advocates-the-golden-rule is the cause of his experience, while the other is convinced that a God-who-desires-his-creatures-to-assert-themselves is back of his religious feeling--can we assume that these two will be as equally happy and live as equally useful and beautiful lives ? Can we expect the same moral conduct from an orthodox Moslem as from an orthodox Christian ?

> Believing that Hitler's Mein Kampf, with its doctrine of the superiority of the so-called Aryan or Nordic race and the Lebensraum (living space) dogma, was the truth, the Germans patterned their concepts of the good and the beautiful after this Weltanschauung. The good was the exterminating of the inferior races, the slaughtering of the weak and the timid, and the subjugation of the recalcitrant. The beautiful was the swastika, the goose step, the screaming of those being cremated or excoriated, and the vicious program of state-sponsored motherhood. Truly, "how man conceives of his relationship to the Infinite and to the whole of reality vitally effects his conscious relationship to his fellow human beings."[31]

The metaphysical tenets which an individual holds are the principles upon which he predicates his actions when living a consistent life; as such their nature is of utmost importance. (2) The layman is most definitely interested in the cause and full meaning of his religious experiences. Furthermore, he wants to know with a reasonable degree of definiteness--with as much certainty as possible in light of the fact mentioned before that no matter-of-fact is ever known to be true--whether a God exists, whether the soul is immortal, and what God, if he exists, demands of his creatures. The number of cheap books

272

and magazine articles of the "Why I Believe in Life after Death" variety that are bought by the man-on-the-street today reflects a strong lay preoccupation with metaphysical issues. Also, the "deadness"--lack of spiritual vitality and appeal to young people and young adults--in so many modernist churches, and the number of conversions to traditional Christianity in the revival meetings conducted by Dr. Billy Graham, et al. give evidence that the layman is searching for some definite knowledge about spiritual matters. Reese's argument is echoed by many today:

> Having departed from the old ways of thinking and having tried the unsatisfactory experiment of living without a philosophy, multitudes are reaching the reflective period. They have come to feel the need of an intelligent, well-rounded theory of life. A minister of wide experience said that he found that nine-tenths of his people were interested most in sermons that presented a philosophical background for the individual's faith. There can be no substitute for a clear, comprehensive, thoroughgoing theory of life. Just as social service, to be effective, must be backed by a valid social philosophy, so must satisfying and ennobling religion be backed by a valid philosophy of life.[32]

I am convinced that the probability of Constructive Religious Empiricism's being able to provide the layman with the religious knowledge for which he seeks, is practically nil. Empirical method by definition produces tentative results, but results vary in their degree of uncertainty according to the data with which they are concerned; and it is clear that as one proceeds from the objective to the subjective (from physics to biology to psychology, for example) empirical results become more and more unstable. The very nebulousness of "religious experience" forces us to conclude that Constructive Religious Empiricism will not give the layman even probably certain religious knowledge. Wobbermin is sadly mistaken when he claims that "the fruitfulness of the religio-psychological method for the problem of the nature of religion is first shown by the fact that it makes possible greater clarity and precision."[33] Only the elusive thing called religious experience (notice below how vaguely Dr. Burtt has to describe it), being the data upon which Constructive Religious Empiricism operates, remains "absolute," while all else in religion becomes extremely tentative:

> Since on these terms no concept--including the concept of God--is final, all definitions being liable to revision in the light of continuing human experience, God is no longer the central fact in religion or the controlling principle in

theology. His place is taken by man's religious experience-- by that selected phase of human doing and suffering which appears to be distinguishable from the secular phases of life and is emphasized in people whom all recognize as especially religious. The religious experience of men and women becomes the decisive fact and the ultimate court of appeal by which we test the validity of any theological concept--the concept of God along with others. No such concept, however defined, is itself any longer absolute or theologically necessary.[34]

William James, in one of his typical flights of fancy, says: "I do not see why a critical Science of Religions . . . might not eventually command as general a public adhesion as is commanded by a physical science. Even the personally nonreligious might accept its conclusions on trust much as blind persons now accept the facts of optics--it might appear as foolish to refuse them."[35] Keeping in mind what James has not-- the nebulousness of religious experience and its ramifications-- one can with a little effort imagine a world in which there is general agreement on the validity of Constructive Religious Empiricism. People are constantly by their radios, listening to the religious experience censuses in progress: "God seems to be holy--no, twelve more individual experience analyses show Him to be more kindly than holy. Salvation seems to be by works rather than by faith for the present, but all results have not as yet been tabulated." One wonders how long (or even if) such an absurd situation could exist! We have to admit that if the search for religious truth must center on empirical analysis of the subjective, even reasonably certain religious truth will in all probability never be found.

The Tyranny of the Subjective

Few people realize the danger of making reality relative to and determined by the subjective, which may be influenced by so many factors. Let us suppose that there is an existing deity with definite characteristics who causes men's religious experiences. We know how physiological factors (lack of sleep, improper food, etc.) and psychological factors (tension, fear, etc.) influence our consciousness. Is it not possible that our religious experiences may be only shadows of the pure experience which, if able to be had, would point us to religious knowledge? Is it not also possible that, even allowing for such physiological and psychological factors, the human being--a finite creature--is incapable of receiving through religious experience any reliable or tangible knowledge of the divine ? Is there not a strong probability that by attempting to discover religious knowledge through our religious experiences, we may be twisting religious truth--knowledge of God if he exists, for example--to fit our fallible, capricious, and easily deluded consciousnesses ? Could we not be tampering with--indeed, tyrannizing over--objective religious truth by making its nature depend upon our attitudes of mind ?

I believe that one of the most significant novels of modern times is George Orwell's 1984. In his work Orwell depicts a totalitarian state which succeeds where others have failed because, through controlling the minds of its subjects, it is able to control objective reality. The subjects of this state are forced by a constant alteration of past history, propaganda, the gradual removal of words from the language which foster "undesirable" thoughts, and where necessary mental compulsion resembling highly refined hypnosis, to see and believe reality to be just as the leaders of the state desire. I quote a few passages from 1984:

> The mutability of the past is the central tenet of Ingsoc. Past events, it is argued, have no objective existence, but survive only in written records and in human memories. The past is whatever the records and the memories agree upon. And since the Party is in full control of all records, and in equally full control of the minds of its members, it follows that the past is whatever the Party chooses to make it. It also follows that though the past is alterable, it never has been altered in any specific instance. For when it has been recreated in whatever shape is needed at the moment, then this new version is the past, and no different past can ever have existed.

> The purpose of Newspeak was not only to provide a medium of expression for the world-view and mental habits proper to the devotees of Ingsoc, but to make all other modes of thought impossible. It was intended that when Newspeak had been adopted once and for all and Oldspeak forgotten, a heretical thought--that is, a thought diverging from the principles of Ingsoc--should be literally unthinkable, at least so far as thought is dependent on words. Its vocabulary was so constructed as to give exact and often very subtle expression to every meaning that a Party member could properly wish to express, while excluding all other meanings and also the possibility of arriving at them by indirect methods. This was done partly by the invention of new words, but chiefly by

eliminating undesirable words and by stripping such words as remained of unorthodox meanings, and so far as possible of all secondary meanings whatever.

"But how can you control matter?" he burst out. "You don't even control the climate or the law of gravity. And there are disease, pain, death--."

O'Brien silenced him by a movement of the hand. "We control matter because we control the mind. Reality is inside the skull. You will learn by degrees, Winston. There is nothing that we could not do. Invisibility, levitation--anything. I could float off this floor like a soap bubble if I wished to. I do not wish to, because the Party does not wish it. You must get rid of those nineteenth-century ideas about the laws of nature. We make the laws of nature."

"But you do not! You are not even masters of this planet. What about Eurasia and Eastasia? You have not conquered them yet."

"Unimportant. We shall conquer them when it suits us. And if we did not, what difference would it make? We can shut them out of existence. Oceania is the world."

"But the world itself is only a speck of dust. And man is tiny--helpless! How long has he been in existence? For millions of years the earth was uninhabited."

"Nonsense. The earth is as old as we are, no older. How could it be older? Nothing exists except through human consciousness."

"But the rocks are full of the bones of extinct animals-- mammoths and mastodons and enormous reptiles which lived here long before man was ever heard of."

"Have you ever seen those bones, Winston? Of course not. Nineteenth-century biologists invented them. Before man there was nothing. After man, if he could come to an end, there would be nothing. Outside man there is nothing."

"But the whole universe is outside us. Look at the stars! Some of them are a million light-years away. They are out of our reach forever."

"What are the stars?" said O'Brien indifferently. "They are bits of fire a few kilometers away. We could reach them if we wanted to. Or we could blot them out. The earth is the center of the universe. The sun and the stars go round it."

Winston made another convulsive movement. This time he did not say anything. O'Brien continued as though answering a spoken objection:

"For certain purposes, of course, that is not true. When we navigate the ocean, or when we predict an eclipse, we often find it convenient to assume that the earth goes round the sun and that the stars are millions upon millions of kilometers away. But what of it? Do you suppose it is beyond us to produce a dual system of astronomy? The stars can be near or distant, according as we need them. Do you suppose our mathematicians are unequal to that? Have you forgotten doublethink?"

Winston shrank back upon the bed. Whatever he said, the swift answer crushed him like a bludgeon. And yet he knew, he _knew_, that he was in the right. The belief that nothing exists outside your own mind--surely there must be some way of demonstrating that it was false. Had it not been exposed long ago as a fallacy? There was even a name for it, which he had forgotten.[36]

Does not the idea of reality becoming completely relative to the human mind, which is able to be easily deluded, terrify the reader? It should, especially in this day when totalitarianism is extending its tentacles like an octopus. Perhaps the philosophical concepts underlying Constructive Religious Empiricism permit this same type of situation to exist in the realm of religion. Statements such as the following abound in the writings of constructive religious empiricists:

No doctrine will be formulated until its meaning for religious experience has first been described and analyzed, psychologically.[37]

Religious experience is the ultimate court of appeal for all scientific study of religion.[38]

It is easy to see how objective religious facts, if such exist, could be distorted by searching for them only or chiefly in the subjective experiences of the human mind.

THE PROBLEM OF "A PRIORI"

Even if the above three difficulties of Constructive Religious Empiricism were surmounted, I believe there to be one further objection to this approach which renders it totally incapable of attaining its desired object, religious truth. The difficulty of which I speak is the following: I believe that Constructive Religious Empiricism is a method of investigation which produces results exactly according to the presuppositions of those who employ it. Obviously, if my contention is true, Constructive Religious Empiricism will have to be rejected, and we will have to look elsewhere for a valid method of acquiring religious knowledge, for a valid method of approaching truth cannot reflect in the answers it gives the convictions of the one who employs it. Such a method would not be discovering universal truth at all; it would simply be reiterating the beliefs of its user. In order to demonstrate the validity of my objection, I shall attempt to prove two theses:

(A) That the results of analyses of religious experience are dictated by the religious experiences which are analyzed;

(B) That the religious experiences analyzed, being dependent upon the criterion of religious experience which is employed, are necessarily determined by the presuppositions of the constructive religious empiricist.

Proof of Thesis (A)

One's data or materials used in any field determine his result or product. A man who would build something of wood is limited in what he builds, and the thing which he would build is limited in its characteristics by the nature of the material which is used. He cannot build a skyscraper out of wood; his product cannot have a metallic appearance or finish; etc., etc. Within the bounds of the characteristics of wood, the builder can do what he likes, but he can never go beyond these characteristics. In the realm of ideas we have the survey or census. Polling agencies realize that their results will be determined by their data, so they make great efforts to survey as many-- not more or less--persons or interest groups as are involved in the given problem to be solved. In attempting to discover political opinion in an area, for example, they make special effort to include all the interest groups (farmers, tradesmen, etc.) in the area, and none outside. They realize that a change in the data (those polled) necessarily means a change in results (political opinion in the given area).

The above statements make clear that the results of Constructive Religious Empiricism (that is, what hypotheses concerned with religious matters are verified) depend upon the religious experiences analyzed, for religious experiences are the data with which the constructive religious empiricist works. Let us see specifically how the verifying of hypotheses would

278

be determined by the religious experiences examined. Worship of Christ is an essential element in the religious experience of the orthodox Christian, while it is repulsive and foreign to the religious experience of the Moslem. Both Christian and Moslem are theists, however. Were orthodox Christian and Moslem religious experiences analyzed together, the hypothesis verified would probably be that worship of God is necessary to salvation, but worship of Christ is optional; whereas the hypothesis that worship of Christ is necessary for salvation would receive complete validation if orthodox Christian religious experiences were used as sole data. John Dewey validly argues:

> The determining factor in the interpretation of the experience is the particular doctrinal apparatus into which a person has been inducted. The emotional deposit connected with prior teaching floods the whole situation. It may readily confer upon the experience such a peculiarly sacred preciousness that all inquiry into its causation is barred. The stable outcome is so invaluable that the cause to which it is referred is usually nothing but a reduplication of the thing that has occurred, plus some name that has acquired a deeply emotional quality.[39]

It is thus not difficult to see that (1) The hypotheses verified by the constructive religious empiricist depend upon the religious experiences which he consults in making his analysis; and (2) The more inclusive the list of religious experiences which the constructive religious empiricist uses as data, the more general are the hypotheses which he verifies. Here we observe a further difficulty with inclusivist (modernist and humanist) Constructive Religious Empiricism: religious convictions are necessarily "watered down" by the approach of constructive religious empiricists. We discussed above the layman's dissatisfaction with modernist platitudes and generalities, and his search for more satisfying and tangible religious convictions. This feeling on the part of the average man offers another practical difficulty to the program of Constructive Religious Empiricism. James, in concluding his Varieties of Religious Experience, honestly admits what other constructive religious empiricists tend to disregard:

> I am well aware that after all the palpitating documents which I have quoted, and all the perspectives of emotion-inspiring institution and belief that my previous lectures have opened, the dry analysis to which I now advance may appear to many of you like an anti-climax, a tapering-off

and flattening out of the subject, instead of a crescendo of interest and result. I said awhile ago that the religious attitude of Protestants appears poverty-stricken to the Catholic imagination. Still more poverty-stricken, I fear, may my final summing up of the subject appear at first to some of you. On which account I pray you now to bear this point in mind, that in the present part of it I am expressly trying to reduce religion to its lowest admissible terms, to that minimum, free from individualistic excrescences, which all religions contain as their nucleus and on which it may be hoped that all religious persons may agree.[40]

Proof of Thesis (B)

Because the constructive religious empiricist tacitly realizes that his conclusions will be influenced by the data with which he works, he is compelled on the one hand not to include in his empirical investigations subjective experiences which will, according to his a prioris, render invalid his conclusions, and on the other hand not to exclude from his analysis experiences which his presuppositions cause him to believe are truly religious. This obviously means that the criteria of religious experience of (and thus religions analyzed by) any particular constructive religious empiricist are determined by his a prioris. Let me by two examples demonstrate that this criticism applies to all constructive religious empiricists regardless of their personal theological convictions.

An exclusivist constructive religious empiricist (e.g., Moslem, Mormon, orthodox Christian), believing that men have true fellowship with the divine--true religious experience--only when they come by the true way (the way provided by his religion), would formulate his criteria of religious experience so as to include his religion and no other. Why? because he is not going to invalidate his empirical study by analyzing subjective experiences which are not truly religious. Could an exclusivist constructive religious empiricist formulate criteria general enough to include faiths other than his own? Certainly not, for to do so would--in his opinion--be to open the floodgates to all manner of false data which would ruin his empirical study. An inclusivist constructive religious empiricist (e.g., Bahaist, humanist), on the other hand, because he believes that no one faith or group of faiths holds a monopoly on religious truth--that adherents of all religions have genuine religious experiences, would formulate his criteria of religious experience so as not to exclude any faiths. Typical examples of such

280

criteria are found in the writings of Fosdick and Horton:

> Whenever anybody thus finds any goodness, truth, or beauty concerning which he feels not that it should give itself to him, but that he should give himself to it and be its loyal servant, that man has entered into an authentic religious experience.[41]

> The adjectives "divine," "holy," "sacred," are rightly applied to anything which humbles him who beholds it and exalts him who rightly adjusts himself to it.[42]

Why are these criteria so broad? because the modernist (inclusivist) constructive religious empiricist is not going to invalidate his empirical study by refusing to analyze subjective experiences which are "truly religious." Could an inclusivist constructive religious empiricist formulate criteria so specific and limited that they would exclude human experiences centering on "goodness, truth, or beauty"? Certainly not, for to do so would--in his opinion--be to reject relevant data, without which he would certainly come to false conclusions as to the nature of religious truth. Thus we see that thesis (B) as well as thesis (A) is valid, and that the hypotheses verified by constructive religious empiricists are more likely reflections of their own presuppositions than universal truths.

A More Searching Analysis of the "A Priori" Problem

Why, we may well ask, has not the true nature of Constructive Religious Empiricism--the fact that it is a machine whose products reflect precisely the interests of the operators who feed it the material they choose--become evident to philosophers and theologians? The vast majority of constructive religious empiricists--as we have pointed out previously--are inclusivists, being modernists and humanists. It is axiomatic that the influence of a priori is manifestly evident when present in exclusivist circles (we are always quick to recognize and condemn the Jehovah's Witness who at our door argues his presuppositionally-riddled theology), but such influence is generally overlooked when present in inclusivist arguments. Few would see "intolerance" in Wobbermin's assertion that "the nature of religion must be that fundamental underlying motive of religious life common to all forms of religious expression."[43] That exclusive religious tenets are ruled out by inclusivists never seems to excite us, whereas the converse makes us boil. The premium placed upon "broadness" and "tolerance" today makes it easy for us to forget that the very general religious "truths" which modernists and humanists state as being the established results of Constructive Religious Empiricism are actually restatements of their own preconceived religious philosophies.[44]

The fact that exclusivists have not employed Constructive Religious Empiricism (for a reason which will be given later) prevents us from seeing what would be completely evident if they did: that by the method of Constructive Religious Empiricism inclusivists must come out with inclusivist religious "truths," while by the same approach to religious knowledge exclusivists must come out with exclusive religious tenets. It does not seem strange to us, because we have no standard of comparison, that modernist and humanist constructive religious empiricists never conclude that particularistic religious tenets are empirically valid.

Before realizing that a priori was a necessary evil of Constructive Religious Empiricism, I felt that only modernist devotees of the method deserved condemnation--and this, not because they were constructive religious empiricists, but because they were inconsistent constructive religious empiricists. My above generalization concerning the inclusiveness of modernist and humanist constructive religious empiricists must be slightly modified in the case of many modernists. Modernism is a peculiar religious philosophy in that it is in reality a transition belief between Christian orthodoxy and humanism. Potter validly argues that "the Modernists have fallen between two stools in trying to sit on both."[45] This fact must be kept in mind if one wishes to come to a full understanding of Constructive Religious Empiricism, and particularly if he desires to understand the work of its founder, Friedrich Schleiermacher. Modernists have carried over their characteristic vacillation on the question of religious inclusiveness into their work as constructive religious empiricists. Although formulating all-inclusive criteria of religious experience, they have permitted their semi-devotion to the Christian tradition to lead them to apply their criteria only to groups within the Christian sphere, thus making their data for analysis and their conclusions "Christian" in a broad sense. They have given necessarily poor excuses for doing this, and have at the same time detracted from their already shaky case by continuing to maintain that salvation and genuine religious experience are not limited to the Christian faith. Schleiermacher well illustrates the various points I have brought out here. In his classical work, The Christian Faith, he states his inclusivist criterion of true religious experience as follows: "The common element in all howsoever diverse expressions of piety, by which these are conjointly distinguished from all other feelings, or, in other words, the self-identical essence of piety, is this: the consciousness of being absolutely dependent, or, which is the same thing, of being in relation with God."[46] Having stated this criterion, Schleiermacher proceeds inconsistently to limit its application to the Christian tradition.

> When Schleiermacher develops his theological reconstruction in detail it is specifically Christian experience that he seeks to interpret, not religious experience in general. He loyally places himself within the Christian tradition and restricts his analysis to those features of experience that are historically traceable to the impact of Christ upon the religious life and feeling of mankind. This means that the range of application of his method is limited by a selective historical commitment and a conscious devotion to the Christian community. Moreover, in view of his particular heritage, this involves a further limitation, namely, to Protestant experience; since, except for his deep appreciation of the social dependencies of religion, Schleiermacher was distinctively Protestant in his fundamental attitudes and convictions. These restrictions, as was above noted, have become characteristic of modernism in its most influential contemporary form. . . .

> Both in the Addresses and in The Christian Faith, he attempts to justify on principle his devout adherence to Christianity. This justification takes the general form of affirming that Christianity empirically discloses its superiority to other religions by providing a more adequate penetration, deeper intensification, and richer development than they of the basic experience which lies at the heart of all religion. But obviously this contention would not seem valid to adherents of other religions.[47]

I must confess that I have little patience with Schleiermacher; I am not convinced by those who attempt to justify his vacillations and contradictions on the ground that he was the innovator of a new science of theology. Schleiermacher was not only the first genuine modernist, he has been typical of all modernists; and present-day constructive religious empiricists of the modernist school make the identical mistakes he did.[48] The cause of their irrationality lies in their essentially unreasonable position--and for adhering to it they have only themselves to blame. It is unfortunate that Horton does not take his self-criticism more seriously:

The modern theologian is in a dilemma. Caught between the pull of traditional wisdom on the one hand and the pull of experimental science on the other, he is apt to steer a somewhat devious course. If he could believe in the infallible authority of Church or Scripture, he might ignore science. If he could believe in the all-sufficiency of science as a guide to life, he might ignore the garnered wisdom of the past. As it is, he can choose neither horn of the dilemma, and appears to halt indecisively between two contrary points of view. From both sides he is exposed to attack. Naturalistic thinkers will characterize him scornfully as a "wabbly modernist," only half released from the shackles of supernaturalism, and a victim of "wishful thinking." Conservative religionists, on the other hand, will regard him as a traitor to religious tradition, already past the halfway mark on the road to atheism. He himself will often wonder if he is not trying to carry water on both shoulders, and his arguments will sometimes seem to start out for one objective and arrive at the reverse. Perpetually losing his intellectual balance in the effort to reach out for larger comprehension, and perpetually regaining it by hasty qualifications and recantations, he is not always a dignified figure.[49]

However, as I have pointed out, the chief trouble with Constructive Religious Empiricism is not that modernists have become irrational by succumbing to their a priori love of the Christian tradition, but that Constructive Religious Empiricism as a method for acquiring religious truth cannot but verify the hypotheses which accord with the presuppositions of the constructive religious empiricist, whether he be modernist, humanist, or exclusivist.[50]

If the religious "truths" derived from the practical application of Constructive Religious Empiricism are determined by the presuppositions of the one performing the analysis, as I believe they are, we might very reasonably ask: what is the evidence for the a priori of the modernist-humanist constructive religious empiricist that true religious experience is not limited to any one faith or group of faiths? The answer that is generally given is that there is an obviously great similarity in emotional feelings among people of all the great faiths.

These widespread and deep-seated resemblances between separated faiths, beginning in primitive religion, as all readers of Frazer's Golden Bough know, and running up into the highly organized religions, have psychological explanations; they are due, not to mutual copying, but to similar

284

emotional reactions to the mystery of the world and the deep
needs of human nature.[5][1]

But is this a convincing argument? Does it refute the orthodox
Christian claim (which is perfectly possible) that all men are
separated from God by their own wrongs (witness two world
wars within three decades), and that only those who come to
God through the way He provided can truly experience Him in
their lives? Both the modernist-humanist constructive religious empiricist and the orthodox Christian seem to have good
arguments for their position; but wait--we are no longer in the
realm of Constructive Religious Empiricism--we are independently investigating the evidence for the presuppositions which
determine the results of analyses of religious experience. And
is this not as it should be? Since the results of applying empirical method to subjective religious experience necessarily
reflect the presuppositions of the constructive religious empiricist who decides on the nature of true religious experience, the
basic question is: What is the evidence for the presuppositions
of the constructive religious empiricist?

And how can this question be answered? If we say by the
empirical analysis of subjective religious experience, we argue
a neat circle. Thus we are left with the methods of arriving at
truth not employed in Constructive Religious Empiricism,
namely: common sense, authority, intuition, or the empirical
investigation of objective phenomena. But this deals the death
blow to Constructive Religious Empiricism as a method for arriving at religious truth, no matter which of these four methods
provide the constructive religious empiricist with his criteria
of religious experience. The religious hypotheses which are
verified by the constructive religious empiricist depend upon
his presuppositions, and his presuppositions depend upon some
method of acquiring truth other than the empirical investigation
of subjective experience. It is clearly evident, therefore, that
religious truth is ultimately to be found outside of the subjective
empirical approach of Constructive Religious Empiricism--that
religious truth will be found where the information on the nature
of true religious experience will be found.

Looking at the matter in another way: what has been the real
cause of the trouble in the approach to truth of Constructive
Religious Empiricism? Not the empirical method, for the a
priori problem being discussed does not exist in other empirical studies such as chemistry or history. The problem lies in
the nature of the material upon which the constructive religious
empiricist performs his empirical analysis, to wit: subjective
experience. Subjective data are incapable of indicating their

own truth-value. Constructive religious empiricists have necessarily determined a priori the nature of "true religious experience," because the subjective experiences themselves have not been able to provide this information. Our discussion agrees with the argument of Carnell that subjective experiences must be "screened from without" for their truth-value:

> Feeling is that apperceptive faculty of the soul by means of which one has an inward impression of the state of some object, person, or relation, as when one has a feeling that he is being followed, or a conviction that certain signs of the zodiac portend things to come. Hunches, inspirations, and feelings, however, are little more than subjective suggestions of the soul; they must be screened from without for their truth or error qualities. Some men feel they are Napoleon himself. Others vow that God has told them to chop their right arm off or fast to death. Still others feel certain that when the crow tips his wing at a ninety degree angle, there will be a large crop of toddy-producing coconuts in Madagascar. Without reason to guide it, feeling is irresponsible--a woman's intuition notwithstanding.[52]

We thus conclude that religious truth will not come from Constructive Religious Empiricism (which requires independent screening), but from the method of arriving at truth which is capable of providing this screening.

IV. THE VALID APPROACH TO RELIGIOUS TRUTH

Empirical Method Applied to Objective Phenomena

Since validation for the presuppositions of Constructive Religious Empiricism is not to be obtained by the empirical investigation of subjective experience, we are compelled to carry our search for religious truth into that area where information on true religious experience can be found. What method for acquiring truth will give us this information? We have previously discussed the fallacies in the lay methods of common sense and authority. We have likewise rejected the intuitive approach. By process of elimination our research is limited to the empirical investigation of objective phenomena--the method of the "exact" sciences and of history.

What would be the nature of objective data which could reveal religious truth? Two alternatives seem possible: written revelation containing divine truths, or the entrance of a divine agent or messenger into history who would state the nature of religious truth. And how could claims to either of these be empirically verified? Certainly not by determining whether they are consistent with religious experience, for that would take us directly back into the presuppositional maze of Constructive Religious Empiricism. It seems that a claim to written revelation could be tested by its systematic consistency,[53] and a claim to the presence of a divine agent or messenger in history by the performance of miraculous deeds by him. Why these tests? All human beings are fallible, so attestation for a historical work alleged to have originated with the divine would involve determining that the writing had no internal contradictions (from a contradiction anything is deducible), and that it exactly fitted the facts of experience. Human beings are limited in their capacities, so attestation for the nature or mission of a divine being would involve determining that he performed acts unable or highly unlikely to be performed by mere human beings.

Obviously such tests as these would not be infallible, because of the very nature of empirical investigation, which precludes absolute proof. It is conceivable that a systematically consistent written work could be produced by mere human beings, and it is likewise possible that a man, in some way having a greater understanding of the workings of the universe than any of his fellow men, could perform acts which would seem to give him divine status. Yet such probabilities are extremely small, and since probability is the key to empirical study, one must make his decisions on the basis of it. We may now make the following generalization: Since the empirical investigation of objective phenomena is the only possibility left for obtaining religious truth, knowledge of the divine stands or falls on the question of whether a divine revelation of either kind described above exists. If such revelation stated only the nature of true religious experience, it would provide us with the necessary data for determining at least some measure of religious truth, for once the valid criterion of religious experience is known, the method of Constructive Religious Empiricism becomes meaningful.

At this juncture we might ask why, since popularly held revelations claim to state the criteria for true religious experience, the exclusivists have not engaged in Constructive Religious Empiricism. Inclusivists have no revelation to tell them what true religious experience is, so they let the powerful belief of our time that one cannot be "intolerant and small" dictate their choice of empirical data. The exclusivist, however, claims to have inside information on the nature of religious experience; why does he not use it to discover religious truth?

The reason is simply that his revelation not only tells him what true religious experience is; it gives him clear answers to the very metaphysical questions which constructive religious empiricists desire to answer. It is conceivable that a revelation could give information only on the nature of true religious experience, leaving other religious truths to be discovered through Constructive Religious Empiricism, but historically this has not been the case. It would seem that the gods of the exclusive religions see considerable force in the first three objections to Constructive Religious Empiricism stated earlier! —for, having taken care of the a priori problem, they, still not trusting Constructive Religious Empiricism, give human beings the religious information which the latter would be inclined to seek by this method of inquiry. The gods of the exclusive faiths, in their revelations, render Constructive Religious Empiricism superfluous.

Hume and the Objective Empirical Approach to Religious Truth

Why have modernists and humanists been quick to apply empirical method to subjective experience in their search for religious truth, and yet generally avoided the empirical investigation of objective phenomena? It would seem that the clear-cut, rigorous nature and more substantial accomplishments of the "exact" sciences, in contrast to the rather inconclusive results of psychology of religion, would have led prospective constructive religious empiricists into the objective rather than the subjective realm.[54] We have already evaluated one reason which constructive religious empiricists give for their approach, viz., that the layman is more interested in the experiential than in the metaphysical aspects of religion; now let us consider a second, and far more significant, reason for their subjectivism.

Since physical law began to take on a formidable, rigorous, Newtonian character, the more left-wing religionists have looked with suspicion and distaste on the idea of the "miraculous." Modernists and humanists have desired to keep up with the Religion of Science, whose doctrinal position--as we have seen--does not allow violations of the natural order of things. Immediately above, the statement was made that objective data capable of yielding religious truth would consist either of written revelation or of the entrance of a divine agent or messenger into history; further, that verification of the former would require establishing the revelation's systematic consistency, and validation of the latter would necessitate proof that the given Being performed miraculous acts. Now, since claims to written revelation generally have recorded within them miraculous acts, establishing the systematic nature of these revelations requires establishing the validity of the miraculous occurrences described in them. Thus the existence of objective empirical data which would indicate the nature of religious truth depends primarily upon the actual occurrence of miraculous events. The aversion of the modernist and humanist to the idea of such events is the major reason why these investigators have dealt with subjective rather than objective data. Potter and Fosdick write:

> The really revolutionary character of Humanism is best seen when one realizes that Humanists not only do not consider belief in the supernatural necessary in religion, but even hold that today such a belief may defeat the purpose of religion. For if religion seeks to unify the personality and relate it to the world without, any belief which hinders either part of the process is detrimental.

> Now a belief in supernatural beings is quite foreign to the modern man's understanding of the scheme of things. His knowledge of science prevents him from finding any room in the world outside himself or the world of personality within himself for either gods or demons. Such beings simply cannot exist for him, in the sense in which they existed for the men of the pre-scientific age.[55]

> Of course, what all humanists desire to escape is supernaturalism, but in this they have the cordial agreement of a great body of theists. Supernaturalism is an obsolete word and it stands for an obsolete idea. Its history displays its irrelevancy to modern thought. Starting with a whimsical world, where everything that occurred was the direct volition of a human or an extrahuman agent, mankind has laboriously discovered a natural world, observed its regularities, plotted its laws, and as one area after another has thus been naturalized, the supernatural inevitably has shrunk. It has become the limbo of the as yet inexplicable, a concept with which we cover our ignorance. The partition of our world into a natural order overlaid by a supernatural order which keeps breaking through is to a well-instructed mind impossible.[56]

The most formidable argument against the miraculous--and that which has generally carried most weight with modernists and humanists--is the argument which Hume stated in his

Enquiry concerning Human Understanding.[57]   The substance of
Hume's argument runs as follows:

A miracle is a violation of the laws of nature; and as a firm
and unalterable experience has established these laws, the
proof against a miracle, from the very nature of the fact, is
as entire as any argument from experience can possibly be
imagined. Why is it more than probable, that all men must
die; that lead cannot, of itself, remain suspended in the air;
that fire consumes wood, and is extinguished by water, unless it be, that these events are found agreeable to the laws
of nature and there is required a violation of these laws, or
in other words, a miracle to prevent them? Nothing is es-
teemed a miracle, if it ever happen in the common course of
nature. It is no miracle that a man, seemingly in good
health, should die on a sudden: because such a kind of death,
though more unusual than any other, has yet been frequently
observed to happen. But it is a miracle, that a dead man
should come to life; because that has never been observed in
any age or country. There must, therefore, be a uniform
experience against every miraculous event, otherwise the
event would not merit that appellation. And as a uniform experience amounts to a proof, there is here a direct and full
proof, from the nature of the fact, against the existence of
any miracle; nor can such a proof be destroyed, or the miracle rendered credible, but by an opposite proof, which is
superior.

The plain consequence is (and it is a general maxim
worthy of our attention), "That no testimony is sufficient to
establish a miracle, unless the testimony be of such a kind,
that its falsehood would be more miraculous, than the fact,
which it endeavors to establish; and even in that case there
is a mutual destruction of arguments, and the superior only
gives us an assurance suitable to that degree of force, which
remains, after deducting the inferior." When anyone tells
me, that he saw a dead man restored to life, I immediately
consider with myself, whether it be more probable, that this
person should either deceive or be deceived, or that the fact,
which he relates, should really have happened. I weigh the
one miracle against the other; and according to the superi-
ority, which I discover, I pronounce my decision, and always
reject the greater miracle. If the falsehood of his testimony
would be more miraculous, than the event which he relates;
then, and not till then, can he pretend to command my belief
or opinion.

The invalidity of Hume's argument lies in his definition of the word "miracle"--a definition entirely in accordance with Newtonian physics, but one which in the physics of today (a physics transformed by the concept of Relativity) no longer has meaning. Hume's definition of miracle is given in the first sentence of the above quoted passage: "a miracle is a violation of the laws of nature." For fear of not making his definition clear, Hume writes in a footnote to this section: "A miracle may be accurately defined, a transgression of a law of nature by a particular volition of the Deity, or by the interposition of some invisible agent" (Italics Hume's). It is evident that were there no rigorous structure of natural law for a miraculous event to violate, it would be impossible a priori to rule out an alleged miracle as Hume has done. Hume says that the ordinary course of events is such powerful evidence against the occurrence of unique events, that the latter can be rejected regardless of the authority or evidence attesting them. Under only one condition would Hume's argument hold, namely, if there were irrefutable evidence for the existence of a rigorous framework of natural law in the universe which would render absurd the idea of its violation.[58] Do we have such evidence? Newton thought so, and so has the traditional Religion of Science.[59] Yet, since Einstein, science has gradually given up this notion. Rather than looking at natural law as a structure which is already present in the universe and which is progressively being discovered, scientists of today see natural law as the human description of what is observed to happen in the universe. Such a conception of natural law is the only truly empirical one, for it places all events, regardless of their uniqueness, on equal footing--all are to be tested for error by a study of the empirical evidence for them, not ruled out a priori because they have not happened as many times as other events.

Laws of nature are a description of what happens, not a handbook of rules to tell us what cannot happen. In choosing his laws of nature, therefore, the scientist "should first consult history, and after deciding by historical evidence what has happened, should then choose his laws within the limits of historical actuality. The non-christian thinker, intent on repudiating miracles, proceeds by a reverse method. He chooses his law without regard to historical limits, and then tries to rewrite history to fit his law. But surely this method is not only the reverse of the Christian method, it is clearly the reverse of rational procedure as well."[60]

That the conception of natural law of Newton and Hume is

indeed the "reverse of rational procedure," may be seen even more clearly by means of an illustration. Gulliver, of Jonathan Swift's Gulliver's Travels, was said to have been shipwrecked on the island of Lilliput--an island inhabited by men six inches high. Before Gulliver's arrival, the Lilliputians had had no contact whatsoever with the rest of the world--no contact whatever with creatures taller than themselves. Suppose the Lilliputians who discovered Gulliver had followed Hume's reasoning: never before had a man one foot, much less six feet, tall been seen-- either by themselves or by anyone within the course of recorded Lilliputian history. Which, then, would be more miraculous-- that they themselves were deluded, or that Gulliver really existed? Obviously the former would be the greater miracle, so Gulliver does not exist at all. He may plead with the Lilliputians to evaluate the overwhelming, objective evidence that he does exist--the fact that he takes up space, eats, etc.--but to no avail. No Lilliputians have ever seen a six foot man; therefore Gulliver a priori does not exist.

Such an example illustrates well the fallaciousness of Hume's argument. In order to determine what natural laws are, it is necessary for us to evaluate, without a priori, the particular evidence for each alleged event, no matter how unique it is. If the evidence for a singular occurrence is equal to that ordinarily required to verify events, we must accept the unique happening, and consider it when plotting or revising the laws of nature.[61] The significance of a miracle does not lie in the fact that it transgresses some universal framework of natural law (we should remember that if God exists, natural law is nothing more than the expression of His will), but in the fact that it is unique--that its very degree of uniqueness gives strong evidence for the truth of the claim of the one who performed it and/or of the claim of the book in which it is recorded.

We pointed out above the distinction between the presuppositions of the Religion of Science and those of empirical or scientific method. It was noted that one can utilize scientific method without agreeing to the presuppositions of the Religion of Science. The more progressive scientists, since Einstein's revolutionary Theory of Relativity, have come to see this distinction, and have gradually abandoned the presuppositions of Science as a Religion, while retaining and re-emphasizing those of empirical method. Our discussion of the miraculous brings this out clearly: specific empirical evidence for an alleged event, not the number of events dissimilar to it which have occurred, is the proper determinant of the validity of the event. The universe, previously closed by Newton, Hume, et al. to the possibility of unique events, now opens to full empirical investigation.

CONCLUSION

The preceding discussion makes clear that a priori arguments against the discovery of religious truth by empirical investigation of objective phenomena are unfounded. Let us now observe more closely the advantages of an objective approach to religious knowledge. (1) This approach at least equals the chief merit of Constructive Religious Empiricism. Above we gave Constructive Religious Empiricism due recognition for utilizing the empirical method, and for setting itself against the rationalistic approach in philosophy and theology. But the objective approach is likewise an empirical method, and one much closer allied to science, which in its "exact" branches applies scientific method to objective, not subjective, data. Furthermore, it is well to note that Constructive Religious Empiricism originated after orthodox Christians had begun to apply--and with great success--empirical method to objective phenomena in their search for religious truth (Schleiermacher's Christian Faith was published in 1821). John Locke, William Paley, Hugo Grotius, Thomas Hartwell Horne, Jean Le Clerc, Charles Leslie,[62] and others had by 1821 shown the worth of the objective empirical approach. Thus Constructive Religious Empiricism cannot claim to have revolutionized theology by making it empirical, for a religious empiricism was being employed--and one utilizing much more stable data--before Constructive Religious Empiricism came into existence. Why did Constructive Religious Empiricism establish itself, then, in the face of a theological approach which we have seen to be better equipped to arrive at religious truth? Perhaps Screwtape has the answer:

> The horror of the Same Old Thing is one of the most valuable passions we have produced in the human heart--an endless source of heresies in religion, folly in counsel, infidelity in marriage, and inconstancy in friendship. . . .

> In the last generation we promoted the construction of . . . a "historical Jesus" on liberal and humanitarian lines; we are now putting forward a new "historical Jesus" on Marxian, catastrophic, and revolutionary lines. The advantages of these constructions, which we intend to change every thirty years or so, are manifold. In the first place they all tend to direct men's devotion to something which does not exist, for

each "historical Jesus" is unhistorical. The documents say what they say and cannot be added to; each new "historical Jesus" therefore has to be got out of them by suppression at one point and exaggeration at another, and by that sort of guessing (brilliant is the adjective we teach humans to apply to it) on which no one would risk ten shillings in ordinary life, but which is enough to produce a crop of new Napoleons, new Shakespeares, and new Swifts, in every publisher's autumn list.[63]

(2) The objective empirical approach avoids the disadvantages of Constructive Religious Empiricism. The objective empirical approach has a greater possibility than Constructive Religious Empiricism of being able to give the layman stable and satisfying religious knowledge. Although the objective approach, since it is also empirical, cannot prove anything with absolute certainty, the fact that it deals with objective data (like chemistry, history, physics) rather than with subjective data (like psychology) makes it more likely to produce definitive results. A well attested miracle occurring many years ago, for example, would provide very stable religious knowledge, for there would be little chance of contradictory evidence arising now to disprove it. Furthermore, the objective empirical approach eliminates the a priori problem which beset Constructive Religious Empiricism; the objective approach has no difficulty in choosing data through whose evaluation to test hypotheses of a religious nature. Whereas Constructive Religious Empiricism, because it deals with subjective phenomena incapable of indicating its own truth-value, has to choose a priori the criteria of true religious experience, the objective approach deals with a definite (and not very large) number of clear-cut claims to revelation whose relevance to religious knowledge is manifest.

In this paper I have evaluated Constructive Religious Empiricism and in doing so have found it incapable of providing men with a stable religious foundation. I have also made an effort to discover what method of acquiring truth must be utilized if sound religious knowledge is to be had. I have pointed out that the results of Constructive Religious Empiricism depend on the criteria of religious experience employed, and that these criteria must be found outside the subjective realm. Since neither common sense, authority, or intuition are valid avenues to the nature of true religious experience, the discovery of religious truth has been seen to depend upon the empirical analysis of objective phenomena, i.e., revelation-claims.

Emphasis has been placed upon the fact that the existence of a valid revelation, while solving the main problem of Constructive Religious Empiricism by providing a criterion of religious experience, would at the same time render the method superfluous by giving to mankind the very religious knowledge for the discovery of which the method originated.[64] We have seen that the objective empirical method avoids the disadvantages and at least equals the advantages of Constructive Religious Empiricism, and is thus a perfectly reasonable method (as well as being the only possible one by process of elimination!) for acquiring religious knowledge. In general: whereas the subjective approach to religious truth can neither identify religious experience nor provide objective religious knowledge, the objective approach is capable not only of giving objective religious knowledge, but also of providing a way of discriminating religious from other subjective feeling. Objective religious knowledge can screen subjective feelings, and distinguish stomach trouble from divine influence.

Thus the problem of acquiring religious truth centers upon an empirical evaluation of the claims to written revelation and/or the entrance of a divine agent or messenger into history. Without such historical revelation, valid religious knowledge seems forever denied us. With it, the secrets of the universe and of the human heart become accessible to man. I can think of no better way to conclude this discussion than to quote Plato, who, in the Phaedo, stated so clearly the issues at stake in the search for religious knowledge:

> With respect to such matters, it seems to me, and perhaps also to you, Socrates, that it is either impossible or very difficult to arrive at certainty in the present life; yet at the same time that a man shows very great weakness if he ceases to examine in every way what is said concerning these matters while he is still able to do so. For with regard to such things it is necessary to do one of the following: either learn from others or discover yourself how they stand, or, if this is impossible, lay hold on the very best and most irrefutable of human reasonings, and, having embarked on this, sail through life as one who risks himself upon a raft, unless a safer and less hazardous passage is possible in a more secure conveyance, to wit, some word of God.[65]

APPENDIX

C. S. Lewis vs. Hume*

The ordinary procedure of the modern historian, even if he admits the possibility of miracle, is to admit no particular instance of it until every possibility of "natural" explanation has been tried and failed. That is, he will accept the most improbable "natural" explanations rather than say that a miracle occurred. Collective hallucination, hypnotism of unconsenting spectators, widespread instantaneous conspiracy in lying by persons not otherwise known to be liars and not likely to gain by the lie--all these are known to be very improbable events: so improbable that, except for the special purpose of excluding a miracle, they are never suggested. But they are preferred to the admission of a miracle.

Such a procedure is, from the purely historical point of view, sheer midsummer madness unless we start by knowing that any Miracle whatever is more improbable than the most improbable natural event. Do we know this?

We must distinguish the different kinds of improbability. Since miracles are, by definition, rarer than other events, it is obviously improbable beforehand that one will occur at any given place and time. In that sense every miracle is improbable. But that sort of improbability does not make the story that a miracle has happened incredible; for in the same sense all events whatever were once improbable. It is immensely improbable beforehand that a pebble dropped from the stratosphere over London will hit any given spot, or that any one particular person will win a large lottery. But the report that the pebble has landed outside such and such a shop or that Mr. So-and-So has won the lottery is not at all incredible. When you consider the immense number of meetings and fertile unions between ancestors which were necessary in order that you should be born, you perceive that it was once immensely improbable that such a person as you should come to exist: but once you are here, the report of your existence is not in the least incredible. With the probability of this kind--antecedent probability of chances--we are not here concerned. Our business is with historical probability.

*C. S. Lewis, Miracles, Ch. XIII ("On Probability"), pp. 121-4.

296

Ever since Hume's famous Essay it has been believed that historical statements about miracles are the most intrinsically improbable of all historical statements. According to Hume, probability rests on what may be called the majority vote of our past experiences. The more often a thing has been known to happen, the more probable it is that it should happen again; and the less often the less probable. Now the regularity of Nature's course, says Hume, is supported by something better than the majority vote of past experiences: it is supported by their unanimous vote, or, as Hume says, by "firm and unalterable experience." There is, in fact, "uniform experience" against Miracle; otherwise, says Hume, it would not be Miracle. A Miracle is therefore the most improbable of all events. It is always more probable that the witnesses were lying or mistaken than that a Miracle occurred.

Now of course we must agree with Hume that if there is absolutely "uniform experience" against miracles, if in other words they have never happened, why then they never have. Unfortunately, we know the experience against them to be uniform only if we know that all the reports of them are false. And we can know all the reports to be false only if we know already that miracles have never occurred. In fact, we are arguing in a circle.

There is also an objection to Hume which leads us deeper into our problem. The whole idea of Probability (as Hume understands it) depends on the principle of the Uniformity of Nature. Unless Nature always goes on in the same way, the fact that a thing had happened ten million times would not make it a whit more probable that it would happen again. And how do we know the Uniformity of Nature? A moment's thought shows that we do not know it by experience. We observe many regularities in Nature. But of course all the observations that men have made or will make while the race lasts cover only a minute fraction of the events that actually go on. Our observations would therefore be of no use unless we felt sure Nature when we are not watching her behaves in the same way as when we are: in other words, unless we believed in the Uniformity of Nature. Experience therefore cannot prove uniformity, because uniformity has to be assumed before experience proves anything. And mere length of experience does not help matters. It is no good saying, "Each fresh experience confirms our belief in uniformity and therefore we reasonably expect that it will always be confirmed"; for that argument works only on the assumption that the future will resemble the past--which is simply the assumption of Uniformity under a new name. Can we say that Uniformity is at any rate very probable? Unfortunately not. We have just seen that all probabilities depend on it. Unless Nature is uniform, nothing is either probable or improbable. And clearly the assumption which you have to make before there is any such thing as probability cannot itself be probable.

The odd thing is that no man knew this better than Hume. His Essay on Miracles is quite inconsistent with the more radical, and honourable, scepticism of his main work.

The question, "Do miracles occur?" and the question, "Is the course of Nature absolutely uniform?" are the same question asked in two different ways. Hume, by sleight of hand, treats them as two different questions. He first answers, "Yes," to the question whether Nature is absolutely uniform: and then uses this "Yes" as a ground for answering, "No," to the question, "Do miracles occur?" The single real question which he set out to answer is never discussed at all. He gets the answer to one form of the question by assuming the answer to another form of the same question.

NOTES

1. Although I do not wish to be pedantic, I feel compelled to state my objection to Dr. Burtt's term "Constructive Religious Empiricism" (see Burtt, Types of Religious Philosophy, Ch. VIII, "Modernism"). The word "constructive" has a definitely positive connotation, which should not be present in a technical term. Such terms should be descriptive; they should not make value judgments. As this paper will show, my researches have led me to believe that Constructive Religious Empiricism is far from "constructive." What improvement do I suggest? It seems to me that "Modernist-humanist Religious Empiricism" or "Subjective Religious Empiricism" would be better terms to employ; the distinction must be clearly made between the subjective religious empiricism of modernists and humanists and the objective religious empiricism of orthodox Christians, concerning which I shall speak later. (I have continued to employ "Constructive Religious Empiricism" in this paper, in order to avoid confusion.)

2. John Dewey, A Common Faith, p. 11.

3. William James, The Varieties of Religious Experience, p. 446. Cf., Walter Marshall Horton, A Psychological Approach to Theology, pp. 23, 232:

> In the light of our general proposals for perpetuating peace and fraternity between science and theology, certain stipulations must at once be laid down. Theology, on the one hand, must not deny the right of psychology to investigate according to its own methods and to explain according to its own presuppositions everything that lies within its proper field, even though this may seem to expose the most sacred recesses of the religious life to the profaning glance of inquisitive and coldblooded scientists. Theology must, moreover, agree without reservation to alter, amend, or cancel altogether whatsoever there may be in the dogmas of the past that is flatly and decisively contradicted by any new facts that psychology may reveal. . . .
>
> God is not merely an object of faith; He is an object of human experience; and as such, He can be scientifically studied and analyzed. Such study and analysis ought to make it progressively more clear precisely what we mean when we say that we rely upon "God" as an "ally" and "moral resource" in time of need.

4. My list of four methods for acquiring truth has been culled from Randall and Buchler, Philosophy: An Introduction (Chs. V - VII, XI); and Edward John Carnell, An Introduction to Christian Apologetics (Ch. III). In both of these works, many more than four methods of arriving at truth are given, but most of these result from a confusion of the problem. "Methods of acquiring truth" and "methods of testing for truth" (e.g., pragmatism, systematic consistency) are intermixed. Randall and Buchler consider even faith as a method of acquiring truth! See also Max Black, Critical Thinking (Ch. XIII); Ambrose and Lazerowitz, Fundamentals of Symbolic Logic, pp. 16-19.

5. Shailer Mathews, The Faith of Modernism, p. 23.

6. Harry Emerson Fosdick, As I See Religion, pp. 4, 9.

7. Georg Wobbermin, The Nature of Religion, p. 227.

8. Charles Francis Potter, Humanism: A New Religion, p. 1.

9. James, op. cit., p. 423.

10. Dewey, op. cit., pp. 8-9, 10. See also pp. 45ff.

11. Horton, pp. 229, 216.

12. Dewey, op. cit., p. 437.

13. Horton, pp. 32, 186-7.

14. Ibid., p. 185. Cf. also D. C. Macintosh, in Wobbermin, op. cit., pp. vi-vii:

> It is a matter of interest to students on this side of the Atlantic that he [Wobbermin] was one of the first to introduce to German readers what was then an almost exclusively American study, namely, the (empirical) psychology of religion. Not only did he make William James' Varieties of Religious Experience available in German translation; he discussed the problems of religious psychology and began definitely to develop in this theology, partly as supplementing but partly in opposition to the more exclusively "religio-historical" method of Troeltsch, what he calls the "religio-psychological" or "James-Schleiermacher" method. Beginning as William James does, with a survey of the varieties of religious experience, we are led, according to Wobbermin, to the discovery that religion is always and everywhere a tendency toward the transcendent, always interested therefore in the truth of its ideas about the transcendent, especially in the truth of its idea of God. If man is to continue to be positively religious he must have ideas which he can believe to be true to guide him in his religious quest and adjustment. At this point, then, man to become or remain religious must go beyond any mere external survey of the varieties of religious experience.

15. Burtt, op. cit., pp. 292-3.

16. Carnell, op. cit., pp. 91-2:

> It may be asked why we make assumptions at all. Why not stay with the facts ? The answer to this is very easy indeed! We make assumptions because we must make

300

assumptions to think at all. All knowledge is inferential and all inferences are assumptions. Knowledge is the mind's construction of meaning, and properly construed meaning is truth. It is therefore useless to say, "Stay with the facts," unless we mean, "Keep your hypotheses in conformity to facts." Facts just are. Knowledge is inference drawn from facts. A fact is any unit of being which is capable of bearing meaning, but it is the meaning, not the fact, which is the knowledge.

17. Randall and Buchler, op. cit., p. 58. See the whole of Ch. VI.

18. Carnell, op. cit., p. 94.

19. See Randall and Buchler, op. cit., Ch. VII.

20. Curtis W. Reese, Humanism, pp. 16-17.

21. Wobbermin says (op. cit., p. 27):

> Due to its inherent nature, Catholicism excludes the search for the nature of religion in the sense of the fundamental problem of all science of religion and theology. The Catholic conception of the Church implies the exclusion of such a question. Ever since the principle of extra ecclesiam nulla salus has gained the upper hand in Catholicism, the problem of the nature of religion has lost its genuine significance for the Catholic mind. For such a principle includes the other: extra ecclesiam nulla religio--outside of the Catholic Church there is no real religion.

See also, James, op. cit., Lecture XVIII ("Philosophy").

22. Burtt, op. cit., p. 196.

23. Carnell, p. 125:

> Internal ineffable experience. This is that activity of consciousness which brings an immediate assurance to the soul of reality that is overwhelming and ineffable, as the mystic experience of being swallowed up in God. We must pass over this for reasons stated earlier. Truth is systematic consistency and must be expressed in communicable propositions. But this is impossible in mysticism.

24. James, op. cit., p. 371. See lectures XVI and XVII ("Mysticism").

25. Potter, op. cit., p. 36.

26. James, op. cit., pp. 488-9.

27. Horton, op. cit., p. 203.

28. Dewey, op. cit., pp. 9-10.

29. Fosdick, op. cit., pp. 20-1.

30. Horton, op. cit., p. 31.

31. Carnell, op. cit., p. 155. For "Germans" read "Nazis"!

32. Reese, op. cit., p. 28. E. E. Slosson, in his Sermons of a Chemist (pp. 39-41) argues this point with telling force:

> In the intellectual crisis of the present, which comes from a sudden influx of novel and unassimilated facts and theories from scientific research, we are not getting the help that we have a right to expect from those who now occupy our pulpits, and I fear that we shall get still less from their successors. For, either from lack of taste or from defect of training, the graduates from our best theological seminaries do not seem to be concerned with such questions. . . . They seem to be smartly up to date and keenly alive on all topics but one, and that is theology. Most of them do not seem to have any, or any interest in any. By theology I do not mean a particular system of dogmatic doctrine, but rather the habit of thinking about the fundamentals of faith and reason, about the metaphysics that lie at the base of physics, the psychology that controls character and motivation, the personal philosophy that is the compass of conduct. It is the schools of science, not the schools of theology, that are turning out the thinkers in such fields.
>
> We are in the midst of the greatest revolution of thought that the world has ever seen, the Einstein theory of relativity, the Planck theory of quanta, the chromosome theory of heredity, the hormone theory of temperament, the new knowledge of the constitution of the universe and of the workings of the human mind. These ideas will

influence the philosophy, theology, religion, and morals of the future as much as the Copernican theory influenced those of the sixteenth century and the Darwinian theory of the nineteenth. Such questions would have aroused the keenest interest in the minds of men like Edwards, Berkeley, Calvin, Wesley, Aquinas, Augustine, or Paul. . . . A student of engineering or biology will sit up half the night discussing these theories and their application to life, but your modern theological graduate is bored by them. He has learned how to give the glad hand to the strangers at the church door and can teach Boy Scouts how they should salute the flag--things that a pumphandle or drill-sergeant could do as well--but he is not qualified to lead his people through the mazes of modern thought. Since sermons have become sociological instead of philosophical, serious-minded people are going elsewhere to get their metaphysics and often getting a poor brand of it from unqualified dispensers. When a young preacher does touch upon such topics--which fortunately is seldom --he is apt to reveal a materialistic conception of matter that sounds amusingly antiquated to his scientific hearers. . . .

Unless the preacher gets accustomed to deep diving while he is young, he is apt to swim shallower and shallower as he gets on in life. Unless he has once thought things through for himself he will be at the mercy of every passing fad that blows. Theological schools ought to teach theology.

Eloquence of tongue and charm of manner will not compensate for want of thought. In time any congregation will tire of a diet exclusively of boneless sermons stewed in cream.

33. Wobbermin, op. cit., p. 41.

34. Burtt, op. cit., p. 293. (Italics mine)

35. James, op. cit., p. 446.

36. George Orwell, 1984, pp. 162, 227, 201-2.

37. Horton, op. cit., p. 33.

38. Wobbermin, op. cit., p. x.

39. Dewey, op. cit., p. 13.

40. James, op. cit., pp. 493-4.

41. Fosdick, op. cit., p. 11.

42. Horton, op. cit., p. 203.

43. Wobbermin, op. cit., p. 42.

44. Potter, op. cit., p. 3:

> It is a new way of looking at religion. You have to make over and broaden your definition of religion to get Humanism in at all, especially if you come from a Christian background. The Humanist splits the seams of all the old coats of religion when he tries them on. The new wine has burst the old wineskins.

Fosdick, op. cit., pp. 27-8, 29-30:

> One immediate effect of such an approach to religious experience as we have been describing is to make its possessor sympathetic and tolerant. Within the framework of many creeds and rituals the inner realities of this experience thrive and grow; and one who cares primarily about the reality is generous toward its diverse and often incongruous settings. In a Buddhist temple I have heard a Japanese peasant praying with passionate devotion to Amida; in a Mohammedan mosque I have worshipped with a vast throng who bowed toward Mecca; at Assisi I have knelt long at the tomb of St. Francis; and in more than one Protestant church, with sermons and hymns representing ways of thinking almost as strange to me as the worship of the Aztecs, I have found God. . . .

> We will not reduce ourselves to any denomination's lowest common denominator; we will not put our necks into the yoke of any official creed. . . .

See also the essay "Tolerance" in Fosdick's Adventurous Religion (pp. 215-31).

45. Potter, op. cit., p. 97. See the entire chapter (VI), entitled, "Fundamentalism, Modernism, and Humanism." Dr. Burtt (op. cit., p. 285) says at the beginning of his chapter on modernism:

The religious philosophy which appears next in the historical order is the most difficult type to expound. Considered from the standpoint of logical coherence, it is not a philosophy but a group of philosophies reflecting no single controlling principle, whether metaphysical, methodological, or ethical. Considered, however, from the standpoint of its historical context and development, it represents a unified tendency in religious thought during the nineteenth and twentieth centuries. Consequently, it is regarded as a distinctive point of view by people concerned with religion who are not sophisticated by habits of philosophical analysis. For that reason it is here treated as such, despite the logical difficulties involved. Our task is to clarify the features that give it unity as a historical tendency, and to note the major lines of divergence which, if emphasized and systematically compared, would compel us to view it as a collection of separate philosophies.

46. Friedrich Schleiermacher, The Christian Faith, Prop. 4, p. 12.

47. Burtt, pp. 297, 301. Cf., Wobbermin, op. cit., p. 99:

If, now, we begin the attempt to complete Schleiermacher's theory of religion upon its religio-psychological foundation, we must be careful at the very beginning to avoid Schleiermacher's errors. As we have seen, there are two of these errors. One is an inadequate consideration of the history of religion, especially of the lower forms of religion.

48. E.g., Harry Emerson Fosdick (see his As I See Religion, pp. 22, 25-27, and the whole of Ch. III, "Religion without God?"); Walter Marshall Horton (see his A Psychological Approach to Theology, pp. 33, 236-7). Wobbermin, a disciple of Schleiermacher and a typical German ("My motto for the religio-psychological method is exclusively this: Back to Schleiermacher and from Schleiermacher forward!") cannot be placed in this category, because he corrects many of Schleiermacher's errors (see the preceding note).

49. Horton, op. cit., pp. 34-5. Potter, op. cit., p. 96:

This "positive presentation of a credible idea of God,"

which Dr. Fosdick admits the lack of, he also admits is
not likely to be composed very soon, confessing that:

> "amid the mass of undigested factual material which
> modern religion faces, the thoughtful Theist knows
> that he often appears vague in his idea of deity. He
> frankly despairs of tossing off on demand a statement
> of Theism philosophically adequate to this new amaz-
> ing universe. He sees in that task work for many
> minds demanding more than one generation, but he is
> still convinced that atheism is no solution of the prob-
> lem and that behind our partial and inadequate ideas
> of God is God."

There could be no better picture of the tragic dilemma of
Modernism, the liberal wing of Christianity.

50. One might think that another fallacy in Constructive Religious Empiricism is that the constructive religious empiricist's a prioris necessarily color the phrasing of the
hypotheses which he tests. Whether or not this objection is
valid, it is certainly unimportant, for the data which the
constructive religious empiricist analyzes is always predetermined by his presuppositions. No matter how the constructive religious empiricist phrases his hypotheses under
these conditions, he will verify only those that accord with
the religious experiences of those he analyzes, i.e., with his
own presuppositions.

51. Fosdick, op. cit., p. 39. Dewey, op. cit., pp. 11-12:

> A writer says: "I broke down from overwork and soon
> came to the verge of nervous prostration. One morning
> after a long and sleepless night . . . I resolved to stop
> drawing upon myself so continuously and begin drawing
> upon God. I determined to set apart a quiet time of
> every day in which I could relate my life to its ultimate
> source, regain the consciousness that in God I live, move
> and have my being. That was thirty years ago. Since
> then I have had literally not one hour of darkness or
> despair."

> This is an impressive record. I do not doubt its authen-
> ticity nor that of the experience related. It illustrates a
> religious aspect of experience. But it illustrates also
> the use of that quality to carry a superimposed load of a
> particular religion. For having been brought up in the

Christian religion, its subject interprets it in the terms of the personal God characteristic of that religion. Taoists, Buddhists, Moslems, persons of no religion, including those who reject all supernatural influence and power, have had experiences similar in their effect.

52. Carnell, op. cit., p. 49.

53. See Ibid., Ch. III ("The Problem of Truth").

54. Modernists and humanists have been some of the most consistent and faithful worshippers at the shrine of Science. Potter's statements are typical (op. cit., p. 44):

> Science alone has been responsible for this change in the status of man, and science, be it remarked, was born of the brain of man and not supernaturally revealed.

> Knowledge of science has given to man the control of forces which hitherto were supposed to be directed by the supernatural power of God. If God still be God, man has stolen his power. Prometheus has returned to earth and has as yet gone unpunished.

55. Ibid., p. 9.

56. Fosdick, op. cit., pp. 83-4.

57. Sec. X ("Of Miracles"). The Enquiry is contained in Burtt's English Philosophers from Bacon to Mill.

58. See C. S. Lewis, Miracles; esp. Chs. VIII and XIII. The reader is referred to the Appendix of this paper for the essence of Lewis' excellent criticism of Hume.

59. Writing as late as 1902, James says (pp. 483-4):

> The God whom science recognizes must be a God of universal laws exclusively, a God who does a wholesale, not a retail business.

Cf., Wobbermin, op. cit., p. 145.

60. Carnell, op. cit., p. 258.

61. It is highly significant that even modernists have been forced to recognize the new conception of natural law and

with it the possibility of unique occurrences. Mathews, The Faith of Modernism, pp. 113-14:

> The Modernist assumes no a priori position relative to the historicity of the stories of miracles in the biblical literature. He recognizes their expressional value in the religion of non-scientific minds. He insists, however, that the records of such events should be tested by the ordinary processes of literary and historical criticism, and by the facts of science. That is to say, he asks not whether they were miracles, but whether they actually took place. If the evidence is strong enough to warrant belief in their having taken place, he at once regards them as belonging to a class of phenomena which have been or will be described in some law. They are not violations of the uniformity of nature. As a religious man he does not abate one whit his belief that whether exceptional or classifiable, whether astounding or accustomed, such events are a phase of the operation of God. If there should be found only one such incident in history, as, for example, the person of Jesus Christ, the Modernist's position brings him reverently to say that therein is the unique revelation of God in accord with biological, psychological and historical processes.

62. See Bibliography.

63. C. S. Lewis, The Screwtape Letters, pp. 126, 117.

64. A valid revelation would not, of course, remove significance from descriptive or psychological studies of religious experience. A revelation, by providing mankind with the essential items of religious knowledge, would render superfluous only the testing of hypotheses concerned with establishing doctrinal truth by the empirical investigation of subjective religious experience.

65. Phaedo, 85d (my translation).

BIBLIOGRAPHY

Ambrose, Alice and Lazerowitz, Morris. Fundamentals of Symbolic Logic. New York: Rinehart and Company, Inc., 1950.

Black, Max. Critical Thinking, An Introduction to Logic and Scientific Method. New York: Prentice-Hall, Inc., 1947.

Burtt, Edwin A. Types of Religious Philosophy. New York and London: Harper and Brothers Publishers, 1939. (A revised edition was issued in 1951.)

Carnell, Edward John. An Introduction to Christian Apologetics. Grand Rapids (Mich.): Wm. B. Eerdmans Publishing Company, 1948.

Clark, Gordon H. A Christian Philosophy of Education. Grand Rapids,(Mich.): Wm. B. Eerdmans Publishing Co., 1946.

Dewey, John. A Common Faith. New Haven: Yale University Press, 1934.

Fosdick, Harry Emerson. Adventurous Religion and Other Essays. New York and London: Harper and Brothers, 1926.

_____. As I See Religion. New York and London: Harper and Brothers, 1932.

Grotius, Hugo. The Truth of the Christian Religion. Ed. by John LeClerc. London: John and Paul Knapton, 1743.

Horne, Thomas Hartwell. An Introduction to the Critical Study and Knowledge of the Holy Scriptures. Philadelphia: E. Littell, 1825. 4 vols.

Horton, Walter Marshall. A Psychological Approach to Theology. New York and London: Harper and Brothers, 1931.

Hume, David. "An Enquiry concerning Human Understanding," The English Philosophers from Bacon to Mill. Ed. by Edwin A. Burtt. New York: The Modern Library, 1939.

James, William. The Varieties of Religious Experience. New York: The Modern Library, 1902.

Kant, Immanuel. Critique of Practical Reason and Other Writings in Moral Philosophy. Trans. and ed. by Lewis White Beck. Chicago: University of Chicago Press, 1950.

Leslie, Charles. The Theological Works of the Rev. Charles Leslie. Oxford: at the University Press, 1832. Vol. I.

Lewis, C. S. Beyond Personality. New York: The Macmillan Company.

_____. The Case for Christianity. New York: The Macmillan Company.

_____. Miracles. New York: The Macmillan Company, 1947.

_____. The Screwtape Letters. New York: The Macmillan Company, 1944. (An augmented edition was published at London by Geoffrey Bles in 1961.)

Locke's Essay for the Understanding of St. Paul's Epistles and LeClerc on Inspiration. Boston: Wells and Lilly, 1820.

Mathews, Shailer. The Faith of Modernism. New York: The Macmillan Company, 1925.

Munro, Robert. Schleiermacher, Personal and Speculative. Paisley: Alexander Gardner, 1903.

Orwell, George. 1984. New York: The New American Library of World Literature, Inc., 1950.

Paley, William. The Works of William Paley, D.D. Philadelphia: J. J. Woodward, 1836.

Potter, Charles Francis. Humanism: A New Religion. New York: Simon and Schuster, 1930.

Randall, John Herman and Buchler, Justus. Philosophy: An Introduction. New York: Barnes and Noble, Inc., 1947.

Reese, Curtis W. Humanism. Chicago and London: The Open Court Publishing Company, 1926.

Schleiermacher, Friedrich. The Christian Faith. Ed. by H. R.

Macintosh and J. S. Stewart. Edinburgh: T. and T. Clark, 1928.

Selbie, W. B. Schleiermacher, A Critical and Historical Study. New York: E. P. Dutton and Company, 1913.

Sellars, Roy Wood. Religion Coming of Age. New York: The Macmillan Company, 1928.

Slosson, E. E. Sermons of a Chemist. New York: Harcourt, Brace and Company, 1925.

Smith, Wilbur. The Supernaturalness of Christ. Boston: W. A. Wilde and Company, 1940.

_____. Therefore Stand. Boston: W. A. Wilde and Company.

Wobbermin, Georg. The Nature of Religion. Trans. by Theophil Menzel and Daniel Sommer Robinson. Intro. by Douglas Clyde Macintosh. New York: Thomas Y. Crowell Company, 1933.

4. A CRITIQUE OF WILLIAM JAMES'
VARIETIES OF RELIGIOUS EXPERIENCE

I. MODUS OPERANDI

The all too obvious disparity between the length of the present critique and that of the work being criticized[1] requires us to indicate at the very outset the approach which we have followed and the self-limitations which have been imposed.

The reader should understand, first of all, that the present study is critical rather than descriptive in character. Summaries[2] and abstracts[3] of the Varieties abound; therefore it has not seemed profitable to go over such ground again. This does not say, however, that we enter upon an evaluation of one of Professor James' greatest works with a feeling of overbearing self-confidence. With regard to our author, it is generally conceded, even by his severest critics, that "as the ocean of time has closed over him he has become one of the immortals, one of the eternal spirits."[4] This we likewise readily admit, and if we do not always follow Horace's dictum "de mortuis nihil nisi bonum," we nevertheless offer the present study as a humble attempt to move a bit closer to the truth ideal--which ideal James himself was so concerned to place beyond the reach of any single individual or generation.[5]

The critical approach to be followed in this paper has been suggested by the two-fold character of the Varieties--the work being both psychological and philosophical in nature.[6] We shall thus criticize the book from these two standpoints, with particular emphasis upon the philosophical-theological issues raised in the work.[7] It will be noted that the psychological and philosophical sections of the paper consist almost entirely of negative criticism; the merits of James' book are collectively set forth in the final section of this essay.

II. PSYCHOLOGICAL CRITICISM

Classic Criticisms

As a background for our personal criticisms of the Varieties from the standpoint of psychology, let us note some of the trenchant observations which have already been made with regard to psychological difficulties in James' book. Here we present for the most part direct quotations from a truly great contemporary work, unfortunately little used by American scholars: J. G. McKenzie's Psychology, Psychotherapy, and Evangelicalism.[8]

(1) James did not give enough attention in his studies to the significant group of religious believers whose experience focuses more on objective realities (e.g. the great theological verities) than on mystical encounters.[9]

The soul has a need to know as well as to feel. This was one of the psychological facts James almost entirely overlooked in his choice of the varieties of religious experience which he describes. James was too much influenced in his choice by the explicit motive to find empirical grounds for a transcendental scheme of things. He was looking for contrasts that might justify his Pluralism. As Dr. Uren has pointed out, James's assertion "that personal religious experience has its roots and centre in mystical states of consciousness" is too narrow and excludes from religious experience those whose fellowship with God "is objective and external rather than mystical." The forgiveness of sin, the love of God, the efficacy of Christ, the experience of a dynamic faith, steady progress in sanctification are just as real to those who have reached those experiences through the external relations of thought--through the attempt to satisfy the need for rational unity--as those whose experience has come to them through mystic intuitions. "Synthetic intuition" is as real in religious as in philosophical experience.[10]

(2) James attributed to constitutional type (i.e., heredity) what should have been attributed to environmental influence; thus he frequently short-circuited complete, scientific explanations.

James made too confident an assertion when he said of the "healthy-minded" that in many of them "happiness is congenital and irreclaimable." Likewise, when dealing with the "sick soul" he commenced with the symptoms but never reached the real causes which led to the sickness. . . .

Most writers on conversion have dealt at length with the abnormal phenomena which often accompany the experience of the dramatic struggle, and resultant experience of conversion. James thought that the phenomena were only found in persons of a psychopathic temperament. This psychopathic temperament, however, is not due to any neurological defect; it is caused by the emotional disturbances and unconscious conflicts which may have been repressed early in childhood.[11]

(3) James became so fascinated with specific conversion accounts[12] that he made little attempt to get at the previous life experiences of the individuals involved--experiences which would undoubtedly have shed much light on the conversion incidents themselves.

> Such isolation of a particular experience is misleading. Continuity is of the very essence of mental life; and to chop off one particular experience as though it had little or no relation to the whole past religious life of the individual is fallacious. . . . The religious sentiment is always prior to the more striking experience with which Starbuck and James dealt. The unexpected and intense conviction of sin, the sudden and dramatic conversion may alter the content of the religious sentiment and does give it a new place in the reorganised inner life, but unless it had been there as a part of the mind's content no religious interest could have been evoked.[13]

(4) As suggested by the last two criticisms, James did not have psychoanalytic insights at his disposal to aid him in interpreting religious experience.[14]

> One of the major defects of Professor James's Varieties was his failure to differentiate between the true "sick soul" and the victim of unconscious tendencies. He concluded too easily that the extreme form was really a true form of the religious experience. Psychotherapy helps us to differentiate clearly between the morbid type of the religious experience and the normal type; and it also helps to explain the difference. . . . If psychotherapy or psycho-analysis has taught us anything it is that all the vital experiences which dispose the mind to stability or the failure to adjust to reality have their origin in our early years, some would say, in our very early years. . . . The doctrines of the Unconscious and Repression have outdated many paragraphs in The Varieties of Religious Experience.[15]

(5) James' distinction between the "healthy-minded" and the "sick" religious personality is a poor one, and does not stand up under close scrutiny.[16]

Professor James confused the "healthy-minded" type of personality with what is known in modern psychology as the "extravert." He classes the healthy-minded with those to whom "the attitude of unhappiness is not only painful, it is mean and ugly." It is very doubtful whether any truly religious man ever sees unhappiness as "mean and ugly." To him unhappiness is always a tragedy eliciting his sympathy and his service.[17]

(6) James' related distinction of the "once-born" and "twice-born" believer[18] is likewise very difficult to maintain.

Many of those of whom we are now thinking have been living on their parents' religious capital; but never till now have they been conscious that they have not reached what we may call "economic maturity" spiritually or morally. They have never made God their own; never appropriated forgiveness; never developed a dynamic faith. Like the "elder brother" they have been content to live under the Father's roof; they are not conscious of having squandered their Father's goods in riotous living. Then gradually or suddenly they became dissatisfied within themselves because they were unsatisfied; discontented because they were uncontented. . . . The emphasis of the "moment of vision" falls on the inadequacy of the values they have been usually satisfied to seek. The "moment of vision" leads them to seek a more vital religious experience; and in the quest of it they make the decision to surrender more fully to Christ. . . . Made aware of their need in that "moment of vision" they have set out to have the need satisfied. There is a new birth in the sense that they have made their own values which they had rather taken for granted than experienced. . . . Their experience is a real evangelical experience; and may in the right spiritual environment be an ever deepening one. Decision is but a beginning not an ending of their struggle. Let us emphasise again that in the case of the "Once-born" there is a true re-orientation within. Religious values and the religious sentiment take a central place in motivation and in the ordering of their lives.[19]

Personal Criticisms

Let us now offer three basic and interrelated psychological criticisms of the Varieties which go beyond the critical material just given.

(1) The experience-overbelief distinction. In examining

315

James' "healthy" vs. "sick" soul, and his "twice-born" vs. "once-born" religious personality, one discovers (as McKenzie has pointed out) that our learned author tends to make sharper distinctions than the facts warrant. This tendency is even more evident, and even more far-reaching in its detrimental effects, when one comes to James' dichotomy between experience and overbelief.

This distinction runs through the pages of James' book like the theme of a great musical composition--sometimes appearing clearly, sometimes evident only if one observes with great care, but always present. This distinction is first suggested in James' opening paragraph (see note 6); it gains clarity when one marks the type of religious experiences excluded by James (see the quotation corresponding to note 10); and it is stated precisely by our author in such passages as the following:

> Our impulsive belief is . . . always what sets up the original body of truth, and our articulately verbalized philosophy is but its showy translation into formulas (p. 73). Religious experience . . . spontaneously engenders myths, superstitions, dogmas, creeds, and metaphysical theologies, and criticisms of one set of these by the adherents of another (pp. 423-4).

> The theories which Religion generates, being thus variable, are secondary; and if you wish to grasp her essence, you must look to the feelings and the conduct as being the more constant elements. It is between these two elements that the short circuit exists on which she carries on her principal business, while the ideas and symbols and other institutions form loop-lines which may be perfections and improvements, and may some day all be united into one harmonious system, but which are not to be regarded as organs with an indispensable function, necessary at all times for religious life to go on (pp. 494-5).

James uses the term "overbelief" (p. 503) to refer to these "myths, superstitions, dogmas, creeds, and metaphysical theologies," which he always considers secondary and distinguishable from original, primary religious experience.

Now there is of course a degree of truth in the distinction made here by James--but truth and error have been mixed as a result of the overly broad denotation given to the term "overbelief." Few would deny that some of the theologizing of Roman and Protestant scholasticism is secondary intellectualism, and has little or no connection with personal religious experience.

316

The list of metaphysical attributes of God which James gives on p. 436, and the lengthy quotation from John Henry Cardinal Newman which precedes it (pp. 430-32), fall into the "overbelief" category without much doubt. But to assume, as James does, that all propositional assertions of faith are secondary and distinguishable from religious experience itself is surely to fly in the face of empirical fact--whether "radically empirical" or not! Christian believers, for example, have never been able to separate their religious experience from positive assertions concerning the nature and offices of Jesus Christ. The "doubting Thomas incident" is a striking illustration of this--especially when we note that it is the climactic event[20] in the apostolic "Gospel of Belief", the Gospel according to St. John. When Thomas had the religious experience of beholding the risen Lord, he responded without hesitation, "My Lord and my God" (ho kyrios mou kai ho theos mou). Such a response can hardly be called an "overbelief" in any semantically valid sense; the experience and the theological assertion are blended into an inseparable unity.

An even more striking empirical contradiction to James' position on theological overbeliefs is the fact that what he would call secondary overbeliefs are the most evident cause of deep religious experiences. The Christian kerygma has through the centuries brought about more deeply meaningful and lasting religious experiences for more people in the Western tradition than has any other single factor (such as the beauties of nature --cf. the case cited by James on p. 69). Take for example the case of John Wesley, who was converted, according to his own testimony, while listening to the reading of the preface to Luther's Commentary on Romans.[21] If the central truths of theology are but a secondary accretion--an overbelief--how are they so consistently able to produce the religious experience which is supposed always to be primary? Thus we see that on two specific counts, James' overbelief-experience distinction contradicts the facts of living religion.

But this is not the only difficulty with the "overbelief" notion. Not only does it do violence to the testimony of religious psychology, but also (as one might expect) it has deadly effects when applied in the realm of practical therapy (i.e., in religious psychiatry). If the psychiatrist follows James in assuming (as not a few do) that immediate religious experiences are primary, and theological opinions are merely mental wallpaper laid over these experiences, then he will be blind to such realistic situations as the following: (a) The common case where a harmful theology, rather than a harmful experience, is the root of the psychological difficulty. For example, the Christian Scientist's refusal, on theological grounds, to see evil in the world can be the cause of more neurotic crackups than any "experience" the Christian Scientist might have. The Jamesian psychologist, however, will be looking in the attic for the termites while the latter are boring away in the cellar. (b) The even more common case where the patient's theology is ennobling and edifying, but he has become neurotic through refusing to admit a lack of conformity to his theology or a refusal to conform to it as he knows he should. One thinks immediately of cases of marital infidelity on the part of those who have been unable to "shake" the Christian ethic. The Jamesian analyst will be prone to suggest that the patient rid himself of his secondary overbelief, rather than conform his emotional life to his theology or ethic.[22]

(2) Obtuseness toward the characteristic qualities of religious experience in particular faiths. The reader has perhaps been perplexed as to the reason for James' blindspot on the overbelief issue. Was not James himself an M.D., and a keen observer of human nature, especially with regard to psychology and religion? The answer to this is of course "yes," but James' keen powers of observation did not prevent him from being influenced by a syncretistic, universalistic attitude of mind. This attitude--very similar to the temperament of Giovanni Pico della Mirandola, who during the Renaissance attempted to synthesize all philosophies (including Plato and Aristotle) in 900 propositions--this attitude naturally caused James to look at differences in religious beliefs as relatively unimportant, and religious experiences as fundamental and universally alike.[23] This approach, however, results in a loss of the characteristic distinctions among the religious experiences of the various faiths; and once such distinctions have gone by the board, the religious experiences themselves are no longer described accurately. But let our author speak for himself:

> When we survey the whole field of religion, we find a great variety in the thoughts that have prevailed there; but the feelings on the one hand and the conduct on the other are almost always the same, for Stoic, Christian, and Buddhist saints are practically indistinguishable in their lives (p. 494).[24]

> The warring gods and formulas of the various religions do indeed cancel each other, but there is a certain uniform deliverance in which religions all appear to meet. . . . When . . . the stage of solution or salvation arrives, the man

318

identifies his real being with the germinal higher part of himself; and does so in the following way. He becomes conscious that this higher part is conterminous and continuous with a MORE of the same quality, which is operative in the universe outside of him, and which he can keep in working touch with, and in a fashion get on board of and save himself when all his lower being has gone to pieces in the wreck. It seems to me that all the phenomena are accurately describable in these very simple general terms. . . . There is probably no autobiographic document, among all those which I have quoted, to which the description will not well apply. One need only add such specific details as will adapt it to various theologies and various personal temperaments, and one will then have the various experiences reconstructed in their individual forms (pp. 498-9).

These "very simple general terms" are of course about as applicable to the Christian religious experience as Feuerbach's "der Mensch ist, was er isst" was to Christian theology. If Christian religious experience means anything, it surely means that "all have sinned and come short of the glory of God"-- that there is no "germinal higher part" of a man that is "continuous" with the Divine. The Christian religious experience begins at the very point where one denies the possibility of "getting on board" and "saving himself."[25] By not recognizing such facts as these, James missed the true character of particular religious experiences; and the Varieties thus has more value as a compendium of documentary material than as a work of profound psychological interpretation.

(3) Superficiality in evaluation. A third difficulty which lessens the psychological value of the Varieties, and which is connected with the two difficulties just described, is the fact that James is unable, because of his universalistic approach, to build a value scale of religious experiences. That the depth and quality of religious experiences vary from person to person and from theology to theology is evident to the most casual observer; yet James, in his attempt not to be particularistic, seldom sees the great gulf between various types of experience. A typical example is the lengthy personal document by an individual who early in life felt himself "curiously related" to a "fundamental cosmical It," and who later lost this "relationship" (pp. 64-65). James cites this experience along with others which so far transcend it that comparison is almost impossible (e.g., see p. 70). Writings of men like the Apostle Paul, who have known the "love of Christ" experientially,

breathe an atmosphere which cannot be found in descriptions of vague, mystical encounters with "cosmic forces."

But James is in no position to see these distinctions, for his universalistic presupposition, backed by his pragmatic epistemology (if an experience "works" for the individual having it, it is "true" for him), allows for no real axiological criteria that can be applied to religious experience. Obviously, a religious experience will "work" in some sense for the one who has it, or it would never get recorded in the literature of the subject; yet who is to say whether a given experience was ultimately good for the experiencer or not? The problem is further complicated by the fact that almost all religions are metaphysically dualistic to some degree--and it is not uncommon for a religion to assert the existence of a personal demonic force that can disguise itself as an "angel of light." This being a live option, when is a religious experience due to the work of benign deity and when to the corrupting influence of satanic activity?[26] Naïve universalism simply assumes that this problem does not exist, and pragmatism--unable as it is to see all the factors-- is impotent to solve it.

But here we leave the realm of psychology[27] for that of

III. PHILOSOPHICAL CRITICISM

As we have just indicated, there is a definite connection between James' universalistic-syncretic point of view and his epistemology. Because his epistemology is so integrally connected with his method and interpretations in the Varieties, we shall devote considerable space in this section to a critical examination of it. Having done this, we shall offer suggestions toward an epistemology which will avoid the psychological errors attendant upon our author's approach.

Let us begin by listening to Professor James' own presentation of his pragmatic epistemology, as he states it in the Varieties:

> The gods we stand by are the gods we need and can use, the gods whose demands on us are reinforcements of our demands on ourselves and on one another. What I then propose to do is, briefly stated, to test saintliness by common sense, to use human standards to help us decide how far the religious life commends itself as an ideal kind of human activity. If it commends itself, then any theological beliefs that may inspire it, in so far forth will stand accredited. If not, then they will be discredited, and all without reference to anything but human working principles. It is but the elimination

of the humanly unfit, and the survival of the humanly fittest, applied to religious beliefs; and if we look at history candidly and without prejudice, we have to admit that no religion has ever in the long run established or proved itself in any other way. Religions have approved themselves; they have ministered to sundry vital needs which they found reigning (pp. 324-25).

The Continental schools of philosophy have too often overlooked the fact that man's thinking is organically connected with his conduct. It seems to me to be the chief glory of English and Scottish thinkers to have kept the organic connection in view. The guiding principle of British philosophy has in fact been that every difference must make a difference, every theoretical difference somewhere issue in a practical difference, and that the best method of discussing points of theory is to begin by ascertaining what practical difference would result from one alternative or the other being true. What is the particular truth in question known as? In what facts does it result? What is its cash-value in terms of particular experience? . . . .

An American philosopher of eminent originality, Mr. Charles Sanders Peirce, has rendered thought a service by disentangling from the particulars of its application the principle by which these men were instinctively guided, and by singling it out as fundamental and giving to it a Greek name. He calls it the principle of pragmatism (pp. 433-5).[27a]

It should be noted that on occasion James lapses from thoroughgoing pragmatism--and this fact serves as a good indication of the inadequacy of the pragmatic epistemology even for its advocates. Two instances of such lapsus philosophi will provide an appropriate transition into the classic objections to pragmatism.

It is the character of inner happiness in the thoughts which stamps them as good, or else their consistency with our other opinions and their serviceability for our needs, which make them pass for true in our esteem (p. 17, italics ours).

I believe that a candid consideration of piecemeal supernaturalism and a complete discussion of all its metaphysical bearings will show it to be the hypothesis by which the largest number of legitimate requirements are met (p. 513, italics ours).[28]

In order to see clearly the weaknesses in the bewitchingly simple pragmatic epistemology, we have culled quotations from several of its most penetrating critics:

(1) Pragmatism's ambiguity (Randall and Buchler):

> We shall consider two forms of the pragmatic conception. One represents the views of James and the British philosopher F. C. S. Schiller (1864-1937), and the other those of Peirce and Dewey. . . .
>
> Objections against this conception of truth must take their starting-point from a consideration of how vague the term "useful" is.
>
> Does Schiller mean that the true is the "useful" in the sense of being applicable technologically, or of affording some practical social satisfaction? If so, then to say that Sophroniscus was the father of Socrates, or that the amoeba reproduces by binary fission, would not be to speak truth, for neither of these truths affords such utility or satisfaction. It would appear that for Schiller those beliefs which ultimately make for human happiness are true, while those which do not are false. But the history of human frustration and misery shows that what men desire to be true, or what if true would make them happy, is thwarted by facts. That a fearful war rages is true, but hardly conducive to the harmony which we seek.
>
> Is a belief "useful" in the negative sense that it causes us no intellectual inconvenience to accept it, or that there is no particular reason why it should not be accepted, or that it fits in well with what we already regard as true? But there was no intellectual inconvenience at one time in regarding the earth as the fixed center of the universe. . . .
>
> Does the fact that the bulk of society prefers a given belief mean that it is true? There certainly is no contradiction in saying, and it is easily conceivable, that a single man may entertain a belief that is true while the rest of society regards it as false. To hold that social acceptance is the criterion of truth is to base the criterion of truth on historical accidents. It confuses an accidental occurrence with a logical method. It is not the fact of social acceptance that is important but the

ground or reason of acceptance. If it should be the case that a minority of one always contradicts the judgment of society, the question which side is right depends on the kind of methods respectively employed, not on the force of numbers.[29]

(2) Pragmatism's lack of vision (Fite):

The pragmatic attitude, speaking in the name reflective intelligence, makes the past life an instrument for the present. As against this I am urging that an intelligence genuinely reflective will refuse to treat any part of life as a mere means to another. Reflection I will identify with "imagination"; and a reflective living of life means that we live each moment in the light of the largest possible range of imagination.[30]

Here Fite argues very plausibly that the pragmatist (holding as he does that the true is that which has "worked") lives in a visionless world where future truth is always determined by past effects. This leads quite naturally to Carnell's criticism.

(3) Pragmatism's hidden assumption (Carnell):

Let us take the proposition, "Helium is lighter than air." This is but virtual knowledge; yet we fully and confidently expect it to lead us without frustration into our experience tomorrow. It is because we believe that the universe is regular, that we trust in the virtual knowledge which is before us. The pragmatist expects the train he rides on to take him to New York City and not to turn into green lizards or peach peacock feathers in five seconds. He expects the world to hold still long enough for him to speak about nature with confident anticipation. What the Christian wants to know is, where has this assurance come from? How can the pragmatist establish a connection between his theory of knowledge and his daily actions? . . .

The rebuttal to this argument is based upon the conviction that we have a right to argue to future regularity upon the basis of past regularity. The sun has always risen; therefore, it is folly to propose that the probability of the sun's rising tomorrow is 50/50. To this we reply that it will not help to argue from the past regularity of the universe to its future regularity unless we have assurance on other grounds that there is a rational connection between the past and the future of things. . . . All the pragmatist can do, if he is consistent, is to wait and see what nature is going to do tomorrow. And if the pragmatist persists in his conviction that the past and the future are organically connected, it seems that his conviction is based more upon a fixation which has resulted from observing past regularities than upon a logically consistent insight into the problem.[31]

(4) Pragmatism's self-contradictory character (Clark):

Instrumentalism is self-contradictory. If truth changes, then the popular instrumentalism that is accepted as true today will be false tomorrow. As Thomism was true in the thirteenth century; so instrumentalism is true in the twentieth century; and within fifty years instrumentalism, in virtue of its own epistemology, will be false. . . . As was said before, these relativistic theories tacitly assume their own absolutism. This or that hypothesis may be tentatively accepted for a limited purpose; but if all statements without exception are tentative, significant speech has become impossible. It follows then that truth must be unchangeable. What is true today always has been and always will be true. . . . Two and two are four; every event has a cause; and even, Columbus discovered America, are eternal and immutable truths. To speak of truth as changing is a misuse of language and a violation of logic.[32]

Closely connected with this criticism is the following:

(5) Pragmatism's lack of certainty (Royce):

Let us suppose that a witness appears, upon some witness-stand, and objects to taking the ordinary oath, because he has conscientious scruples, due to the fact that he is a recent pragmatist, who has a fine new definition of truth, in terms of which alone he can be sworn. Let us suppose him, hereupon, to be granted entire liberty to express his oath in his own way. Let him accordingly say, using, with technical scrupulosity, my colleague's definition of truth: "I promise to tell whatever is expedient and nothing but what is expedient, so help me future experience." I ask you: Do you think that this witness has expressed, with adequacy, that view of the nature of truth that you really wish a witness to have in mind?[33]

This tentative character of the pragmatic epistemology seems to make it a particularly inappropriate criterion of truth to apply in the religious realm. Contrast with the "oath" just given these words of Bishop Carpenter: "Jesus Christ had, indeed, no esoteric gospel. . . . What there was to teach was to be taught to all nations, to every creature under heaven, without restriction, frankly and fully."[34] It is interesting, moreover, how little satisfied with the tentative pragmatic approach the "practical" North American of this era seems to be; his feeling is apparently that we no longer have time to "wait and see" the effects (and thus determine the validity) of employing atomic weapons, germ warfare, etc. internationally--that the time has come to decide beforehand, on entirely different and far more solid grounds, what ought to be our standards of truth and value.[35]

(6) Pragmatism's inability to achieve its purpose--especially in the religious realm (Brightman):[36]

> It is . . . evident that untrue ideas may lead to results which, in the long run, appear to be practical. Christian Science and Roman Catholicism, for example, are both systems of belief that have led to practical results; yet both cannot be true at the same time unless the universe is a mad house. It helps us no whit to say that the results are due to the truth in each system; for, since each system is believed entire by its adherents, the results furnish no criterion of what parts of either or both systems may be true. . . . Pragmatism may include the untrue or exclude the true. Human desires may be satisfied just as well to believe in fairies as to believe in self-consciousness.[37]

A More Adequate Epistemological Approach to Religious Experience

The preceding criticism of pragmatism by Brightman becomes particularly pertinent when we recall the grave psychological errors into which James fell when he coupled epistemological pragmatism with a universalistic point of view. His pragmatism led him to feel that a religious experience was true if it "worked" for the individual who had it; the religious experience of virtually all faiths (including Christian Science and Roman Catholicism!) seemed to satisfy their adherents; this fact confirmed James' universalistic tendencies,[38] and resulted in his separating religious experience from "overbelief," his neglecting the characteristic and unique elements in the religious experiences of particular faiths, and his overlooking the great axiological variation among religious experiences.

325

If one does not hitch himself to pragmatism's star, however (and for the numerous reasons given above it seems hardly desirable to do so), one is under no compulsion to duplicate James' psychological errors. Only if one uses the superficial criterion that all religions are "true" if they seem to "work" experientially for their adherents, does one need to fly in the face of empirical fact and relegate religious beliefs to a secondary position as compared with immediate religious experiences. And only if one utilizes this same criterion of religious truth will he need to deëmphasize the crucial differences among the religious experiences of particular faiths--which differences, as we have seen, are often more central and vital to the religious person than the beliefs which his religion has in common with others. And, finally, only if one enters the sphere of religious experience with the pragmatic monkey on his back will he feel it necessary to consider all religious experience to be axiologically on almost the same plane.

But to disengage ourselves from an excessively superficial criterion of truth is hardly to solve the problem of interpreting religious experience. Some criterion of truth must be employed to bring order out of the welter and confusion of religious beliefs and experiences; and, as has been said, it must be a criterion which gives full weight to the integral connection between religious experiences and religious beliefs, and which recognizes the importance of particularist religious tenets to religious experience, and which gives some technique for establishing a value scale corresponding to the undeniable axiological variations among religious experiences.

We need not repeat the criticisms which numerous philosophers have leveled against common epistemologies such as instinct, intuition, feeling, custom, tradition, authority, consensus gentium, sense experience (narrowly conceived), and correspondence.[39] Few today would attempt to defend philosophically these supposed criteria of truth. A word should be said, however, concerning Brightman's widely accepted "coherence" or "systematic consistency" epistemology. Few seem to realize that in this criterion empirical reality ("fitting the facts") can suffer at the hands of rationalism ("logical consistency"). Life is often greater than logic,[40] and the advocate of coherence can (and often does) make the grave error of forcing the facts to fit a coherent system. This is of course the standard criticism which the scientist levels against the philosopher--and it cannot be thrown off with a shrug of the shoulders. One is rather relieved, for example, that Brightman's epistemology was not employed by physicists engaged in determining the nature of

light. Empirical fact clearly indicates that light is composed
of waves and yet of particles--but such a notion is inconsistent
by any logical standard. The photon is not the result of a "coherence" approach in Brightman's sense of the term. This difficulty with the "coherence" criterion (the fact that it does not
subordinate logical consistency to fitting the facts) becomes
especially acute in the field of philosophy of religion. Brightman is very correct when he writes, "The human mind has always struggled against the demands of reason, or (to take a
more historical view) has come very slowly to a recognition of
its universal claims, especially in the field of religion";[41] what
he does not see is the ground for such unwillingness to assert
the "universal" applicability of reason--whether in the
"Aristotelian-Kantian" or "Platonic-Hegelian" sense.[42] Sensi-
tive men have always been too humbled by the vastness of reality to assume readily that it conforms to reason's dictates;
and in the realm of religion--which deals as it does with cosmic
powers and purposes beyond our ken--there seems to be even
less room for rationalistic presumption.

A criterion of truth which does not prostrate itself before the
great god reason is the one termed by Randall and Buchler
"success in inquiry."[43] By this approach (which is really the
equivalent of the experimental method), "truth means scientific
success, or as we ordinarily say, 'verification,' with all that
this term implies. . . . Thus we call the belief that the earth is
one among planets and not the fixed center of the universe
'true,' not because it was always believed by a majority, but
because all who subscribe to the method of science would be
brought to this view if they persisted in the exercise of the
method." The experimental method is well set forth in four
steps by Professor Beaver: (1) The clear recognition and accurate statement of the problem to be solved, (2) The formulation of working hypotheses which appear to explain the problem
and the suggestion of methods of investigation, (3) The accurate
collection of data, (4) The formulation of conclusions by correct interpretation of the data.[44] This epistemology (which,
needless to say, is not to be confused with dogmatic, authoritarian "scientism" or "logical positivism")[45] has been a constructive force in the numerous fields of endeavor where it has
been employed. In the physical sciences it has transformed the
tight, presuppositionally mechanistic world of Newton into the
relativistic universe of Einstein--in which "anything can happen." In the psychological field, it has led to serious experimentation in the once-tabooed realm of extra-sensory
perception.[46] Thus the "success in inquiry" epistemology does

not subordinate life to logic as does the "coherence" view; nor does it confuse utility with truth, as does pragmatism.

When applied in the religious realm, experimental inquiry can cut the Gordian knot of conflicting truth claims and varied spiritual experiences--an accomplishment which we have seen to be beyond the ability of James' pragmatism. If the "problem to be solved" (to use Beaver's terminology) is set as "Which exclusive religious truth-claim is valid ?," and the validity of each religious system is considered as a possible hypothesis-- with each faith marshalling its evidence, the results will be somewhat as follows: The great Eastern religions (which are rightly termed "non-historical" in character because their doctrinal validity does not depend on historical occurrences) will be unable to offer attesting data beyond the pragmatic satisfactions which their beliefs give them.[47] Such evidence is unsatisfactory, as we have noted above, for the "satisfactions" could as well be the work of a clever devil as of a good deity. The historical religion of Islam will offer Mohammed's self-conscious claims to prophetic status, but will be unable to offer evidence that Mohammed was in fact what he claimed to be--the final and authoritative Prophet of Allah. Judaism will offer its claim to be the immutable revelation as given to His chosen people Israel, but God's history of the Jewish people will indicate to the impartial observer either that Yahveh was a tribal god who was unable to preserve his people, or that, if in times past their god was indeed the Lord of Heaven and Earth, He no longer considers them His peculiar and chosen people. Finally, Christianity will offer its claim to truth--a claim which consists merely of a finger pointing back through time to an historical Figure who divided world history into two parts--to Jesus of Nazareth--to His statements concerning Himself and true religion, and to the life He led attesting the statements He made. An honest, historically accurate, scientific investigation of these data (involving chiefly a study of the documents collected in the New Testament)[48] will show that Jesus claimed to be God Incarnate, that He described the only true (but not the only possible) religion as consisting of fellowship with Himself,[49] and that He attested His claims by a sinless life which profoundly affected everyone who crossed His path, and by a Resurrection which left no doubt in the minds of eye-witnesses that He was in fact the true God.[50]

To an honest "inquirer" then (in Randall's sense of the term) only Christianity will stand up under objective, empirical investigation;[51] but once this is admitted, the pieces in the jigsaw puzzle of religious experience will fit together as they never do in James' Varieties. One will not be under any stress to violate empirical fact by wrenching "overbeliefs" from religious experiences; on the contrary, one will see how vital particular beliefs are to such experiences (especially the belief held concerning Jesus Christ). One will be able, moreover, to judge the ultimate value of given religious experiences--something which James' vague pragmatic criterion was incapable of achieving. The axiological principle will be: how does Jesus Christ--the only true Way to God--figure into the religious experience in question? To the extent that God's Son is avoided or His mediatorship denied, to that extent religious experience becomes diabolically rather than divinely oriented (see note 49). It is to be emphasized, however, that real religious experiences do take place even in the most extreme instances of Christ-denial (e.g. in the Black Masses of the late mediaeval period), for Schleiermacher with real insight saw the essence of religion as "dependence." God help us, however, if our dependence is on ourselves, on a cosmic process, or on the great adversary; as a counteractant to such possibilities, we urge each reader, if he has not already done so, to pursue the forthright inquiry which will lead him to the One in whose presence no further questions of truth or value need be asked.

IV. THE MERITS OF
THE VARIETIES OF RELIGIOUS EXPERIENCE

Even though Professor James was not a psyche kathara (pure soul) in the Christian sense of the term, it is certain that, in the realms of psychology and philosophy, thanousa ou thane (dying he did not die).[52] Let us conclude with a catalog of some of the chief merits of his classic work on religious experience. We shall again employ a psychological-philosophical division.

Psychological Merits

(1) A legitimate stress on "extreme cases." James has, in my opinion, been unjustly criticized for emphasizing the more volatile and expressive examples of religious experience. Modern psychiatry realizes full well that until psychoses are comprehended, neuroses are not understood; the starting point for psychological analysis should be the experience which most clearly exemplifies the phenomenon under consideration. But listen to James' own, very adequate defense of his approach:

It is a good rule in physiology, when we are studying the meaning of an organ, to ask after its most peculiar and characteristic sort of performance, and to seek its office in that one of its functions which no other organ can possibly exert. Surely the same maxim holds good in our present quest. The essence of religious experiences, the thing by which we finally must judge them, must be that element or quality in them which we can meet nowhere else. And such a quality will be of course most prominent and easy to notice in those religious experiences which are most one-sided, exaggerated, and intense (p. 45).[53]

(2) Tolerance. James' universalistic-syncretic approach has a good side to it, in that our author deals sympathetically with a wide diversity of religions and religio-philosophical viewpoints. The fact that he can speak even of Annie Besant as a "high-souled woman" (p. 24) is evidence of his benign attitude.[54]

(3) Recognition of the universality of religious experience. Although James was apparently not aware of the negative origin of many of the religious experiences with which he dealt (cf. notes 26 and 49), he did realize that man was an incurably religious animal. His treatment of atheism brings this out quite well:

Non-religious as some . . . reactions may be, in one sense of the word "religious," they yet belong to the general sphere of the religious life, and so should generically be classed as religious reactions. "He believes in No-God, and he worships him," said a colleague of mine of a student who was manifesting a fine atheistic ardor; and the more fervent opponents of Christian doctrine have often enough shown a temper which, psychologically considered, is indistinguishable from religious zeal (p. 36).

(4) The "apperceptive mass" he provides is a magnificent contribution to the field of religious psychology. Even though James' criterion of truth and many of his interpretative techniques must be considered inadequate, the data he provides in the Varieties will not cease to be a gold mine of information for those interested in the field of religious psychology. The desire which James expressed in the following paragraph was fully realized in the Varieties:

The mass of collateral phenomena, morbid or healthy, with which the various religious phenomena must be compared in order to understand them better, forms what in the slang of pedagogics is termed "the apperceiving mass" by which we comprehend them. The only novelty that I can imagine this course of lectures to possess lies in the breadth of the apperceiving mass. I may succeed in discussing religious experiences in a wider context than has been usual in university courses (p. 26).

Philosophical Merits

(1) James' distinction between origin and value is tremendously significant--especially at present when anthropological-sociological thinking is so predominant. James rightly makes the "medical materialist" appear foolish:

Perhaps the commonest expression of this assumption that spiritual value is undone if lowly origin be asserted is seen in those comments which unsentimental people so often pass on their more sentimental acquaintances. Alfred believes in immortality so strongly because his temperament is so emotional. Fanny's extraordinary conscientiousness is merely a matter of overinstigated nerves. William's melancholy about the universe is due to bad digestion--probably his liver is torpid. Eliza's delight in her church is a symptom of her hysterical constitution (p. 11).[55]

(2) James recognized mysticism's great failing: "Although mysticism is entirely willing to corroborate religion, it is too private (and also too various) in its utterances to be able to claim a universal authority" (p. 421; see also the whole of Lectures XVI and XVII).

(3) James likewise saw the limitations of rationalism; he did not fall into the mire of logical positivism, though he himself was a competent scientific thinker.[56]

If we look on man's whole mental life as it exists, on the life of men that lies in them apart from their learning and science, and that they inwardly and privately follow, we have to confess that the part of it of which rationalism can give an account is relatively superficial. It is the part that has the prestige undoubtedly, for it has the loquacity, it can challenge you for proofs, and chop logic, and put you down with words. But it will fail to convince or convert you all the same, if your dumb intuitions are opposed to its conclusions. If you have intuitions at all, they come from a deeper level of your nature than the loquacious level which rationalism inhabits (pp. 72-73).

(4) He was quite right in rejecting the traditional rationalistic proofs for God's existence, as well as the transcendental

idealism exemplified by Principal Caird (pp. 427-45).

(5) As the preceding two merits obliquely suggest, Professor James saw quite clearly the basic distinction which has received so much emphasis in recent theological thinking--the fundamental difference between passive, academic knowledge about God, and the vital, personal, "I-thou," existential[57] relationship with one's Maker and Redeemer. With the following significant quotation from our author, we close:

> Knowledge about a thing is not the thing itself. You remember what Al-Ghazzali told us in the Lecture on Mysticism--that to understand the causes of drunkenness, as a physician understands them, is not to be drunk. A science might come to understand everything about the causes and elements of religion, and might even decide which elements were qualified, by their general harmony with other branches of knowledge, to be considered true; and yet the best man at this science might be the man who found it hardest to be personally devout. Tout savoir c'est tout pardonner. The name of Renan would doubtless occur to many persons as an example of the way in which breadth of knowledge may make one only a dilettante in possibilities, and blunt the acuteness of one's living faith. If religion be a function by which either God's cause or man's cause is to be really advanced, then he who lives the life of it, however narrowly, is a better servant than he who merely knows about it, however much (pp. 478-9).

NOTES

1. Five hundred and sixteen closely printed octavo pages in the Modern Library edition. All references to the Varieties in this paper will be concerned with this edition.

2. E.g. Gardner Murphy, Historical Introduction to Modern Psychology, rev. ed. (N.Y., Harcourt, Brace, 1951), pp. 202-5.

3. E.g. Selected Papers on Philosophy by William James (Everyman's Library, no. 739), pp. 245-73; Thomas S. Kepler, Contemporary Religious Thought (N.Y., Abingdon, 1941), pp. 241-46.

4. Murphy, op. cit., p. 208.

5. See his statement and defense of "radical empiricism" in the preface to The Will to Believe and Other Essays in Popular Philosophy (N.Y., Longmans, 1910), pp. vii-ix; see also his A Pluralistic Universe (N.Y., Longmans, 1943).

6. In his preface to the Varieties, James seems to state that his book is solely psychological in character: "The unexpected growth of the psychological matter as I came to write it out has resulted in the second subject [the satisfaction of man's religious appetites through philosophy] being postponed entirely, and the description of man's religious constitution now fills the twenty lectures" (p. xvii). However, even the most cursory survey of the work will show that it deals with many vital philosophical issues (Lecture XVIII is entitled "Philosophy"!), and philosophical assumptions raise their heads throughout the book. Statements like the following (which abound) should not mislead us: "In these lectures I propose . . . to consider as little as possible the systematic theology and the ideas about the gods themselves, and to confine myself as far as I can to personal religion pure and simple" (p. 30). James here merely illustrates the truth of the Hegelian principle which he refers to on p. 440: "to be conscious of a negation is already virtually to be beyond it." In defending the importance of psychology of religion in comparison with philosophy of religion, James necessarily has much to say concerning the latter.

7. We shall not of course concentrate on elements in James' personal philosophical position which are referred to only obliquely in the Varieties (e.g. his polytheistic, finite pluralism). Our main concern will be with his "overbelief" idea and his epistemological pragmatism.

8. First published in 1940 (London, George Allen and Unwin). McKenzie, who is Jesse Boot Professor in Social Science at the University of Aberdeen, is the author of several other works on the relation of psychology to evangelical Christian faith.

9. Compare with this criticism James' apparent desire to make the Varieties purely psychological (see note 6, supra).

10. McKenzie, op. cit., p. 77.

11. Ibid., pp. 46-47, 99. See also pp. 58-59.

333

12. As supplied largely by the Starbuck and Flournoy MSS. collections (see the Varieties, p. xviii).

13. McKenzie, op. cit., pp. 46-48.

14. The psychoanalytic movement was just getting under way when James delivered what was to become the Varieties as the Gifford Lectures for 1901-2. Freud's Interpretation of Dreams was published in 1900.

15. McKenzie, op. cit., pp. 45, 46, 83.

16. This distinction is set forth in Lectures IV-VII. It seems quite clear to me that had James understood Luther's basic dictum that the Christian religious believer is "simul iustus et peccator," he would not have made this blunder. That James at least unconsciously recognized the difficulty of his distinction is shown by the fact that Luther appears in the "sick soul" category (p. 135), while Lutheran theology (based on the sola fide principle) is used to illustrate "healthy-minded" religion (p. 106 ff).

17. McKenzie, op. cit., pp. 74-75. See also the quotation corresponding to note 11.

18. Varieties, p. 163 etc. (esp. Lectures IX-X). In this connection the reader should certainly not neglect Harold Begbie's writings: Twice-born Men, a Clinic in Regeneration: A footnote in narrative to Professor William James' "The Varieties of Religious Experience" (N.Y., Revell, 1909) [also published under the title, Broken Earthenware]; Souls in Action: Expanding the narrative of Twice-born Men (N.Y., Doran, 1911).

19. McKenzie, op. cit., pp. 73-74. The type of "conversion" experience just described has been brought to the attention of almost everyone who has done church work in a pastoral or semi-pastoral capacity.

20. Thus, for example, maintains E. C. Colwell, the eminent N. T. scholar (Journal of Biblical Literature, v. 52 [1933], pp. 12-21). The Thomas incident occurs at the end of John 20; some feel that John 21 is a later addition to the text.

21. Wesley's own words are quoted in Kenneth Scott

Latourette's History of Christianity (N.Y., Harper, 1953),
p. 1025. Wesley's conversion occurred on May 24, 1738.

22. With the points made in the preceding paragraphs, cf. John
Morrison Moore (Theories of Religious Experience, N.Y.,
Round Table Press, 1938, pp. 73-74): "A less favorable
judgment must be passed on James's assumption that religious experience, in the sense of immediate feeling, is the
essential and originative aspect of religion. This view is
weak both historically and psychologically. It cannot be
maintained that all of the rites, doctrines, and institutions
of religion have originated in personal religious experience,
for these external aspects of religion antedate and condition
all the personal experience of which we have any record.
Religious experience, the religion of the spirit, is an all-
important aspect of religion, but it cannot exist by itself,
and it is not the source of religion or even of all that is
progressive and highest in it. At this point James was mis-
led by his own extreme individualism and by the assumptions which were predominant in his generation."

23. James' universalistic syncretism seems on the surface to
carry on a tug of war with his pluralism. Yet there is a
real connection between the two: if the number of possible
viewpoints is legion, then they all must have some validity
and therefore something in common.

24. See also pp. 27, 28, 29, 32, 423, 445-46, 498.

25. The little German poem which James quotes on p. 51 is another example of a point of view foreign to kerygmatic
Christian experience ("Entbehren sollst du", etc.). Begbie
(Souls in Action, p. 19) magnificently expresses the contrast between Christian experience and that of another great
world religion: "Christianity is janua vitae; Buddhism,
janua mortis. Christianity is an ardent enthusiasm for
existence; Buddhism a painful yearning for annihilation.
Christianity is a hunger and thirst after joy; Buddhism a
chloral quest for insensibility. The Christian is bidden to
turn away from sin that he may inherit the everlasting joy
of eternity; the Buddhist is told to eradicate all desire of
any kind whatsoever lest he be born again. Buddha sought
to discover an escape from existence; Christ opened the
door of life. Buddha forbade desire; Christ intensified

aspiration. Buddha promised anaesthesia; Chi.st promised everlasting felicity."

26. J. S. Bixler (Religion in the Philosophy of William James, Boston, Marshall Jones, 1926, p. 202) writes: "The hypothesis of the subconscious self as an intermediary between man and the Deity, a sort of 'apex mentis,' to use the phrase of mediaeval mysticism, has probably today outlived the major portion of its usefulness. We now know that intimations diabolical as well as divine come over the threshold."

27. It will be noted that we have not dealt specifically with James' attitude toward "mysticism" or "saintliness" (i.e., sanctification). Many of our general criticisms are pertinent to the Jamesian treatment of these subjects; but limitations of space and time forbid us to enter these fertile areas in a thoroughgoing manner.

27a. The reader should also be referred to James' appropriately entitled work, Pragmatism (London, Longmans, 1907), esp. pp. 43-81.

28. Cf. James' revealing footnote (note 1) on p. 500. The passages we have quoted in our text irresistibly remind one of Brightman's coherence criterion of truth (A Philosophy of Religion, N.Y., Prentice-Hall, 1940, pp. 128-9).

29. J. H. Randall, Jr. and Justus Buchler, Philosophy: An Introduction (N.Y., Barnes and Noble--College Outline Series, 1942), pp. 137-40. The ambiguity criticism has of course been leveled at pragmatism by many authors.

30. Warner Fite, Moral Philosophy (N.Y., Lincoln MacVeagh-Dial Press, 1925), p. 116.

31. Edward John Carnell, An Introduction to Christian Apologetics (Grand Rapids, Eerdmans, 1950), pp. 53-55. Carnell is Professor of Apologetics at Fuller Theological Seminary, Pasadena, California. He holds a Ph.D. in philosophy from Boston University, and a Th.D. from Harvard.

32. Gordon H. Clark, A Christian View of Men and Things (Grand Rapids, Eerdmans, 1952), p. 319. Clark is Chairman of the Philosophy Department at Butler University.

33. Josiah Royce, The Philosophy of Loyalty (N.Y., Macmillan, 1908), pp. 331-32.

34. Boyd Carpenter, Forty Days of the Risen Life (N.Y., Dodd, Mead, 1898 [Little Books on Religion, ed. by W. Robertson Nicoll]), pp. 2-3.

35. A pamphlet like Professor Charles W. Morris' Pragmatism and the Crisis of Democracy (Chicago, University of Chicago Press, 1934 [Public Poling Pamphlet, No. 12]) has a hollow ring to it today.

36. E. S. Brightman, An Introduction to Philosophy (N.Y., Holt, 1925), p. 56.

37. In referring to the classic criticisms of pragmatism, one must not overlook Brand Blanshard's telling refutation of the pragmatic approach in his Nature of Thought (v. 1, Ch. 10).

38. Whether James' syncretic-universalistic attitude of mind led him to accept a pragmatic epistemology, or the reverse, is a "which-comes-first? the-chicken-or-the-egg" type of question. Undoubtedly the two formed what chemists would term a "reversible reaction" (symbolized appropriately by the double arrow).

39. See, for example, refutations by Brightman (A Philosophy of Religion, pp. 122-26); Carnell (op. cit., Ch. 3).

40. Zeno's paradoxes still cause a lingering feeling of doubt in the realm of rationalistic philosophy.

41. A Philosophy of Religion, p. 123.

42. Ibid., pp. 183-6. The "Platonic-Hegelian" approach, which Brightman espouses, has much in common with James' universalistic-syncretic presupposition. Syncretism, it should be noted, can be as bigoted and a priori as exclusivism--though Brightman does not seem to realize it.

43. Op. cit., pp. 140-42.

44. William C. Beaver, Biologic Science in Laboratory and Field, 4th ed. (St. Louis, Mosby, 1952), pp. 13-16.

Professor Beaver is Head of the Biology Department at Wittenberg University. His biology text and accompanying laboratory manual are in use in numerous colleges and universities throughout the United States.

45. Of course the experimental method has its presuppositions too (Kant forever blasted the notion that one can begin with pure empirical fact), but these presuppositions (as set forth, for example, by Edwin A. Burtt in his Types of Religious Philosophy) are minimal, and lead to the discovery of truth, rather than restrict its scope (in contrast to many philosophical a prioris).

46. Interestingly, James himself was open minded enough to be seriously concerned with ESP; see his "What Psychical Research Has Accomplished," in The Will to Believe (N.Y., Longmans, 1910), pp. 299-327; and William James on Psychical Research, ed. by Gardner Murphy and R. O. Ballou (N.Y., Viking, 1960).

47. Doctrines such as karma and nirvana are of course not subject to proof or disproof in any accepted sense of the term.

48. The historical worth of these records is set forth clearly by F. F. Bruce in his The New Testament Documents; Are They Reliable? (London, Inter-Varsity Fellowship, 1960).

49. Jn 14:6: "I am the Way, the Truth, and the Life; no man comes to the Father but by me." Jn 8:41-44 (Jesus conversing with Jews who did not accept Him): "Then said they to him, . . . We have one Father, even God. Jesus said unto them, If God were your Father, ye would love me. . . . Ye are of your father the devil. . . . He was a murderer from the beginning, and abode not in the truth, because there is no truth in him."

50. We refer again to the "doubting Thomas" incident in John 20. Christ's Resurrection is as much a "fact" as Columbus' discovery of America (see the Clark quotation in the text above, corresponding to note 32). The attesting value of the Resurrection (for those who are not committed to Hume's a priori, mechanistically based argument against the probability of the miraculous) is greater than many non-Christians (or Christians!) realize. See Wilbur Smith,

Therefore Stand; also, his The Supernaturalness of Christ (Boston, W. A. Wilde).

51. If one asks why many who accept the "experimental inquiry" epistemology are not committed Christians in the Biblical sense of the term, we reply (1) that one must "be willing to do His (Christ's) will" before he will know whether Christ's doctrine is valid (Jn 7:17), (2) that Western civilization seems to be so preoccupied with applying scientific method to building bigger and better refrigerators, TV sets, and atomic bombs, that little time is left for applying this same method to an issue that will influence one's situation in eternity.

52. We refer to the lines which Ralph Barton Perry placed at the beginning of v. 1 of his classic Thought and Character of William James (Boston, Little, Brown, 1935): ō psychē kathara; thanousa gar ou thanes (Behold a pure soul! for though dying you did not die).

53. See also pp. 23, 39, 50 of the Varieties.

54. Charles M. Bakewell writes in his Introduction to Selected Papers on Philosophy by William James (cit. supra): "James also possessed in a wonderful degree what might be called sympathetic imagination--the ability to get as it were on the inside of the other fellow's vision; and whenever he ran across, in the work of another thinker, however humble and obscure, evidence of some fresh and original interpretation of genuine experience, he heralded it as a veritable discovery. It was a new document to be reckoned with. He was, in fact, singularly free from what he has called 'a certain blindness in human beings.' How free, a reading of the Varieties of Religious Experience will show" (p. xi).

55. James' entire argument on this issue is worthy of careful perusal--see the Varieties, pp. 5-22. It might seem on the surface that we have fallen into the very error James condemns--for have we not validated Christianity by showing that it has its origin in the Divine Christ? The answer to this is simply that we have arrived at the Christ through the legitimate technique of "truth by inquiry," and that in the single instance where such a Deity is involved, origin does in fact indicate value, for whatever the Christian God says is both factually true and comprehensively valuable.

56. Read James on "the powers and limitations of science" in
The Philosophy of William James: Drawn from His Own
Works, with an Introduction by Horace M. Kallen (N.Y.,
Modern Library, 1925), pp. 197-213.

57. It should be noted, however, that when James uses the word
"existential" in the Varieties (e.g., p. 6), he is not employing it in the Kierkegaardian sense. What James means
here by "existential" might better be termed "factual" or
"phenomenal."

5. THE DEPENDABILITY AND VALUE OF THE EXTANT GOSPEL MANUSCRIPTS

by

Edward J. Barnes, B.A., M.A.
Lecturer in Latin and Ancient History
Waterloo Lutheran University

The original manuscripts of the gospels[1] in their complete form have been lost beyond any reasonable hope of recovery. They were evidently written on papyrus, a comparatively cheap material which deteriorates rapidly. Numerous early papyrus fragments[2] of the New Testament writings have recently been found preserved in the dry sands of Egypt, but they by no means comprise a complete N. T. text. From what, then, are scholars able to constitute a text of the gospels sufficiently firm to stand as a basis for Christian belief?

In the absence of the complete originals, the textual critic of the gospels turns first to the oldest copies available.[3] Seven of these, written on papyrus, were considered by Nestle[4] to be very valuable. They date from the second century A. D. to the sixth, and they contain only parts of the complete gospels as we know them. Their value is that they provide an early check on parts of the text contained in later MSS. They also are evidence that the gospels were at an early date known more or less in their present form.

These few early papyrus fragments are only a small fraction of the total number of extant MSS; there are in fact almost four thousand MSS containing the complete N. T. or parts of it.[5] Thirty-seven of these[6] are listed by Nestle (ibid.) as exemplary, and they date from the fourth century right through to the eleventh. Also used by scholars for constituting an acceptable text of the gospels are early translations from the Greek into Syriac, Egyptian, Ethiopic, Armenian, Latin, and writings by the Church Fathers (from the early second century A. D.), who probably quote from non-existent texts older than the extant ones which we possess. Here, then, are the "raw materials" from which the textual critic of the N. T. works.

Many persons, however, question the validity of these documents. They point out, for example, that some of these writings about Christ did not appear until a century after his supposed death (ca. A. D. 30) and that the "best" of them were not written until three or four centuries later. They feel that these documents appeared too long after the events described in them to be of more than gossip or apocryphal value.

These critics further insist that there are blatant contradictions among the different gospel accounts of the works and teachings of Christ. They feel justified in demanding greater agreement among evangelist biographers dealing with a person as important as Christ is claimed to have been. From here it is but a short step to questioning the intentions of these biographers, that is, whether they were not perpetrating a hoax around a character largely mythical, thus rendering their work essentially fictional. We claim that the extant gospel MSS are dependable for the purpose of preparing a text of the gospels which comes as close as we are capable of making it to what the original versions by Matthew, Mark, Luke, and John must actually have contained. Consequently these objections must be met.

Turning first to the problem of the dates, we discover by analogy with the extant MSS of other ancient writings that the gospels are in an enviable position. Let us take as our first example Lucretius, a Roman poet who finished his De Rerum Natura ca. 55 B. C. The oldest extant MSS of his work date from the ninth and tenth centuries A. D., and, in all, only some half dozen good MSS survive. Yet it is pretty well agreed that our present text of Lucretius' poem, based on these few extant copies from the Middle Ages, is (except for minute variations here and there, as well as some gaps which cannot be filled) fairly close to what Lucretius actually published.[7] Another Roman writer, Tacitus, brought out his Annals ca. A. D. 115. The oldest MS copies of this work date from the eleventh century A. D., and only some twenty MSS in all preserve the bulk of the text in reasonably good form. Although Tacitus wrote in 115, the period covered by the Annals is A. D. 14-66; nonetheless he is considered to be a first-rate authority for this period. Let us go back even farther. Aristotle wrote his Poetics ca. 350 B. C. Of this work thirty-one MS copies survive to form the basis for our present editions. Most of these MSS date from the fifteenth century of our era, that is, about eighteen hundred years after the text was first written; of the others, none dates earlier than the eleventh century, so that the oldest is still more than a thousand years later than Aristotle's original version. Yet again the text of the Poetics is acceptable as it stands. Finally there is the text of the History of the Peloponnesian War by the Greek political scientist, Thucydides.

Now, it is true that Thucydides was contemporary with the people and events about which he writes; but our oldest MSS of his History were not written until thirteen hundred years after his time. Furthermore, like Tacitus, Thucydides is considered, on the basis of these MSS, to be an A-1 historian of his time.

If we now examine data of similar nature pertaining to the gospel MSS, we shall discover that our present text exists under much more favorable auspices. The central event of the Gospel, the Crucifixion and Resurrection of Jesus, occurred, so far as historians can determine, ca. A. D. 30. With reasonable certainty we can affix the following dates to the original composition of the works of the first three evangelists:[8] Mark at about A. D. 60; Luke, a bit later;[9] and Matthew, shortly after 70; in all, only thirty to forty years after the Crucifixion and at a time when many persons were still alive who could remember what our Lord had done and said. Compare this proximity with the date at which Tacitus wrote about the death (A. D. 14) of Augustus, a full hundred years after the event. Clearly the likelihood of our going astray in determining the original text of the gospels is greatly minimised.

In fact, one can with confidence declare that the original versions of the gospels are far better attested by our extant MSS than are any other ancient works.

By many critics, nonetheless, work of a religious nature is open to suspicion, and more corroborative evidence of its validity is demanded than for any other kind of writing. The historian, however, proceeds in a strictly empirical manner, and applies identical standards to documents be they secular or religious. As to the gospels, it is true, the historian disinterestedly cites as corroborative evidence works by contemporary and later ancient writers who were Christians. He would not be a good historian if he did not do this. Equally without prejudice he explores the pertinent ancient writings by non-Christian authors. The first of these authors to be mentioned here is Thallus (writing ca. A. D. 52), who was an enemy of certain Christians in Rome. We are told that he explained the darkness during the Crucifixion as the result of a solar eclipse.[10] This story is important because it shows not only that the traditional story of the Passion was known in Rome among non-Christians by about A. D. 50, but also that the enemies of Christianity even as early as this were attempting to explain the facts recorded in the Christian tradition as natural phenomena.

Josephus wrote during the years A. D. 70-80. Early in life he had been a militant Jewish nationalist and later was a favorite of the emperor Vespasian. Josephus was never a Christian, yet his writings include historical references to persons and events recorded in the gospels, for example, the trial conducted by Pilate.[11] Between his account and that of the gospels we observe no historical discrepancies. In fact, a comparison of the texts reveals, paradoxically, that, while Josephus nowhere quotes from the gospels, his brief account of matters pertaining to Christ and the Christians is, in effect, a compilation of the events related by the evangelists. We have in Josephus' work the same tradition presented by a completely independent commentator.

Tacitus, whom we have already mentioned, also gives the story of Pilate[12] basically identical with that told by Josephus. He sets his account in the time of Tiberius, and he refers to Jesus as Christus.

In A. D. 112, a well-known Roman orator and administrator writes a letter[13] as governor of the Imperial Province of Bithynia-Pontus, in Asia Minor, to Trajan in Rome. Pliny asks advice on how to handle the treasonous Christians, persons who recognized neither the Roman gods nor the authority of the emperor. Much bad gossip, he reports, had been heard about them, such as their secret meetings (which included both sexes) and their crimes. But investigation, he declares, showed that these rumours had little basis in fact. Indeed, Pliny remarks on the high moral character of these people. We are free to observe, however, that the Sacrament of Holy Communion was being practised at this time, and that among non-Christians it was obviously misrepresented and distorted, sometimes even as cannibalism.

We have seen, then, that within a hundred years after the Crucifixion the Christian way of life was spreading throughout the eastern Mediterranean, and that the Christian ethic as we know it from the gospels was making its impact on historians and even on the home government in Rome. The important point to note for our immediate purpose is that we have learned these things from non-Christian, even hostile writers.

But we must return to the N. T. documents themselves. It was pointed out earlier that, in some details concerning Christ's life, the gospels differ in emphasis. Some critics unfairly call these differences "contradictions."[14] That there should be differences is understandable. In the first place, the gospels are records of Christ's life and ministry written for colonies of Christians living in widely separated parts of the Roman world; different audiences must be approached in different ways. Secondly, the evangelists, when they came to write their different versions, used varied sources.[15] Consider instead the ways[16] in which the gospels agree and in which coincidence can play no part. The general tradition of the Resurrection common to all four gospels must have been established very soon after the Crucifixion.[17] In our terms, it must be admitted, thirty years is a long time for a story to spread, for today we think of such things in a context of newspapers, radio, and other forms of telecommunications. In the days of the apostles, however, telecommunications was unknown. Tales were told chiefly by word of mouth, around campfires and in the bazaars of large towns. The evangelists set down in writing what they could learn of Christ's life so that no changes (or, technically, "corruptions," as the literary critic calls them) could enter the tradition and cause the faith to be spoiled. And because this transcribing to the permanency of book form began only thirty years or so after the Crucifixion, there were many still alive who were willing to guarantee as authentic what they had seen and what their belief, therefore, consisted in.[18] The ambitious and serious gospel-writer had at his disposal ample means of cross-referencing and justifying the things he was told.

But not only are the accountable differences among the gospels questioned: doubts have been raised as well concerning the intent of the gospel-writers. "What was their interest in propagating this myth?" the skeptic may ask. "What did they stand to gain?" The skeptic who poses this kind of question will not quibble with the textual critic concerning the soundness of the gospel text as we now have it. Although he may even concede that we have substantially what the evangelists wrote, he refuses to trust the early apostolic band themselves. But why not trust them? Their wages were oppression, hunger, torture, often even death. Some of them tell us in writing that they were warned of the danger of their task. Yet they accepted it as their duty to truth, and they were willing to travel the known world to proclaim it, for they were convinced of this truth. Their faith in Jesus Christ was an existential fact, and their endeavour was to make that faith an existential fact for others. That they succeeded is proved by the existence of our gospels. These documents, which are the <u>result</u> of the campaigning carried on by those first priests[19] of Christ, had no conceivable pragmatic or materialistic value. They represent, instead, a facing of the reality of life and death; they reveal an obligation contracted with God through His Son, an obligation which must be faced; and they are evidence that courage may be engendered through His courage, and that life may be lived with joy and honesty as He lived it. Short of hearing Christ's teachings from His own mouth, there could be no sounder bulwark of the Christian faith than these gospel documents.

NOTES

For innumerable critical suggestions on the precision of my prose style I have to thank Dr. Evelyn Mae Boyd, of the English Department of Waterloo Lutheran University. Her time and acumen have, throughout the writing of this paper, been always at my disposal.

1. In this paper, "gospels" will be used to designate the first four books of the N. T. canon, named after Matthew, Mark, Luke, and John; "the Gospel," however, refers to the central theme of these books, viz. the life, Passion, and Resurrection of Jesus Christ.

2. The Rylands 457 fragment (John 18) at Manchester is exemplary; it is dated in the second century A. D. Cf. Eb. Nestle, Novum Testamentum Graece, rev. Erwin Nestle (Stuttgart, 1952), p. 14*; this work will hereinafter be referred to as Nestle.

3. It is of the nature of manuscripts that, owing to repeated copying by hand, errors creep into the text over a period of centuries. Consequently, the older the MS, the more likely it is to give the correct reading or "tradition." This rule, however, does not always hold true; the degree of error in any MS depends on the care and accuracy spent in its copying by the scribe himself, and on the care of the scribes before him who wrote the MSS to which his owes its origin.

    In this paper, the designation "MSS" will refer to the extant copies; where the originals are meant, this will be specified.

4. Op. cit., p. 14*, the MSS numbered "p^1," "p^{22}," etc.

5. Cf. F. F. Bruce, The New Testament Documents: Are They Reliable? (London: Inter-Varsity Fellowship, 1960), 5th ed. rev., p. 16; this work will hereinafter be referred to as Bruce.

6. The two most important, both almost complete, are the Codex Vaticanus and the Codex Sinaiticus of the mid-fourth

century. These are the greatest literary treasures
Christianity possesses.

7. The textual problems involved with the MSS O and Q, as well
   as the other good MSS, are competently discussed by Cyril
   Bailey, Titi Lucreti Cari De Rerum Natura Libri Sex
   (Oxford, 1947; repr. corr. 1950), 3 vols.: I, pp. 37-51. It
   is not considered necessary for the purpose of this paper
   to direct the reader also to comprehensive editions of
   Tacitus, Aristotle, and Thucydides.

8. For the date of the Crucifixion, cf. Bruce, pp. 11-12; for the
   dates of the Synoptic gospels, ibid. pp. 12-13 and p. 12 n. 4,
   particularly under A. Harnack.

9. I have no intention here of doing any more than to mention
   the "Proto-Luke" problem, for which cf. Bruce, p. 13 and
   his n. 2 ad loc., and p. 43.

10. On Thallus cf. Bruce, p. 113 and nn. ad loc. One should
    note that Christ was crucified during the Passover, that is,
    at the full moon, when solar eclipses cannot occur. The
    problem remains.

11. Pilate in the gospels has sometimes been considered a du-
    bious figure by modern historians, but pertinent ancient
    records are discussed by G. A. Müller, Pontius Pilatus der
    fünfte Procurator von Judäa (1888); some of the early
    sources are Josephus Jewish Antiquities XVIII.4.2, 89;
    Tacitus Annals XV.44.3 (vid. infra n. 12); Philo Leg. ad
    Gaium 38; Eusebius H. E. 2, 7. A letter (British Museum,
    Roy. 13cxiv), purporting to be from Pilate to Tiberius and
    relating the life (strangely like a synopsis of the gospels)
    and condemnation of Christ, has been ascertained to be a
    forgery. Finally cf. a news-release, "Stone Slab is Clue to
    the Life of Pilate," Toronto Daily Star (Reuters), August
    19, 1961, which reports:
    Caesarea, Israel — Four lines written in Latin on a lime-
    stone slab more than 1,900 years old are being studied
    eagerly by archaeologists here who believe it may produce
    knowledge of Pontius Pilate, the Roman procurator of Judea,
    who ordered the crucifixion of Christ.
    The slab, found in the ruins of a Roman theatre, which
    once seated 5,000, is 32 inches long, 24 inches wide, and 6
    inches thick.

Two of the four lines in Latin stand out, the others are obscured; but the letters ". . . tius Pilata" (Latin for Pilate) stand out.

Biblical scholars and archaeologists here claim it is the first concrete evidence of Pilate. Previously, he was known only [sic] through the Gospels and the writings of the Jewish historian, Josephus Flavius.

The word "Tiberium," discernible on one line, indicates to experts here that the theatre was dedicated to the emperor Tiberius, who ascended the throne in A. D. 14. Pontius Pilate was governor of Judea from A. D. 26 to A. D. 36.

A team of Italian archaeologists found the slab. They reported that it would be subjected to modern archaeological techniques in an effort to bring out the printing on the lines blurred by time. It was found ten miles south of Haifa.

With regard to this newspaper article I have been graciously helped by Miss Grace Schmidt, Reference Librarian, the Kitchener Library.

12. Tacitus does, as Sir Ronald Syme indicates (Tacitus [Oxford, 1958], II, p. 469), register "the origin of the name 'Christiani' with documentary precision;" cf. Annals XV.44.3, "auctor nominis eius [sc. 'Christiani'] Christus Tiberio imperitante per procuratorem Pontium Pilatum supplicio affectus erat." Tacitus also mentions the Great Fire in Rome that occurred A. D. 64. He says that Nero blamed it on the Christians to remove the blame from himself; cf. Annals XV.44.2, 5. The evidence of Tacitus for the dating in the reigns of Tiberius and Nero is important for the Christian argument, particularly since his text is not disputed at these points. Serious doubt has recently been articulated, however, that there ever was a persecution of Christians especially prompted by Nero; for the evidence briefly discussed cf. now F. M. Heichelheim and C. A. Yeo, A History of the Roman People (Englewood Cliffs, N. J.: Prentice-Hall, Inc., 1962), pp. 326-327 and note ad loc.

13. Pliny Epistulae X.96; Trajan's reply: X.97.

14. With regard to alleged "contradictions" in the accounts of Christ's Resurrection, W. M. Smith writes: "The so-called

348

variations in the narratives are only the details which were most vividly impressed on one mind or another of the witnesses of our Lord's Resurrection, or on the mind of the writers of these four respective Gospels. The closest, most critical, examination of these narratives throughout the ages, never has destroyed and can never destroy their powerful testimony to the truth that Christ did rise from the dead on the third day, and was seen of many" (The Supernaturalness of Christ [Boston: W. A. Wilde and Co., 1940], p. 205).

15. The fruits of Literary Criticism, Source Criticism, and Form Criticism are briefly displayed by Bruce as follows: a general discussion of the problems, pp. 30-35; Mark, pp. 35-37 (holding that "Mark is, by and large, [the] oral preaching written down," derived chiefly from the apostle Peter); Matthew and Luke, pp. 37-40 (a discussion of the postulated Q document, the Logia, or "Sayings," of Jesus); Matthew, pp. 40-41 (on a separate or "Matthaean" Logia, as well as other collections); Luke, pp. 41-45 (on the Matthaean Logia and a separate set known as L, peculiar to Luke; on "Palestinian informants" and "Christian Hellenists;" on Philip and Mark); the Synoptists generally, pp. 45-46; John, pp. 46-61 (a magnificent study of the circumstances under which this remarkable and individual book was written).

16. For the most important, vid. supra n. 15.

17. At the most, thirty years; see date for original writing of Mark, supra the text at n. 8. If we can accept what is told about Thallus in the year 52, this would set the difference down to little more than twenty years: in other words, by 52 there was in Rome a group of Christians who accepted the Crucifixion.

18. St. Paul himself provided his readers with this information, making it clear that others were alive to support his word, I Corinthians 15:5-8: "[Christ] appeared to Cephas: then to the twelve: then he appeared unto five hundred brethren at once, of whom the greater part remain until now, but some are fallen asleep: then he appeared to James: then to all the apostles: and last of all, as unto one born out of

due time, he appeared to me also" (italics mine); <u>cf.</u> also Bruce, pp. 44-45.

19. On this expression, <u>cf.</u> I Peter 2:5, 2:9; Revelation 1:6, 5:10.

6. THE PETRINE THEORY EVALUATED BY PHILOLOGY AND LOGIC

I. The Argument Stated.

1. The disputed Biblical passage (Matt. 16:13-19):

> Now when Jesus came into the district of Caesarea
> Philippi, he asked his disciples, "Who do men say that
> the Son of man is ?" And they said, "Some say John the
> Baptist, others say Elijah, and others Jeremiah or one
> of the prophets." He said to them, "But who do you say
> that I am ?" Simon Peter replied, "You are the Christ,
> the Son of the living God." And Jesus answered him,
> "Blessed are you, Simon Bar-Jona! For flesh and blood
> has not revealed this to you, but my Father who is in
> heaven. And I tell you, you are Peter, and on this rock I
> will build my church, and the powers of death shall not
> prevail against it. I will give you the keys of the kingdom
> of heaven, and whatever you bind on earth shall be bound
> in heaven, and whatever you loose on earth shall be
> loosed in heaven."

2. The Roman Doctrine.

   a. "Christ appointed the Apostle Peter to be the first of
   all the Apostles and to be the visible Head of the whole
   Church, by appointing him immediately and personally to the primacy of jurisdiction. According to
   Christ's ordinance, Peter is to have successors in
   his Primacy over the whole Church and for all time.
   The successors of Peter in the Primacy are the bish-
   ops of Rome." (De fide, quoted in Ludwig Ott, Fundamentals of Catholic Dogma, ed. in English by James
   Canon Bastible, and tr. from the German by Patrick
   Lynch [St. Louis, Mo.: Herder, 1954; Nihil Obstat
   and Imprimatur, October 7, 1954], pp. 279-82.)

   b. "Si quis dixerit, beatum Petrum Apostolum non esse a
   Christo Domino constitutum Apostolorum omnium
   principem et totius Ecclesiae militantis visibile caput;
   vel eundem honoris tantum, non autem verae

351

propriaeque iurisdictionis primatum ab eodem
Domino Nostro Jesu Christo directe et immediate
accepisse. A.S." (Vatican Council of 1870; Denzinger,
par. 1823.) Translation: "If anyone says that the
blessed Apostle Peter was not constituted, by Christ
the Lord, Prince of all the Apostles and visible head
of all the Church Militant [i.e., Church on earth]; or
that he [Peter] directly and immediately received
from Our Lord Jesus Christ a primacy of honour only
and not one of true and proper jurisdiction, let him be
anathema."

3. A Roman interpretation of the Matt. 16 passage.

"The primacy was promised on the occasion of the
solemn confession of the Messiahship in the house of
Caesarea Philippi (Mt. 16, 17-19). . . . God in Heaven
will confirm whatever obligations Peter will impose or
dispense from on earth" (Ott, loc. cit.).

4. The argument in syllogistic form:

(1) Major premise: Christ founded the church on Peter
and gave absolute spiritual authority in the church to
him.

(2) Minor premise: Peter passed this spiritual authority
on to his successor-bishops of Rome.

(3) Conclusion: The pope in any age has the right to absolute spiritual authority over Christendom.

II. The Difficulties in This Argument

1. The Meaning of the Matt. 16 Passage

a. In the Greek, the root of the name "Peter" is PETR-,
and the meaning of this root is "rock." Thus there is
"a happy play of words" in the Matt. 16 passage (A. B.
Bruce, in the Expositor's Greek Testament, ed. W.
Robertson Nicoll). The question is: What does this
play on words signify? Does it indicate (as the Ro-
manists argue) that the foundation of the church is
Peter?

b. It is of utmost importance to note that the Greek text
does not read, "You are Petros, and on this petros I
will build my church," but "You are Petros, and on
this petra I will build my church." Two different

Greek words are employed. These words have the
same root (PETR-) but different connotations.
Liddell and Scott (the authoritative lexicographers of
Classical Greek) state: "Properly, petra is a fixed
rock, petros a stone"; they assert that petros must
be "distinguished from petra" (Liddell's Intermediate
Lexicon, founded upon the 7th edition of Liddell and
Scott). G. Abbott-Smith, professor of Hellenistic
Greek in McGill University and an authority on the
vocabulary of the New Testament, defines petra as "a
mass of live rock as distinct from petros, a detached
stone or boulder" (Manual Greek Lexicon of the New
Testament, 3rd. ed.). This difference in connotation
is further supported by Alexander Souter's definition
of petra in the New Testament as "solid rock, native
rock, rising up through the earth," and by the fact that
in Arndt and Gingrich's revision-translation of
Bauer's lexicon of the New Testament and other early
Christian literature, "stone" is given as the basal
meaning of petros, but "rock" as the basal meaning of
petra (the latter is translated "stone" only in two
New Testament instances, and these are both quotations of the Old Testament phrase "stone of
stumbling/offence" in Is. 8:14). The fact that two
different words, rather than the same words, are used
in the Matt. 16 passage suggests that Peter and the
foundation of the church are not being identified; whatever the precise denotation of petra in Matt. 16, it is
clear that some difference between Peter and the
foundation is meant, or the word petros would simply
have been repeated. To state it another way: The
play on words was not made as tight as it could have
been, and there must be a reason for this.

c. But, it is sometimes objected, were not the two different words simply used for stylistic variation? The
answer involves a fundamental point of linguistic interpretation, namely, that "style" must never be appealed to over against specific meanings, unless
specific meanings can be shown to break down in the
given situation. This point is nowhere better made
than by Bloomfield, the greatest modern linguistic
authority: "Our fundamental assumption implies that
each linguistic form has a constant and specific meaning. If the forms are phonemically different, we suppose that their meanings also are different. . . . We

353

suppose, in short, that there are no actual synonyms.
. . . [This] general truth is presupposed not only in
linguistic study, but by all our actual use of language"
(Language, par. 9.5). Thus the burden of proof does
not rest on the interpreter who says that two different
words have at least connotative distinctions of meaning; it rests on the one who argues that the difference
is of no consequence and that "style" explains all.
The style argument, seen in this light, often turns out
to be no more than an asylum of ignorance.

d. However, others argue, the use of two words in Greek
is of no consequence, for the original dialogue between
Jesus and Peter took place in Aramaic, and undoubtedly but a single word (Kepha, "Cephas") was used in
the Aramaic conversation. The fallacy in this argument (as in virtually all such arguments based on
proto-Aramaic New Testament conversations and/or
documents) is that it involves a reasoning from the
unknown to the known rather than from the known to
the unknown. The only means we have of knowing
what in fact Jesus said to Peter on the given occasion
is via the Greek record; thus if a valid distinction is
made in the Greek, we must assume (if we accept the
reliability of the record) that a like distinction was
made in the original conversation. This does not say
how the distinction was made in Aramaic (perhaps it
was only by inflection or gesture), but it does say that
a distinction was made. To argue otherwise is really
to say that one cannot express a given idea in a given
language, i.e., that languages carry their own metaphysics with them. This is a serious confusion of
linguistics and philosophy, and reminds one of the old
farmer who, on being asked directions to a city, replied after puzzling over the problem for a while:
"Well, I guess ye jest can't git there from here."
Linguistically, you can always "git there," though
perhaps not by as direct a route in one language as in
another.

e. What, then, is the denotation of petra if not Peter ?
The total context of the passage (see above) suggests that the "live rock" on which the church is
founded is Peter's confession of Jesus as the Christ,
or, better, Christ Himself, who elicits this confession
from believers. Scripture must not contradict

354

Scripture, and to take Peter as the foundation flatly contradicts I Cor. 3:11, which asserts that "no other foundation can anyone lay than that which is laid, namely Jesus Christ." Cf. also I Cor. 10:4: "They drank from the spiritual rock (petra) which followed them, and the rock (petra) was Christ." It is very significant that in the New Testament Peter refers to Christ - and not to himself - as the rock: "Jesus is the stone rejected by the builders which has become the keystone" (Acts 4:11; Peter preaching); "Come to him [Christ], our living Stone - the stone rejected by men but choice and precious in the sight of God. . . . For those who have no faith, the stone which the builders rejected has become not only the corner-stone, but also 'a stone to trip over, a rock to stumble against.' They stumble when they disbelieve the Word" (I Peter 2:4-8).

f. Note that the interpretation just presented was a common one held by many theologians of the early church. Mantey (co-author with Dana of the basic Manual Grammar of the Greek New Testament) writes: "Chrysostom, . . . of the fourth century, perhaps the greatest preacher of his generation, has left no doubt as to his conception of Peter's relationship to Christ and others: 'On this rock; that is, on the faith of his confession. He did not say upon Peter, for it was not upon man, but upon his faith.' Chrysostom's interpretation of this passage was advocated also by Gregory of Nyssa, Isidore of Pelusium, Hilary, Theodoret, Theophanes, Theophylact and John of Damascus. It is evident that Augustine, the eminent Catholic theologian, writing even as late as the fifth century, did not hold the viewpoint of present-day Catholics with reference to Peter's having primacy over others, and not at all as to his transmitting to others any special spiritual authority. For in his sermon on Matthew 16:18 he stated that the Church was built not on Peter but on Christ: 'Simon he was called before; but this name of Peter was given him by the Lord and that in figure to signify the Church. For because Christ is the Rock (Petra), Peter (Petros) is the Christian people. For the Rock (Petra) is the principal word (principale nomen est). Therefore Peter (Petros) is from Petra, not Petra from Petros: As Christ is not called from the Christian, but the Christian from

Christ. "Thou art therefore," saith He, "Peter, and upon this Rock which then thou has recognized, 'Thou art the Christ, the Son of the living God,' I will build my Church. Upon me I will build thee, not me upon thee."" (Julius R. Mantey, Was Peter a Pope? [Chicago: Moody Press, 1949], pp. 20-21.)

2. Other Fallacies in the Roman Argument.

   a. The spiritual authority ("power of the keys") given to Peter in the Matt. 16 passage is given to all the apostles in Matt. 18:18 and John 20:22-23; note that the same words are used: "Truly, I say to you [plural], whatever you bind on earth shall be bound in heaven, and whatever you loose on earth shall be loosed in heaven." Jesus "breathed on them, and said to them, 'Receive the Holy Spirit. If you forgive the sins of any, they are forgiven; if you retain the sins of any, they are retained.'" Thus the Matt. passage gives Peter no unique authority - no authority which the other apostles did not possess as well. Cf. Eph. 2:19-22: "So then you [believers] are no longer strangers and sojourners, but you are fellow citizens with the saints and members of the household of God, built upon the foundation of the apostles and prophets, Christ Jesus himself being the chief cornerstone, in whom the whole structure is joined together and grows into a holy temple in the Lord; in whom you also are built into it for a dwelling place of God in the Spirit."

   b. Peter received no infallible church authority from Jesus, even in matters spiritual (ex cathedra), for Paul refuted Peter to his face on the matter of circumcising Gentile converts. Paul wrote: "When Peter came to Antioch I opposed him to his face, because he stood condemned" (Gal. 2:11).

   c. There is not a particle of historical evidence that Peter ever passed on any authority to anyone; and what is more important, there is no New Testament evidence at all that Christ commanded Peter to pass on any authority. Without such a clear command of Christ, the "successors" of Peter must be regarded as having arrogated authority to themselves, rather than having received it from Christ.

III. Conclusion

"The Church's one foundation is Jesus Christ, her Lord;
She is His new creation by water and the Word;
From heaven He came and sought her to be His holy Bride,
With His own Blood He bought her, and for her life He died."

-Samuel John Stone, 1866.

Bibliographical Note:

For the best and most comprehensive discussion of Peter's place in the early church, read Oscar Cullmann, Peter: Disciple - Apostle - Martyr, tr. from the German by Floyd V. Filson (Philadelphia: Westminster Press, 1953), $4.50 (also in paperback).

7. A CRITICAL EXAMINATION OF EMIL BRUNNER'S THE DIVINE IMPERATIVE, BK. III

The Content of Book III of "The Divine Imperative"

Those who have read one or more of Professor Brunner's publications--whether in the original German or in authorized English translation--need not be told that the author's style is so lucid and his organization of material so well conceived that detailed précis of his works have doubtful value. The present examination of The Divine Imperative, Book III, does not, therefore, attempt to provide a complete restatement of the contents of the volume; yet, because accurate exposition is the only sound basis for meaningful criticism, a summary of the author's argument and a review of the high points of his presentation will be set forth before proceeding to a critique of the work.

The title of Book III of The Divine Imperative indicates the book's subject-matter: "The Orders," i.e., the Divine orders, or orders of Creation (Schöpfungsordnungen). For Brunner's definition of the term "orders," one should turn first to Chapter 14 of Book I, where the following explanation is given:[1]

> It is characteristic of our present existence (as an actuality created by God, and yet sinful) that it is embedded in a framework of "orders" of a most varied kind. The individual human being does not enter into the sphere of social and natural relations as a free master of himself but, as a psycho-physical and historical being, he is born into the life which is already present, and--as always--already "ordered," and he grows--at first instinctively, more or less unconsciously, within this "organism" composed of a people and of humanity as a whole, as one of its "members." When conscious self-determination and faith awaken, man has already been moulded both by nature and by history, he has already been absorbed into the intricate web of human life with its manifold claims; duties of all kinds chain him to a certain way of living; he is burdened and tied down by a thousand ties.

According to Brunner, then, an order is first and foremost a necessary configuration of human existence, within which the individual finds himself by the very fact of his humanity. Werner Elert likewise points up this characteristic of the orders when he asserts that they "have validity in individual situations" and that their "existential orderliness always becomes apparent in the fact that they allow no substitution."[2] But something more is involved in the concept of the orders. In the Introduction to Book III, Brunner writes: "We see not merely particular spheres of life within which we are to act, but orders in accordance with which we have to act, because in them, even if only in a fragmentary and indirect way, God's Will meets us. Hence we call them 'Divine orders'" (p. 291). Thus the orders must be viewed not only as structures required by the nature of human life, but also as areas in which God meets man and requires of him responsible existence. Elert has this latter aspect in mind when he states that the "formal criterion" of the orders is "the fact that man can break them and that they are therefore subject to divine legislation."[3]

As background for his discussion of the particular Divine orders, Brunner begins Book III with a general treatment of "The Individual, the Community, and the Orders of Society." Here he points out that the traditional opposition between individualism and corporate life is a false dichotomy which can be solved only in the agape-love of the Christian faith; for "real communio is simply and solely love without conditions, which is only possible in reply to God's way of loving, which is without conditions," and "the individual essence of a human being only prospers where its development is not deliberately sought" (pp. 306, 307). The author deals in a very penetrating manner with the fundamental ethical problem of the relation between God, the neighbor, and the self; he affirms correctly that "there are no duties towards God, in the way in which there are duties towards our neighbour. We do not bring anything to God, we simply receive" (p. 310),[4] and he notes that "the command to love one's neighbour 'as oneself' is not to be understood as an imperative but as an indicative" (p. 316).[5] The fact that "the distinctive mark of the Christian Ethos--not merely of the Middle Ages, with its ascetic errors, but also of Primitive Christianity and of all genuine Christianity--is passive love, self-sacrificing surrender--which, from the psychological point of view is the highest activity" leads one to ask, "What am I to do if these [individual neighbor-] claims conflict with each other ?" (p. 328). The answer to this question necessarily involves the author in the whole problem of the orders--within which responsible human action is to be carried out. The various orders, being the product of Divine creation and yet also suffering from sinful human perversion, are all to be viewed by the Christian with "a watchful, aggressive, determined attitude of hostility to all that is contrary to the will of God within human life; but this critical and reforming temper must always be based upon a grateful acceptance of human life, coupled with a readiness to serve wherever we may be" (p. 338). At this point the author has laid a sufficient foundation for discussing each of the Divine orders individually.

Marriage and family are treated first. Brunner begins by setting forth a methodological principle which will govern his discussion both of this order and of the others to follow:

> Just as it is useless to appeal to tradition on this question, so also it is useless to appeal to isolated passages in the Bible. Devotees of the literalist interpretation of the Bible are particularly prone to this practice, especially on this question, but such procedure reveals a very unevangelical, legalistic idea of the authority of the Bible. . . . We may . . . demand of a theological ethic that it should not make its statements as apodictic doctrines without considering whether they have any relation to human reality or not, but that it should develop its doctrines in view of reality, and that means the reality of the present day. (Pp. 341-42.)

The case for monogamy is built on two arguments, one objective, the other subjective. The former presents what Brunner terms a "trinity of being"--the fact "that every human being is irrevocably the child of one man and one woman, that every father, with this woman, and every mother, with this man, is, irrevocably, the father and the mother of this child" (p. 345). The subjective argument for monogamy is the assertion that "genuine natural love is in its essence monistic" (p. 347). These objective and subjective considerations are bound together in the concept of Divine Creation. "Only where--in the recognition of the order of creation--husband and wife bind themselves together in love and know themselves bound-- marriage means 'binding'--has a marriage (on its subjective as well as on its objective side) been 'concluded'" (p. 348). Such marriage serves as "a symbol and a way of approach to true community" (p. 350). Human sin colors the picture, however; one must recognize that marriage is indeed a remedium concupiscentiae, and that monogamy "is the optimum which, as experience has proved, lies between complete asceticism and a form of sex relation which is more accommodating to the sex desire" (p. 352). Moreover, since in thought if not in actual deed "we are all adulterers, the difference between the different orders of the sex relation become relative" (p. 353). This latter conclusion leads logically to such statements as the following: "It is conceivable that a case might arise in which, in order to obey the Divine Command, one might have to act 'against the law.' Such a case, for instance, would occur if the dissolution of a marriage had become a duty" (p. 354). "A marriage without love, and this means also without sex attraction, should never be contracted. . . . For the sake of the love of our neighbour the only moral thing to do is to dissolve a marriage of this kind" (p. 361). "The worth of a law is to be measured not by its 'strictness' in the abstract sense, but by the wisdom with which the legislation is adjusted to reality, in order to attain a maximum of social health and decency. From this point of view it is even possible that the State may have to resolve to renounce the exclusive protection of monogamous marriage, and be compelled to extend it to sex relations which are still further removed from monogamous marriage, since, in any case, the present form of marriage can be easily dissolved" (p. 363). "It must certainly be admitted that the gratifying decline in the number of prostitutes is due in whole or in part to the increase in the practice of free relationships among 'decent people'" (p. 653). Brunner concludes his discussion of the order of marriage and the family with a plea for "responsible motherhood" (in reference to the birth-control issue), for an understanding of the economic difficulties which today confront young people seeking marriage, and for a recognition of the complex role which modern Western civilization has forced upon both the wife and the unmarried woman.[6]

The economic order is next examined. The author begins by stressing the basic principles that God wills that men work; that He also desires that they experience sufficient rest and constructive recreation; and that He regards as demonic any unrestrained attempt to dominate the world or any form of enslavement to the things of this world. "It is essential to the Divine purpose of labour that labour can only make people happy in so far as it fulfils its purpose, that is, in so far as it helps man to be truly man, and serves the purpose of life in community" (p. 393). The economic order--involving the soil, tools, human workers, finished goods, and the consumption of these goods--is both the product of Divine creation ("If any will not work, neither let him eat"--II Thess. 3:10), and an area in which sin has particular power ("On the one hand, it has been spoilt by its false tendency to become an end in itself, and on the other by egoistic exploitation by the individual which always works out both as sin and as a curse"--p. 399). Granting this, however, "the first question the Christian ought to ask in this economic world should not be: 'How can I alter it?' but: 'How can I serve within it?'" (p. 401). Brunner answers this latter question via three principles: (1) "Man is not to engage in economic activity for its own sake, but in order to live, to live in a human way" (p. 402). (2) "The economic system should never be regarded merely as an individual concern, but also as the concern of the community" (p. 404). It follows from this, of course, that private property can per se neither be affirmed nor be denied. (3) "Every person capable of rendering service is under an obligation to render service" (p. 406). As a means of adjusting the "comparative monopolies" which exist in the economic sphere due to differences among individuals and among groups, the capitalistic system is vigorously rejected as the "objectification of the striving for gain" (p. 419 - from Sombart in the Handwörterbuch der Soziologie). Capitalism is "irresponsibility developed into a system" (p. 423); yet a Christian must not shirk his economic responsibility even where this system is present, for "none of us knows whether he will ever know any better order" (p. 424). Communism offers no more desirable economic Weltanschauung, for "it is just as much opposed to the Divine order in creation as its counterpart; it is the same system, with the signs reversed" (p. 427).[7] Certain socialistic approaches (e.g., the English consumers' Co-operative and the Danish agricultural producers' co-operative Movement--see p. 670) offer fruitful suggestions toward a more Christian economic approach; however, we should never allow ourselves to think that any economic program--regardless of its attractiveness--can cancel out the radical selfishness of fallen man. Within whatever economic system the Church finds itself, it is called to preach the Gospel, engage in social service, offer prophetic criticism of existing evils and idols, and present an example of genuine community based on love.

The order of the State now comes under discussion. The author's concern is not with political theory (the Idea of the State--whether Positivistic, Idealistic, or Romantic), but with political reality; and in every actual State three elements exist: community, disciplinary order, and the exercise of power. True community is of course not created by the State, for compulsion, not love, is its principle of action; yet the State, like the family, provides men with a faint approximation of the interdependent life which characterizes God's Kingdom. The nature of the State as the Divine institution of the power of order is evidenced by its numinous authority--expressed in

rational legislation and in irrational power. And it is axiomatic
that "the greater the power of the State, and the certainty that
every one who breaks the law will be dealt with by the law, the
less will the power of coercion be felt" (p. 453).[8] However, the
State has no right to assume totalitarian control over the other
orders.[9] "A too close connection with the State, or even a sub-
ordination in principle of these spheres of life to the State, must
take away their meaning and destroy their vitality; and--this
should be noted as very significant--it must also destroy the
force and meaning of the State" (p. 458). Brunner holds that
"in itself there is no Christian and non-Christian form of the
State" (p. 465); whether one proceeds from the standpoint of
the twofold purpose of the State (to achieve both the most competent form of government and the maximum degree of community), or from the fact of sin and evil in the State, one is
forced to conclude that "neither complete autocracy nor unqualified government by the people, that is, democracy (which
is the ideal of Liberalism), can, as a rule, be the right form of
government" (p. 466). The author rejects absolute pacifism as
not taking into account the extent of human depravity, but suggests that modern war may have become a greater evil than any
alternative to it. With regard to the penal treatment of crimi-
nals, Brunner declares that punishments must expiate the
wrongs both of society as a whole and of the lawbreakers themselves; he believes that "forcible education" (p. 477) at state
expense is the best means of achieving this.

The several cultural orders are next analyzed.[10] Here
especially Christian faith must perform its regulative function,
for "the symbol of all actual--but not true--creation of culture
is the Tower of Babel" (p. 488). The particular danger inherent in science is its "one-sided emphasis on the freedom of
man from the world, without any consideration for the fact that
man belongs to the world" (p. 492). Art, on the other hand, can
easily lend support to mysticism and pantheism; it is often
"sought because it does not demand decision, as faith does, but
merely the attitude of a spectator, or of one who is swayed
hither and thither by the artistic influences around him" (p.
500). To be sure, science and art, like the other orders, are
Divine gifts and tasks; Christians are to participate in them
with thankfulness to God and in reliance upon His grace. With
respect to education, Brunner makes several interesting
points:[11] The Idealistic philosophy of education needs to be
corrected and supplemented by the Christian stress on integrating the individual into the community and increasing his sense
of personal responsibility toward his fellows. Education is

primarily the concern of the family--not of the school, or even of the State; indeed, "the State as a legal organization requires centralization, the building up from above, downwards. Culture, which begins, essentially, with the individual, and as a fellowship, needs the intimacy of the small group, requires to be built up from below" (p. 513). The Church, though it should employ sound pedagogical method, is "not an education institution, but it is the community of the redeemed" (p. 511). The "free forms of community" (friendship, custom, public opinion) receive brief treatment. "As friendship is the nearest approach of the natural spiritual element to personal community, so, on the other hand, custom is the impersonal medium between the truly ethical and the natural" (p. 519). Public opinion is "a kind of secular parallel to the 'invisible Church'" (p. 521), and "it is the duty of Christendom to create public opinion, in the sense that through it and in it Christ should exercise His Sovereignty even over those who do not know Him, so far as this is possible" (ibid.).

Lastly, Brunner deals with the Church as a Divine order. He defines the Church by combining the three classic statements of its nature: coetus electorum; communio sanctorum; corpus Christi; and at the same time he makes quite clear that "the Church and perfection are mutually exclusive ideas; the Church is the community of those who are still sinners" (p. 526). This Divine-human institution is characterized primarily by the preaching and believing of the Word (even where only two or three are gathered); but it must also move out into the community of faith with other believers (here the Sacraments and Church order enter the picture) and into a community of love with those who do not believe (here the missionary effort and social service come into play). Brunner distinguishes between the "Church of faith" and the "worshipping community"; the former "makes its influence felt beyond the bounds of the worshipping community in the natural secular relations between human beings, in the natural orders of the family, the economic order, the State and culture" (p. 535). Church discipline is necessary to prevent the Church as worshipping community from becoming absorbed in the world. The significance of the worshipping community lies in the fact that it "is the preferred, distinctive necessary order, which in far greater measure than the other orders, because in more direct and necessary connexion with it, serves the Church of faith" (p. 538). Church union "ought never to be achieved at the expense of the primary element; the primary element is that the local congregation should fulfil its particular calling, as fully as it possibly can, a calling which is unique and wholly peculiar to itself" (p. 540). No denomination or type of Church-State relationship (State Church, National Church, Free Church) can honestly be considered the "true" Church--for sin exists in all. Sin within the churches shows itself especially in legalism--which either "confuses the letter of Scripture with the Word of God" (p. 545) or blurs "the distinction between the human confession of faith (dogma) and the Word of God" (ibid.), or identifies ecclesiastical legislation ("canon law") or church organization with the Word of God. "True ecclesiasticism . . . consists in the fact that the divine and the human are not separated, but also that they are not regarded as identical with one another" (p. 562). "False churchmanship, or clericalism," on the other hand, "does not consist in an excessive concern for the visible Church, but it is churchmanship which lacks any real foundation because it seeks that foundation in itself. . . . The watchword of genuine churchmanship is never 'the Church,' but always and only 'Jesus Christ'" (pp. 565-66).

A Critique of Book III of "The Divine Imperative"

Brunner's analysis of the Divine orders is almost sure to leave the Christian reader with two equally strong, but conflicting, impressions. One of these is that in many respects the author succeeds wonderfully in showing the application of the Christian message to the real world of human experience. When he deals with science and art, Brunner does not attempt to force from the Christian revelation standards of propositional truth or of aesthetic value by which to judge the work of scholars, researchers, and artists.[12] In his presentation of the political and economic orders, he wisely observes the sin rampant in all the various human panaceas and programs, and therefore refuses to justify any existing economic or political system from the standpoint of Christ's Gospel.[13] In all these areas the author employs the Christian message as a regulative principle, thereby pointing up the idolatrous tendencies which inhere in each of them; yet at the same time he stresses the responsibility which believers have to enter these spheres and serve the Creator to the best of their ability in them.

But this positive impression is not the only one which the Christian reader carries away with him after studying The Divine Imperative, Book III. Brunner's discussion of the Church as a Divine order is characterized by an unfortunate vagueness. No denomination, in his opinion, deserves the designation of the "true" Church; with this almost all

Protestant Christians would agree, but since every Christian is duty-bound to align himself with other believers in a worshipping community, some criteria should be presented for choosing among the welter of denominational bodies. Brunner gives no such criteria; his assertion that the sine qua non of the Church is the preaching of the Word offers little help, for he cautions us not to confuse the letter of Scripture, or confessions of faith, with that Word. Similar vagueness is manifested in his attitude toward church union. No principles of union are stated; in fact, as we have seen, the author recommends that such union ought not to be considered as important as the local congregation's fulfilment of its "wholly peculiar" calling. Brunner's discussion of the marital order reveals further difficulties. From the truth that we are all adulterers, if only in thought, the author makes the questionable deductions that divorce is normally justifiable when marriage has occurred "without sex attraction," and that the State would be right in renouncing "the exclusive protection of monogamous marriage" if by doing so greater "social health and decency" would be promoted.

How are we to view such doubtful or inadequate arguments as those just cited? Do we have here merely isolated examples of lapsus theologi? Or is there a more basic explanation for the difficulties in certain areas of Brunner's presentation, as contrasted with a thoroughgoing soundness in other areas? I believe that a fundamental problem lies at the root of Brunner's treatment of the orders--a problem which exists also in more than a few other analyses of the Schöpfungsordnungen.

The problem of which I speak has to do with the relationship between the two defining characteristics of an order which were stated at the outset of this paper. Brunner and Elert (and other theologians who have dealt with the orders) agree that an order is (1) a necessary configuration of human existence, and (2) an area of life in which God encounters man and requires of him responsible existence. Now a basic question (given no precise answer by Brunner) is: How does one determine the proper content of an order--i.e., the content which accords with the Divine Will? Is the proper content of an order already inherent in it as a necessary structure of existence? Or does the "necessity" of the orders refer merely to their form (their proper content being determined only by Special Revelation)? Or does the proper content of an order stem in part from the already-existing order, and in part also from God's revealed Will? If the latter is the correct answer, what is the final arbiter when the actually-existing order and God's Revelation concerning that order are at variance? The importance of this problem becomes evident when one realizes that by assuming no more than a natural content for the political order, Gogarten and other German theologians of the Third Reich concluded that the Nazi régime was consistent with God's Will; and that by assuming a revealed content for the artistic order, Zwingli and others refused to allow music to be employed in Divine services.

The final determinative of the content of an order must be the Divine Revelation--for the orders have been, and continue to be, corrupted by sin. Once this latter fact is admitted, it necessarily follows that the existing content of an order need not be identical with God's Will for that order; and that without some Word from outside the orders themselves, it would forever be impossible to determine their proper content. However, this does not say that God's Revelation has fully or equally outlined the proper content of each order; it simply says that wherever the Revelation does speak with regard to an order, its assertions must be taken as final.

Brunner, however, does not approach the orders with this principle as his guide. His fear of being classed with Biblical literalists and fundamentalists causes him again and again to warn that "the Bible itself is not simply the Word of God" (p. 528),[14] and to base his statements with regard to the proper content of the orders not principally upon Scriptural ground, but primarily upon "the reality of the present day" (p. 342).[15] The result is not particularly serious where Scripture is silent or virtually silent on the content of an order, but it becomes a matter of real concern where Scripture makes detailed apodictic assertions on the Divine Will for an order. And when does Scripture speak on the content of orders? Brunner himself suggests the answer in another connection when he writes: "The further the sphere of science is from the personal sphere the more autonomous does the science become, the more legitimate is its abstract conception of scientific law; the nearer it is to the personal sphere, the more the real human being needs to be known, the more faith gains not merely a regulative but a constitutive significance" (p. 496). A careful study of Scriptural statements bearing directly on the orders will show, I am convinced, that the more personal the order, the more the Christian Revelation has to say about its proper content; and the less personal the order, the less the Bible deals with its content. Brunner's discussion of the orders is, then, understandably strongest where the orders are the most impersonal (science, art, the State, economics)--where, in other words, the content of the orders is not a matter of Revelation, and where faith acts largely as a regulative, not a constitutive, principle. And Brunner's presentation is weakest, as we have seen, in the highly personal orders of the Church and the family, where Scripture has much to say in criticism of the current content of these orders.

More specifically: If the orders are arranged in a continuum from less personal to more personal, it will be seen that the single continuum represents both an increasing amount of Scriptural teaching on the proper content of the orders, and a decreasing strength in Brunner's treatment of these same Divine configurations.

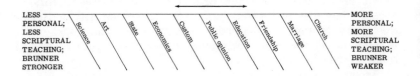

Where science and art are involved, Scripture presents only simple regulative principles, e.g., "Avoid the . . . contradictions of what is falsely called knowledge, for by professing it some have missed the mark as regards the faith" (I Tim. 6:20-21),[16] and "Little children, keep yourselves from idols" (I Jn. 5:21). Such principles as these Brunner has competently developed in The Divine Imperative, Book III. With regard to the slightly less impersonal realms of the State and economics, Scripture is only a bit more full in its assertions (Rom. 13:1-7 and similar passages; Acts 5:29; II Thess. 3:10); these passages, though of vital importance, are still regulative, not constitutive, in character, and Brunner, as we have seen, presents their implications quite effectively. Custom Brunner rightly calls "the impersonal medium between the truly ethical and the natural" (p. 519), and here again Scripture does not attempt to set down absolute rules as to proper or improper customs;[17] the regulative principle is, "Whether you eat or drink, or whatever you do, do all to the glory of God" (I Cor. 10:31). Brunner catches the spirit of this Apostolic approach when he writes, "It should be an urgent concern of the Church that custom should be moulded into shape as a deposit of faith and not of unbelief, of personal responsibility and not of irresponsibility" (p. 519). Unfortunately, however, he does not in this connection work out the full implications of such a passage as Phil. 4:8.

The Christian Revelation is at many points concerned with public opinion--that "secular parallel to the 'invisible Church.'"

Again and again the New Testament exhorts Christians to conduct themselves in the world in such a way that the best possible climate of opinion is created for the furtherance of God's Kingdom; such a verse as Mt. 5:16 is representative: "Let your light so shine before men, that they may see your good works and give glory to your Father who is in heaven" (cf. also Phil. 1:27; II Cor. 6:3-8). Brunner, however, in his brief discussion of public opinion, does not directly present any Biblical teaching on the subject. "Education," the author agrees, in that it "has more to do with the personal centre than any other aspect of cultural life, has a particularly close connexion with faith or with its opposite" (p. 507), but he does not apparently recognize the wealth of Scriptural material on this very personal sphere of life. Brunner stresses as the proper aim of education "integrating the individual into the community and increasing his sense of personal responsibility toward his fellows"--goals which closely parallel those of American progressive educationists. The Biblical Revelation, on the other hand, emphasizes the educational importance of thoroughly comprehending the objective works of God in nature and history (Deut. 6:6-7; Ps. 104; II Tim. 2:15, 3:14-17). Community and responsibility are of course genuine Biblical concerns, but from the standpoint of the "fruits of the Spirit," not as an educational goal. The sphere of friendship thrusts us even more into the personal realm, and by that very fact it places us more definitely within the area of Scriptural teaching. The close connection between philia (love as friendship) and agape is evidenced by Jn. 21:15-17 (Gk. txt.); and the New Testament tells us that our closest associations should be made within the circle of true believers (II Cor. 6:14ff.; II Jn. 10-11), but also that we should seek worldly friends for the sake of spiritual goals (Lk. 16:9). These constitutive principles receive no mention in Brunner's work.

The marital order is more personal in character than any other order except the Church (cf. Eph. 5:23-32), and Scripture makes far more constitutive assertions about it than with regard to the configurations to the left of it in the continuum given above. Monogamy was instituted prior to the Fall; polygamy, concubinage, and easy divorce were permitted under the Old Covenant only due to the hardness of human hearts (Mk. 10:2-12; Mt. 19:3-9), and with the coming of Christ, who fulfilled the Law, the situation is radically and unalterably changed (Mt. 5:27-32). The content of the marital order is clearly defined by Revelation--it is permanent monogamy; and current cultural trends, population statistics, etc. have nothing to do with the issue. The fact that all are adulterers before God because of sins of the heart in no way provides an escape-hatch for church or state policy on the marriage and divorce problem. We must find our solutions within the framework of Scriptural teaching, not by circumventing it. More time spent in evangelism, pre-marital counselling, sex education, etc., and less on speculations concerning polygamous solutions to a high female birth-rate, and the hygenic advantages of pre-marital intimacies among "decent people," will accord better with the total Christian ethos.

The most personal of the Divine orders is the Church, for through it men enter into a living, intimate relationship with the Lord of the universe. The Christian Revelation sets forth the content of this Church in greater detail than it does for any of the other orders. Brunner instinctively recognizes this when he terms this order "the Church," and not simply "Religion." From the purely natural viewpoint, one might well assert that Religion, but not the Christian Church, is a necessary configuration of existence for human beings. Only Revelation tells us that one religion alone--Christianity--is truly worthy of the designation "Divine order" (Jn. 14:6; Acts 4:12)--even as only that same Christian Revelation tells us that one form of marriage alone--monogamy--is Divinely ordered. But our author does not attempt rigorously to examine Scriptural teaching on the Church; instead he concentrates on the Church as one actually finds it in the world, as if its legitimate content can be determined naturally like that of science or the State--as if Scripture sets up only regulative principles to govern the Church's life. Brunner presents the work of the local congregation as of more fundamental significance than the larger perspective of church cooperation and world-wide witness; yet Scripture clearly stresses the latter to a much greater degree than the former (Jn. 17:20-21; Mt. 28:18-20; Acts 1:7-8). Moreover, the New Testament Revelation is in no sense indifferent to the problem of the "true" Church; true doctrine determines the truth of a church body (Acts 2:42; Gal. 1:6-9); and it is safe to say that if Christians were really convinced of this, efforts in the ecumenical direction might not be quite as frustrating as they have been in the past.

In conclusion, then, the central point growing out of this critique may well be reiterated, namely, that it is not legalism, or bibliolatry, or fundamentalism to take the Scriptural Revelation seriously when it speaks--to let "our consciences become captive to the Word of God," both in the written and in the living sense. Thomas Campbell's motto provides an excellent guide

370

for all those who would understand the Divine orders: "Where the Scriptures speak, we speak; where the Scriptures are silent, we are silent."[18]

NOTES

1. Emil Brunner, The Divine Imperative, tr. by Olive Wyon (Philadelphia, Westminster Press, c1947), p. 140. All succeeding page references to The Divine Imperative assume this edition.

2. Werner Elert, The Christian Ethos, tr. by Carl J. Schindler (Philadelphia, Muhlenberg Press, c1957), p. 79. (A 2d and revised edition of this translation has now been published.)

3. Elert, op. cit., p. 78.

4. Cf. Paul Ramsey, Basic Christian Ethics (New York, Scribner, c1950), pp. 116ff. ("Is Love for God Part of the Meaning of Christian Love?").

5. Ramsey emphasizes this also: "Pointing to the existence of self-love is one thing, making it an injunction would be another. The words, 'You shall love your neighbor as yourself,' certainly contain a reference to love for self, yet they by no means include a commandment, 'You shall love yourself'" (op. cit., p. 100).

6. These latter issues are also carefully examined by Harold Haas in his chapter on "Christian Faith and Family Life" in Christian Social Responsibility, Vol. III (Life in Community), ed. by Harold C. Letts (Philadelphia, Muhlenberg Press, c1957), pp. 148ff.

7. The fundamental individualism at the root of Marxist Communism as well as of Western Capitalism is seldom noticed. Karl Löwith (professor of history at Heidelberg) points up this individualism when he writes, "In a perfect communist commonwealth each individual has realized his human essence as a common sociopolitical existence" (Meaning in History [Chicago, University of Chicago Phoenix Books, c1949], p. 50).

8. Cf. the principle stated in Justinian's Institutes: "Melius

est in tempore occurrere, quam post causam vulneratam remedium quaerere" (2 Inst. 299).

9. For thought-provoking literary depictations of such totalitarianisms, see Thomas Hobbes' Leviathan and George Orwell's 1984.

10. A very valuable work on this subject is Emile Cailliet's The Christian Approach to Culture (New York, Abingdon-Cokesbury, c1953).

11. Note in this connection Gordon H. Clark's A Christian Philosophy of Education (Grand Rapids, Eerdmans, 1946).

12. Fundamentalists have been especially prone to judge scientific work by what they believe to be the "truth of revelation"; Calvinists have done the same in the artistic realm.

13. Brunner thus does not fall into the error committed by the many theologians who have identified an economic system (Capitalism, Communism, etc.) or a political system (Nazism, Americanism, etc.) with the Christian faith. C. S. Lewis sums up this failing when he has Screwtape write: "The real trouble about the set your patient is living in is that it is merely Christian. . . . What we want, if men become Christians at all, is to keep them in the state of mind I call 'Christianity And.' You know--Christianity and the Crisis, Christianity and the New Psychology, Christianity and the New Order. . . . Substitute for the faith itself some Fashion with a Christian colouring" (The Screwtape Letters [New York, Macmillan, 1944], p. 126).

14. This distinction, frequently made today (e.g. by Joseph Sittler among Lutherans), between the Scriptures and the living Word of God (Christ) is very misleading and results in more difficulties than it resolves. The only "living Word" any Christian knows is the Word whose characteristics are set forth in the "written Word"; any inner experience of Christ which contradicts the Christ of Revelation is, ipso facto, not the real Christ. Moreover, the Bible does not merely contain the Word of God, it is the Word of God--otherwise, as the Lutheran Confessions have asserted unequivocally (Formula of Concord, para. 1), it could not be the standard by which all other writings and teachings are to be judged, but would itself have to be judged by some

372

other standard. Professor Lavik correctly notes that the Brunner-Sittler view "assumes as a philosophic and rationalistic principle that the finite is not capable of the infinite (finitum non est capax infiniti)"--a tenet which harks back to Greek philosophical conceptions of the Absolute (John R. Lavik, The Christian Church in a Secularized World [Minneapolis, Augsburg, c1952], p. 73). Brunner recognizes that he deviates from the Reformers on this matter; he writes: "This is the point at which the theology and the Church of the present day must move most definitely away from the view of the Reformers. . . . Calvin . . . and Luther . . . at this point . . . were more closely bound by the ecclesiastical tradition than we have any right to be" (p. 716). Recent Lutheran doctrinal affirmations have fortunately followed the Reformers and not the Neo-Orthodox; the Federation of Evangelical Lutheran Churches in India stated in 1951: "All believers will, as our Lord and His apostles did with regard to the Holy Scriptures of the Old Testament, listen to every word and passage of the biblical text with the reverent faith that is due to the holy Word of God" (Doctrinal Statement Presenting the Confessional Basis of the Federation of Evangelical Lutheran Churches in India [Guntur, India, Lutheran Press, 1951], p. 14).

15. The basic role to be played in theology by "the reality of the present day" is, as Tillich so well points out, not to offer theological solutions in contradistinction to those of Revelation, but to reveal the vital and truly significant questions and problems to which Revelation must supply the answers. See Paul Tillich, Systematic Theology, Vol. I (Chicago, University of Chicago Press, c1951), pp. 3 ff.

16. Scripture does not necessarily present constitutive scientific data in such passages as Gen. 1-2. The Hebrew employed in the Creation account is highly poetic in character, and the clear intention of the writer is theological, not cosmological or scientific.

17. One might at first glance think that the New Testament makes a considerable number of apodictic, constitutive assertions with regard to customs (e.g. the "braided hair" passages--I Tim. 2:9; I Pet. 3:2-3). Here, however, the principle applies in Biblical interpretation which has been universally accepted in Anglo-American common law: "The reasoning, illustrations, or references contained in the

opinion of a court are not authority, not precedent, but only
the points in judgment arising in the particular case before
the court" (L. & N.R.R. Co. v. County Court of Davidson
County, 1 Sneed [Tenn.] 637). The New Testament writers
use such matters as braided hair simply as examples to
illustrate their point that women "should adorn themselves
modestly and sensibly in seemly apparel."

18. Quoted by Kenneth Scott Latourette, A History of Christianity (New York, Harper, c1953), p. 1042.

8. HISTORY: PUBLIC OR PRIVATE?
A DEFENSE OF JOHN WARWICK MONTGOMERY'S
PHILOSOPHY OF HISTORY*

by

Paul D. Feinberg, Th.D., Ph.D. (Cand.)
Division of Philosophy of Religion
Trinity Evangelical Divinity School

In Professor Ronald H. Nash's "The Use and Abuse of History in Christian Apologetics" he seeks to clarify and correct a view of history most prominently associated with John Warwick Montgomery. While Nash admits that his philosophy of history has on the whole been an influence for good in the Christian community, he feels that the time has come to note that at least at some points it "cannot be supported" (p. 218). I take it from his critique that these points have to do with objectivity in history and historical writing (pp. 218-221) and the relationship which the facts of history bear to their interpretation (pp. 221-224).

I would like to examine these criticisms, evaluate briefly the constructionist view of history, pointing out the possible dangers and difficulties which I see in such a philosophy, and finally draw some conclusions.

I

The first issue is that of objectivity. Montgomery's position requires that history can be written objectively. Nash admits that he and Montgomery differ on the meaning of objective history (p. 220). Montgomery means that "systematic historical reconstruction is open to criticism,"[2] while Nash claims to take the "more natural meaning" of "freedom from value judgment." Nash then proceeds to refute the possibility of objective history in his sense. He suggests that the two most damaging arguments against the value-free history are that language itself is value-charged and that the notion of history is intrinsically value-laden (pp. 220 ff.). It may come as a surprise to some, but Nash and Montgomery are in agreement

*Reprinted from **Christian Scholar's Review**, I, 4 (Summer, 1971), pp. 325-331.

on this point. Montgomery too has argued that history free from value-judgments is both impossible and undesirable.[3] As a matter of fact, it is just for this reason that he argues that historical writing must have complete openness to criticism.

But what does Nash's refutation have to do with Montgomery? Nothing at all. It provides interesting biographical information about Nash. It is also an example of what Passmore calls an interesting feature of philosophical words which makes it possible to define them in such a way that they can become vacuous or meaningless in either of two directions. On the one hand, they may become vacuous by applying to everything, while, on the other hand, they may become meaningless by applying to nothing. In both instances the word or words have lost their usefulness as a mode of distinguishing.[4] But the refutation is irrelevant to Montgomery's philosophy of history. It is clear that he does not hold the rejected view of objectivity. For Nash's criticism to be damaging, he must show either that Montgomery's view of history necessarily entails the refuted meaning of objectivity (the argument for that I see nowhere in Nash's critique) or that Montgomery's understanding of objectivity is impossible (a position I cannot conceive anyone taking). The claim of Nash that his interpretation of objectivity is more natural or in accord with ordinary usage is neither here nor there. It is not my purpose to contest this point. For, as long as Montgomery has clearly defined his usage of the term, all that is required is that the definition is not contrary to ordinary usage.[5] The former condition I have shown to have been met above, the latter can be verified by examination of a dictionary or philosophies of history.[6]

The fundamental issue connected with historical objectivity, as Montgomery sees it, is not whether history should be free from value judgments, but whether these judgments are justified sui generis or are open to criticism in light of the facts of history. What I take to be Montgomery's position is clearly stated by Wittgenstein, "If language is to be a means of communication there must be agreement not only in definitions but also (queer as this may sound) in judgments."[7]

II

This leads us to the crux of the debate. What is the relationship between the facts of history and their interpretation? Nash's handling of this issue is extremely unfortunate. It is indeed a shame that he did not consult some of Montgomery's other works, particularly "The Theologian's Craft."[8]

Nash correctly claims that Montgomery holds that the facts of history carry their own interpretation (p. 221), but seldom has the meaning of a view been missed by so much. Nash's difficulties arise from his understanding of Montgomery's claim. It does not mean that interpretations "in some way ride piggy-back on the events of history" (p. 222). Interestingly enough, the correct meaning of that statement is quoted by Nash just a paragraph above (p. 221). It is "that the facts in themselves provide adequate criteria for choosing among variant interpretations of them."[9] Montgomery means that meanings are public in the Wittgensteinian sense, as opposed to private or personal. Meanings are learned by public use. To escape the predicament of philosophical puzzle-ment (Wittgenstein likens this to being a fly in a fly bottle: we buzz around in the same confined space, but are unable to escape), one must abandon an a priori, oversimplified view of words and their functions. Wittgenstein says, "One cannot guess how a word functions. One has to look at its use and learn from that."[10] Pitcher commenting on Wittgenstein puts it clearly:

> What determines whether the words "meaning" and "understanding" can appropriately be applied to a person P in any given situation is the nature of the situation and its wider context—for example, what sort of person P is, how much P knows about the matter at hand, what it is he is alleged to mean or understand, what led up to the situation, and especially how P does, or would under suitable conditions, act after the situation. What goes on in P's mind, if any thing, is rarely, if ever, the circumstance which warrants the correct application of the terms "meaning" and "understanding."

Consequently, Wittgenstein argues that since meanings are public, there are public criteria for their application. This extends not only to things which are physically external, but to pain and sensation language, long the favorite argument of those who argue for the necessity of private language.[12] The criterion or criteria must be satisfied in the context which the claim is made, and consist of both verbal and non-verbal behavior. This is what Montgomery means by events carrying their interpretation with them. I cannot shake the conviction that Montgomery and Wittgenstein are right on this issue. Further, I agree with Montgomery who holds that this must be the fundamental assumption of a Christian philosophy of history or, for that matter, any philosophy of history.[13]

Having come to a proper understanding of the relationship which interpretations have to events, the other difficulties suggested are easily solvable. Nash seems to indicate that Montgomery's view falls to the ground in that there are no such things as "facts" (p. 222). This difficulty arises from Nash's understanding of "fact." It appears that for him a "fact" is the combination of a brute event plus a mind-dependent interpretation. Since the interpretation

377

then is internal and not somehow "out there" piggy-back upon the event, there are no "facts." Nash himself says, "There is no such thing as a fact apart from some interpretation and some imputed significance" (p. 222). I would submit that this is indeed a queer way of speaking about "facts." A "fact of history" is at least roughly synonymous with "event of history." A "fact" is something that exists or existed.[14] A "fact" may be interpreted or uninterpreted, meaningful or meaningless. "Facts" carry with themselves the possibility of interpretation and the criteria for choosing among variant interpretations. They may, as Nash points out, be simple or complex (cf. Caesar and the Rubicon). However, the fact that they are complex does not detract from the truth that they are "facts" any more than the fact that a sentence is conplex makes it any less a sentence.

What seems to bother Nash most about Montgomery's view of history is that significance is imputed to events, and that there are interpretations rather than an interpretation. Nash appears to feel that if facts carried their interpretation, this should be impossible (pp. 222 ff.). Again, the dilemma arises from a wooden and stilted view of the relationship between meaning and event. Significance may arise from various sources. However, significance is not imputed by the mind. The mind properly only recognizes the significance which the event "out there" bears. Significance arises from the nature of the event. Death, for instance, is significant because it is an ultimate human existential concern.[15]

If indeed the event only provides us with an adequate criterion for choosing among interpretations,[16] the possibility of interpretations is infinite. This Montgomery has never denied. All this shows is that there is the possibility of many more false interpretations than true. What is important is that there is some method of telling what is the correct meaning. Let's take the example given by Nash of the virgin birth of Christ. I suggest that all along the events or facts supplied criteria for arriving at the correct interpretation. Even before the angel arrived, the truth of a virgin birth was supported by the fact that Mary had not had intercourse with a man. True, the announcement of the angel removed the puzzlement, but this too was part of the event or fact. Why must events or facts be restricted merely to the configuration of objects and persons? Events are made up both of acts and words (in this case divine revelation).[17]

Nash's contention that "there is no necessary connection between any alleged fact and its interpretation" (p. 222), I suggest, is either trivial or false. If Nash means by this that there is no formal or logical necessity connecting a fact with its interpretation, then what he says is trivial. Such necessity is precluded by the very nature of history which is empirical. If we are to understand by

378

this that it is possible for someone to think up interpretations without regard to the facts, this too is true but quite trivial. As a matter of fact, society thinks so little of this type of behavior that if one persists in it, he will find himself confined to a mental institution. If, however, Nash means empirical necessity, I submit that there exists this kind of necessity between a fact or event and its <u>correct</u> interpretation. If not, the consequences are disastrous, for there would be no hope of discriminating between competing positions. The very foundations of human knowledge would be jeopardized.

Let us consider an example from recent history. It can be substantiated that some 6 million Jews died under German rule in the second World War. Let me suggest two mutually exclusive interpretations. First, these events may be interpreted as the actions of a mad man who was insanely anti-Semitic. The deaths were murders, atrocities. Second, it might be asserted that Hitler really loved the Jews. He had a deep and abiding belief in heaven and life after death. After reviewing Jewish history, Hitler decided that the Jews had been persecuted enough, and because of his love for them he was seeking to help them enter eternal blessedness. If no necessity exists between events and interpretation, then there is no way of determining which meaning is correct. We would never be justified in claiming that one holding the latter view is wrong. This is both repugnant and absurd. There must be an empirical necessity that unites an event or fact with its correct interpretation.

Finally, Nash suggests that Montgomery's philosophy of history "implies that the historian is a passive observer of the past" (p. 223). This is clearly <u>not</u> Montgomery's position.[18] The fact that some of his followers might make this claim is irrelevant to the truth claim of Montgomery's view of history. These disciples are just wrong. This should not be held against Montgomery's position, as this only shows that a methodology, even though correct, can be misapplied.

III

What if history is viewed from the constructionist sense? Frankly, it is difficult to say much concrete about this position, because Nash's citations are from Meiland's <u>Scepticism and Historical Knowledge</u> coupled with a disclaimer saying that he disagrees with many of the points made in the book (p. 224). However, if Nash means by constructionist philosophy of history that "the past cannot be observed directly" (p. 223) and that "all knowledge of the past is inferential and indirect" (p. 223), and if he means that the reconstructions of the past are subject to objective, empirical criteria for their validity, then Nash and Montgomery are in substantive agreement. But if he means that "the historian remakes

379

the past in his own image" (p. 224) and that "the historian constructs or creates parts of the past" (p. 224), and if this is to be construed as a construction in accord with his own a priori Weltanschauung, then to my mind Nash's view of history must be avoided at all costs. This latter view of history can only lead to a purely verbal escape from the scepticism which Nash and Meiland attribute to Montgomery [19] and to historical solipsism. Historiography of this type suffers from the same methodological deficiency as post-Bultmannianism. [20] Nash, if he does indeed hold a position similar to the one I am criticizing, is correct in objecting to being put generally in the same class with Bultmann and his followers. The content of their theology and history is vastly different, and for this I am grateful. However, their methodology and its resultant solipsism are similar. If constructionism leads to solipsism, then there is no criterion for choosing between Nash and Bultmann. [21]

IV

What is at stake in a discussion of this sort? Is it a case of two philosophers arguing from their ivory towers about their abstract views of history? I think not. If we are doomed to historical scepticism and solipsism, a compelling witness to the unbeliever is impossible. The evangelist can never escape the charge of circularity. If, on the other hand, Montgomery is correct and the particular historic events of the Christian faith constitute both a necessary and sufficient ground for belief, the unbeliever is without excuse. He can be shown that the difficulty is not with the evidence but with a rebellious will. He has been blinded by the evil one that the glory of the gospel should not dawn upon him. As evangelists and philosophers, let us never forget that religious epistemology is related to human volition. None are so blind as those who will not see.

NOTES

1. Ronald H. Nash, "The Use and Abuse of History in Christian Apologetics," Christian Scholar's Review, I, 3 (Spring, 1971), pp. 217-226.

2. J. W. Montgomery, Where is History Going? (Minneapolis: Bethany Fellowship, Inc., 1969), p. 195. See also "The Theologian's Craft," The Suicide of Christian Theology (Minneapolis: Bethany Fellowship, Inc., 1970), pp. 267 ff. and The Shape of the Past (Ann Arbor: Edwards Bros., 1962), pp. 138 ff. In light of the passages cited I fail to see how Nash's claim that there is ambiguity surrounding Montgomery's

discussion is justified, but I shall leave a decision on this matter in the hands of the reader.

3. Shape, op cit., pp. 13-17, 73.

4. J. A. Passmore, "The Objectivity of History," Philosophical Analysis and History, ed. William H. Dray (New York: Harper & Row, 1966), pp. 75 ff.

5. Irving M. Copy, Introduction to Logic (Third edition, New York: The Macmillan Co., 1968), pp. 100, 101.

6. Philosophical Analysis, op. cit., pp. 75 ff., and Max Fisch, "The Philosophy of History: A Dialogue," Philosophy (Tokyo), 1959, p. 167.

7. Ludwig Wittgenstein, Philosophical Investigations, 3rd ed., trans. by G. E. M. Anscombe (New York: The Macmillan Co., 1968), Sect. 242, p. 88e.

8. Suicide, op. cit., pp. 274 ff. This essay appears also in Concordia Theological Monthly, February, 1966 and Journal of the American Scientific Affiliation, September, 1966.

9. J. W. Montgomery, "Clark's Philosophy of History" in The Philosophy of Gordon H. Clark, ed. Ronald Nash (Philadelphia: Presbyterian and Reformed Publishing Co., 1968), p. 375.

10. Philosophical Investigations, op. cit., sec. 340.

11. George Pitcher, The Philosophy of Wittgenstein (Englewood Cliffs: Prentice Hall, 1964), p. 257.

12. Philosophical Investigations, op. cit. secs. 199-300 passim. See also decisive articles on private language in G. Pitcher, Wittgenstein: The Philosophical Investigations (New York: Doubleday & Co., 1966).

13. Where, op. cit., p. 203.

14. Verify this by checking a good dictionary.

15. Herman Feifel, ed., The Meaning of Death (New York: McGraw Hill Book Co., 1959) and Jacques Choron, Death and Western Thought (New York: Collier Books, 1963). This has significance in light of Nash's discussion of Montgomery and the resurrection.

16. Clark, op. cit., p. 374.

17. James Barr, The Semantics of Biblical Language (London: Oxford University Press, 1961), p. 230.

18. Suicide, op. cit., p. 290: On the role of the historian's existential involvement Montgomery says, "The historian cannot stop with an external, objective examination of facts and records; as Benedetto Croce and R. G. Collingwood have so well shown, he must relive the past in imagination—re-enact it by entering into its very heart."

19. I think that the claim of scepticism for all empiricism is misplaced, but the refutation of such a position would be a paper in itself.

20. For decisive refutations of this methodology see J. W. Montgomery, In Defense of Martin Luther (Milwaukee: Northwestern Publishing House, 1970), chapter two; and E. D. Hirsch, Validity in Interpretation (New Haven: Yale University Press, 1967), particularly appendix II.

21. A suggested escape from this charge is that coherence determines validity. Surely not! There have been numerous systems whose internal consistency cannot be questioned, but both Nash and I would properly reject them. If the answer is: "But these are not as comprehensively coherent," one must surely answer that only empirical evidence can determine the relative validity of de facto coherence. This, however, defeats the claim. At best one can only suggest some further criteria. Then, the alternatives are either solipsism or an infinite regress.

INDEX OF NAMES

This index includes the names of all individual persons - ancient and modern, real and mythical - discussed or cited in the book. A name which appears both in a text passage and in a note corresponding to that passage is indexed only where it occurs in the text.

Bloch, Marc 10, 16, 18
Bloomfield, Leonard 353-354
Blum, H. F. 32
Boccaccio 49
Boileau-Despréaux, Nicholas 16
Bolingbroke 66
Boman, Thorlief 60
Bonaparte, Louis 242
Boring, E. G. 102
Bornkamm, Heinrich 51
Boyd, Evelyn Mae 346
Boyer, Blanche B. 62
Bradley, F. H. 21
Brandi, Karl 28
Brightman, Edgar Sheffield 325, 326-327, 336, 337
Brilioth, Yngve 60
Brinton, Crane 154
Brown, Robert E. 109
Bruce, A. B. 352
Bruce, F. F. 168, 173, 338, 346, 347, 349, 350
Brunner, Emil 64, 119-120, 124, 156, 159, 176, 358-374
Brunner, Peter 63, 64
Bruno, Saint 220
Brutus 91
Buchler, Justus 241, 256, 299, 301, 310, 322, 327
Buchner, Ludwig 218-219
Buckle, Henry Thomas 72, 73, 74
Bultmann, Rudolf 11, 120-122, 123, 127, 128, 130, 142, 143, 152-154, 162, 167
Burckhardt, Jakob 70, 76-77, 78, 81, 93
Burtt, Edwin A. xi, 172, 254, 257, 264, 267, 273, 301, 304, 305, 307, 309, 338
Bury, J. B. 79-80, 88, 96
Butterfield, Herbert 4, 101, 145, 146, 149, 178, 182
Byron, George Gordon, Lord 253

Caesar, Julius 91
Cailliet, Emile 372
Caird, John 332
Cairns, David 159
Calhoun, Robert L. 187
Calogero, Guido 110
Calvin, John 50, 52, 303, 373
Campbell, Thomas 370-371
Caponigri, A. Robert 69, 97
Carlyle, Thomas 70, 76, 87, 89

Carnell, Edward John 63, 140, 170, 197, 214, 240, 254, 266, 286, 299, 300, 301, 302, 307, 309, 323, 337
Carnot, N. L. S. 231
Carpenter, Boyd 325
Carr, E. H. 147
Carr, Wildon 29
Carroll, Lewis 17
Cassirer, Ernst 97
Catlin, George 222, 228, 230, 238, 241, 242, 243, 253, 254
Cattaneo, Carlo 200, 214
Cellini, Benvenuto 49
Charlemagne 45
Charles V, Holy Roman emperor 28
Charles XII, king of Sweden 96
Chaumette 95
Christina, queen of Sweden 17
Chrysostom, St. John 355
Churchill, Charles 217
Churchill, Sir Winston 178
Chytraeus, David 50, 162
Clark, Gordon H. 62, 309, 324, 338, 372
Clark, R. E. D. 173
Clausius, R. J. E. 231
Clement XII, pope 193
Clement of Alexandria 135
Clinton, Henry 104
Cochrane, C. N. 58
Cocker, B. F. 61
Coleridge, Samuel Taylor 199
Collingwood, R. G. 10, 11, 50, 58, 62, 63, 91-92, 93, 97, 98, 105, 215
Columbus, Christopher 324, 338
Colwell, E. C. 173, 334
Commines 49
Compton, Arthur H. 197, 214
Comte, Auguste 72, 74, 91, 99
Condillac, Étienne Bonnat de 223
Copernicus, Nicolaus 303
Corsini, Cardinal 193
Coué, Émile 118
Craig, Samuel G. 171
Croce, Benedetto 11, 90-91, 93, 97, 100, 188, 191, 192, 194, 196, 201, 202, 203, 206, 207, 208, 210, 214, 215
Cromwell, Oliver 8, 67
Cúccaro, Jacinto J. 206
Cullmann, Oscar 59, 357
Cyrus 52

Daalen, D. H. van 177

Guillebaud, H. E. 176

Haas, Harold 371
Hadrian 84
Haines, C. R. 58
Haldane, J. B. S. 173
Hamilton, Edith 37
Hammond, T. C. 169, 197, 215
Harbison, E. Harris 64, 155, 177, 179
Harland, Gordon 160
Harnack, Adolf 347
Harrisville, Roy A. 170, 174
Hastie, W. 96
Hayes, Patrick, Cardinal 215
Heath-Stubbs, John 178
Hebert, A. G. 60
Hegel, G. W. F. 21, 70-71, 74, 76, 77, 78, 86, 87, 128, 187, 219, 221, 222-224, 327, 333
Heichelheim, F. M. 348
Heick, O. W. 61
Heidegger, Martin 127, 153
Heilbroner, Robert L. 178
Heim, Karl 177
Heisenberg, Werner 197
Helmholtz, H. L. F. von 221, 232
Henry, Carl F. H. 171
Heraclitus 181
Heraclius 57
Herberg, Will 107
Herder, J. G. von 203, 206, 208, 216
Herodotus 36, 38, 79
Herrmann, Wilhelm 153
Hertz, Karl 65
Hesiod 36
Hicks, Edward 61
Hilary of Poitiers 355
Himmelfarb, Gertrude 101
Hippocrates 58
Hitler, Adolf 15, 76, 135, 178, 272
Hobbes, Thomas 208, 216, 218, 223, 255, 372
Hocking, William Ernest 196, 215
Hogarth, William 12, 217
Holl, Karl 54
Homer 36, 57, 204
Horace 39, 241, 312
Hordern, William 156, 160, 163
Horn, Edward T., III 60-61
Horne, Thomas Hartwell 176, 293, 309
Horney, Karen 103, 164
Horton, Walter Marshall 262, 269, 271, 281, 283-284, 299, 300, 303, 305, 309
Hoselitz, Bert F. 111
Hostie, Raymond 102
Hughes, Philip E. 159

Huizinga, Johan 92-94, 139
Hume, David 170, 187, 216, 288-292, 296-298, 309, 338
Huxley, Julian S. 173
Hyppolite, Jean 98

Ibn-Rushd (Averroës) 210
Irenaeus 44
Isaac 130
Isaiah 136
Isidore of Pelusium 355
Isis 60

Jacob 130
Jacob de Saint-Charles, Louis 53, 64
James II, king of England 75
James (the Lord's brother) 349
James, Henry 32
James, William 19, 90, 161, 168, 257-258, 260, 268, 269, 274, 279, 300, 301, 307, 309, 312-340
Jeremiah 246, 351
Jesus Christ passim
Jevons, Frank B. 201
Jewett, Paul K. 157
Joachim of Floris 48, 166
John (the Apostle) 61, 136, 153, 159, 235, 256, 317, 341-350
John the Baptist 73, 246, 351
John of Damascus 355
Johnson, Edgar N. 205, 216
Jones, Ernest 103, 104
Joseph of Arimathea 251
Josephus, Flavius 343-344
Judas Iscariot 250
Jung, Carl Gustav 81
Justin Martyr 169
Justinian I, Byzantine emperor 371

Kallen, Horace M. 340
Kant, Immanuel 21, 22, 67-68, 70, 132, 141, 187, 257, 310, 327, 338
Kantonen, T. A. xi, 77
Kaphahn, F. 100
Kaufmann, Walter 121, 130
Keats, John 25
Kennedy, John F. 178
Kepler, Thomas S. 332
Khrushchev, Nikita 178
Khvostov 102
Kierkegaard, Søren 113, 153, 159, 340
Kirk, Russell 155, 165, 166, 167
Kochan, Lionel 101
Köhler, Walter 156
Koheleth 78, 149

SUPPLEMENTAL INDEX

Works by John Warwick Montgomery

Published by Bethany Fellowship:

Christianity for the Tough-minded
Crisis in Lutheran Theology (two volumes), 2nd ed.
Damned Through the Church
Demon Possession*
God's Inerrant Word*
How Do We Know There Is a God?
The Law Above the Law
Myth, Allegory, and Gospel*
Principalities and Powers: The World of the Occult, 2nd ed.
The Quest for Noah's Ark, 2nd ed.
The Shape of the Past: A Christian Response to Secular
    Philosophies of History, 2nd ed.
Situation Ethics: True or False? (with Joseph Fletcher)
The Suicide of Christian Theology
Where Is History Going?

Published by Editorial Betania:

¿Como sabemos que hay un Dios? (in Spanish)

Available from Other Publishers:

The Altizer-Montgomery Dialogue (with Thomas J. J. Altizer)
Chytraeus on Sacrifice: A Reformation Treatise in Biblical
    Theology
Computers, Cultural Change, and the Christ (trilingual: English,
    French, German)
Cross and Crucible (two volumes)
Ecumenicity, Evangelicals, and Rome
¿Es confiable el Cristianismo? (in Spanish)
History and Christianity
In Defense of Martin Luther
International Scholars Directory *
The 'Is God Dead?' Controversy
Jurisprudence: A Book of Readings *
La Mort de Dieu (in French)
A Seventeenth Century View of European Libraries *
A Union List of Serial Publications in Chicago-Area Protestant
    Theological Libraries *
Verdammt durch die Kirche? (in German)
The Writing of Research Papers in Theology

---

*Works edited by Dr. Montgomery